CAMBRIDGE

C000121576

PREP∆RE

TEACHER'S BOOK

❚ Wayne Rimmer   **❚ Second Edition**

A2

LEVEL 3

Cambridge University Press
www.cambridge.org/elt

Cambridge Assessment English
www.cambridgeenglish.org

Information on this title: www.cambridge.org/9781108385954

© Cambridge University Press and UCLES 2015, 2019

First published 2015
Second Edition 2019

20 19 18 17 16 15 14 13 12 11 10 9 8 7 6 5 4

Printed in Italy by Rotolito S.p.A.

A catalogue record for this publication is available from the British Library

ISBN 978-1-108-38595-4 Teacher's Book with Downloadable Resource Pack
(Class Audio, Video, Photocopiable Worksheets)
ISBN 978-1-108-43329-7 Student's Book
ISBN 978-1-108-38060-7 Student's Book and Online Workbook
ISBN 978-1-108-38094-2 Workbook with Audio Download

CONTENTS

CAMBRIDGE

DEAR TEACHERS

I'm delighted that you've chosen our official preparation materials to prepare for a Cambridge English Qualification.

We take great pride in the fact that our materials draw on the expertise of a whole team of writers, teachers, assessors and exam experts. These are materials that you can really trust.

Our preparation materials are unique in many ways:

- They combine the skills and knowledge of the teams at Cambridge Assessment English, who create the tests, and the teams at Cambridge University Press, who create the English Language Teaching materials.

- They draw upon the experience of millions of previous exam candidates – where they succeed and where they have difficulties. We target exercises and activities precisely at these areas so that you can actively 'learn' from previous test takers' mistakes.

- Every single task in our materials has been carefully checked to be an accurate reflection of what test takers find in the test.

In addition, we listen to what you tell us at every stage of the development process. This allows us to design the most user-friendly courses, practice tests and supplementary training. We create materials using in-depth knowledge, research and practical understanding. Prepare for Cambridge English Qualifications with confidence in the knowledge that you have the best materials available to support you on your way to success.

We wish you the very best on your journey with us.

With kind regards,

Pamela Baxter
Director
Cambridge Exams Publishing

PS. If you have any feedback at all on our support materials for exams, please write to us at cambridgeexams@cambridge.org

 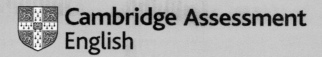

EXPERTS TOGETHER

Our aim is to deliver the materials you tell us you need. Exclusive insights from test development and candidate performance guarantee expert content. The result is a unique Exam Journey in each course, ensuring every student is ready on exam day.

From skills development to exam tasks, language discovery to real-world usage, we create better learning experiences, together.

REVISED EXAMS 2020

In 2020, the A2 Key, A2 Key for Schools, B1 Preliminary and B1 Preliminary for Schools exams are being updated!

Look out for all our new materials this year so that you can prepare in advance!

TO FIND OUT MORE VISIT

www.cambridgeenglish.org/**key-and-preliminary**

WELCOME TO PREPARE

STUDENT'S BOOK OVERVIEW

Each unit begins with **About you**, where students can talk about themselves and their lives.

EP **Vocabulary sets** are informed by English Vocabulary Profile to ensure they are appropriate for the level.

Motivating, topic-based **texts** specifically chosen to engage and inform students.

All reading texts are recorded, giving the option to listen and read or listen and check answers where appropriate.

Clear **grammar presentation** and practice is extended in the Grammar reference and practice section at the back of the book.

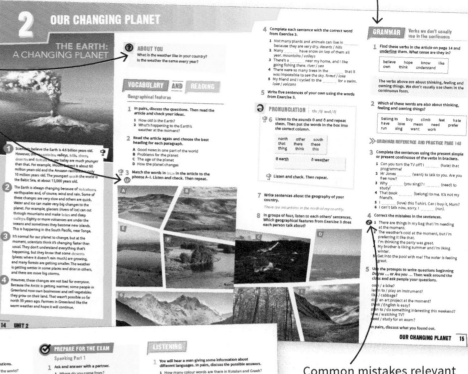

Common mistakes relevant to your students' level are identified in the grammar activities marked with the **Cambridge Learner Corpus icon.** 👁

Prepare for the exam provides practice of every part of the *A2 Key for Schools* exam.

Useful tips in **Prepare to write** help students learn to prepare, plan and check their writing.

Talking points provides opportunities to personalise language and encourage students to say what they think about the topic of the unit.

There is comprehensive coverage of **pronunciation** in the Student's Book.

Video interviews show real teens giving their opinion on the topic of the unit. Each video comes with a worksheet containing comprehension and discussion questions.

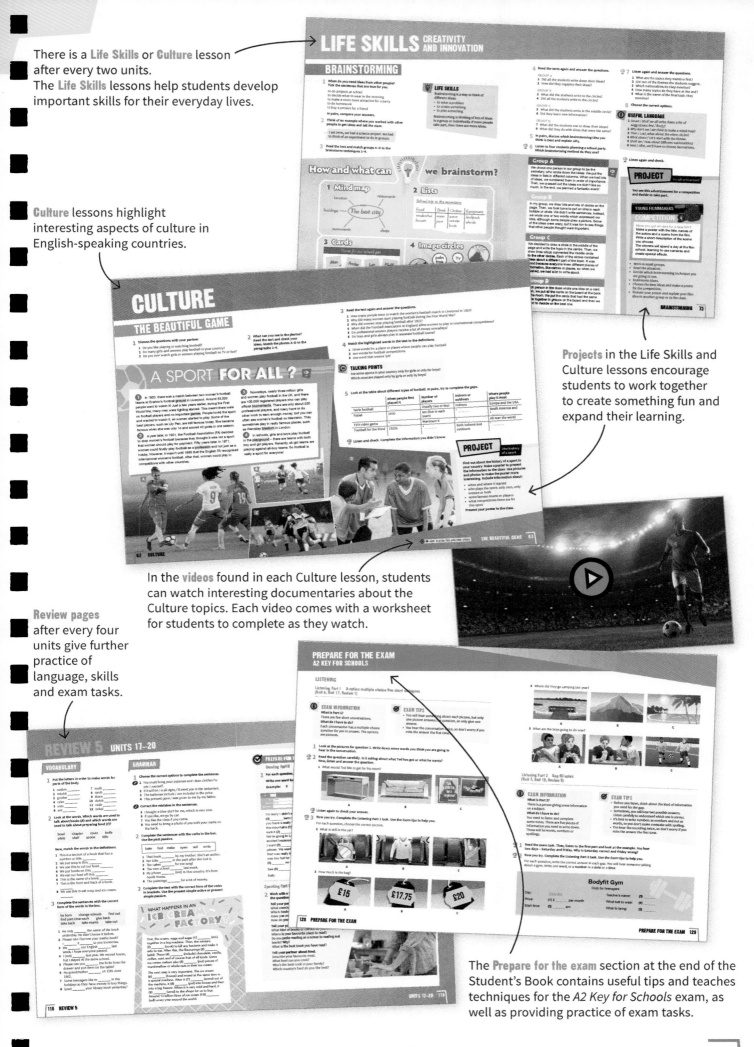

There is a **Life Skills** or **Culture** lesson after every two units.
The **Life Skills** lessons help students develop important skills for their everyday lives.

Culture lessons highlight interesting aspects of culture in English-speaking countries.

Projects in the Life Skills and Culture lessons encourage students to work together to create something fun and expand their learning.

In the **videos** found in each Culture lesson, students can watch interesting documentaries about the Culture topics. Each video comes with a worksheet for students to complete as they watch.

Review pages after every four units give further practice of language, skills and exam tasks.

The **Prepare for the exam** section at the end of the Student's Book contains useful tips and teaches techniques for the *A2 Key for Schools* exam, as well as providing practice of exam tasks.

COMPONENT LINE UP

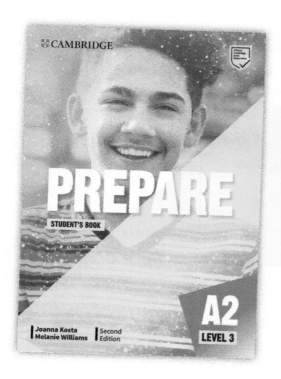

Student's Book

The Student's Book combines teen-appeal topics with preparation for the revised 2020 *A2 Key for Schools* exam. With twenty lively core units, Reviews, Culture and Life Skills sections, a Vocabulary list, and a Grammar reference and practice section, the Student's Book has all the material you need to create interactive, personalised lessons. Full audio and extensive video to accompany the Student's Book is available for teachers online or to download.

Workbook with Audio Download

The Workbook gives additional practice of all the language from the Student's Book. It also provides students with comprehensive skills development work and further exposure to exam tasks. The Workbook is suitable for use both in the classroom and for homework. Learners can access and download the audio files from e-Source using the code provided.

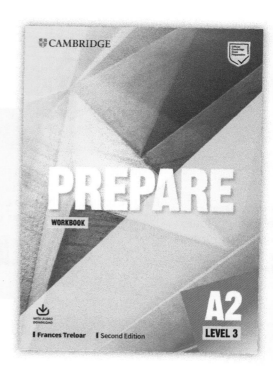

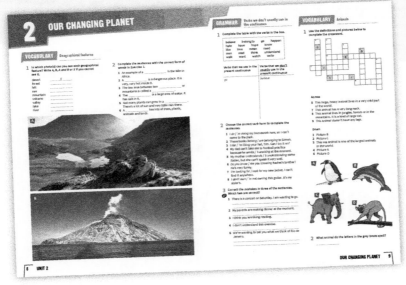

Online Workbook

The Online Workbook, delivered via the Cambridge Learning Management System, is a digital version of the Workbook with interactive exercises and tasks which provide further practice of the language and skills in the Student's Book. The Online Workbook also allows you to track your students' progress, highlighting areas of strength and weakness for ongoing performance improvement.

Teacher's Book with Downloadable Resource Pack

The interleaved Teacher's Book contains complete teaching notes for all of the Student's Book tasks, in addition to answer keys and audioscripts. With a wealth of lesson ideas, warmers, coolers and extension tasks, the Teacher's Book helps you manage mixed-ability classes and work with fast finishers. Information panels include background information about themes, topics and cultural events. Prepare for the exam information boxes provide detailed descriptions of each task found in the *A2 Key for Schools* exam, as well as useful tips on how to approach the tasks. Clear indications direct you to additional resources which support and extend learning.

The Downloadable Resource Pack, accessed via e-Source, includes Class Audio, Video and Photocopiable Worksheets. These provide an extensive suite of downloadable teacher's resources to use in class and include:

- Grammar worksheets (available at two levels of challenge: standard and plus)
- Vocabulary worksheets (available at two levels of challenge: standard and plus)
- Review games
- Literature worksheets
- Speaking worksheets
- Writing worksheets
- Video worksheets
- Culture video worksheets

In addition, you can find videos showing two complete *A2 Key for Schools* speaking exams and accompanying worksheets.

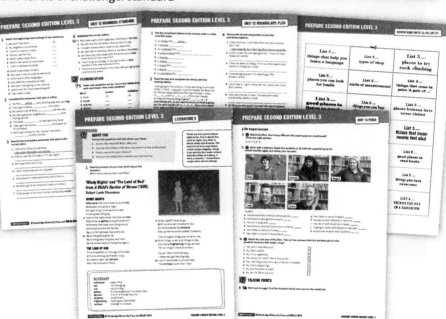

Presentation Plus

Presentation Plus is easy-to-use, interactive classroom presentation software that helps you deliver effective and engaging lessons. It includes all the Student's Book and Workbook content and allows you to present and annotate content, and link to the photocopiable worksheets.

Test Generator

The Test Generator allows you to download ready-made tests for each unit, term and end-of-year assessment or to build your own tests easily and quickly. All the tests are available at two levels of challenge: standard and plus, to help assess learners of mixed abilities.

THE PREPARE EXAM JOURNEY

The *Prepare* Exam Journey combines teen-appeal topics with extensive preparation for Cambridge English Qualifications. Levels 2 and 3 of *Prepare* Second Edition take students on a two-year journey towards the revised 2020 *A2 Key for Schools* exam. This approach builds confidence every step of the way from the first experiences of exam tasks to skills development, from language discovery to understanding how English works in the real world.

LEVEL 2

Prepare Level 2 gradually introduces authentic *A2 Key for Schools* exam tasks, ensuring students become familiar with every part of the exam.

■ Exam tasks are discreetly labelled with the exam icon in **Level 2 Student's Book.** ✅

 2
35

Listen to five short conversations. For each question, choose the correct picture (A, B or C).

1 What was Bella happy with at the party?

■ **Level 2 Workbook** offers further exposure to each part of the exam.

2 For each question, choose the correct answer.

Mexican blankets
Different sizes
Buy one for £20 or two for £35
Today only!

A The blankets are all big.
B There's a special offer on these blankets.
C The blankets are only £35 each today.

■ Information for each part of the exam is included in **Level 2 Teacher's Book.**

🔊 2
35

A2 Key for Schools Listening Part 1.

✅ In this part of the exam, students listen to five short conversations and answer a question by choosing the correct picture, A, B or C. They listen to each conversation twice. Before they listen, ask the students to read each question again and say how each of the three pictures answers it. Do the first as an example: *What was Bella happy with at the party? In A Bella was happy about the people, in B she was happy about the food and in C she was happy about the music.* The students then listen to the three conversations and choose the right picture for each one. After they listen for the first time, encourage them to compare their answers with a partner and to say why they think their answer is correct. Play the recording for a second time for the students to check their ideas. With a weaker class, play the recording for a third time and stop it after the correct answer is given. With a stronger class, ask the students to say why the other pictures are not correct, e.g. *In 1 Bella says the music wasn't great and there weren't many people there.* They can do this by listening again.

LEVEL 3

Prepare Level 3 provides complete coverage of the *A2 Key for Schools* exam, driving students to exam success.

■ Each exam task is highlighted clearly in the *Prepare for the Exam* features in **Level 3 Student's Book.**

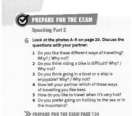

✅ **PREPARE FOR THE EXAM**
Speaking Part 2

6 Look at the photos A–K on page 20. Discuss the questions with your partner.

1 Do you like these different ways of travelling? Why? / Why not?
2 Do you think riding a bike is difficult? Why? / Why not?
3 Do you think going in a boat or a ship is enjoyable? Why? / Why not?
4 Now tell your partner which of these ways of travelling you like best.
5 How do you like to travel when it's very hot?
6 Do you prefer going on holiday to the sea or in the mountains?

» PREPARE FOR THE EXAM PAGE 134

■ The *Prepare for the exam* section at the end of **Level 3 Student's Book** includes further guidance and support with practice tasks.

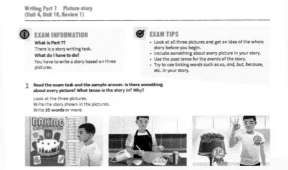

Writing Part 7   Picture story
(Unit 4, Unit 18, Review 1)

ⓘ **EXAM INFORMATION**
What is Part 7?
There is a story writing task.
What do I have to do?
You have to write a story based on three pictures.

✅ **EXAM TIPS**
• Look at all three pictures and get an idea of the whole story before you begin.
• Include something about every picture in your story.
• Use the past tense for the events of the story.
• Try to use linking words such as *so, and, but, because,* etc. in your story.

1 Read the exam task and the sample answer. Is there something about every picture? What tense is the story in? Why?

Look at the three pictures.
Write the story shown in the pictures.
Write **35 words** or more.

■ **Level 3 Workbook** consolidates each exam task and includes Exam tips.

✅ **PREPARE FOR THE EXAM**
Listening Part 5

1 For each question, choose the correct answer.
🔊 You will hear Martha talking to a friend about a trip to the zoo. Which animal was each person most interested in?

People
0 brother   E
1 sister
2 dad
3 mum
4 grandad
5 grandma

What they liked best
A bears   E monkeys
B dolphins   F penguins
C elephants   G snakes
D giraffes   H wild dogs

EXAM TIPS
• Always read the instructions, the questions (1–5) and all the answer options (A–H) before you listen.
• You can only use an answer A–H once. Remember you can't use the example!

■ **Level 3 Teacher's Book** details each part of the exam and suggests teaching tips for the classroom.

✅ **PREPARE FOR THE EXAM**

A2 KEY FOR SCHOOLS
Listening Part 5

In this part, students listen to a dialogue. They need to match five items to eight options. They are listening for specific information such as objects, places and feelings. They hear the recording twice.

Tip Tell the students that there are five questions plus an example, and eight answers, so there are two answers they don't need to use. They may hear two or more words from the list of answers for each question, but only one will be correct. They must listen for the meaning to choose the right one.

PAPER / TIMING	PART	WHAT DO CANDIDATES HAVE TO DO?	☑ PRACTICE IN LEVEL 3
Reading and Writing 1 hour Reading	**Part 1** Six 3-option multiple choice questions	Read six short real-world texts for the main message.	Student's Book pages 66, 75, 102, 120–121 Workbook pages 46, 73
	Part 2 Seven 3-option multiple matching questions	Read seven questions and three short texts on the same topic, then match the questions to the texts.	Student's Book pages 22, 70, 104, 122 Workbook pages 14, 50, 74
	Part 3 Five 3-option multiple choice questions	Read one long text for detailed understanding and main ideas.	Student's Book pages 34, 56, 88, 123 Workbook pages 22, 38, 62
	Part 4 Six 3-option multiple-choice cloze questions	Read a factual text and choose the correct vocabulary items to complete the gaps.	Student's Book pages 48, 53, 61, 124 Workbook pages 34, 42
	Part 5 Six open cloze questions	Complete gaps in an email (and sometimes the reply too) using one word.	Student's Book pages 78, 110, 119, 125 Workbook pages 54, 78
Writing	**Part 6** One guided writing task	Write a short email or note of 25 words or more.	Student's Book pages 61, 83, 97, 126 Workbook pages 43, 59
	Part 7 One picture story task	Write a short story of 35 words or more based on three picture prompts.	Student's Book pages 25, 31, 105, 127 Workbook pages 19, 75
Listening About 30 minutes	**Part 1** Five 3-option multiple choice questions	Identify key information in five short dialogues and choose the correct picture.	Student's Book pages 27, 31, 101, 128–129 Workbook pages 19, 71
	Part 2 Five gap fill questions	Listen to a monologue and complete gaps in a page of notes.	Student's Book pages 45, 111, 119, 129 Workbook pages 31, 79
	Part 3 Five 3-option multiple choice questions	Listen to a dialogue for key information and answer five 3-option questions.	Student's Book pages 71, 75, 115, 130 Workbook pages 50, 83
	Part 4 Five 3-option multiple choice questions	Identify the main idea, message, gist or topic in five short monologues or dialogues and answer five 3-option questions.	Student's Book pages 49, 53, 90, 131 Workbook pages 35, 67
	Part 5 Five matching questions	Listen to a dialogue for key information and match five items.	Student's Book pages 17, 39, 97, 132 Workbook pages 10, 26
Speaking 8–10 minutes: Part 1, 3–4 minutes; Part 2, 5–6 minutes	**Part 1** Interlocutor asks questions to each candidate in turn	Respond to questions, giving factual or personal information.	Student's Book pages 13, 31, 93, 97, 119, 133
	Part 2 Discussion task with visual stimulus	Discuss likes, dislikes and give reasons.	Student's Book pages 21, 42, 53, 134–135

Key to symbols:

ə Pronunciation   ✅ *A2 Key for Schools* exam task   ▶ Video

LISTENING	SPEAKING	WRITING	VIDEO
World cities quiz Six short conversations	Making requests in different situations		▶ Favourite cities
A conversation about going to the cinema ✅ Listening Part 3		An invitation to the cinema	
✅ Listening Part 3			
An interview with an explorer	Doing your own Life Quiz		▶ Life experiences
A conversation about a birthday picnic		An email ✅ Writing Part 6	
			▶ Famous markets
Three young people talk about free-time activities A talk about an unusual hobby	An interview about an unusual hobby		
Five short conversations ✅ Listening Part 4 A talk about different languages		Information about your English class	▶ Different languages
✅ Listening Part 5	✅ Speaking Part 1	✅ Writing Part 6	
Five short conversations ✅ Listening Part 1	Giving advice		▶ Health
A talk about a reading competition		A story ✅ Writing Part 7	
			▶ How teens read
A talk about a cooking competition ✅ Listening Part 2	Talking about a recipe		▶ Favourite foods
A conversation about a new school ✅ Listening Part 3		A biography	
✅ Listening Part 2	✅ Speaking Part 1		

1 IT'S A CHALLENGE!

The Duke of Edinburgh's Award

This is a great way to have fun, make new friends and learn new things. The award has four parts:

- **VOLUNTEERING** – Give your time to make a difference to people's lives.
- **FITNESS** – Do some exercise and get fitter.
- **SKILLS** – Learn something new – or get better at something you like.
- **EXPEDITION** – Go camping and hiking in the countryside.

If you complete everything, you get a certificate.

Write an email to Mr Jones, The Duke of Edinburgh's Award leader at our school. Describe yourself and say why you want to do the award.

? ABOUT YOU

Do you have any awards or prizes?
If yes, what did you win them for?
If no, do you know about any awards or prizes for young people in your country?

VOCABULARY AND READING

Adjectives of personality

1 Read the poster and look at the photos. Then answer the questions in pairs.

1 What is The Duke of Edinburgh's Award?
2 What kind of activities do students do for the award?
3 Can you do an award like this at your school?
4 If not, would you like to do one?

2 Read the students' emails on page 11 and answer the questions with *Daniel* or *Grace*.

1 Who plays two instruments?
2 Who is happy with a piece of work they're doing?
3 Who is preparing a surprise for another person?
4 Who is teaching another person how to do something?

3 Check the meaning of the words in the emails on page 11. Then use them to complete the sentences.

1 My brother's very _____. He lies in bed until midday and never does any work.
2 My grandpa's 70, but he's still really _____. He cycles everywhere and plays tennis.
3 Sonia is very _____. She always thinks of other people and is good to them.
4 Everyone likes Toby. He's the most _____ boy in the school.
5 Our teacher is so _____. She always makes us laugh.
6 When I speak to adults, I try to be _____.
7 Sara is very _____. She smiles a lot and she's easy to talk to.
8 Most people in my class talk a lot, but Fred is _____ and doesn't say much.
9 I wasn't sure how to do my project, but the teacher was very _____. She told me about some great websites.
10 Suchitra is very _____. She can paint and draw, and she writes excellent stories.

Listen and check. Then repeat.

4 Write sentences about your partner using the adjectives in Exercise 3. Give the sentences to your teacher to read out for the class to try and guess who they are about.

Unit Overview

TOPIC	Activities and personal interests
VOCABULARY AND READING	Adjectives of personality
	The Duke of Edinburgh's Award
GRAMMAR	Present simple and present continuous
READING	Register to do the Duke of Edinburgh's Award
VOCABULARY	Personal details
PRONUNCIATION	The alphabet
LISTENING	A conversation about the Duke of Edinburgh's Award
SPEAKING	Talking about yourself
EXAM TASK	Speaking Part 1

Resources

GRAMMAR REFERENCE AND PRACTICE: SB page 147; TB page 264
PREPARE FOR THE EXAM: SB page on TB page 249; TB page 258
WORKBOOK: pages 4–7
PHOTOCOPIABLE WORKSHEETS: Grammar worksheet Unit 1; Vocabulary worksheet Unit 1
TEST GENERATOR: Diagnostic test; Unit test 1

WARMER

If students did Level 2 together, this activity gets them using simple English again after the break; if they didn't, it helps them get to know each other.

Write the words *food*, *sport*, *city*, *animal* and *colour* on the board. Give students one minute to write down their favourite thing in each category. Start by giving them an example for each, e.g. *ice cream*, *basketball*, *Milan*, *elephant* and *green*.

In pairs, students then compare and discuss their answers. Demonstrate with a stronger student:

'What's your favourite food, Mario?'

I love sushi. There's a great sushi place near my house. What about you?

As a variation, all students should walk around the class asking and comparing answers to see which items in each category are the most popular.

ABOUT YOU

Pre-teach **award** (a prize you give to someone for something good they did), then ask students for examples of awards or prizes it is possible for young people to win, for example in sports competitions, youth movements or school exams. Put students into groups to discuss the questions. Encourage students to brainstorm other awards and prizes in their country. (If you have students from different countries, the discussion is more interesting if you put different nationalities together.) Then exchange ideas as a class. As an extension activity, put students into pairs to think of funny awards for their class for this year: for example, for the student who smiles the most, the student who asks the most questions.

VOCABULARY AND READING

Adjectives of personality

BACKGROUND INFORMATION

The Duke of Edinburgh's Award is a registered charity which aims to develop young people's social and physical skills so that they can make a fuller contribution to adult life, for example by finding a better job. Prince Philip, Duke of Edinburgh, founded the Duke of Edinburgh's Award in the UK in 1956. Now each year around 300,000 young people in about 145 countries take the award. A number of different organisations run the Duke of Edinburgh's Award and these include schools, colleges, youth centres and businesses. Around 50,000 volunteers act as leaders and trainers. The minimum time to complete the programme is two years (it must be finished before you are 25) and there are three levels, Bronze, Silver and Gold, which increase in the level of challenge and commitment. The Gold level has an extra residential requirement where participants have to do an activity away from home for five days.

1 Ask students to look at the poster and the heading. Ask, 'Who is the Duke of Edinburgh?' (*Prince Philip, husband of the queen of England, Elizabeth II*). Pre-teach **volunteering** (offering to do something without expecting payment), **expedition** (an organised journey, especially a long one for a particular purpose) and **hiking** (the activity of going for a long walk for pleasure outdoors). Point out the pronunciation of *Edinburgh* (/ˈed.ɪn.bər.ə/). If necessary, read out the background information to help students. Ask, 'Who is Mr Jones?' (*the school's Duke of Edinburgh's Award leader*). Put students into pairs to read and answer the questions; then check the answers as a class.

Answers

1 It's an achievement award.
2 They volunteer, do fitness activities or exercise, learn something new and go on an expedition.
3 and 4 Students' own answers

FAST FINISHERS

Tell fast finishers to write down three skills which they have, for example, *I can play the piano, I can cook quite well, I am learning to draw*. Then tell fast finishers to work in pairs, compare their skills and ask one another questions about them, for example, *Can you make borscht?*

CONTINUED ON PAGE 18

2 Ask students to look at the emails. Ask, 'Who tells a lot of jokes?' (*Daniel*). Tell students to answer the questions. Check the answers then ask students, 'Who sounds more interesting, Daniel or Grace?'

Answers

1 Daniel 2 Grace 3 Grace 4 Daniel

The Reading text is recorded for students to listen, read and check their answers.
01

3 Ask concept-checking questions about the words. For example, 'Are friendly people nice or not nice?' (*nice*). Let weaker students translate the words. Drill all the words. Then tell students to complete the sentences. Put students into pairs to compare their answers.

Answers
02

The answers are recorded for students to check and then repeat.
1 lazy 2 active 3 kind 4 popular 5 funny 6 polite
7 friendly 8 quiet 9 helpful 10 creative

4 Put students into pairs and have them write four sentences about their partner using adjectives. Tell them not to name their partner but to use *they* instead, for example, *They don't talk very much.* Collect the sentences then read them out for the class to guess the student. Write the sentences which have mistakes on the board and tell students to correct or improve them.

MIXED ABILITY

Tell stronger students to write six sentences and choose four of the sentences to read out. Put students who need more support in pairs and have them write two sentences each about the same student in another pair.

GRAMMAR Present simple and present continuous

1 Write on the board:

Daniel plays the guitar.

Daniel is playing the guitar.

Ask students, 'Which is present simple?' (*the first*) and 'Which is present continuous?' (*the second*). Tell students to complete the table. Check answers as a class.

Answers

Present simple: I'm a friendly person, I often make people laugh, I work hard, I play hockey and go swimming every week, I hope I can do this award, I don't talk much, I like to be busy , I often go shopping with her, She always tells me I'm kind, she doesn't know about it
Present continuous: I'm learning to play the keyboard, I'm also teaching my brother to swim , I'm doing a big painting, it's going well, My mum and I are planning a party for her

2 Ask, 'When Daniel writes "I work hard", does he mean only now?' (*no*). Tell students to complete the rules. Check as a class.

Answers

1 continuous 2 simple

>> **GRAMMAR REFERENCE AND PRACTICE ANSWER KEY TB PAGE 264**

3 Tell students to look at the first sentence. Ask, 'Is this something happening now or something that happens regularly?' (*something that happens regularly*) and 'How do you know?' (*It happens every week.*). Tell students to choose the correct form in the other sentences. Check as a class.

Answers

1 watch 2 do you usually eat 3 'm practising 4 are learning
5 don't always do 6 is teaching

4 Write *It is raining every day* on the board. Have students correct the sentence (*It rains every day.*). Tell students to correct the sentences. Check as a class.

Answers

1 It's **raining** a lot at the moment.
2 In my free time, I **usually go** to the cinema.
3 I'm **selling** my English book. Would you like to buy it?
4 Right now, I'm **watching** basketball.
5 I **usually wear** a jacket, even when it's hot.
6 We **swim and sunbathe** every day.

5 Tell students to look at the photos on page 10. Look at the examples and ask some questions, for example, 'What are they wearing?'. Put students into pairs to talk about the photos then share ideas as a class.

Answers

Students' own answers

6 Tell students to make notes. Share ideas as a class then tell students to write their emails.

Possible answer

To: Mr Jones
From: Sophia
I really want to do this award! I work hard at school and I'm not lazy. People say I am kind and friendly.
In my free time I love swimming and reading. I am learning English and I am planning to go to Edinburgh one day!

>> **GRAMMAR WORKSHEET UNIT 1**

COOLER

Dictate this. Students listen and draw it.

Daniel is hiking in the countryside. He is wearing shorts and a T-shirt and he is walking under some trees. Some birds are flying over the trees and the sun is shining in the sky. Daniel is feeling happy and he is smiling.

Students can then draw their own pictures and dictate descriptions to each other.

To: Mr Jones
From: Daniel
Subject: The Duke of Edinburgh's Award

I'd love to do The Duke of Edinburgh's Award. I'm a **friendly** person and I'm **popular** at school. I'm **funny** – I often make people laugh, but I work hard and I'm **polite** to the teachers.

Music is important to me. I'm good at the guitar and I'm learning to play the keyboard. I'm a very **active** person – I play hockey and go swimming every week. I'm also teaching my brother to swim.

To: Mr Jones
From: Grace
Subject: The Duke of Edinburgh's Award

I hope I can do this award. I'm a **quiet** person – I don't talk much, but I'm very **creative**. Art is my favourite subject. At the moment, I'm doing a big painting, and it's going well.

I like to be busy – I'm not a **lazy** person. I'm also **helpful**. My neighbour's quite old, and I often go shopping with her. She always tells me I'm **kind**. It's her birthday soon. My mum and I are planning a party for her, but she doesn't know about it!

GRAMMAR — Present simple and present continuous

1 Complete the table with examples of the present simple and present continuous from the two emails.

Present simple	Present continuous
I often make people laugh	*I'm learning to play the keyboard*

2 Look at the examples in Exercise 1 and complete the rules.

> **1** We use the present _____ to talk about things happening now, around now and at the moment.
> **2** We use the present _____ to talk about things that are always true or happen regularly.

>> **GRAMMAR REFERENCE AND PRACTICE PAGE 147**

3 Choose the correct form of the verb.

1 I *watch / am watching* Spartak Moscow play football every week.
2 What *do you usually eat / are you usually eating* for dinner?
3 Sorry, I can't talk now, I'm busy. I'*m practising / practise* the piano.
4 We learned about rivers last term, and now we *learn / are learning* about forests.
5 I'm quite lazy – I *don't always do / 'm not always doing* my homework.
6 My dad *is teaching / teaches* me how to play tennis at the moment.

4 Correct the mistakes in the sentences.

1 It rains a lot at the moment.
2 In my free time, I'm usually going to the cinema.
3 I sell my English book. Would you like to buy it?
4 Right now, I watch basketball.
5 I'm usually wearing a jacket, even when it's hot.
6 We are swimming and sunbathing every day.

5 Work with a partner. Look at the photos on page 10. Say what the people are doing. Then say how often / when you do the activities in the photos.

> She's playing the guitar.

> I never play the guitar, but I sometimes play the piano.

6 Imagine you are writing an email like Grace's and Daniel's. Make notes. Think of some:

- adjectives to describe yourself
- sports and hobbies you usually do
- things you are learning / planning / doing now

Now write your email.

IT'S A CHALLENGE! 11

REGISTER TO DO THE **DUKE OF EDINBURGH'S AWARD**

HOME	NEWS	ACTIVITIES	PHOTOS	MESSAGES	SEARCH:

YOUR LEADER: MR JONES

Today, you are going to start using The Duke of Edinburgh's Award part of our school website. This has all your details on it, and it shows the activities you are doing. You can also get news and messages from Mr Jones here.

What you need to do:
- Fill in the online form with all your details.
- Choose your activities. You have to discuss and agree these with Mr Jones first.

Here are some ideas, but there are lots more on the DofE website:

Volunteering – helping older people, picking up rubbish or working with animals

Fitness – dance, sport or exercise classes

Skills – playing an instrument, studying a language, learning chess or improving your drawing skills

- You have to do each activity you choose for at least an hour a week for three months. Take lots of photos, and write about what you are doing. Put all this information on the website. When you finish, you can use it to print a book about your time doing the award. This costs about £20.

PERSONAL DETAILS

FIRST NAME:	Grace
SURNAME:	Hopkins
AGE:	14
FIRST LANGUAGE:	English

CONTACT DETAILS

EMAIL ADDRESS:	g.hopkins@topnet.com
ADDRESS:	44 Meadow Avenue, London N24 6BG
HOME TELEPHONE:	020 7946 0945
MOBILE:	0770 900 573

ACTIVITIES:

READING

1 **Read the web page quickly. Who is it for?**

2 **Read the information on the website. Are the sentences right (✓) or wrong (✗)?**

1 Mr Jones is going to put news and messages on the website.
2 Mr Jones is going to fill in the students' forms.
3 Students need to talk to Mr Jones before they choose their activities.
4 If students don't like the ideas, they can choose others.
5 Students have to spend several hours a week doing each activity.
6 Students can put information about their activities on the website.
7 Every student gets a free book about their time doing the award.

TALKING POINTS

Which parts of the award do you think are most useful? Why?
Which look most fun? Why?
Why is it a good idea to do awards like this?

VOCABULARY Personal details

1 **Read Grace's details. Match questions 1–7 to the words and phrases on the form above.**
EP
1 What's your family name?
2 How old are you?
3 Where do you live?
4 What do you speak at home?
5 What numbers can we call you on?
6 What's your email address?
7 What's your first name?

🔊 04 **Listen and check. Then repeat.**

🔊 05 2 **Listen to Grace's contact details. Then repeat them.**

1 g.hopkins@topnet.com
2 44 Meadow Avenue, London N24 6BG
3 020 7946 0945
4 0770 900 573

WARMER

Read out five sentences, some present simple and some present continuous, about yourself. Students must decide if they are true or false. For example:

I get up at six o'clock every day.

My husband/wife plays the guitar.

I am wearing green socks.

My grandmother speaks English very well.

I am doing the Duke of Edinburgh's Award.

Students do the same in pairs.

1 Ask students to repeat the last sentence you read out in the Warmer. Use this to remind students of what you studied in the last lesson and ask some questions: 'What is the Duke of Edinburgh's Award?', 'How many parts are there?' and 'Which teacher is the leader at Daniel and Grace's school?'. Refer students back to page 10 if they can't remember.

Then ask students, 'What information could there be on a website for the Duke of Edinburgh's Award?'. Get different ideas from the class. Give students one minute to look at the website and have students answer the question in the book. Check the answer and then ask some extra questions, 'Is this the Duke of Edinburgh's Award website?' (*No, it's the school website.*), 'Does everyone do the same activities?' (*No, there is a choice.*) and 'How can you prove you have done an activity?' (*by taking photos*).

Answers

Students who want to do the Duke of Edinburgh's Award.

2 Say to students, 'There are only four skills you can do – true or false?' (*False*) and ask 'How do you know this?' (*This website gives examples of only four skills but it says there are lots more ideas on the main website.*) Tell students to read the sentences, decide whether they are right or wrong and correct the wrong ones. Check as a class and have students say how they know the answer. Go through the sentences together if you are short of time or the class needs more support.

Answers

1 ✓   2 ✗   3 ✓   4 ✓   5 ✗   6 ✓   7 ✗

FAST FINISHERS

Tell fast finishers to write down one extra suggestion for Volunteering, Fitness and Skills. For example: Volunteering – teaching your own language to children who have come to your country. Then put fast finishers together to compare and discuss whether they would like to do any of these extra activities and which are most difficult.

🔊 The Reading text is recorded for students to listen, read and check their answers.
03

Put students into small groups to discuss the questions. Monitor and collect examples of strong language and mistakes for feedback. Ask students to share answers with the class then write the language you have collected on the board and draw attention to the strong language and ask students to correct the mistakes themselves.

VOCABULARY   Personal details

1 Ask students, 'What personal information would the school need to know about each person doing the award?'. Get different suggestions then tell students to look at the information about Grace and check if it includes their ideas. Tell students to look only at the information and try and make each question themselves. (You can help students by giving the question word for each question.) Then have students look at the questions and match them to the words and phrases. Ask students what N24 6BG in the address means. (*It is the postcode.*)

Get students to practise asking the questions. Make sure that students ask the questions with a falling tone. (*yes/no* questions usually have a rising tone and *wh*-questions a falling tone.)

Answers
04

The answers are recorded for students to check and then repeat.

1 Surname   2 Age   3 Address   4 First language
5 Home telephone/Mobile   6 Email address   7 First name

 2 Nominate students to read aloud the contact details for them to predict the pronunciation. Tell students that . and @ in emails are written and pronounced *dot* /dɒt/ and *at* /æt/ and that a zero in telephone numbers is usually pronounced *oh* /əʊ/. Play the recording for students to check and repeat. Make sure that they break the phone numbers into groups of digits, with a pause between, as this is easier to say, hear and remember. Put students into pairs so one student is Grace and the other student asks the questions. When they finish they swap roles.

ə PRONUNCIATION | The alphabet

3 There are lots of fun alphabet songs on YouTube. Alternatively, with books closed, tell students to write down the alphabet. The first person to finish wins. Nominate students to say each letter of the alphabet.

4 🔊 06 Write *B F T* on the board. Ask students which letter has a different sound (*F – the vowel sound is* /e/ *not* /iː/). Tell students to identify the letter with the different sound in the groups given. Play the recording for students to listen and check.

> **Answers**
> **1** U /juː/ not /eɪ/ **2** M /em/ not /iː/ **3** Y /waɪ/ not /e/
> **4** K /keɪ/ not /iː/ **5** X /eks/ not /juː/ **6** O /əʊ/ not /iː/

5 Ask students questions about Sam and Jo, for example, 'Where does Sam live?' Pre-teach *Can you repeat that, please?* as students will need this. Put students into pairs. One student is Sam and the other student asks Sam questions. They then change roles.

Students repeat with the information about Jo. Monitor and make sure students are making the questions and pronouncing the answers correctly. As an extension activity, have students make up the contact details of a famous person, for example Frankenstein or Jennifer Lawrence, and go round the class asking for one another's contact details.

LISTENING

1 🔊 07 Tell students to read Grace's and Daniel's emails on page 10 again and try and predict what they will talk about. Ask students who Finn could be and what relationship he has with Grace and Daniel. Then play the recording to check students' predictions.

> **Answers**
> They are talking about which activities to choose for the Duke of Edinburgh's Award.
> Finn is a new student at the school.

2 🔊 07 Play the recording for students to complete the table. Check answers then ask students, 'Who has chosen the most interesting activities?'

> **Answers**
> **Grace:** Skill – art, Fitness – modern dance
> **Daniel:** Skill – drums, Fitness – hockey
> **Finn:** Skill – chess, Fitness – running

🔊 08 Tell students they are going to listen to the end of the conversation again. Play the recording. Students check their answers in pairs. Then play the recording again and check as a class.

Ask students, 'What else would you like to know about Finn?'. Then have students make the questions to get this information.

> **Answers**
> **1** 33 Alloway Road **2** 0734 667 378
> **3** f.townsend56@facemail.com

» **AUDIOSCRIPT TB PAGE 286**

✓ PREPARE FOR THE EXAM

> **A2 KEY FOR SCHOOLS**
> **Speaking Part 1**
>
> In this part (and the whole exam) students are in pairs. Part 1 lasts 3–4 minutes and there are two phases.
>
> In Phase 1 the examiner will ask each student factual information of a personal kind. In the exam students will not be not asked their address, email address or phone number.
>
> In Phase 2 the examiner will ask questions on two topics. The topics could be about family, school, hobbies, home, etc. The examiner will speak to both students but will ask each one different questions. After the candidates have answered two questions each about a topic, one of the candidates will be asked an extended response question, i.e. Now, please tell me something about … . If candidates don't understand a question, the examiner will ask the question in another way to help them.
>
> **Tip** Tell students that the examiner can only mark what the students say, so it is important for them to answer the questions as fully as they can.

1 Tell students to work in pairs and ask and answer the questions. If students need more support, go through the questions first as a class. Monitor and make sure students are saying full questions and answers. At the end have students check with each other that they have written down the correct information.

> **Answers**
> Students' own answers

> **MIXED ABILITY**
>
> Put students in mixed ability pairs to do this activity. Have stronger students ask the questions first as this is more difficult. Students who need more support then have a model to use when it is their turn to ask questions.

2 Tell students to ask and answer the questions. Monitor and make sure students are giving full answers to all the questions. Then put students into different pairs to repeat both activities.

> **Answers**
> Students' own answers

» **PREPARE FOR THE EXAM TEACHING NOTES AND ANSWER KEY TB PAGE 258**

> **COOLER**
>
> Write this sentence on the board, teach *fox*, and ask the students what is special about the sentence:
>
> *The quick brown fox jumps over the lazy dog.*
>
> If the students don't know, go through the alphabet, crossing off the letters in the sentence until they understand that it uses every letter of the alphabet.
>
> Arrange the students into groups. They must write their own sentence which uses as many letters of the alphabet as possible. The winner is the group with a grammatical sentence with the most different letters.

PRONUNCIATION | The alphabet

3 Practise saying the letters of the alphabet.

A B C D E F G H I
J K L M N O P Q R
S T U V W X Y Z

4 Decide which letter has a different sound in each group.

1 H J U
2 E M P
3 Z L Y

4 K P V
5 W X U
6 C O G

🔊 **Listen and check.**
06

5 In pairs, ask and answer questions using the contact details for Sam and Jo.

> What's your email address?

> My email address is sam.brown@coolmail.com

> How do you spell that?

Sam

sam.brown@coolmail.com

289 Sandy Lane, Oxford O22 3PG

Tel 01865 995478

Mob 06968 133 254

Jo

jo.marsh@melly.co.uk

72 Hale Street, Manchester M4 8QT

Mob 07473 964 443

LISTENING

🔊 **1** Listen to the conversation. What are Grace and Daniel talking about? Who is Finn?
07

🔊 **2** Listen again. Complete the table with the activities the friends choose.
07

	Grace	Daniel	Finn
Skill			
Fitness			

🔊 Listen to the end of the conversation again. Complete Finn's contact details.
08

1 Address: _____
2 Phone number: _____
3 Email address: _____@facemail.com

SPEAKING

✓ PREPARE FOR THE EXAM

Speaking Part 1

1 In pairs, ask and answer questions to complete the form for each other. Spell your surnames.

FIRST NAME:
SURNAME:
AGE:
ADDRESS:
EMAIL ADDRESS:
PHONE NUMBER:

2 In pairs, ask and answer the questions.

School:
How much homework do you get?
What's your favourite subject?
Tell me something about your school.

Free time:
What do you do in your free time?
Who do you spend your free time with?
Tell me something about what you did last weekend.

» PREPARE FOR THE EXAM PAGE 133

IT'S A CHALLENGE! 13

THE EARTH: A CHANGING PLANET

? ABOUT YOU

What is the weather like in your country?
Is the weather the same every year?

VOCABULARY AND READING

Geographical features

1 In pairs, discuss the questions. Then read the article and check your ideas.

   1 How old is the Earth?
   2 What's happening to the Earth's weather at the moment?

2 Read the article again and choose the best heading for each paragraph.

   A Good news in one part of the world
   B Problems for the planet
   C The age of the planet
   D How the planet changes

3 Match the words in blue in the article to the photos A–I. Listen and check. Then repeat.

1 Scientists believe the Earth is 4.6 billion years old. However, the **mountains**, valleys, **hills**, **rivers**, **deserts** and **forests** we see today are much younger than that. For example, Mount Everest is about 60 million years old and the Amazon rainforest is only 10 million years old. The youngest **sea** in the world is the Baltic Sea, at about 15,000 years old.

2 The Earth is always changing because of **volcanoes**, earthquakes and, of course, wind and rain. Some of these changes are very slow and others are quick. Water and ice can make very big changes to the planet. For example, glaciers (rivers of ice) can cut through mountains and make **lakes** and deep **valleys**. Eighty or more volcanoes are under the oceans and sometimes they become new islands. This is happening in the South Pacific, near Tonga.

3 It's normal for our planet to change, but at the moment, scientists think it's changing faster than usual. They don't understand everything that's happening, but they know that some **deserts** (places where it doesn't rain much) are growing, and many forests are getting smaller. The weather is getting wetter in some places and drier in others, and there are more big storms.

4 However, these changes are not bad for everyone. Because the Arctic is getting warmer, some people in Greenland now own businesses and sell vegetables they grow on their land. That wasn't possible so far north 50 years ago. Farmers in Greenland like the warm weather and hope it will continue.

14 UNIT 2

2 OUR CHANGING PLANET

Unit Overview

TOPIC	The world around us
VOCABULARY AND READING	Geographical features The Earth: a changing planet
PRONUNCIATION	th: /θ/ and /ð/
GRAMMAR	Verbs we don't usually use in the continuous
READING	Learning about the giant panda
VOCABULARY	Animals
LISTENING	A conversation about animals
WRITING	An article about an animal
EXAM TASK	Listening Part 5

Resources

GRAMMAR REFERENCE AND PRACTICE: SB page 148; TB page 264
PREPARE FOR THE EXAM: SB page on TB page 248; TB page 258
WORKBOOK: pages 8–11
PHOTOCOPIABLE WORKSHEETS: Grammar worksheet Unit 2; Vocabulary worksheet Unit 2
TEST GENERATOR: Unit test 2

WARMER

To practise the new vocabulary and alphabet sounds from Unit 1, play *Battleships*.

Ask the students to make two 8 by 8 grids in their notebooks. They label the bottom of each grid A–H and the side I–P. In one grid they write six new words from Unit 1, horizontally, vertically or diagonally, one letter in each cell. The other grid they leave blank. Arrange students into pairs. They take turns to guess each other's letters by reading out coordinates (the alphabet letters) and try to find their partner's six words. For example:

Student A: *B/P?*

Student B: *No, my turn. D/J?*

Student A: *Yes, the letter K.* (Student B writes K in square B/P on their blank grid.)

⑦ ABOUT YOU

Ask students, 'What's the weather like today?' and 'Is the weather usually like this at this time of the year?'. In pairs, students discuss the questions. Share ideas as a class.

VOCABULARY AND READING

Geographical features

BACKGROUND INFORMATION

Climate change is caused by a combination of natural and human factors. The natural factors include variations in the amount of light we get from the sun and the movement of land plates. The biggest human factor is the release of gases like carbon dioxide into the atmosphere

and this is known as global warming as it is causing temperatures to rise. Although there is much regional variation, scientists agree that global warming is more significant in climate change than natural factors. There are three main ways of reacting to climate change. The first, and most preferable, is to limit gas emissions; the second is to find ways to adapt to the reality of global warming; the third, and most ambitious, is to change the climate itself through advanced technologies on Earth or in space.

1 Ask students, 'What is changing in our world now?'. Ask them to think about changes in different categories like climate, animals and people, giving some examples, e.g. *people are moving around more*. Get some ideas then put students into pairs to discuss the questions in the book. Share ideas as a class. Pre-teach **earthquake** (it's easier to demonstrate by shaking the desk!) and tell students to check their ideas in the reading text. Check answers as a class.

Answers

1 4.6 billion years old
2 The weather is changing faster than usual. The weather is getting wetter in some places and drier in others, and there are more storms.

2 Tell students to look at heading A and say what information they are looking for (*something positive in a specific place*). Ask students to match the headings to the paragraphs. Check as a class and have students tell you why they match. Then ask students to find all the places mentioned in the text, for example Mount Everest, on a map.

🔊 The Reading text is recorded for students to listen, read
09 and check their answers.

Answers

1 C 2 D 3 B 4 A

FAST FINISHERS

Fast finishers can write down a business idea, like the one some people in Greenland have, which would work because of climate change. For example, *Build hotels on the new islands in the South Pacific and get tourists*. Put fast finishers into pairs to compare ideas.

3 See if students can name any of the features in the photos without looking back at the text. Tell students to match the words to the photos. You can help by giving definitions, for example, *people climb these* (*mountains*).

🔊 **Answers**
10
The answers are recorded for students to check and then repeat.
A desert B hills C volcano D sea E lake F river
G mountains H forest I valley

4 Write an example on the board.

There is a very high <u>mountain / lake</u> in the middle.
(mountain)

Tell students to complete the sentences. Check as a class.

| Answers

1 deserts 2 mountains 3 river 4 forest 5 lake

5 Tell students to write five sentences of their own with two alternatives to test other students. Check the sentences are correct and then put students into pairs to complete one another's sentences.

| Answers

Students' own answers

PRONUNCIATION | th: /θ/ and /ð/

6 These sounds are specific to English, so you will need to show how the sounds are made, by exaggerating how the tongue makes contact with the upper teeth. The difference between them is 'voicing' and you can demonstrate this by asking the students to put their hands over their ears and hearing the buzzing for /ð/. A good contrast is *breath* /θ/ versus *breathe* /ð/ but you will need to demonstrate the meaning of these words.

Play the recording of the two sounds. Students then complete the table.

| Answers

The answers are recorded for students to check and then repeat.
/θ/ earth: north, south, thing, think
/ð/ weather: other, that, there, these, this

7 Tell students to use the vocabulary on page 14 to write five sentences about their country. (If students are all from the same country, for variety you could ask them to write about different regions.) Monitor and make sure students are using the vocabulary correctly.

| Answers

Students' own answers

MIXED ABILITY

Give students who need more support sentence frames to use to write their sentences. For example:

In my country there are (a lot of) …

We have some / don't have many … because …

There aren't many … but …

You can see … in …

---

8 Put students into groups to listen and tick the geographical features in Exercise 3 that the other students say. Ask if they disagree with any of the information given.

GRAMMAR | Verbs we don't usually use in the continuous

1 Ask students to underline the verbs and say what tense they are in. Check as a class. Elicit from students that these verbs are about thinking, feeling and owning things.

| Answers

present simple

---

2 Have students underline the verbs which are about thinking, feeling and owning things. Check as a class. Point out that *have* can be used in the present continuous in phrases like *have a shower*; *think* is used in the present simple for giving opinions, e.g. *What do you think about climate change?* but in the present continuous to describe the thought process, e.g. *What are you thinking about?*

| Answers

belong to, hate, have, love, prefer, need, want

» **GRAMMAR REFERENCE AND PRACTICE ANSWER KEY TB PAGE 264**

3 Write an example on the board:

This is a beautiful house. Who _____ (own) it? (owns)

Tell students to complete the sentences in the correct tense. Check as a class.

| Answers

1 hate 2 wants 3 are you singing, need 4 belongs 5 love
6 am running

4 Say some sentences for students to correct, for example:

Simon's not at home because he works. (~~works~~ is working)

Students correct the sentences. Check as a class.

| Answers

1 There are things in my bag that I **need** at the moment.
2 The weather's cold at the moment, but I **prefer** it like that.
3 I **think** the party was great.
4 My brother **likes** summer and I **like** winter.
5 Get into the pool with me! The water **feels** great.

5 Tell students to write the questions, ask one another and then report back to each other in pairs. You could divide the class into two or more groups during the mingle stage and then form pairs of students from different groups so that the pairs have different information to share. Monitor and make sure students are using the correct tense.

| Answers

Do you own a bike?
Are you learning to play an instrument?
Do you like cabbage?
Are you doing an art project at the moment?
Do you think English is easy?
Are you planning to do something interesting this weekend?
Do you love watching TV?
Are you studying for an exam at the moment?

» **GRAMMAR WORKSHEET UNIT 2**

COOLER

Write these sentences on the board (or dictate them) and ask students to correct them.

1 A mountain is a small hill. (~~small~~ big)

2 A volcano is water with land around. (~~volcano~~ lake)

3 It is dry in a storm. (~~dry~~ wet)

4 *Thing* and *this* begin with the same sound. (~~the same sound~~ different sounds)

5 She is understanding the question. (~~is understanding~~ understands)

6 It rains now. (~~rains~~ is raining)

7 Are you knowing your neighbours? (~~Are you knowing~~ Do you know)

---

4 Complete each sentence with the correct word from Exercise 3.

1 Not many plants and animals can live in _____ because they are very dry. *deserts / hills*
2 Many _____ have snow on top of them all year. *mountains / valleys*
3 There's a _____ near my home, and I like going fishing there. *river / sea*
4 There were so many trees in the _____ that it was impossible to see the sky. *forest / lake*
5 My friend and I cycled to the _____ for a swim. *lake / volcano*

5 Write five sentences of your own using the words from Exercise 3.

∂ PRONUNCIATION | th: /θ/ and /ð/

🔊 **6** Listen to the sounds θ and ð and repeat
11   them. Then put the words in the box into the correct column.

north	other	south
that	there	these
thing	think	this

θ ear**th**	ð wea**th**er

🔊 Listen and check. Then repeat.
12

7 Write sentences about the geography of your country.

There are mountains in the north of my country.

8 In groups of four, listen to each others' sentences. Which geographical features from Exercise 3 does each person talk about?

GRAMMAR | Verbs we don't usually use in the continuous

1 Find these verbs in the article on page 14 and <u>underline</u> them. What tense are they in?

believe	hope	know	like
own	think	understand	

The verbs above are about thinking, feeling and owning things. We don't usually use them in the continuous form.

2 Which of these words are also about thinking, feeling and owning things?

belong to	buy	climb	feel	hate
have	love	mean	need	prefer
run	sing	want	work	

» **GRAMMAR REFERENCE AND PRACTICE PAGE 148**

3 Complete the sentences using the present simple or present continuous of the verbs in brackets.

1 Can you turn the TV off? I _____ (hate) that programme!
2 Mr Jones _____ (want) to talk to you. Are you free now?
3 Why _____ (you sing)? I _____ (need) to study!
4 That book _____ (belong) to me. It's not my friend's.
5 I _____ (love) this T-shirt. Can I buy it, Mum?
6 I can't talk now, sorry. I _____ (run).

4 Correct the mistakes in the sentences.

👁 1 There are things in my bag that I'm needing at the moment.
2 The weather's cold at the moment, but I'm preferring it like that.
3 I'm thinking the party was great.
4 My brother is liking summer and I'm liking winter.
5 Get into the pool with me! The water is feeling great.

5 Use the prompts to write questions beginning *Do you ...* or *Are you ...* Then walk around the class and ask people your questions.

own / a bike?
learn to / play an instrument?
like / cabbage?
do / an art project at the moment?
think / English is easy?
plan to / do something interesting this weekend?
love / watching TV?
need / study for an exam?

In pairs, discuss what you found out.

OUR CHANGING PLANET 15

1 Look at the picture below. In pairs, write down three things you know about pandas. Read the article once to check your ideas.

2 Are these sentences right (✓) or wrong (✗)?

1 The writer helped to look after giant pandas on her trip.
2 It's possible to find wild pandas in several countries.
3 Pandas only eat bamboo.
4 Baby pandas are very light when they are born.
5 Pandas start eating bamboo at the age of 18 months.
6 Scientists know exactly how many wild pandas there are.
7 It's possible to see a panda in Mexico.

Learning about the
GIANT PANDA 🔊 13

When I planned my trip to China, one of things I really wanted to do was to work at the Dujiangyan Panda Base in Chengdu. I spent seven days there, looking after the pandas, giving them food and cleaning their enclosures.

While I was there, I learned a lot about pandas. Wild pandas live in bamboo forests, high in the mountains of central China. In the past, they also lived in other parts of China and in Myanmar and Vietnam, but they don't any more. They spend about 12 hours a day eating bamboo, but they sometimes eat other plants or small animals. At Dujiangyan, we also gave them fruit, like apples, and special panda cakes made of rice, eggs and flour and other things.

Adult giant pandas weigh between 75 and 135 kilograms. Females usually only have one baby panda, or cub, at a time. The cubs only weigh about 85 grams when they are born! The little cub drinks milk for about four months and then begins to eat bamboo. Young pandas stay with their mothers for around 18 months.

Scientists think there are now between 1,500 and 2,000 pandas in the wild. This is a low number, but it's double what it was in the 1970s. The reason the number is going up is because of all the work scientists are doing at places like the Dujiangyan Panda Base in Chengdu. There are also about 325 pandas in zoos in a number of different countries, including the United States, Mexico, Japan and Germany.

🔊 14 **EP** 1 Match the words in the box to the photos A–J. Listen and check. Then repeat.

dolphin   elephant   giraffe
monkey   parrot   penguin
polar bear   snake
tiger   whale

2 Answer the questions about the animals in Exercise 1.

1 Where do the animals come from?
2 Where do they live (sea, mountains, forest)?
3 Which are dangerous?
4 Look at each photo carefully. Are the animals in a zoo or are they wild?
5 How many other animals can you name in English?

💬 **TALKING POINTS**

What are your five favourite animals?
Why do you like them?
How often do you go to zoos?
Do you like them?

16   UNIT 2

WARMER

Ask students, 'What pets do you have?'. Ask them to say what is good and bad about having a dog. Get different ideas, for example, (good) *A dog can look after the house,* (bad) *You need to go for a walk with your dog in the winter.* Tell students to write down one good thing and one bad thing about having each of these pets: a cat, fish, a rabbit, a bird. Put students into small groups to compare ideas.

1 Books closed. Ask students, 'Which animal is black and white and lives in China?' (*a panda*). Put students in pairs to write down three pieces of information about pandas. Give an example: *They are bears.* As an alternative, or extension, ask the students to write three things which they would like to know about pandas, for example, *Do they eat other animals?.* Share ideas as a class.

Books open. Ask some questions about the photo: 'What are the people doing?', 'Do you think they are enjoying it?' and 'Would you like to do this?'.

Pre-teach **bamboo** (a tall tropical grass with hard, hollow stems, or the stems of this plant), **enclosure** (an area surrounded by fences or walls) and **the wild** (the natural place for animals to live, not a zoo). Books open. Give students three minutes to check their ideas in the text.

Answers

Students' own answers

2 Ask students, 'The writer knew about the panda base before they went to China. Right or wrong?' (*Right*) 'How do you know?' (*The writer knew about it when they planned their trip.*).

Tell students to answer the questions in the book. When you go through the answers, make the students tell you what is wrong with the 'wrong' answers. Then ask students some open comprehension questions: 'Where in China do pandas live?' (*in central China*), 'What are panda cakes made of?', (*rice, eggs and flour and other things*), 'Is the number of pandas increasing or decreasing?' (*increasing*) and 'Do most pandas live in the wild or in zoos?' (*in the wild*).

Answers

1 ✓
2 ✗ Pandas are only found in the mountains of central China.
3 ✗ They sometimes eat other plants or small animals.
4 ✓
5 ✗ They start eating bamboo when they are about four months old.
6 ✗ They think there are about 1,500 to 2,000.
7 ✓

🔊
13 The Reading text is recorded for students to listen, read and check their answers.

FAST FINISHERS

Fast finishers write three more right/wrong questions for the other fast finishers to answer.

1 Ask, 'Which of these animals do you know?' before the matching. Play the recording for students to check and repeat the words. Ask some questions about the animals: 'Which has a long neck?' (*the giraffe*), 'Which can fly?' (*the parrot*) and 'Which can climb very well?' (*the monkey*). Then have students cover up the words, look at the pictures and say what the animals are.

🔊
14 **Answers**

The answers are recorded for students to check and then repeat.
A monkey B elephant C snake D polar bear E whale
F giraffe G tiger H parrot I penguin J dolphin

2 Put students in small groups to answer the questions. Check as a class. Then ask students for other ways to categorise the animals, for example, one colour / different colours; I've seen some / I haven't seen any.

As an extension activity, choose one of the animals from Exercise 1 and tell students they must guess which one it is. Students can ask you ten questions (but not *What is it?*) to find out which animal it is. Give the students useful questions and frames to help them, for example:

Where does it live?

Is it (big)?

What does it eat?

Can it … ?

When you have demonstrated, put students into pairs to do the same.

Possible answers

1 Monkeys come from many countries in Africa, South America and Asia; elephants come from Africa and Asia; snakes are on every continent; polar bears come from the Arctic which includes parts of Canada, Russia, Alaska, Greenland and Norway; whales live in the oceans; giraffes come from Africa; tigers come from Asia; parrots come from Africa, Asia and South America; penguins come from southern Africa, the tip of South America, Australia, New Zealand and Antarctica; dolphins live in seas around the world.
2 Sea: dolphin, whale (penguins and polar bears live close to the sea)
Mountains: monkey, parrot, snake
Forests: elephant, monkey, parrot, snake, tiger
Other: giraffe
3 monkeys, elephants, snakes, polar bears, tigers
4 They look as though they are wild.
5 Students' own answers

» **VOCABULARY WORKSHEET UNIT 2**

💬 **TALKING POINTS**

This could be done in pairs or, to maximise speaking opportunities, as a class survey with students asking the questions to as many other students as they can in a time limit. As an extension, students could turn the results of the first question into a pictograph. They make a graph with the number of pictures of the animal corresponding to how many students like it. (Look up 'animal pictograph' on Google for examples.) This could be done on paper or electronically.

LISTENING

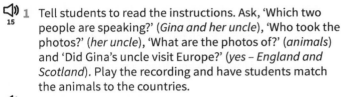

A2 KEY FOR SCHOOLS
Listening Part 5

In this part, students listen to a dialogue. They need to match five items to eight options. They are listening for specific information such as objects, places and feelings. They hear the recording twice.

Tip Tell the students that there are five questions plus an example, and eight answers, so there are two answers they don't need to use. They may hear two or more words from the list of answers for each question, but only one will be correct. They must listen for the meaning to choose the right one.

🔊 **1** Tell students to read the instructions. Ask, 'Which two
15 people are speaking?' (*Gina and her uncle*), 'Who took the photos?' (*her uncle*), 'What are the photos of?' (*animals*) and 'Did Gina's uncle visit Europe?' (*yes – England and Scotland*). Play the recording and have students match the animals to the countries.

🔊 **2** Have students check in pairs then play the recording
15 again to check as a class.

Answers

1 C 2 B 3 H 4 G 5 E

» **AUDIOSCRIPT TB PAGE 286**

» **PREPARE FOR THE EXAM TEACHING NOTES AND ANSWER KEY TB PAGE 258**

3 Tell students to look at the photos and teach the pronunciation of *kakapo* /ˈkɑːkəpəʊ/. Put students into pairs and tell one student to go to the information about the kakapo on page 136 and one student to go to the information about the sand cat on page 138. Have students ask one another questions using the question prompts. Monitor and make sure students are asking the questions correctly and replying with full answers.

As feedback, nominate students to give you information about each of the animals.

Answers

Possible questions
1 What kind of animal is it?
2 Where is it from?
3 Where does it live?
4 What does it eat?
5 How much does it weigh?
6 How many are left in the wild?
7 What are its babies called?
8 How many babies do the females have?
9 How long do the babies stay with the mother?
Possible answers for the kakapo
1 It's a kind of parrot.
2 It comes from New Zealand.
3 It lives on two islands.
4 It eats plants, fruit and nuts.
5 An adult weighs from two to four kilos.
6 There are about 127 kakapos left in the wild.
7 Kakapo babies called *chicks*.
8 Females have two to three chicks every two years.
9 The chicks stay with their mother for 10 weeks.

Possible answers for the sand cat
1 It's a kind of cat.
2 It comes from Africa and Asia.
3 It lives in deserts.
4 It eats insects, birds and other small animals.
5 An adult weighs from one to three kilos
6 No one knows how many there are in the wild.
7 Sand cat babies are called *kittens*.
8 Females have one to eight kittens every year.
9 The cubs stay with their mother for about six months.

MIXED ABILITY

Put weaker students together and go through all the questions before they start the speaking activity. Make sure students make the questions correctly and drill the questions. Stronger students can try and do the task without looking at the question prompts.

WRITING

✎ PREPARE TO WRITE
An article about an animal

GET READY Ask students some questions to remind them about the panda text, for example, 'What food do pandas eat most?' (*bamboo*). Have students underline the prepositions and say which two have the same meaning (*around/about*). Tell students to complete the sentences. Check as a class.

Answers

1 between 2 about/around 3 including 4 between
5 including

PLAN Tell students to choose an animal and make notes for each paragraph. Students could get information from the internet, reference books or by asking one another.

WRITE Tell students to write their article and encourage them to use the prepositions from *Get ready*. This stage could be done for homework to save time.

IMPROVE Have students work in pairs and make suggestions for how to improve one another's articles. Tell students to correct grammar and spelling mistakes and suggest different words. Students could then make changes. Have students read out their articles to the whole class.

COOLER

Have a quiz about the unit content.

1 Which is older – Everest or the Amazon rainforest? (*Everest*)

2 Could you grow vegetables in Greenland 50 years ago? (*no*)

3 What is a baby panda called? (*a cub*)

4 How many hours a day do pandas spend eating? (*about 12*)

5 How long does the kakapo stay with its mother? (*10 weeks*)

6 What do sand cats eat? (*insects, birds, small animals*)

PREPARE FOR THE EXAM

Listening Part 5

1 You will hear Gina talking to her uncle about some photos of animals. Where did he take each photo? For each question, choose the correct answer.

Photographs	Countries
0 lion *D*	**A** Argentina
1 monkey	**B** England
2 snake	**C** India
3 penguin	**D** Kenya
4 dolphin	**E** Mexico
5 elephant	**F** New Zealand
	G Scotland
	H South Africa

2 Listen again and check.

>> **PREPARE FOR THE EXAM PAGE 132**

3 Work in pairs. Look at the photos of the two animals below. Use the prompts 1–9 to write questions about these animals.

1 What kind of animal / it?
2 Where / from?
3 Where / live?
4 What / eat?
5 How much / weigh?
6 How many / left in the wild?
7 What / babies / called?
8 How many babies / female have?
9 How long / baby stay with / mother?

>> Student A, go to page 136. You have information about the kakapo there.

>> Student B, go to page 138. You have information about the sand cat there.

PREPARE TO WRITE

An article about an animal

GET READY Underline the prepositions *between*, *about*, *around* and *including* in the article about pandas on page 16. Think about their meaning. Which two have the same meaning in the article?

Complete the sentences with *between*, *about*, *around* or *including*.

1 This competition is for anyone _____ the ages of 10 and 14.
2 There are _____ 40,000 African lions left in the wild.
3 All my friends, _____ Tariq, are interested in animals.
4 The zoo is closed _____ January and March.
5 I've got lots of pets, _____ a rabbit and two cats.

PLAN Plan your article about an animal. Choose one of the animals in Vocabulary Exercise 1 or a different one. Write three paragraphs. Make notes for what to include in each paragraph.

Paragraph 1	the kind of animal it is / where it lives / what it eats
Paragraph 2	what it weighs / information about its babies
Paragraph 3	how many are left in the wild / in zoos

WRITE Write your article. Try to include the prepositions from *Get Ready*.

IMPROVE In pairs, compare your articles. Can you improve them?

Kakapo

Sand cat

OUR CHANGING PLANET **17**

CULTURE

NATIONAL PARKS

1 Discuss the questions in pairs.

   1 What is a national park?
   2 Have you ever been to one?
   3 Can you name a national park in your country?
   4 What can you see there?

2 Where is Yellowstone National Park? What do you know about it? Read the text and check your ideas.

3 Match the texts 1–5 with the photos A–E.

Yellowstone National Park

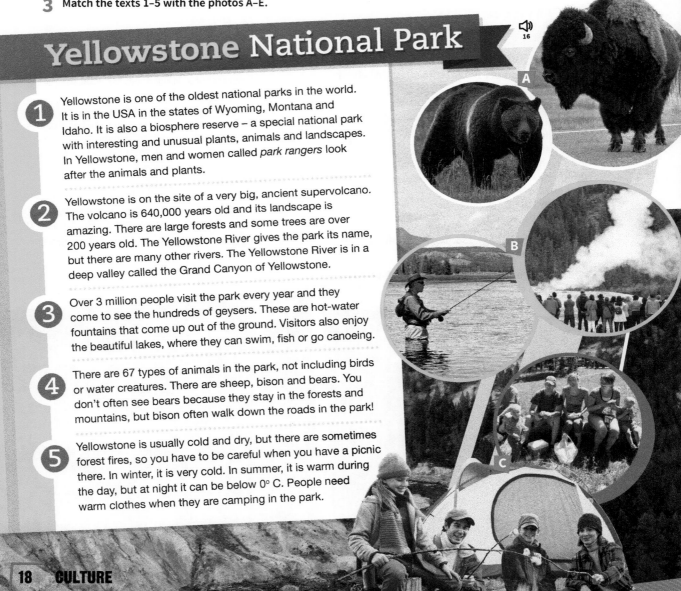

1 Yellowstone is one of the oldest national parks in the world. It is in the USA in the states of Wyoming, Montana and Idaho. It is also a biosphere reserve – a special national park with interesting and unusual plants, animals and landscapes. In Yellowstone, men and women called *park rangers* look after the animals and plants.

2 Yellowstone is on the site of a very big, ancient supervolcano. The volcano is 640,000 years old and its landscape is amazing. There are large forests and some trees are over 200 years old. The Yellowstone River gives the park its name, but there are many other rivers. The Yellowstone River is in a deep valley called the Grand Canyon of Yellowstone.

3 Over 3 million people visit the park every year and they come to see the hundreds of geysers. These are hot-water fountains that come up out of the ground. Visitors also enjoy the beautiful lakes, where they can swim, fish or go canoeing.

4 There are 67 types of animals in the park, not including birds or water creatures. There are sheep, bison and bears. You don't often see bears because they stay in the forests and mountains, but bison often walk down the roads in the park!

5 Yellowstone is usually cold and dry, but there are sometimes forest fires, so you have to be careful when you have a picnic there. In winter, it is very cold. In summer, it is warm during the day, but at night it can be below 0° C. People need warm clothes when they are camping in the park.

18 CULTURE

CULTURE

Learning Objectives

- The students learn about Yellowstone National and the importance of national parks in general.
- In the project stage, students find out about a national park in their country and make a presentation about it for the class.

Vocabulary

park ranger unusual look after ancient amazing go canoeing creatures picnic

Resources

CULTURE VIDEO AND CULTURE VIDEO WORKSHEET: Glacier National Park

BACKGROUND INFORMATION

The oldest national park is actually Bogd Khan Uul National Park in Mongolia, established in 1778. The park is a mountain about 2,200 metres high and overlooking the capital of Mongolia, Ulaanbaatar. The mountain was sacred and religious services used to be held there with food and even money being given to the spirits of the mountain.

One of the first national parks in Europe was the Swiss National Park, established in 1914. It is located in the Alps mountain range in eastern Switzerland and borders Italy. The rules for visitors to the park are very strict: you cannot leave the marked paths, light fires or walk your dog there.

The Royal National Park in Australia was the first to have national park in its name when it was established in 1879. Just south of the largest city Sydney, it is very accessible and there are over 100 kilometres of walking paths. The 30-kilometre coast walk is often done as part of the Duke of Edinburgh Award. Because of the dry climate, bush fires are a threat and the park is sometimes closed if there is a fire risk. The park is on the coast so there are plenty of beaches and rock pools. It is not recommended to go into the rock pools as they contain the blue-ringed octopus, one of the most dangerous sea animals because although it is only about 5 centimetres long it releases a poison which can kill very quickly.

The largest national park is the Northeast Greenland national park covering 972,000 km² of the interior coast of Greenland, which is itself the biggest island in the world. Most of the park is on an ice sheet and an animal population which includes polar bears, walruses and seals reflects this. In the park you can also find the Arctic hare, a type of hare with a thick layer of fat that allows it to live in the extreme cold. There is no permanent human population in the park but there are military bases and research stations.

Thailand has the most national parks, about 150, covering 20% of its territory. The first marine national park in Thailand was Khao Sam Roi Yot on the south-east coast. A rare animal found there is the fishing cat, which can swim long distances, even under water, to find food. If you are very fit you can do the mountain climb to reach Phraya Nakhon Cave and enjoy its outstanding natural beauty.

WARMER

Ask students where these places with colour words in them are: The White House (*Washington DC, the USA*), The Black Forest (*Baden-Württemberg, Germany*), Red Square (*Moscow, Russia*), Greenland (*near Canada*). The Red Sea (*The middle east*), Yellowstone.

For Yellowstone, ask students to read the text and find out.

1 Ask students about the best places in their country to enjoy nature. Tell students to read the box about national parks. Put students into pairs to discuss the questions. Share ideas as a class. Ask students, 'Why do we need national parks?' (*To protect the environment and wildlife there and make the place accessible and attractive to tourists.*).

   Answers

   Students' own answers

2 Ask students some specific questions about Yellowstone, for example, 'Why is it called Yellowstone?', 'What can visitors do there?'and 'What's the weather usually like?'. Give students a time limit to read and check their ideas. Ask students if any of the information particularly impressed or surprised them.

   Answers

   The USA in the states of Wyoming, Montana and Idaho

3 Use the photos to pre-teach the vocabulary **bison** (point out that *bison* is both singular and plural), **fish** (verb), **geyser** and **valley**. Tell students to match the photos to the texts. Check as a class.

   Answers

   1 D 2 E 3 B 4 A 5 C

FAST FINISHERS

Tell fast finishers to write a sub-title which could go before each paragraph. For example, paragraph 1 *Welcome to Yellowstone!*, paragraph 2 *Where we are*.

4 Give some oral examples first: Yellowstone is a new national park. (*Wrong – it is one of the oldest.*) A geyser has boiling water. (*Right*) Tell students to mark the sentences in the book as right or wrong and correct the ones which are wrong. Check as a class. Ask students what they would do if they saw a bison on the road.

Answers

1 ✗ It is in three states.
2 ✓
3 ✗ Glaciers are not mentioned.
4 ✓
5 ✓
6 ✗ You can swim or go canoeing.
7 ✓
8 ✓

5 Tell students to match the words and definitions. Point out that 2 and 5 are phrases. Check as a class. Ask some questions using the vocabulary, for example, 'How often do you have picnics?' 'Have you ever been canoeing?' 'Is there anything unusual in your town or area?'

Answers

1 unusual 2 look after 3 ancient 4 amazing 5 go canoeing
6 creatures 7 picnic

🔊 The Reading text is recorded for students to listen, read
16 and check their answers.

6 Ask students what the best time of year would be to go for a walk in Yellowstone. Then have students say what you could see on a walk in Yellowstone: which natural features and animals.

Possible answers

a canyon, mountains, geysers, volcanic rocks, fields, plants, wild flowers, hot water pools, a waterfall, lots of animals including sheep, foxes and bison.

🔊 7 Pre-teach **mystic** (relating to or involving mysterious
17 religious or spiritual powers). Go through the questions and have students predict what they are listening for. For example, in gap 1 students need a noun. Tell students to listen and complete the information. Check as a class.

Answers

1 fruit 2 sheep 3 film 4 9 (nine) 5 notebook 6 waterfall
7 6 (six)

≫ **AUDIOSCRIPT TB PAGE 287**

💬 **TALKING POINTS**

Put students into pairs to say which walk they would prefer to do and why. Share ideas as a class.

MIXED ABILITY

Give weaker students some phrases to structure their speaking:

I'd prefer to go on … because …

The most interesting thing for me about … would be …

It would be great to … because …

I could … and that would be fun because …

Encourage students to give reasons for their choices in full sentences.

PROJECT *Description of a national park*

Students could do this project individually or work in small groups. Students can use the internet or reference books to find details about their national park. The presentations will be more interesting if there are a variety of national parks so ask students to tell you what they have chosen so that you can make sure there is not too much repetition. If students are working individually and have chosen the same place, you could ask them to work together. As an alternative, you could have students find out about a national park in a different country.

Tell students first to make notes about their national park. Then they should decide which information to include in their presentation. Tell students that they could use technology like Powerpoint for their presentation or they could make a poster. When students present their information, give them a time limit and have the rest of the class ask them questions. Give feedback to students at the end of all the presentations on the content, language and style of presentation. You could put the presentations on social media or the class website or, if they are posters, put them on the classroom walls.

PROJECT EXTENSION

Plan a class trip to a national park or area of natural beauty near you. Tell students to do some research and present to the class information about the best place to visit and the most economical in terms of time and money. The class can then vote for which place to visit. If you can't actually physically visit this place, plan the trip as if you were going and make an itinerary like the ones in Exercise 7.

▶ **CULTURE VIDEO:** Glacier National Park
01 When students have completed the lesson, they can watch the video and complete the worksheet.

COOLER

Read out these places in the USA and get students to write them in two columns: with *the* and without *the*. The answers are given in brackets.

Examples: USA (the), America (–)

- Yellowstone park (–)
- 5th Avenue (–)
- Hudson River (*the*)
- Empire State Building (*the*)
- Macy's Department Store (–)
- Lake Superior (–)
- Rocky Mountains (*the*)
- White House (*the*)
- Wall Street (–)
- Central Park (–)
- Golden Gate Bridge (*the*)

Students could then find out information about these places from the internet or a library.

4 Are these sentences right (✓) or wrong (✗)?

1 Yellowstone is part of one state in the USA.
2 Park rangers protect the animals and plants in Yellowstone.
3 Yellowstone has a famous glacier.
4 The park contains very old plants.
5 The geysers in the park are popular with tourists.
6 You can't go in the water in the park.
7 People regularly see bison in the park.
8 The temperature can be very different on summer days and nights.

5 Find words in the text that match the definitions.

1 different from others (paragraph 1)
2 keep safe (paragraph 1)
3 very old (paragraph 2)
4 fantastic (paragraph 2)
5 travel in a small type of boat (paragraph 3)
6 animals in general (paragraph 4)
7 a meal outside (paragraph 5)

6 What can you see on a walk in Yellowstone Park? Make a list. Then, listen and check your ideas.

7 Listen and complete the information about two guided walks in Yellowstone Park.

	Mount Washburn	Mystic Falls
Leave hotel at	10 am	[4] _____ am
Transport	bus	bus
Lunch	sandwiches, [1] _____ and cold drinks	hamburgers and chicken
Things to take	a light jacket and a camera	a [5] _____
Landscape you see	the Grand Canyon of Yellowstone and the Teton Mountains	In Biscuit Basin there are geysers and hot-water pools and a [6] _____ in Mystic Falls.
Animals you see	[2] _____ and maybe foxes	bison
Arrive back at	4 pm	[7] _____ pm
After trip activity	a [3] _____ about geography	a meeting to share photos

💬 **TALKING POINTS**

Which walk would you prefer to go on? Explain why.

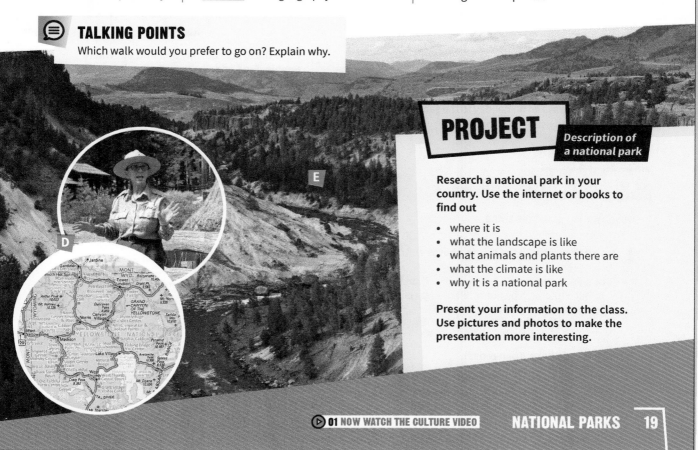

PROJECT

Description of a national park

Research a national park in your country. Use the internet or books to find out

- where it is
- what the landscape is like
- what animals and plants there are
- what the climate is like
- why it is a national park

Present your information to the class. Use pictures and photos to make the presentation more interesting.

▶ **01 NOW WATCH THE CULTURE VIDEO**   **NATIONAL PARKS** 19

3 ON HOLIDAY

FIRST HOLIDAYS WITH FRIENDS

Most of us can't wait to go on holiday without our parents. We can choose where to go, what to do and who to go with. But are first holidays with friends always great? Read about Sophie, Fred and Chris. Where did they go? Did they have a good time?

Last summer, after we finished our exams, I invited my friend Paula to go on holiday to Greece with me. We got a flight to Athens and then we went by ship to the island of Milos. We were really tired when we got there, but we both wanted a swim, so we went to the beach. You can guess! We lay down and closed our eyes and when we woke up TWO hours later, we were really hot and thirsty – and red! Never again! Sophie, 16

My first holiday was a weekend in London. Jim, Simon and I travelled by tram from my house to the bus station. When we arrived there, I put my hand in my pocket but my wallet wasn't there! Where was it? I think I lost it on the tram. Jim and Simon each lent me money for the coach. We stayed at Jim's aunt's house in London and we had a fantastic weekend. Fred, 13

My first holiday was with my friend Tom at a campsite in a forest near our town. We didn't want my parents to drive us there, so we went by bus and then on foot. It was a long walk to the forest and it was raining! I put the tent up quickly because I knew how to do it, but all our things were wet. Then the sun came out the next day. We dried everything and had a great time! Chris, 12

? ABOUT YOU

Where do you like going on holiday?
How often do you go on holiday?
Do you always go on holiday to the same place?
How do you usually get there?

VOCABULARY AND READING

Holidays: Ways of travelling

1 Match the words in the box to photos A–K.

> **EP**
> by bike   by boat   by coach   on foot
> by helicopter   by motorbike   by plane
> by scooter   by ship   by tram
> by underground

🔊 **18** Listen and check. Then repeat.

2 Decide whether each type of transport from Exercise 1 moves in the air, on land or in the water.

3 Read the article quickly and find out where Sophie, Fred and Chris went on holiday. How did each of them get there?

4 Read the article again and answer the questions.

1 What does the article mean by 'first holidays'?
2 What did Sophie and Paula do when they arrived on the island?
3 What happened while they were sleeping?
4 What did Fred lose?
5 How did he pay for the coach?
6 What was the weather like when Chris and Tom were putting up the tent?

ə PRONUNCIATION | Silent letters

5 In pairs, read the words aloud. Which are the silent letters?

climb	flight	guess	half
island	knew	two	where

🔊 **20** Listen and check. Then repeat.

3 ON HOLIDAY

Unit Overview

TOPIC	Holidays and travelling
VOCABULARY AND READING	Holidays: Ways of travelling
	First holidays with friends
PRONUNCIATION	Silent letters
GRAMMAR	Past simple
READING	Teen Travel Tips: Moscow
VOCABULARY	Holiday vocabulary
LISTENING	A conversation with a hotel receptionist
SPEAKING	A conversation at a tourist information centre
EXAM TASKS	Speaking Part 2; Reading Part 2

Resources

GRAMMAR REFERENCE AND PRACTICE: SB page 149; TB page 264

PREPARE FOR THE EXAM: SB pages on TB pages 238 and 250–251; TB pages 253 and 259

WORKBOOK: pages 12–15

PHOTOCOPIABLE WORKSHEETS: Grammar worksheet Unit 3; Vocabulary worksheet Unit 3

TEST GENERATOR: Unit test 3

WARMER

Tell students to come to the middle of the room. Tell everyone to run to the left wall if the noun you say needs the preposition *at* and to the right wall if it needs *on*: 'two o'clock' (*at*), 'Wednesday' (*on*), 'the phone' (*on*), 'school' (*at*), 'home' (*at*), 'your way home' (*on*), 'TV' (*on*), 'night' (*at*), 'holiday' (*on*).

ABOUT YOU

Ask students, 'What places are popular for holidays in (y)our country?'. Then have students answer the questions in pairs. Share ideas as a class.

VOCABULARY AND READING

Holidays: Ways of travelling

1 See if students know any of the transport words already. Then ask students to match the words to the photos. Ask students, 'Which preposition is different?' (*on foot*).

Answers

The answers are recorded for students to check and then repeat.
A by helicopter **B** by motorbike **C** on foot **D** by coach **E** by boat **F** by plane **G** by tram **H** by bike **I** by ship **J** by underground **K** by scooter

2 Ask students, 'Does a bike move in the air, on land or in the water?' (*on land*). Tell students to decide what the other words do. Check then have students work in pairs and add as many words as they can to the categories air/land/water in a time limit. (Other A1–B1 examples are given in the answer key in italics.)

Answers

Air: by helicopter, by plane, *by jet*
Land: by bike, by coach, on foot, by motorbike, by scooter, by tram, by underground, *by ambulance, by bus, by train, by lorry, by van*
Water: by boat, by ship, *by ferry*

3 Pre-teach **campsite** (an area where people can stay in tents for a holiday). Give students three minutes to read the text then ask the question as a class.

Answers

Sophie went to Athens by plane and then to Milos by ship.
Fred went to London by tram and by coach.
Chris went to a campsite in a forest by bus and on foot.

4 Ask, 'Which of the friends is the youngest?' (*Chris*) and 'Where is Athens?' (*Greece*). Check the answers as a class. Ask, 'Where would you like to go on holiday without your parents?'.

Answers

1 First holidays means people's first holidays without their parents.
2 They went to the beach to have a swim.
3 They got sunburnt.
4 He lost his wallet.
5 His friends, Jim and Simon, lent him the money.
6 It was raining.

 The Reading text is recorded for students to listen, read and check their answers.
19

MIXED ABILITY

For students who need more support with open questions write two-option answers on the board:

1 It means people's first holidays **A** without their parents **B** in their life

2 They went to the beach to have **A** a sleep **B** a swim

3 **A** They got sunburnt. **B** They woke up at two o'clock.

4 He lost **A** his wallet. **B** his money for the coach.

5 **A** Jim's aunt **B** Jim and Simon … lent him the money.

6 **A** It was sunny. **B** It was raining.

7 **A** No. All their clothes were wet.
B Yes. The sun came out the next day.

PRONUNCIATION | Silent letters

5 Ask students, 'What season comes after summer?' (*autumn*). Elicit that we don't pronounce the *n* at the end of *autumn*; it is silent, i.e. it is written but not said.

In pairs, students read the words and underline the silent letters. Play the recording. Students check and repeat. Elicit any more examples of silent letters the students might know, e.g. *often, talk, night*.

Answers
20

The answers are recorded for students to check and then repeat. The silent letters are underlined.
climb, flight, guess, half, island, knew, two, where

A2 KEY FOR SCHOOLS
Speaking Part 2

In this part, the examiner will start by asking the students a general question about the five pictures, for example, 'Do you like these different ways of travelling? Why? / Why not?' Students then have 1–2 minutes to talk together and give their answers. Students need to name what they see and then talk about whether they like or dislike it and say why. Following that, they are each asked one or more questions about some of the pictures, such as 'Do you think riding a bike is difficult? Why? / Why not?' Then each student is asked individually which they like best.

Tip Tell students that they should interact well with their partner by listening to what their partner says, asking questions and making comments. They could look ahead to page 51 for phrases to keep the conversation going and interrupt politely.

6 Put students into pairs to discuss the questions. Share ideas as a class.

≫ **PREPARE FOR THE EXAM TEACHING NOTES AND ANSWER KEY TB PAGE 259**

GRAMMAR Past simple

1 Say, 'Give me an example of a regular past simple verb' (e.g. *walked*) and elicit the rule (base form + *ed*). Then say, 'Tell me some verbs which are not like this, which are irregular' (e.g. *do–did, go–went*). Tell students to underline the past simple verbs in the sentences given. Ask for the base forms of the irregular verbs too.

> **Answers**
> 1 Where <u>did</u> they <u>go</u>?
> 2 Where <u>was</u> it?
> 3 <u>Did</u> they <u>have</u> a good time?
> 4 We <u>closed</u> our eyes.
> 5 Jim and Simon and I <u>travelled</u> by tram to the bus station.
> 6 My wallet <u>wasn't</u> there.
> 7 My first holiday <u>was</u> with my friend Tom.
> 8 We <u>didn't want</u> my parents to drive us, so we <u>went</u> by bus and then on foot.
> 9 We <u>dried</u> everything.
>
> 1 closed, travelled, didn't want, dried
> 2 did (they) go, was, Did (they) have, wasn't, went
> 3 be

2 Books closed, ask students if they can remember any more examples of the past simple in the article. Books open, ask students to check and underline all the past simple verbs. Check as a class.

> **Answers**
> got went were got wanted went lay woke were
> was arrived put was lost lent stayed had
> was was was put knew were came out had

3 Go through the sentences orally first then tell students to write them. Check as a class. For extra practice, have students make the questions positive sentences, make the positive verb forms negative and the negative verb forms positive (students will need to change some of the words too).

> **Answers**
> 1 Did you go 2 didn't travel, was 3 wanted, didn't have
> 4 Did the plane arrive 5 wasn't, enjoyed 6 Were you

FAST FINISHERS

Tell fast finishers to complete the sentences with other past simple verbs where possible. For example: **1** Did you travel … , **2** They didn't go …

4 Tell students to look back at the text and complete the answers to the questions. Before students work out the rules for making past simple sentences make sure they understand what a subject and object is by using a simple example: *Paula likes Fred.* – subject verb object

Check answers as a class. Give an extra example with *What*: What dried everything? (*What* = subject, so *did* is not used). What did the sun dry? (*What* = object, so *did* is used)

> **Answers**
> a Paula b Fred
> 1 a 2 past simple without 'did' 3 the object 4 the subject

5 Ask students to identify whether *Who* is a subject or object of the verb in each sentence (**1** = object, **2** = subject). Have them choose the answers then check as a class. Then give an answer and have students make the question, for example, *She bought a cake.* (What did she buy?)

> **Answers**
> 1 b 2 a

≫ **GRAMMAR REFERENCE AND PRACTICE ANSWER KEY TB PAGE 264**

6 Tell students to complete the sentences. Check as a class.

> **Answers**
> 1 did you eat 2 took 3 did you go camping 4 booked
> 5 did you go 6 bought

7 Write an example on the board and have students correct it: *I couldn't swim so I feeled afraid.* (*feeled – felt*)

Tell students to correct the sentences. Check as a class.

> **Answers**
> 1 I **made** two new friends on my holiday.
> 2 Sorry we couldn't meet yesterday. I **went** shopping and then cycling with my mum.
> 3 It was a rainy day on Saturday, so I **spent** the day at home.
> 4 I **watched** TV and played on the computer yesterday evening.
> 5 It was a pity you **left** the party early last Friday.

8 Books closed, mix the words up in the questions, write them on the board and have students rearrange them. Books open, students check with the book and then discuss the questions in pairs. Compare ideas as a class.

≫ **GRAMMAR WORKSHEET UNIT 3**

COOLER

Arrange students into groups. Ask them to write the alphabet A–Z down a page of their notebooks. For each letter they must think of a verb, for example, *Ask, Break*, etc. Give a time limit and see which group can give a verb for the most letters of the alphabet. Students then write the past simple for each verb: *Asked, Broke*, etc.

PREPARE FOR THE EXAM

Speaking Part 2

6 **Look at the photos A–K on page 20. Discuss the questions with your partner.**

1 Do you like these different ways of travelling? Why? / Why not?
2 Do you think riding a bike is difficult? Why? / Why not?
3 Do you think going in a boat or a ship is enjoyable? Why? / Why not?
4 Now tell your partner which of these ways of travelling you like best.
5 How do you like to travel when it's very hot?
6 Do you prefer going on holiday to the sea or in the mountains?

»» PREPARE FOR THE EXAM PAGE 134

GRAMMAR   Past simple

1 **Underline the past simple forms in the sentences.**

1 Where did they go?
2 Where was it?
3 Did they have a good time?
4 We closed our eyes.
5 Jim, Simon and I travelled by tram to the bus station.
6 My wallet wasn't there.
7 My first holiday was with my friend Tom.
8 We didn't want my parents to drive us, so we went by bus and then on foot.
9 We dried everything.

Now answer these questions.

1 Which past simple verbs are regular?
2 Which past simple verbs are irregular?
3 Which verb never has *did* in questions and negatives?

2 <u>Underline</u> all the examples of the past simple in the article.

3 **Complete the sentences using the past simple of the verb in brackets.**

1 _____ (you / go) on holiday with your family last year?
2 They _____ (not travel) by boat to the island because the weather _____ (be) bad.
3 We _____ (want) to visit the museum, but we _____ (not have) time.
4 _____ (the plane / arrive) on time?
5 The holiday _____ (not be) great, but I _____ (enjoy) the afternoons on the beach.
6 _____ (you / be) in the mountains for the whole holiday?

4 **Read questions a and b and complete the answers. Then answer questions 1–4.**

a Who did Sophie invite to go on holiday with her? She invited _____ to go on holiday with her.
b Who lost his wallet? _____ lost his wallet.

1 Which past simple question uses *did* + infinitive, **a** or **b**?
2 What is the verb form in the other question?
3 Is question **a** asking for information about the subject or object?
4 Is question **b** asking for information about the subject or object?

5 **Choose a or b for each question.**

1 Who did the boy see?
  a His mother saw him.
  b He saw his mother.

2 Who saw the boy?
  a His mother saw him.
  b He saw his mother.

»» GRAMMAR REFERENCE AND PRACTICE PAGE 149

6 **Complete the sentences using the past simple of the verbs in brackets.**

1 What _____ (you / eat) when you were on holiday in Italy?
2 Who _____ (take) you to the airport?
3 Where _____ (you / go camping) last summer?
4 Who _____ (book) the flights, your mum or your dad?
5 Who _____ (you / go) on holiday with last summer?
6 Who _____ (buy) you your new bike? Was it your parents?

7 **Correct the mistakes in the sentences.**

1 I maked two new friends on my holiday.
2 Sorry we couldn't meet yesterday. I go shopping and then cycling with my mum.
3 It was a rainy day on Saturday, so I spended the day at home.
4 I watch TV and played on the computer yesterday evening.
5 It was a pity you lefted the party early last Friday.

8 **In pairs, ask and answer the questions.**

1 Where did you go on your last holiday?
2 Who did you go with?
3 How did you get there?
4 What did you do there?
5 What was the best thing you did? Why?

READING

1 Look at the photos of Moscow. Do you know any of these places? Read the text quickly and find out who visited which place.

Red Square

The Kremlin

Old Arbat

Aquarium at VDNKH

Moscow Metro

Yuri Kuklachev Cat Theatre

✈ TEEN TRAVEL TIPS ▶ MOSCOW

21

MONIQUE

Moscow is great for sightseeing! I took photos everywhere I went. The only problem was that I don't speak Russian, so it was hard to get a taxi, and I hate walking. My advice is to take some Russian lessons before you go. I went to the aquarium on my first day. I enjoyed it, but there were a lot of tourists. I preferred the quieter streets with little shops selling postcards and presents. After I got gifts for my friends, I didn't have much money left!

CARLA

The underground, or metro, is a great way to travel around, but too crowded for me. My favourite place was Red Square. The buildings are amazing. But don't spend all your time taking photos – I didn't. I bought postcards from the little shops. You don't need Russian. Everyone speaks English. Oh, and I loved the street food and ate lots of it, but it wasn't cheap! The aquarium is fantastic. If you only go to one place, go there.

OLIVIA

My favourite place was Old Arbat, one of the oldest streets in Moscow. I wanted to get presents for my mum and dad, but all the shops had the same presents, so I didn't buy much. I mostly ate street food because it didn't cost much, and it was delicious. I went to the metro to look at the amazing stations, but I didn't travel on it. I went everywhere on foot. You see so much that way.

✅ PREPARE FOR THE EXAM

Reading Part 2

2 For each question, choose the correct answer. Write *M* for Monique, *C* for Carla or *O* for Olivia.

1 Who thinks walking is the best way to travel around Moscow?
2 Who found the street food in Moscow expensive?
3 Who says it's important not to miss the aquarium?
4 Who spent a lot of money on presents?
5 Which person enjoyed visiting the metro?
6 Who says you should learn some Russian before going?
7 Who said it was better to buy postcards than to take photos?

» PREPARE FOR THE EXAM PAGE 122

💬 TALKING POINTS

In pairs, look at the photos of the six places in Moscow in Exercise 1. Discuss which ones you think look more interesting to visit.

VOCABULARY — Holiday vocabulary

1 Match the words in the box to the things in the photo A–E. There are three words for A. There are two words for D.

EP

| guest | guidebook | luggage | map |
| receptionist | suitcase | tourist | visitor |

22
Listen and check. Then repeat.

WARMER

Arrange students into pairs. Ask them to write down eight things that you need to take on holiday, for example, a passport, money. They then compare lists and say why you need each thing, for example, *An umbrella is good because it isn't nice to get wet.*

BACKGROUND INFORMATION

Moscow is the capital of the Russian Federation and has a population of about 13 million people. It has not always been the capital of Russia and when Moscow is first mentioned in official records, in 1147, it was just a small town on the river Moskva. However, today Moscow is a very modern city which has hosted the 1980 summer Olympics and the final of the 2018 FIFA World Cup. However, the most famous image of Moscow and Russia is St Basil's Cathedral in Red Square, built in the sixteenth century. The Yuri Kuklachev Cat Theatre is not mentioned in the text but it is the only cat theatre in the world (cats are notoriously difficult to train). The cats have a number of performances from fairy tales to circus stunts.

1 Books closed, write the word MOCKBA (*Moscow* in Russian letters, pronounced /mæskˈvæ/) on the board and ask the students if they can read it. Ask students what they know about Moscow and Russia, for example, 'Where were the 2014 Winter Olympics?' (*Sochi*), 'What three colours are the Russian flag?' (*red, blue, white*). Books open, ask some questions about the photographs. Match Monique's text to the photo of the aquarium, showing that the key words are *aquarium* and *fish*. Students then continue individually.

Answers

Monique – Aquarium
Carla – Metro, Red Square, Aquarium
Olivia – Old Arbat, Metro

A2 KEY FOR SCHOOLS
Reading Part 2

In this part, students have to read three short texts on the same topic. Students have seven questions and they need to choose the right answer (A, B or C) for each.

Tip Tell students to first read the texts quickly to get an idea of what they are about and where the key information is. Then they should read each question carefully and locate the information. Tell students to look for words and phrases which mean the same as the ones in the questions. Students should be careful not to choose an answer because the word in the question is repeated in the text as the word in the question might appear in two texts, or even in all three texts. Sometimes the key idea in the question is expressed using a different word or phrase in the text.

2 If necessary, do the first one together. 'Who talks about walking?' (*Monique and Olivia*), 'Does Monique like walking?' (*no*), 'What phrase does Olivia use to mean walking?' (*on foot*) and 'Did Olivia think walking was useful?' (*Yes, she says 'you see so much'.*). Let students do the rest individually then check as a class. Have them tell you where they identified the information. Then ask students, 'Who do you think had the best time in Moscow?'

Answers

1 O (Olivia) 2 C (Carla) 3 C (Carla) 4 M (Monique)
5 O (Olivia) 6 M (Monique) 7 C (Carla)

» **PREPARE FOR THE EXAM TEACHING NOTES AND ANSWER KEY TB PAGE 253**

FAST FINISHERS

Tell fast finishers to underline all the examples of the past simple in each text.

 The Reading text is recorded for students to listen, read and check their answers.

TALKING POINTS

Ask students what they think they would see at each place. If you have the technology, you could show short YouTube clips to give students more information about them. Put students into pairs to discuss the photos. Share ideas as a class.

VOCABULARY   Holiday vocabulary

1 Ask students, 'What is the name of the place in a hotel where you get your key?' (*reception*) and tell them to open their books, look at the photo and match the words. Draw students' attention to the fact that *luggage* is uncountable but *suitcase* (and *bag*) is countable.

Play the recording, check the meaning of the vocabulary and drill it. Concept-check the vocabulary: 'Who is the person who gives you your room key?' (*receptionist*), 'And the person who takes the key is the … ?' (*guest*), 'This person does not stay in a place all the time.' (*visitor*), 'This person travels for fun not business.' (*tourist*), 'If you are lost, you need a … ?' (*map*), 'You put your clothes and things in a bag called a … ?' (*suitcase*), 'A lot of suitcases together are … ?' (*luggage*) and 'You use a … to learn about a new city or country.' (*guidebook*).

Answers

The answers are recorded for students to check and then repeat.
A guest, tourist, visitor B map C receptionist
D luggage, suitcase E guidebook

2 Have students complete the sentences in the book orally then write the words down. Tell them they may need to make the words plural. Check as a class.

> **Answers**
>
> **1** map **2** tourists **3** guidebook **4** suitcase **5** guests
> **6** luggage **7** receptionist **8** visitors

MIXED ABILITY

Divide the sentences into two sets: 1–4 and 5–8. Give students first the answers, mixed up, to 1–4, then the answers, mixed up, to 5–8, so the task is more closed. For students who are stronger, tell them to do the task without looking back at Exercise 1.

---

3 Put students into small groups to discuss the questions. Get ideas as a class. Then ask, 'Which are more useful, paper maps or online maps?'

> **Answers**
>
> Students' own answers

>> VOCABULARY WORKSHEET UNIT 3

LISTENING

1 Put students into pairs to describe the photo.

> **Possible answers**
>
> 1 the reception of a hotel
> 2 There is a boy, who is probably a guest, and a receptionist.
> 3 The boy is checking in/has just arrived at the reception of a hotel. He has got a bag next to him on the floor. The receptionist is showing him a map.

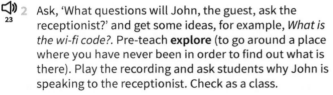 **2** Ask, 'What questions will John, the guest, ask the receptionist?' and get some ideas, for example, *What is the wi-fi code?*. Pre-teach **explore** (to go around a place where you have never been in order to find out what is there). Play the recording and ask students why John is speaking to the receptionist. Check as a class.

> **Answers**
>
> Because he wants some information about sightseeing in Moscow

3 Ask, 'John has been to Moscow before – right or wrong?' (*wrong*). Play the recording again and have students do the exercise. Check as a class and have students correct the answers which are wrong.

> **Answers**
>
> 1 ✗ (He has a sister.)
> 2 ✓
> 3 ✗ (It's not very far.)
> 4 ✗ (It's on the other side of the street map.)
> 5 ✓
> 6 ✗ (No, it isn't his.)
> 7 ✓
> 8 ✓

>> AUDIOSCRIPT TB PAGE 287

SPEAKING

 1 Ask, 'What information might John want?' and get some ideas.

Play the recording and ask students what John and his family's plans are. Check as a class.

> **Answers**
>
> They want to go to the space museum.

2 Go through the phrases and ask students who said which one, John or the receptionist. Play the recording twice. The first time, students should read and listen to the phrases. Pause the recording after each phrase to give them enough time to repeat it. The second time, students should repeat after the recording without looking at the text.

3 Give an example yourself first of an interesting city and four sights. Brainstorm cities and sights on the board. Arrange students into pairs. One student should be a tourist and the other person should be a clerk in a tourist information office. They swap roles when they have finished. Change the pairs after the first conversation so they can have a different conversation when they change roles. Monitor and encourage students to use the phrases from Exercise **2**.

4 Remind students that the . in web addresses is pronounced *dot*. Have students make the questions then put them in pairs to ask and answer them. Check as a class then repeat the activity with students in different pairs.

> **Answers**
>
> 1 What's the address? It's 24 Green Street.
> 2 Is it open every day? No, it isn't. It's closed on Sundays.
> 3 What time does it close? It closes at 5 pm.
> 4 How much are the drinks? All the drinks are 50p.
> 5 What's the web address? It's www.tourvisit.com

COOLER

Write these groups of words on the board. Students must find the odd one out. Do the first one together to demonstrate, then students work in groups. There could be different answers.

1 Red Square the Kremlin the Metro Big Ben (*Big Ben – the others are in Moscow*)

2 flight ship climb island (*ship – the others have silent letters*)

3 ride fly walk drive (*fly – the others are on the ground*)

4 tourist guest pilot visitor (*pilot – this is a job*)

5 plane helicopter bike car (*bike – it has no engine*)

Students could make their own odd-one-outs.

---

2 Now complete the sentences with the words from the box in Exercise 1.

1 You can find the names of streets on a _____ of the city.
2 Millions of _____ visit Moscow every year.
3 It's always a good idea to buy a _____ to help you plan activities for your holiday.
4 I've only got one small _____ for all my clothes. I hope I can get everything in it.
5 We stayed in a really small hotel in Moscow. It only had room for eight _____.
6 We put all our _____ in the back of the taxi. We didn't want to have the bags on the seats.
7 When we arrived at the hotel, the _____ gave us our room key.
8 The Space Museum in Moscow has lots of _____ every year.

3 In pairs, ask and answer the questions.

1 How much luggage do you take with you on holiday?
2 Who packs your suitcase?
3 What do you put in your suitcase when you go on summer holidays?
4 Do you or your parents usually buy a guidebook when you go on holiday?
5 Do you use maps? When was the last time you used a map?
6 Do many tourists come to visit your town? What do they like to see?
7 What does a receptionist do?
8 Did you stay in a hotel on your last holiday? Did you like it?

LISTENING

1 Look at the photo in Vocabulary Exercise 1. In pairs, discuss the questions.

1 What can you see?
2 Who are the people?
3 What are they doing?

🔊 23 **2** Listen to the conversation between John, a student on holiday in Moscow with his parents, and the hotel receptionist and check your ideas.

Why is John speaking to the receptionist?

🔊 23 **3** Listen again. Are the sentences right (✓) or wrong (✗)?

1 John is an only child.
2 John wants to look around the city in the afternoon.
3 The tourist information centre is a long way from the hotel.
4 The receptionist hasn't got an underground map.
5 John thinks taxis are faster than the underground.
6 John forgot his bag.
7 The guest before John had several suitcases.
8 There is a lift in the hotel.

SPEAKING

🔊 24 **1** John phones the tourist information centre for some more information. Listen to his conversation. What are John and his family going to do that day?

🔊 24 **2** Listen again and repeat the phrases from the conversation.

John: Can you give me some information about the space museum, please?
Clerk: Yes, certainly. The museum's near the centre, and you can book online. You'll really enjoy it.
John: That's perfect. Thanks.
Clerk: It's the best way to learn about the history of our country.
John: That's a really good idea. Oh, by the way, have you got any information about the Kremlin?
Clerk: Yes, of course. It's all on our website. Have a good day.

3 In pairs, choose a city you both know. What four places would tourists like to visit in this city? Role-play a conversation at a tourist information centre. Use phrases from Exercise 2 to help you.

4 Make questions. Then in pairs, ask and answer them using the information below.

1 address?
2 open every day?
3 what time / close?
4 how much / drinks?
5 web address?

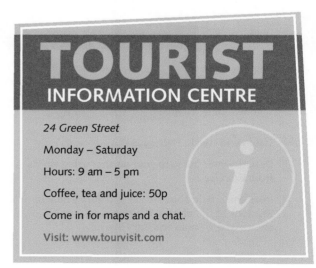

TOURIST
INFORMATION CENTRE

24 Green Street

Monday – Saturday

Hours: 9 am – 5 pm

Coffee, tea and juice: 50p

Come in for maps and a chat.

Visit: www.tourvisit.com

4 MY PLACE

A New HOME

🔊 26

ABOUT YOU

▶ **02 Watch the video and discuss the questions.**

Where do you live? Who do you live with?
How many bedrooms are there in your home?
Do you share a bedroom?
What's the most interesting thing about your room?
Would you like to live in an unusual house?

VOCABULARY AND READING

Homes

1 Match the words in the box to A–K in the picture.

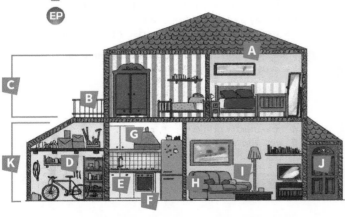

balcony	ceiling	cooker	cupboard
entrance	first floor	garage
ground floor	lamp	sink	sofa

🔊 **Listen and check. Then repeat.**
25

2 Describe your home to your partner using words from Exercise 1.

3 Read the article about Paula and Gary's homes and look at the photos. Which photo, A or B, shows where Paula and Gary live now?

Paula and Gary lived in a modern house. It had a living room and a kitchen on the ground floor and on the first floor two bedrooms, one with a balcony and a bathroom. Next to the house they had a garage for their car, and they even had a small garden with a little gate painted green. It sounds perfect!

But Paula and Gary weren't happy. They both wanted to live somewhere more interesting, so they started to look for a new home. They were looking at homes on the internet one day, when Tim, Gary's dad, had an idea. Tim had his own lorry business and he was selling one of his lorries. Why didn't Paula and Gary buy it and make it into their new home? Gary and Paula thought this was a brilliant idea and bought it that same day.

It was a busy year: Gary was building everything for their new home, while Paula was working. He built cupboards around the cooker and the sink and he even built the shower. They bought a small sofa because there wasn't enough space for a big one.

Finally, six months ago, Gary finished the work on the lorry and they moved in. Gary and Paula love their new home! Paula thinks the best thing

B

is the entrance made of wood and glass and Gary loves the high ceiling because he's tall.

There's no place like home!

4 Read the text again. Answer the questions.

1 How many floors did Paula and Gary's old house have? What was on each floor?
2 Why did Gary and Paula want to leave their old home?
3 What did Gary and Paula buy from Tim?
4 Who built the things for the new home?
5 When did Gary and Paula move into their new home?
6 What do Paula and Gary like most about their new home?

4 MY PLACE

Unit Overview

TOPIC	Home
VOCABULARY AND READING	Homes A new home
PRONUNCIATION	/iː/ and /ɪ/
GRAMMAR	Past continuous and past simple
READING	Strange Houses
VOCABULARY	Adjectives to describe homes
LISTENING	Five short conversations
WRITING	A description of a home
EXAM TASKS	Writing Part 7; Listening Part 1

Resources

GRAMMAR REFERENCE AND PRACTICE: SB page 150; TB page 264

PREPARE FOR THE EXAM: SB pages on TB pages 244–245 and 243; TB pages 255 and 256

WORKBOOK: pages 16–19

VIDEO AND VIDEO WORKSHEET: Homes

PHOTOCOPIABLE WORKSHEETS: Grammar worksheet Unit 4; Vocabulary worksheet Unit 4

TEST GENERATOR: Unit test 4

WARMER

Ask students to make two columns in their notebooks, one for regular and one for irregular verbs. Dictate this list of verbs for students to write in the correct column:

ask, break, call, carry, do, draw, go, jump, laugh, leave, ride, shout, swim, visit, worry.

After you have checked the answers together, students then give the past simple of the irregular verbs.

Answers

Regular: ask, call, carry, jump, laugh, shout, visit, worry
Irregular: break (broke), do (did), draw (drew), go (went), leave (left), ride (rode), swim (swam)

ⓘ ABOUT YOU

▶ You can begin the class and introduce the topic of the unit
02 by showing the video and asking students to complete the video worksheet. Then, read the questions in the *About you* box and students answer questions in pairs.

VOCABULARY AND READING

Homes

1 Brainstorm words connected to the home, for example *downstairs, mirror* and *wall* are all A1–A2. Then ask students to match the words to the picture.

Play the recording for students to check and repeat. Point out that /p/ is pronounced in *lamp* but not in *cupboard*. Concept-check some of the vocabulary, for example, 'You prepare food with this' (*cooker*), 'The

opposite of floor' (*ceiling*), 'You wash plates here' (*sink*). Ask students where in the home they could find these things, for example, 'entrance' (*at the front*), 'garage' (*next to the house*).

🔊 Answers
25

The answers are recorded for students to check and then repeat.
A ceiling B balcony C first floor D garage E sink F cooker
G cupboard H sofa I lamp J entrance K ground floor

2 Describe your home first as a model. Ask students to write down which of the words from Exercise 1 you use. Then put students into pairs to do the same. You could also set this up as a picture dictation where one student describes their home and the other student draws and labels it.

3 Pre-teach or elicit **lorry** (a large vehicle used for transporting goods). Ask students to describe the photos. Ask students, 'Where is this text from?' (*a magazine*). Have students read the first line and ask students to predict the text: 'What will happen to Paula and Gary?' (*They will move house.*), 'Why do you think they decide to move?' (*They don't like where they live now.*) and 'Why don't they like it?' (*Maybe they live in a bad neighbourhood or their home is too small.*).

Give students a time limit to read the whole text and choose the photo. Check as a class. Also check if they were right about their predictions.

Answers

They live in a lorry home, photo B.

4 Ask students, 'How many rooms did their old house have?' (*five*) and 'Who is Tim?' (*Gary's father*). Tell students to answer the questions in the book and check as a class. Ask students, 'Would you prefer to live in their old home or their new home?', 'Have you ever moved home?' and 'Why did you move?'.

Answers

1 It had two floors with a living room and a kitchen on the ground floor and two bedrooms and a bathroom on the first floor.
2 Because they wanted to live somewhere more interesting.
3 They bought a lorry from him.
4 Gary built the things for the new home.
5 They moved into their new home six months ago.
6 Paula loves the entrance made of wood and glass. Gary loves the high ceiling.

🔊 The Reading text is recorded for students to listen, read
26 and check their answers.

FAST FINISHERS

Tell fast finishers to write down advantages and disadvantages of living in the lorry home. For example: advantage – *if they don't like where they are, they can drive to a new place and live there*; disadvantage – *people might think they are strange.*

🔊 PRONUNCIATION | /iː/ and /ɪ/

27 5 Say /iː/ and /ɪ/ and give *beat/bit* as an example minimal pair in case students don't know the symbols. Elicit the sounds in the two words then play the recording for students to listen to the words and check their answer. Show the students how /iː/ in *ceiling* is pronounced: the lips are open wide, the top part of the tongue is near the top of the mouth, and the sound is long. Then contrast the /ɪ/ sound in *sink*: the lips are loosely spread, the tongue is nearer the centre of the mouth, and the sound is shorter. Play the recording for students to repeat the words.

> **Answers**
> /ɪ/ sink   /iː/ ceiling

6 Have students work in pairs and match the words to the sounds then check with the recording and repeat.

28 🔊 **Answers**
> *The answers are recorded for students to check and then repeat.*
> /iː/ eat, he's, feet, leave, he'll, seat
> /ɪ/ it, his, fit, live, hill, sit

GRAMMAR | Past continuous and past simple

1 Tell students to underline and identify the verbs. Check as a class.

> **Answers**
> a Gary <u>was building</u> everything for their new home, while Paula <u>was working</u>
> b They <u>were looking</u> at homes on the internet one day, when Tim, Gary's dad, <u>had</u> an idea.
> c Finally, Gary <u>finished</u> the work on the lorry and they <u>moved</u> in.
> Past simple: had, finished, moved
> Past continuous: was building, was working, were looking

2 Pre-teach **interrupt** by demonstrating it: ask one student to count to ten and then interrupt her in the middle. Draw timelines on the board to show the sequence of events in the sentences:

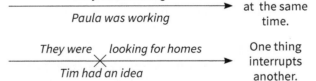

Explain that *when* and *while* are words which join parts of a sentence and say when something is happening.

Tell students to match the descriptions to the examples. Check as a class.

> **Answers**
> i c   ii a   iii b

3 Choose the words as a class.

> **Answers**
> To form the past continuous we use the *past* simple of the verb *be* and the *present* participle.

» **GRAMMAR REFERENCE AND PRACTICE ANSWER KEY TB PAGE 264**

4 Have students complete the sentences. Check as a class. Where both tenses are possible, ask students to explain the difference in meaning.

> **Possible answers**
> NB where more than one answer is possible, students need to be aware of the different meanings of the different answers.
> 1 was helping   2 lived   3 was cooking   4 ate
> 5 was leaving / left   6 were watching

5 Have students correct the sentences. Check as a class.

> **Answers**
> 1 I felt very nervous while we **were watching** the match.
> 2 We **were waiting** at a bus stop when we first met.
> 3 We were amazed when we **found** so much money.
> 4 While I **was cleaning** the kitchen I saw the broken window.
> 5 It **was** snowing when we went outside.
> 6 I **left** the house just after you called me.

» **GRAMMAR WORKSHEET UNIT 4**

✓ PREPARE FOR THE EXAM

A2 KEY FOR SCHOOLS
Writing Part 7

In this part, students have to write a short story or description of at least 35 words based on three pictures.

Tip Students should look at the three pictures carefully and understand what story or description they show. When they write, students should show their range of vocabulary and grammar, for example by using complex sentences with past simple and past continuous.

6 Put students into pairs to tell the story using past tenses. Check as a class. Then have students write their stories individually. Ask some students to read out their stories.

> **Model answer**
> While Jane was drinking some coffee, she felt hungry. She wanted to have a cake but when she opened her cupboard there was no food. So Jane went to the supermarket and bought one.

» **PREPARE FOR THE EXAM TEACHING NOTES AND ANSWER KEY TB PAGE 255**

MIXED ABILITY

Write the model answer as a gap-fill on the board for students who need more support.

---

7 Put students into pairs to speak. Ask some students to tell the class some of their sentences.

> **Answers**
> Students' own answers

COOLER

Give students one minute to write down as many words with the /ɪ/ and /iː/ sounds as they can. Then write some of their examples on the board. Mouth one of the words to the class: put your mouth into the right position for the word but don't say it aloud. The students have to recognise the word from your lip movements. Repeat, and when the students get the idea, they can play in groups.

PRONUNCIATION | /iː/ and /ɪ/

5 Listen to the two words. Which has an /iː/ sound and which has an /ɪ/ sound?

s**i**nk   c**ei**ling

6 In pairs, match the words to the sounds in Exercise 5.

eat	feet	fit	he'll
he's	hill	his	it
leave	live	seat	sit

Listen and check. Then repeat.

GRAMMAR — Past continuous and past simple

1 Look at the example sentences from the text. Find and <u>underline</u> all the verbs in the sentences. Which verbs are past simple and which verbs are past continuous?

a Gary was building everything for their new home, while Paula was working.
b They were looking at homes on the internet one day, when Tim, Gary's dad, had an idea.
c Finally, Gary finished the work on the lorry and they moved in.

2 Match i–iii to sentences a–c in Exercise 1.

i One action follows the other.
ii The actions are happening at the same time.
iii One action interrupts the other.

3 Choose the correct words to complete the sentence.

To form the past continuous, we use the *present* / *past* simple of the verb *be* and the *present* / *past* participle.

» GRAMMAR REFERENCE AND PRACTICE PAGE 150

4 Complete the sentences using the past simple or the past continuous. Sometimes more than one answer is possible.

1 While my brother was painting his bedroom, my sister _____ (help) our mum in the garden.
2 We _____ (live) in an apartment for a year and then we moved to a house.
3 My dad _____ (cook) dinner in the kitchen when I arrived home from school.
4 I did my homework and we _____ (eat) dinner in the kitchen.
5 When Mum phoned me, I _____ (leave) my classroom with my friends.
6 While my parents _____ (watch) TV, I was playing computer games with my friends.

5 Correct the mistakes in the sentences.

1 I felt very nervous while we watched the match.
2 We waited at a bus stop when we first met.
3 We were amazed when we were finding so much money.
4 While I cleaning the kitchen, I saw the broken window.
5 It is snowing when we went outside.
6 I was leaving the house just after you called me.

PREPARE FOR THE EXAM

Writing Part 7

6 Look at the three pictures. Write the story shown in the pictures using the past simple and past continuous. Write 35 words or more.

» PREPARE FOR THE EXAM PAGE 127

7 In pairs, take turns to describe what you did yesterday.

Use the past simple and past continuous with *when* and *while*.

While I was having breakfast …

When I got to school …

READING

1 Look at the photos of the unusual homes. What do you think they are like inside?

2 Read the article and match the photos A–D to paragraphs 1–4.

STRANGE HOUSES 🔊 29

Most of us live in an apartment or in a house. Our homes often look similar to our neighbours' from the outside, but on the inside they can be very different. Most of us like our homes to be cosy and comfortable, but we have very different ideas about what that means. Some people like to have bright colours and lots of furniture, others prefer a cool, modern-looking home.

However, some houses look very unusual from the outside. Have a look at these four photos.

1 Do you like flying? Then, this attractive house is for you. It's in Lebanon and is the shape of a plane. It's got small windows, so it's not very light inside, but in a warm country, small windows keep a house cool in summer.

2 This very unusual house is in Mexico. It looks like part of the rock – and it is! The walls and the roof of the house are part of a very big rock. The family made the house more than 30 years ago. We can't see inside, but it looks quite dark, cool and peaceful.

3 In 1968, a group of swimmers first had the idea to build this tiny house on a rock in the middle of the River Drina in Serbia. It's not only small but, as you can see, it's also not easy to get there. In winter it can be quite cold, so people use it mostly in summer.

4 A Japanese company designed this football-shaped house in 2006. It's got 32 sides and four legs and can sit on top of water. It's very small but has big windows, so there is lots of light. What a great place to live!

B

C

D

3 Read the article again and answer the questions.
1 What does the house in Lebanon look like?
2 Why are small windows important in a warm country?
3 What is the Mexican house made of?
4 How old is the house?
5 What can you find in the middle of the River Drina?
6 When do most people use the house? Why?
7 What does the Japanese house look like?
8 Why is it very bright inside?

💬 **TALKING POINTS**

Which of these houses would you like to live in? Why?
Which of these houses would you not like to live in? Why?
Do you know about any other unusual homes? Tell your partner about them.

VOCABULARY Adjectives to describe homes

1 🔊 Find these words in the article and complete the table.
EP

attractive	bright	cold	comfortable
cool	cosy	dark	light	peaceful
tiny	unusual	warm

🔊 Listen and check. Then repeat.
30

Opinion	Size	Temperature	Sound	Light

WARMER

Arrange students into pairs. Write these times on the board:

10.00, yesterday, 19.00, two days ago, last Saturday evening, on my birthday, in the summer holidays, this time one year ago

Students must tell each other what they did or were doing at these times. For example, *At ten o'clock yesterday we were having a maths test.*

1 Ask students, 'Is there anything unusual about your home?'. Give some examples: it is next to a fire station, you have a big garden. Then ask, 'What was unusual about Gary and Paula's house?' (*It was a lorry.*). Put students into pairs to describe the photos and discuss what they look like inside. Share ideas as a class.

> **Answers**
> Students' own answers

2 Give students a time limit to read the article and match the photos to the paragraphs. Check as a class.

> **Answers**
> 1 A 2 D 3 B 4 C

3 Ask students, 'Which four countries are the houses in?' (*Lebanon, Mexico, Serbia, Japan*). 'Which is the newest house?' (*the Japanese one*)

Have students answer the questions in the book then check as a class.

Ask students, 'Why do you think people decided to make these houses?' and 'What is the difference between a house and a home?'.

> **Answers**
> 1 It looks like an aeroplane / an Airbus A380.
> 2 Because they keep the house cool in summer.
> 3 It is made of/from rock.
> 4 The house is more than 30 years old.
> 5 A small house on a rock.
> 6 Most people use the house in summer because it's too cold to use it in winter.
> 7 It looks like a football.
> 8 Because it has big windows.

🔊 **29** The Reading text is recorded for students to listen, read and check their answers.

BACKGROUND INFORMATION

Other unusual homes include:

- The Keret house in Poland. Just 92–152 cm wide, this is the world's narrowest home. There are two floors but the house is not wide enough for stairs so you need a ladder to go upstairs.

- House NA in Japan. This is made of glass and completely transparent. The inspiration for the house comes from early humans who lived in trees.

- The Hobbit House in Wales. This is a replica of Bilbo Baggins' home in Tolkien's *The Hobbit* and it is also very eco-friendly because it is built with completely natural materials and designed to cause minimal damage to the environment. A family made it themselves in four months.

- Major Oak in Sherwood Forest, England. This tree is 800–1,000 years old and ten metres wide. There is a legend that Robin Hood and his gang of outlaws lived here. The tree has an official birthday, 20th February: the same as the Major Rookes who gave the tree its name.

- 432 Park Avenue in New York. This is the tallest residential building in the world (425 metres). The largest apartment has six bedrooms, seven baths and a library, and a great view of course.

📧 **TALKING POINTS**

Put students into pairs to discuss the questions. Then put pairs together into small groups to compare their ideas. Vote as a class on the house which is most and least popular.

> **Answers**
> Students' own answers

VOCABULARY   Adjectives to describe homes

1 Tell students to underline the words in the text. Go through them and see if students know them or can work out their meaning from the context. Then have students put them in the table. Play the recording for students to check and repeat.

Concept-check some of the vocabulary. For example, 'very small' (*tiny*), 'it looks nice' (*attractive*), 'the opposite of bright' (*dark*), 'calm' (*peaceful*).

🔊 **30** **Answers**

> *The answers are recorded for students to check and then repeat.*
> Opinion: attractive, comfortable, cosy, unusual
> Size: tiny
> Temperature: cold, cool, warm
> Sound: peaceful
> Light: bright, dark, light

2 Put students into pairs to describe their homes.
   Encourage them to use the adjectives in Exercise 1. Ask
   some students to tell the whole class.

3 Give some more examples of unusual places. Give real
   examples from Background Information or use fantasy
   examples, for example, a house which you can fold away
   into a suitcase. In pairs, students choose an unusual
   place and decide how to improve it. Tell them to look
   back at the homes vocabulary on page 24 to help them.
   They then present their idea to the class. Have the class
   vote for the most unusual house.

> **MIXED ABILITY**
>
> Put stronger students together with students who need
> more support. The stronger students can do the more
> difficult parts, such as explaining why they have designed
> the house as they have; their partners can do the less
> demanding parts, such as pointing out where things are.

>> **VOCABULARY WORKSHEET UNIT 4**

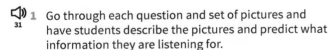

A2 KEY FOR SCHOOLS
Listening Part 1

In this part, students are tested on their ability to
identify simple factual information in five separate short
conversations. Students listen for information such as
prices, numbers, times, dates and descriptions. They have
to choose one of three pictures as the answer.

Tip Tell students to listen carefully for meaning, as they
will hear something about all three pictures, but only
one answers the question. They should listen all of the
way through, as the answer could come at the beginning,
middle or the end of the conversation.

🔊 1 Go through each question and set of pictures and
31   have students describe the pictures and predict what
        information they are listening for.
        Question 1: 'What can you see in the three pictures?' (*a
        door with a number*), 'Maria visits her friend Simon at
        number 5 and then goes home to house 15. Where does
        she live?' (*B*)
        Question 2: 'Who lives here?' (*Jason*), 'Which house has
        no stairs?' (*B*) 'Which house has the most floors?' (*C*)
        Question 3: 'Who is Jenny?' (*a school student*) 'Which
        time is latest?' (*C*), 'What two ways can you say the time
        in B?' (*three fifty, ten to four*)
        Question 4: 'What is Ben going to paint?' (*his bedroom*),
        'Which bedroom is going to be blue?' (*A*)
        Question 5: 'Who do you think Sarah is talking to?' (*a
        friend*), 'What is she doing in C?' (*making a cake*)
        Play the recording twice. Check answers as a class. For
        speaking practice, students read the dialogues in pairs.

   Answers

   1 B **2** A **3** B **4** A **5** C

>> **AUDIOSCRIPT TB PAGE 288**

>> **PREPARE FOR THE EXAM TEACHING NOTES AND ANSWER KEY TB PAGE 256**

**WRITING**

✎ **PREPARE TO WRITE**
   A description of a home

GET READY Ask students, 'Is it better to live in an
apartment or a house?'. Have students say what are the
advantages and disadvantages of each, for example, you
need to use a lift if you live in an apartment; a house is
more expensive.

Read out Fernanda's email to students. Ask, 'Would
Fernanda prefer her own bedroom?' (*yes*).

Write this on the board: *Luiza is my friend. Luiza is 15. I like
Luiza and Luiza likes me.*

Ask, 'Does it look strange?' (*yes*).

Change the sentence on the board:

Luiza is my friend. She is 15. I like her and she likes me.

Ask, 'What are the words *she*, *her* and *me*?' (*pronouns*).

Get students to say what nouns the underlined pronouns
replace in Fernanda's email in the book. Check as a class.

Students read the text about David. Ask, 'Is David older
than Mia?' (*yes*), 'Which of his parents is a nurse?' (*his dad*).

Have students replace the underlined nouns with
pronouns. Check as a class.

> **Answers**
>
> Fernanda lives in São Paolo. Her family's apartment has five
> rooms.
> It = the apartment, She = Luiza, We = Luiza and Fernanda, The
> house = It and it, Helen and Francisco = They

PLAN Ask students the questions. Students then use the
questions to make notes about their own home. As a
variation, students could write about the unusual home
they gave a presentation about in Exercise 3 page 26.

WRITE In their description, encourage students to use the
vocabulary from Exercise 1 page 24 and Exercise 1 page 26.

IMPROVE Tell students to check their work to make sure
that the sentences are grammatical and there is not a lot of
repetition of nouns. In pairs, they check one another's work.

> **Model answer**
>
> I live in a small apartment in Granada, Spain. It's cosy and
> very comfortable. There is a kitchen, a bathroom, a living
> room, two bedrooms and a balcony. I share a bedroom with
> my sister, Gabriela. She's very tidy but I'm not!

> **FAST FINISHERS**
>
> Write anagrams of words from the descriptions of
> Fernanda's and David's homes on the board, e.g. ehkcitn
> (*kitchen*), knitlag (*talking*).

> **COOLER**
>
> In groups, students choose furniture for the bedroom
> in their new apartment. They have $300 to spend. They
> choose from:
>
> small bed $100, big bed $150, bookcase $50, armchair
> $80, chair $30, desk $40, cupboard $50, computer table
> $40, sink $50

2 In pairs, tell your partner about your home. Use the words in the box to help you.

3 In pairs, choose one of the unusual places in the article and decide how you can make it into a comfortable and cosy home. Present your unusual home to the class.

LISTENING

 PREPARE FOR THE EXAM

Listening Part 1

1 For each question, choose the correct answer.

1 What is the number of Maria's house?

2 Which is Jason's house?

3 What time is Jenny going to leave school today?

4 What colour does Ben want to paint his bedroom?

5 What is Sarah going to do this afternoon?

➤➤ **PREPARE FOR THE EXAM PAGE 128**

WRITING

 PREPARE TO WRITE
A description of a home

GET READY Read Fernanda's description of her home. Which city does she live in? How many rooms does her family's apartment have?

Hi, I'm Fernanda. I live with my family in an apartment in São Paulo, Brazil. It's on the ninth floor of a big block near the city centre. It's got a kitchen, a living room, a bathroom and two bedrooms. I share one of the bedrooms with my sister, Luiza. She's 15. I'd like my own bedroom, but it's OK sharing with Luiza. We like the same things and we enjoy talking at night.

We use pronouns instead of nouns, so we don't have to repeat nouns. Which nouns do the underlined pronouns in Fernanda's description replace? Now replace the underlined nouns in this paragraph with pronouns.

David lives with his family in a small house in York. The house is quite new and the house has two bedrooms. David shares his bedroom with his baby sister, Mia. Mia is two and a half. David's mum, Helen, is a doctor and his dad, Francisco, is a nurse. Helen and Francisco both work at the local hospital.

PLAN Think about your home. Where is it? What kind of home is it? Who lives there? How many rooms has it got? Do you have your own room, or do you share a bedroom? Make notes.

WRITE Write a description of your home. Use pronouns for some of the nouns.

IMPROVE Read your description and look for mistakes. Check that you included all the information from your plan and that you have used some pronouns.

LIFE SKILLS CRITICAL THINKING

ACCEPTING OTHER PEOPLE'S OPINIONS

LIFE SKILLS

Other people's ideas
- can help us learn
- can be fun
- make life interesting

We should listen to other people and enjoy learning new things when we discuss opinions.

1 Make sentences that are true for you.

I	always often sometimes never	agree with my parents. agree with my best friends. agree with my teachers. change my opinion. like new ideas.

In pairs, compare your sentences. Did you have the same ideas?

2 Explain why each sentence is true for you.

> I sometimes agree with my parents because they know more than me, but other times they are too strict.

3 Look at the words in the box. In pairs, discuss the questions.

> films   food   holidays
> homework   music   sports

1 Do you talk to your friends or family about these topics?
2 Do you always have the same opinions?

4 Do the quiz and choose the two best options. Then in pairs, compare your answers.

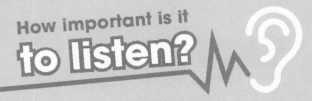

How important is it to listen?

We talk to other people and give our opinions every day. Maybe you talk about what to do after school with your friends, or about plans for the weekend with your family. It's important to give your opinions, but it is also important to listen to other people's opinions and think about the best option. How good are you at listening? Do the quiz.

1 When you listen to someone, do you ...
 a look at him/her and smile?
 b say, 'That's interesting' or 'That's a good idea'?
 c interrupt and give your own opinion as soon as possible?

2 When someone has an idea, do you ...
 a always agree with him/her and think his/her ideas are good?
 b ask questions about the idea to get more information?
 c always disagree with him/her and often think he/she is wrong?

3 When you have a different opinion to someone else, do you ...
 a ignore him/her by not listening and turning your head away?
 b think about his/her opinion before you say you don't like it?
 c explain your opinion and ideas?

4 How can a group of people agree when they have different opinions?
 They can ...
 a explain their reasons for their opinions.
 b exchange ideas with each other by talking and listening.
 c not work together.

5 Is it good to change your opinion when you listen to other people's ideas?
 a Sometimes. I respect other people and know I am sometimes wrong.
 b Never. I'm always right and I don't like to change.
 c Maybe. If I have a good reason.

32

28   LIFE SKILLS

LIFE SKILLS

Learning Objectives

- The students learn that it is important to take account of other people's opinions and respect what everyone has to say.
- In the project stage, students prepare a timetable for a visit to their school by students from a different country.

Vocabulary

interrupt agree with ignore exchange respect

BACKGROUND INFORMATION

There are strong social and cultural factors which influence the extent to which people feel entitled to give their own opinions and accept the opinions of others. These factors include age, gender, status and nationality. For example, in many societies, young people are expected to respect older people and not give opinions which seem to challenge what their elders say or make them feel uncomfortable. In these settings, age is equated with experience and wisdom so it seems logical that the opinions of older people are more valuable and should be followed rather than questioned. Younger people are therefore largely expected to confirm the opinions of their elders and show appreciation of their input.

The context of communication is also important as there may be more restraints on the freedom with which people feel free or qualified to give opinions when there is a high-stakes situation such as a business negotiation. When there are major consequences of making a mistake by giving or accepting the wrong opinion, people will be much more careful about both what they say and how they interpret the words of others. There may also be pressure to back up opinions with factual information so that speakers' positions seem to be more objective and informed.

It is important that people are sensitive to such factors when they are in situations and with people they don't know or don't know well. Trying to impose the norms of your own society and culture on people from different backgrounds is not likely to result in effective communication and could even cause lasting damage to your relationship. The key to skilful communication is to keep an open mind and understand that you can still make progress even if you have to adapt to a different way of expressing yourself.

WARMER

Tell students this puzzle and see if they can work out the solution.

'A man goes to a pet shop and buys a parrot. The shop assistant tells him that the parrot will repeat every word that it hears the man say. Two days later the man comes back to the shop and complains that the parrot hasn't said a word. Why?'

(*The parrot is deaf and so can't hear what the man says.*)

Ask students if they ever have the feeling that nobody is listening to them and how they feel and what they do in this situation.

LIFE SKILLS
ACCEPTING OTHER PEOPLE'S OPINIONS

Tell students to read the information and check vocabulary as necessary. Invite students to say if they agree or disagree with any of the points in the text and to give their reasons. Encourage open-class discussion and help students make connections between their contributions.

1 Tell students to write down the five sentences that apply to them. Put students into pairs to compare and see how similar their answers are.

2 Tell students to give one another situations and examples which explain their sentences. Put students into new pairs and repeat the exercise. As feedback, ask some students to explain to the class why their sentences in Exercise 1 are true.

3 Have students discuss the questions in pairs. Ask students, 'Which topics are most difficult for you to discuss or agree on?' 'Are there any topics which you can't discuss with anyone?'

FAST FINISHERS

Tell pairs which finish early to think of two more topics, for example diet and pocket money, and discuss the same questions about these topics.

4 Books closed, tell students to make a list of situations when it is important to be a good listener, for example, a friend tells you about a problem, a teacher explains a grammar point, your coach is giving you instructions. Ask students, 'Are you a good listener?'. Most students will say *yes* so ask, 'How do you know you're a good listener?'. Books open, have students do the quiz. Put students into pairs to compare their answers and say why they chose them. Ask students if they had answers which were not one of the three choices.

5 Remind students that advice is uncountable so we would say *some advice* or *a piece of advice*. Have students match the questions to the advice. Check as a class. Ask students whether they agree with this advice and to think of situations when they have or haven't followed it.

> **Answers**
> a 3 b 5 c 1 d 4 e 2

6 Tell students to match the words to the definitions. Check as a class. Ask, 'Which two words have a negative meaning?' (*ignore* and *interrupt*)

> **Answers**
> 1 ignore 2 agree with 3 interrupt 4 respect 5 exchange

> **MIXED ABILITY**
> Weaker students might find it difficult to match the words to paraphrases so translate the words into their language and have them match the words to the translations. After this they could try the original exercise.

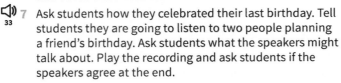 The Reading text is recorded for students to listen, read and check their answers.

7 Ask students how they celebrated their last birthday. Tell students they are going to listen to two people planning a friend's birthday. Ask students what the speakers might talk about. Play the recording and ask students if the speakers agree at the end.

> **Answers**
> They agree

8 Tell students to listen and answer the questions. Check as a class. Ask students, 'Do you think the party will be fun?' and 'Can you think of another present for Martha if the shop doesn't have the T-shirt in her size?'.

> **Answers**
> 1 Because they did that last year and it's boring to do the same every year
> 2 because Martha likes films
> 3 It's going to be sunny
> 4 everyone, but not Martha
> 5 David
> 6 a T-shirt

9 Tell students to complete the sentences. Play the recording again for students to check. Ask students to find examples of how the speakers are being good listeners, for example, Jenny gives her own opinions but she also asks David what he thinks.

> **Answers**
> 1 Maybe but 2 Yes, but 3 great idea 4 I'm sure
> 5 I'm not sure

» AUDIOSCRIPT TB PAGE 288

10 Tell students to decide if each statement is True or False. Then put students into pairs to discuss them. Encourage students to follow the advice in Exercise 5 and use the phrases in Exercise 9. Afterwards, ask some students to give their opinion to the whole class and start a class discussion.

PROJECT *Planning an exchange visit*

Ask students why students from another country might want to visit their school, for example, they are learning Spanish and want some practise with native speakers of their own age. Put students into small groups. Have them read the situation and tell each student to think of an activity that would be useful for their foreign guests. Write some examples on the board to give students ideas: a sports competition, a visit to a local museum, a mini-lesson in another subject such as geography. Have the group choose the best activities and make a timetable for the day. Encourage students to follow the advice in Exercise 5 and use the phrases in Exercise 9 when giving opinions and listening to one another. Then students should make a poster containing text, pictures and photos for their guests. Give students some ideas about the content: the programme for the day, information about your school and class, interesting facts about your town/area. Each group then takes it in turn to present their poster to the class. One way of doing this would be to put the posters on the classroom walls. One member of each group would stay with the poster to answer questions about it and the other students would go round the other posters.

PROJECT EXTENSION

Tell students to imagine that they are doing the second half of the exchange – they are visiting their guests in their home country. Put students into groups to agree on where the students come from (it can be any English-speaking country) and plan a timetable for their visit. Each group presents their plan to the rest of the class.

COOLER

See how good students' listening skills are by playing Chinese whispers. Arrange students in a line (put students into large groups if you have a very large class). Whisper a word with a sound contrast, for example *ship* or *sheep*, to a student at the start of the line. That student whispers it to the next student who repeats it to the next until it reaches the last student, who must tell you the word so you can check it is the one you said. When you play again, change the order of students in the line so different people have to confirm the word. You could also play this with sentences.

5 Match the questions 1–5 in Exercise 4 to the advice a–e.

a It's important to have your own opinions. Don't always agree immediately.

b Sometimes you can change your opinion because you listen and decide another idea is better.

c You should be polite to other people and listen carefully when they are speaking.

d It's best to talk to other people when there is a problem and think of ideas that make everyone happy.

e It is important to listen to other people's opinions and decide if the ideas are good or bad. Don't get angry or stop listening. Maybe they are really good ideas!

6 Match the highlighted words in the quiz to the definitions.

1 not pay attention to _____

2 have the same opinion as _____

3 speak when another person is speaking _____

4 be polite to _____

5 give and receive _____

7 Listen to David and Jenny discussing what to do for their friend Martha's birthday. Do they agree in the end?

8 Listen again and answer the questions.

1 Why doesn't David like the idea of a surprise party?

2 Why does Jenny think the cinema could be a good idea?

3 What's the weather going to be like on Saturday?

4 Who will pay for the food and drink?

5 Who will send the invitations?

6 What does Jenny want to give Martha?

9 Listen again and complete the sentences with the phrases in the *Useful language* box.

! USEFUL LANGUAGE

great idea   I'm sure   Yes, but

I'm not sure   Maybe, but

Jenny: We did it last year and it was fun.
David: **(1)** _____ why not do something different?
Jenny: We could go to the cinema.
David: **(2)** _____ the cinema is expensive.
Jenny: You're right. Do you like the idea of a picnic in a park?
David: Yes, I do. That's a **(3)** _____ .
David: Do you think she wants to go to the park in the centre for her birthday?
Jenny: **(4)** _____ that's the best place.
David: Do you think Martha likes orange or lemon?
Jenny: **(5)** _____ . What do you think is best?

10 Are the statements true (T) or false (F) for you? In pairs, compare your answers and explain your opinion. Be polite!

I think …

1 football is more interesting than basketball.

2 pizza is better than pasta.

3 cats are nicer than dogs.

4 maths is easier than history.

PROJECT *Planning an exchange visit*

A group of students from another country are coming to visit your school. Your teacher wants you to plan some activities for the day. Prepare a timetable for the day.

- Work in small groups.
- Read the situation.
- Individually, think of an activity you could do with the students and think of a reason why it is a good idea.
- Write your ideas in your notebook.
- In your group, decide what activities to do and prepare a timetable for the day. Use the *Useful language* from Exercise 9 to discuss the best options.
- Make a welcome poster for the visiting students to see when they arrive. Include pictures and photos to make it attractive.
- Present your poster to another group or to the class.

ACCEPTING OTHER PEOPLE'S OPINIONS 29

VOCABULARY

1 Write the missing letters to complete the word for each set.

0 dolphin   penguin   giraffe
a *n i m a l s*

1 receptionist   luggage   tourist
h _ _ _ _ _ _ _

2 land   hill   sea
E _ _ _ _ _

3 tram   underground   scooter
t _ _ _ _ _ _ _ _ _

4 balcony   ceiling   cupboard
h _ _ _ _ _

5 address   age   surname
i _ _ _ _ _ _ _ _ _ _

2 Complete the sentences with the correct words.

1 I don't want to go in the car to the beach. Walking is good for us, so let's go _____.

2 My parents packed our _____ for our skiing holiday last night.

3 Have you got a _____ of the city? I want to see where the museum is.

4 We've got a _____ in our apartment block, but I don't use it. I always use the stairs.

5 Do you ever come to school _____ bike?

6 _____ are large white animals and they live in the cold Arctic.

7 _____ are birds with brightly coloured feathers. Some of them can talk.

8 _____ are birds too, but they can't fly. They spend a lot of time swimming in the ocean.

3 Read the descriptions of some nature words. Write the missing letters to complete the words.

0 This place is water, but has land all around it.
l a k e

1 This place is very dry. It's hot in the day and often cold at night.
_ _ _ _ _ r _ _

2 This place has lots of trees.
_ _ r _ _ _ _

3 This place is all water and it moves all the time.
_ i _ _ _ _

4 This place is low and is often between two mountains.
_ _ _ _ l _ _ _

5 This place is a kind of mountain, but it has a hole in the top.
v _ _ _ _ _ _ _

GRAMMAR

1 Choose the correct options to complete the sentences.

1 I like to watch swimming competitions because *I'm swimming / I swim* too.

2 Of course everyone *wants / want* to have more friends.

3 The weather was really hot, but I still *have / had* a great time there.

4 In my town, *there is / there are* a lot of shopping centres and sports centres.

Correct the mistakes in the sentences.

5 I visited Thao Cam Vien zoo, but I didn't liked it.

6 Every day we doing different tests or exams at school.

7 Do you liked the competition?

8 I can't go shopping today because I working.

2 Complete the sentences. Use the present simple or present continuous.

0 I *really like* (really like) my new bedroom. I *am painting* (paint) it blue.

1 I _____ (think) that's Olivia over there. What _____ (she / do)?

2 Sorry, I _____ (not know) where the station is. I _____ (come) from another town.

3 That aeroplane _____ (fly) very low. I _____ (hope) everything's OK.

4 My aunt _____ (travel) a lot, but she _____ (not travel) at the moment.

5 I'm sorry, I _____ (not understand). Can you say it again, please?

3 Complete the text about Gabby using the past simple and past continuous.

Gabby wants to do dance for the fitness part of a competition. Last month, she
(0) *bought* (buy) a dance DVD, so she
(1) _____ (can) learn at home.

But it was quite difficult because while she **(2)** _____ (watch) the DVD, she
(3) _____ (also practise) the dance steps. When her mum **(4)** _____ (come) home, she **(5)** _____ (say) to Gabby, 'Why don't you join a dance class? It's a much better way to learn.' 'That's a good idea,'
(6) _____ (answer) Gabby.

Overview

VOCABULARY	Adjectives of personality; personal details; geographical features; animals; holidays: ways of travelling; holiday vocabulary; homes; adjectives to describe homes
GRAMMAR	Present simple and present continuous; verbs we don't usually use in the continuous; past simple; past continuous and past simple
EXAM TASKS	Listening Part 1; Writing Part 7; Speaking Part 1

Resources

PHOTOCOPIABLE WORKSHEETS: Grammar worksheets Units 1–4; Vocabulary worksheets Units 1–4; Review game Units 1–4; Literature worksheet; Speaking worksheet; Writing worksheet

WARMER

Read out these sentences. Students must say true or false.
- The past tense of buy is bought. (*True*)
- Your surname is your family name. (*True*)
- We can use the verb like in the continuous. (*False*)
- Luggage is an uncountable noun. (*True*)
- We usually use while with the past simple. (*False*)
- A hill is bigger than a mountain. (*False*)
- Travel is a regular verb. (*True*)

VOCABULARY

1 Show the example and ask students to write the words which describe the vocabulary sets. Check as a class. Ask students to add other words in each category, for example, animals – monkey, whale, polar bear.

> **Answers**
> 1 holidays 2 Earth 3 transport 4 homes / house
> 5 information

2 Write an example on the board to demonstrate:

We travelled by _____ on the river. (*boat*)

Have students complete the sentences in the book. Tell them that 1 and 6 are two words. Check as a class. Books closed, write the answers on the board and see if students can work in groups and write down the sentences the words were in (give them some clues like the start of the sentences.)

> **Answers**
> 1 on foot 2 suitcases / luggage 3 map 4 lift 5 by
> 6 Polar bears 7 Parrots 8 Penguins

3 Show the example and ask students to complete the words. Check as a class. With stronger students, you could do this with books closed as an oral exercise.

> **Answers**
> 1 desert 2 forest 3 river 4 valley 5 volcano

FAST FINISHERS

Tell fast finishers to look back at the vocabulary on page 14 and make two examples of their own. For example: *It is very high but there is a great view from the top.* (mountain); *You go up and down this.* (hill)

You could also ask fast finishers to make sentences about any of the new words in the first four units.

GRAMMAR

1 Before you begin this section, briefly review the grammar covered in Units 1–4. First, revise the present simple and present continuous. Write these sentences on the board.

Susan walks to school.   Susan is walking to school.

Elicit that the first sentence is present simple and the second is present continuous. Ask students what the difference in meaning between the sentences is (*the first sentence describes Susan's regular routine, the second shows what she is doing now*).

Then revise the past simple and past continuous. Write this sentence on the board and ask students to put it in order beginning with Susan.

while saw walking she friend was Susan her (*Susan saw her friend while she was walking.*)

Draw a time line on the board to show that Susan saw her friend in the middle of an activity in the past.

Then have students complete sentences 1–4 in Exercise 1 and correct sentences 5–8. Check as a class.

> **Answers**
> 1 I swim 2 wants 3 had 4 there are
> 5 I visited Thau Cam Vien zoo, but I didn't **like** it.
> 6 Every day we **do** different tests or exams at school.
> 7 Do you **like** the competition? / **Did** you **like** the competition?
> 8 I can't go shopping today because I'm working.

2 Have students complete the sentences with either the present simple or present continuous. Check as a class.

> **Answers**
> 1 think, is she doing 2 don't know, come 3 is flying, hope
> 4 travels, is/'s not travelling 5 don't understand

3 Tell students to complete the text with either the past simple or past continuous form of the words in brackets. Check as a class. Ask students if they like dancing and if they think it is better to learn in a class than by yourself.

> **Answers**
> 1 could 2 was watching 3 was also practising 4 came
> 5 said 6 answered

A2 KEY FOR SCHOOLS Listening Part 1

1 Briefly review what students need to do in this part of the exam and if necessary read out the A2 Key for Schools box on TB page 50. Ask students questions about each question:

Question 1: 'Which date is closest?' (*9th August*)

Question 2: 'Are the tickets for one person?' (*No, they're for a family*).

Question 3: 'What are the two ways of saying the time in B?' (*three fifteen, a quarter past three*)

Question 4: 'What can you see in all three pictures?' (*a door*)

Question 5: 'What are these three objects?' (*a poster, a book shelf, a lamp*)

Play the audio twice and have students answer the questions. Ask students what they would like to buy for their bedrooms.

> **Answers**
> 1 B   2 B   3 A   4 B   5 C

>> **AUDIOSCRIPT TB PAGE 289**

A2 KEY FOR SCHOOLS Writing Part 7

2 Briefly review what students need to do in this part of the exam and if necessary read out the task description and tip on TB page 46. Ask students questions about the pictures: 'What is the man doing?' (*walking by a river*), 'What is he carrying?' (*an umbrella*), 'Why does he open his umbrella?' (*It starts to rain*), 'What happens to his umbrella?' (*It breaks.*) and 'So what does he do?' (*He stands under a tree.*). Give students time to write their stories. Encourage them to use both simple and continuous forms (either present or past). Take the stories in, mark them and give them back to students in the next class with corrections and suggestions for improvement.

> **Model answer**
> A man was walking next to the sea on a cloudy day. It started to rain and he opened his umbrella. The umbrella broke while he was opening it. So the man stood under a tree while it was raining.

MIXED ABILITY

For weaker students, write the model answer on the board with alternative words. Students copy out the story with the correct words.

A man was walking *next to / on top of* the sea on a cloudy *night / day*. It *started to rain / stopped raining* and he opened his umbrella. The umbrella broke while he *was opening / opened* it. So the man stood under *the / a* tree while it *was raining / rained*.

A2 KEY FOR SCHOOLS Speaking Part 1

3 Briefly review what students need to do in this part of the exam and if necessary read out the task description and tip on TB page 22. Have students make the questions individually. Check and drill the questions. Tell students that the intonation would normally go down on these questions and *do* and *you/your* would not be stressed. Put students into pairs to ask one another the questions. Encourage students to answer in full sentences, for example *I come from Santiago* rather than just *Santiago*.

> **Answers**
> 1 What's your name?
> 2 How old are you?
> 3 Where do you live?
> 4 Where do you come from? / Where are you from?

4 Give students time to read the questions. Tell students that the last question is more difficult because it is an open question. Ask students to think of at least three sentences to answer each open question and write them on the board. For example, *Tell me something about your bedroom.* (*It's not very big. I share it with my sister. There's a computer in the corner. I usually do my homework there.*) Put students into pairs and have them ask one another the questions. Weaker students may need to write the answers to the questions before they answer them orally. You could repeat the task with new pairs for more speaking practice. This time students could also add their own questions for each topic, for example, *How far is your home from school? Does your school have a basketball team?* As feedback, ask the questions to the whole class.

> **Answers**
> Students' own answers

COOLER

Play a back-to-the-board vocabulary game with the words from this review unit. Ask one student to sit so they are not facing the board. Write *underground* on the board. The students who can see the word must explain the word to the student so they can guess it, for example, *You use it to get to school in the morning.* When students understand, put them in small groups to play. (Each group can use an A3 piece of paper rather than a board.)

PREPARE FOR THE EXAM

Listening Part 1

1 **For each question, choose the correct picture.**

🔊 **1** What day does Antonio play football?
34

A TUESDAY 9 August   **B** THURSDAY 11 August   **C** FRIDAY 12 August

2 How much is a family ticket to the zoo today?

A £22   **B** £25   **C** £28

3 What time does the girl's coach arrive?

A   **B**   **C**

4 What is the number of Rosa's house?

A 16   **B** 17   **C** 18

5 What did Marco buy for his bedroom?

A   **B**   **C**

Speaking Part 1

3 **Work in pairs. Make questions and then ask and answer with your partner. Take turns to speak.**

1 Name?   3 Live?
2 Age?   4 Country?

4 **Take turns to ask and answer the questions in the table.**

Now let's talk about your home.	Now let's talk about your school.
5 When did your family move into this home?	**5** When do you arrive at school in the mornings?
6 How many rooms has your home got? What are they?	**6** Which languages do you learn at school?
7 What colour is the furniture in the living room?	**7** How many students are there in your class?
8 Which is your favourite room?	**8** What's your favourite subject?
9 Tell me something about your bedroom.	**9** Tell me something about your classroom

Writing Part 7

2 **Look at the three pictures. Write the story shown in the pictures. Write 35 words or more.**

5 SCHOOL

 ABOUT YOU

▶ **03 Watch the video and discuss the questions.**

How many different subjects do you study?
How much homework do you usually get each day?

VOCABULARY AND READING

School subjects

1 Match the school subjects in the box to the pictures A–L.

EP

> biology   chemistry
> design and technology   drama
> foreign languages   geography
> history   ICT   maths
> PE   physics   science

🔊 35 **Listen and check. Then repeat.**

2 Read the article about schools in Finland and choose the best title.

A Starting young
B New ways of learning
C Time for homework

3 Read the article again and answer the questions.

1 At what age do Finnish students go to school?
2 How long are they at school every day?
3 Do students have any homework?
4 Do subject words appear on all school timetables?
5 How do some experts think our brains work?
6 In Finland, do students
  a complete a project at the same time as they learn school subjects, or
  b study school subjects and then complete a project?
7 What subjects do students learn when they do the project on Pompeii?

4 In pairs, ask and answer the questions.

1 Which are your favourite subjects?
2 Which subjects don't you enjoy as much?
3 Which subjects are you best at?

🔊 36

In international tests of maths, science and reading, students in Finland do well. This is good news! But when you look more carefully at the schools, it's not easy to explain. Finnish students don't start school until they are seven years old. The school day is short, about five hours, and there are only three or four classes a day. Students don't have much homework and there are no exams. So, why don't they do badly in tests? Perhaps something else can explain it.

There is another unusual feature of schools in Finland. For most of us, the school timetable is a list of subjects, for example ICT, history, foreign languages, geography, with one lesson following another. But some experts believe our brains work in a different way. They say our brains don't divide our learning into subjects. Our brains learn better when they get new information in context. This is why some Finnish schools don't teach subjects separately. Instead, they give students a project, such as 'the weather', and then bring school subjects into the project.

So how do some experts believe we learn most easily? Here's an example of a project with a class of 12-year-olds. Students watch a video re-enactment of the end of the city of Pompeii. Then on their laptops they compare ancient Italy under the Romans with modern Finland. Groups look at different parts of the topic and then share their ideas. They also use 3D printers to make a tiny Roman building. Later, they use the pieces of the building for a game. This project includes history, ICT, and design and technology.

Unit Overview

TOPIC	School
VOCABULARY	School subjects
AND READING	New ways of learning
PRONUNCIATION	Word patterns
GRAMMAR	Comparative and superlative adverbs
READING	Clarissa's blog
VOCABULARY	take
LISTENING	An interview about homeschooling
SPEAKING	Describing your perfect school
EXAM TASKS	Reading Part 3

Resources

GRAMMAR REFERENCE AND PRACTICE: SB page 151; TB page 265

PREPARE FOR THE EXAM: SB page on TB page 239; TB page 253

WORKBOOK: pages 20–23

VIDEO AND VIDEO WORKSHEET: School subjects

PHOTOCOPIABLE WORKSHEETS: Grammar worksheet Unit 5; Vocabulary worksheet Unit 5

TEST GENERATOR: Unit test 5

WARMER

Draw a 5 by 5 grid on the board and write a word diagonally left–right. Ask students to give you words to fill in each row horizontally. For example:

L				
	E			
		A		
			R	
				N

L	O	R	R	Y
L	E	M	O	N
P	L	A	Y	S
S	O	R	R	Y
A	G	A	I	N

When students understand, tell them to play in groups, one student choosing a diagonal word to begin.

⑦ ABOUT YOU

▶ 03 You can begin the class and introduce the topic of the unit by showing the video and asking students to complete the video worksheet. Then, read the questions in the *About you* box for students to answer in pairs.

VOCABULARY AND READING

School subjects

1 See if students can tell you the name of the subjects they studied yesterday. If you know the students' teachers, say a teacher's name and have students say the subject that they teach. Then ask students to describe the pictures and match them to the subjects.

Play the recording for students to check and repeat. Ask students, 'What is PE?' (*Physical Education*) and 'What is ICT?' (*Information and Communications Technology*).

Ask students, 'Are there any of these subjects which you don't study?' and 'Do you have a subject which is not in the pictures?' (for example, *music*). Have students say what they study and do in each subject, for example, *In biology we learn how our bodies work.* Then have students cover up the names of the subjects, look at the pictures and tell you what they are.

◁» 35 Answers

The answers are recorded for students to check and then repeat.

A biology B chemistry C drama D science E geography
F foreign languages G ICT H Design and technology I PE
J history K maths L physics

2 Have students describe the photograph and ask, 'Is it like your school? Why? / Why not?'. Ask students what each title would be about. For example, *Starting young* – why it is important to teach children from a very young age. Pre-teach **feature** (a typical quality, or an important part of something) and **re-enactment** (making something happen again in exactly the same way that it happened the first time, often as entertainment or as a way to help people remember certain facts about an event). Give students a time limit to read and choose the title. Check the answer as a class.

Answer

B

3 Tell students that Pompeii was a city near Naples that was destroyed by an earthquake in 79 AD. Ask, 'Do Finnish students do exams?' (*no*) and 'How old were the children doing the Pompeii project?' (*12*). Give students time to read and answer the questions. Check answers as a class. Ask these questions for students to discuss: 'Do you think students learn better when the school day is shorter?' and 'When there is no exam do you think students study hard?'.

Answers

1 They start at the age of 7.
2 For about five hours.
3 They have a little.
4 Yes, they do.
5 They think our brains understand better when knowledge is connected.
6 a
7 History, ICT, design and technology.

FAST FINISHERS

Put fast finishers together to think of a project which would include different school subjects. They should write down the name of the project, what students need to do and how it involves the different subjects. When the rest of the class has finished, fast finishers should explain their project idea to them.

◁» 36 The Reading text is recorded for students to listen, read and check their answers.

CONTINUED ON PAGE 62

4 Put students into pairs to discuss. Share ideas as a class. Ask, 'Do you think students learn more efficiently when they study subjects or when they study a topic?' and 'How do you think students learn the most easily?'.

PRONUNCIATION | Word patterns

 5 Write the word *university* on the board and say the word with the syllables spelled out: *u-ni-ver-si-ty* (5). Say, 'Is it univerSIty or uniVERsity?' (*uniVERsity, the stress is on the third syllable*). Mark the stress pattern on the board.

Go through the example words in the table. Play the recording and get the students to identify where the stress is. Play the second recording for students to check and repeat.

As an extension activity, put students in teams and give them two minutes to add as many words to the first two categories as they can, for example:

topic Oo: orange, window, chocolate

audience Ooo: holiday, beautiful

Answers
The answers are recorded for students to check and then repeat.

Oo	topic, classroom, history, science
Ooo	audience, chemistry, favourite, languages
oOoo	communicate, biology, geography, technology

GRAMMAR | Comparative and superlative adverbs

1 Say to students, 'You pronounced those words beautifully' and then write this on the board. Ask students, 'What kind of word is *beautifully*?' (*an adverb*) and 'Does it describe *what* you do or *how* you do it?' (*how*). Tell students that *beautifully* is a simple adverb, *more beautifully* is a comparative adverb and *most beautifully* is a superlative adverb.

Ask students to read the sentences. Draw their attention to *well* and *better* and explain that they are irregular adverb forms from the adjective *good*: *well – better – the best*.

Ask students to decide whether the adverbs are simple, comparative or superlative.

Answers
Simple adverbs: well, badly, hard
Comparative adverbs: more carefully, better, more efficiently
Superlative adverbs: the most easily

MIXED ABILITY

Some students may need a presentation which is less book-based. Ask students to repeat the alphabet A–Z. Arrange them in pairs. One student says the alphabet as quickly as they can; the other times them. Then they swap roles.

Next ask all the students to line up according to their time, the slowest on the left and the quickest on the right. Go down the line and compare the students:

Tomas said it more quickly than Ivo. Sandra said it the most quickly. Christina said it less quickly than Lionel.

Highlight the comparative forms on the board and ask students to make sentences comparing themselves, for example, *I said it more quickly than most of the class.*

2 Answer the question as a class.

Answer
the

3 Tell students to complete the table. Check as a class. Explain the difference in meaning and word order between the adverbs *hard* and *hardly* with these examples:

Jane studies hard. She is a good student.

Jane hardly studies. She is a bad student.

Answers
1 badly **2** good **3** well **4** better **5** careful **6** carefully
7 more carefully **8** efficient **9** more efficiently
10 the most efficiently **11** easier **12** more easily
13 most easily **14** hard **15** hard **16** the hardest

» **GRAMMAR REFERENCE AND PRACTICE ANSWER KEY TB PAGE 265**

4 Go through the exercise orally first then have students write the answers. Check answers as a class.

Answers
1 quickly **2** the fastest **3** better **4** more slowly **5** the worst
6 harder

5 Write these examples on the board and ask students what is wrong and why.

I couldn't do it more quicker. (the correct form is *quickly*)

She shouted loudly something. (*loudly* should be at the end of the sentence because the adverb cannot go between the verb and the object)

Tell students to correct the sentences. Check answers as a class.

Answers
1 You speak English really **well**.
2 I made friends **much more easily** at my new school.
3 Drama classes helped me speak **more clearly** and better.
4 Catch this bus and you can get **home more quickly**.
5 My brother **likes the music class the best**.

6 Put students in pairs and tell them to turn to page 136. Students take it in turns to make sentences combining a verb with a comparative or superlative adverb form of one of the adjectives. You could give students a time limit to see which pair can make the most sentences.

» **GRAMMAR WORKSHEET UNIT 5**

COOLER

Tell students to read out each question in the *About you* box on page 32. Now tell them to read them again quickly, then more quickly, then slowly, then quietly, then quickly and quietly, then slowly and loudly. You could also ask students to suggest adverbs for how to read the questions, for example *angrily* and *happily*.

PRONUNCIATION | Word patterns

5 Listen and look at the word patterns in the table. Then put the words in the box into the correct column.

Oo	Ooo	oOoo
topic	*audience*	*communicate*

| biology | chemistry | classroom | favourite | geography |
| history | languages | science | technology | |

🔊 **Listen and check. Then repeat.**
38

GRAMMAR | Comparative and superlative adverbs

1 Look at the adverbs in the sentences. Decide which ones are simple adverbs, comparative adverbs or superlative adverbs.

1 In international tests of maths, science and reading, students in Finland do well.
2 When you look more carefully at the schools, it's not easy to explain.
3 So, why don't they do badly in tests?
4 Do students learn better when the school day is shorter?
5 When there is no exam, do students study hard?
6 Do students learn more efficiently when they study subjects or when they study a topic?
7 So, how do some experts believe we learn the most easily?

2 Look at the comparative and superlative adverbs and in Exercise 1 again and answer the question.

> Which word do we often use before superlative adverbs?

3 Complete the table.

Adjective	Simple adverb	Comparative adverb	Superlative adverb
bad	1	*worse*	*the worst*
2	3	4	*the best*
5	6	7	*the most carefully*
8	*efficiently*	9	10
easy	11	12	13
14	15	*harder*	16

≫ **GRAMMAR REFERENCE AND PRACTICE PAGE 151**

4 Write the correct form of the adverb for the adjective in brackets.

1 Laura often makes mistakes because she always does her homework very _____ (quick).
2 Hans speaks _____ (fast) in our class.
3 You speak English much _____ (good) than me.
4 Please can you speak _____ (slow)? I didn't understand you before.
5 None of us did well in the exam, but I did _____ (bad)!
6 I think I work _____ (hard) in English lessons than I do in science.

5 Correct the mistakes in the sentences.

👁 **1** You speak English really good.
2 I made friends much easier at my new school.
3 Drama classes helped me speak clearer and better.
4 Catch this bus and you can get more quickly home.
5 My brother likes best the music class.

6 ≫ **Work with a partner. Go to page 136.**

SCHOOL **33**

1 Read Clarissa's blog quickly. Where is she studying now, at home or at school?

Clarissa's blog

31 July 2018

A few years ago, I wasn't very happy at school and I wasn't doing well in tests. So, when I was eight, Mum and Dad decided to teach me at home.

Homeschooling – great, I thought! I could stay in bed all day! Well, it wasn't quite like that! My parents found out what I needed to learn. Sometimes I had lessons, but most of the time I studied things I liked and found interesting. That's how homeschooling works best.

My favourite hobby was playing computer games, so, with Dad's help, I began to write my own computer programs. But I liked making models too, and for that I needed … maths! At school, maths was boring, but now it was useful for making my models. I made a model boat and I needed to understand science and maths to do that – oh, and design and technology too!

So were there any bad things about homeschooling? Not really. I missed my friends, but I saw them at weekends and we talked about school! They told me about their week at school, and I told them about mine. Mine always seemed more fun to me. Some weeks I studied more than they did. Other weeks I didn't study much at all. And I never had homework!

I'm 15 now, and I'm back at school because I need to take exams. I don't mind. It's nice to study with my friends again.

PREPARE FOR THE EXAM

Reading Part 3

2 Read Clarissa's blog again. For each question, choose the correct answer.

1 Why did Clarissa's parents teach her at home?
   A Her parents didn't like her school.
   B She was too old for her school.
   C She was having problems at school.

2 What does Clarissa say about homeschooling in the second paragraph?
   A She only learned what her parents told her to.
   B She chose what she wanted to learn.
   C She studied in bed a lot of the time.

3 Clarissa preferred doing maths at home because
   A her dad was able to explain it to her.
   B it helped her do things she enjoyed.
   C she had more time to spend on it.

4 What was the difference between Clarissa's and her friends' school experiences?
   A Clarissa didn't have to do any homework.
   B Clarissa always had more work to do than they did.
   C Her friends enjoyed themselves more.

5 What does Clarissa say about homeschooling in her blog?
   A It's important to have daily lessons.
   B It's hard to find time to see friends.
   C Learning doesn't always have to come from books.

» PREPARE FOR THE EXAM PAGE 123

TALKING POINTS

What do you like about going to school?
What are the good things about homeschooling?
What are the bad things about it?
Would you like to study at home? Why? / Why not?

WARMER

Tell students that you will read out some teacher-student jokes. Students should write down ways of completing them with what the student said.

- Teacher: If I had six oranges in my left hand and seven in my right hand, what would I have? (*Big hands!*)

- Teacher: Sara, did you miss school yesterday? (*No, not a bit.*)

- Teacher: You're bad at spelling so I told you to write this word ten times. Why did you only write it four times? (*I'm bad at maths too.*)

Put students into groups to think of another joke about school. Have each group tell their joke.

BACKGROUND INFORMATION

Until the nineteenth century, and the growth of state schools and introduction of compulsory education in developed countries, homeschooling was the most common type of education. The family would teach their own children as only the very rich could afford personal tutors. Homeschooling declined once free state education became available but in the middle of the twentieth century numbers increased again as some parents became dissatisfied with the educational system. However, only a small number of children are homeschooled, less than five percent in the USA for example. There are two main reasons why parents choose homeschooling for their children. The first is that they think their children need a more personalised approach, perhaps because of special needs and requirements they have; the second is because parents want to be actively involved with their children's education. Regulation of homeschooling, for example control over the content and methodology of the educational programme parents can offer, varies from country to country. Homeschooling is not legal in every country, for example it is not legal in Germany, and there is some criticism of it. Some people believe that education needs to be done by qualified professionals, teachers not parents. There is also the concern that studying at home harms students' social skills by isolating them from other children.

1 Tell students to look at the photograph and ask, 'What is she doing?' 'How is she feeling?' Elicit or pre-teach **blog** (a record of your activities or opinions that you put on the internet for other people to read and that you update regularly). Ask students if they keep a blog or read any blogs. Give students a time limit to read the blog then ask where Clarissa is studying now.

Answer

At school

A2 KEY FOR SCHOOLS
Reading Part 3

In this part, students have to read one long text adapted from authentic material like a newspaper or magazine. Students answer five three-option multiple-choice questions about the main ideas and specific details in the text.

Tip Tell students to first read the text quickly to get an idea of what it is about and which ideas and words or expressions are repeated to show the key information. Then students should read each question carefully, underlining the key words, and locate the information. Tell students that usually there are four paragraphs with one question on each paragraph. Questions 1–4 come in the same order as the information in the text. Tell students that the last question can be a more global question and tests, for example, the main point, the writer's purpose, attitudes or opinions.

2 Ask students some general questions about the text: 'How old was Clarissa when she started homeschooling?' (*eight*) and 'What was her hobby?' (*computer games*). 'When did she see her friends?' (*at the weekends*). Point out that the first four questions test details of the text and that question 5 is about the text generally. Have students answer the questions. Check as a class and have students tell you where they found the answer. For example, in question 1 *wasn't doing well in tests* has a similar meaning to *having problems at school*.

Answers

1 C 2 B 3 B 4 A 5 C

>> PREPARE FOR THE EXAM TEACHING NOTES AND ANSWER KEY TB PAGE 253

FAST FINISHERS

Tell fast finishers to make a timetable for one day of Clarissa's week when she is homeschooling. The timetable should show when and what Clarissa studies on that particular day. When the other students have finished and you have checked the answers, fast finishers can present their timetables to the class and students can say which of the days sounds most interesting and useful.

The Reading text is recorded for students to listen, read and check their answers.
39

TALKING POINTS

Ask students, 'Do you know anyone who has homeschooling?' and 'Is it common in this (your) country?'. Then have students discuss the questions in groups. Write down the advantages and disadvantages of homeschooling on the board and discuss them as a class.

1   Write the sentence on the board but leave a gap for *take*. Ask students what word is missing and what it means here.

| **Answer**
| to do

2   Say to students, 'Take a pen and underline the sentence.'. Then, 'So you can take an exam and take a pen, anything else with *take*?' Have students match the meanings to the words. Check answers as a class.

Answers
The answers are recorded for students to check and then repeat.
a take an umbrella
b take photos or pictures
c take exams
d take a subject
e take the second turning
f take medicine
g take a train

3   Go through the different uses of *take* on the mind map and give your own examples before students give theirs. Encourage students to use monolingual dictionaries (print or online) to get example sentences. Also encourage students to personalise the examples so that they are about themselves and people they know.

4   Demonstrate with an example on the board:
When you take a long _____ journey, what do you do not to get bored? (*train*).

Get some answers from the class. Then have students complete the questions in the book. Check as a class. Ask students to write answers to the questions.

| **Answers**
| 1 umbrella 2 turning 3 subject 4 photos 5 train
| 6 medicine 7 exam

5   Put students into pairs to compare their answers from Exercise 4. Share ideas as a class.

» VOCABULARY WORKSHEET UNIT 5

LISTENING

1   Ask students to describe the photograph. Pre-teach **camper van** (a large motor vehicle that is designed to be lived in while travelling. It contains cooking equipment, one or more beds, and sometimes a toilet). Ask students, 'Where is Bali?' (*Indonesia*) and 'What do you know about Bali?' (*It is popular with tourists.*).

Play the recording and ask students to tell you what phrase Ethan uses to describe the education on the trip.

| **Answers**
| World Schooling

2   Go through the questions and see if students can confirm or correct them already.

Play the recording again and have students check their ideas. As an extension activity, put students into groups to think of another *-schooling*, for example, playschooling where students learn through games.

Students should present their type of schooling to the rest of the class and this information could be included in the perfect school presentation later in the lesson.

Answers
1 ✓
2 ✗ (Ethan's mum lost her job.)
3 ✗ (Ruth and Ethan went to an ordinary school before they went travelling.)
4 ✗ (Their family and neighbours thought Ethan's mum and dad were mad so they must have told them.)
5 ✓
6 ✓
7 ✗ (Ethan wanted to go back to school.)
8 ✗ (Ethan says he worked much harder when he was travelling.)

MIXED ABILITY

To help students with weaker listening skills, pause the recording after you hear the answer to a question, or two questions if the information comes close together, and then ask the questions. This breaks up long recordings and students don't get lost. You can still cater for stronger students by asking them extra questions about what they have just heard. So after students hear 'That was two years ago. My sister, Ruth, she's 11 now, and I were doing OK at school. Mum lost her job and Dad loved travelling …', pause so students can answer questions 1 and 2. Ask stronger students, 'How old was Ruth when they went travelling?' (*nine*)

» AUDIOSCRIPT TB PAGE 289

3   Ask students for the advantages and disadvantages of world schooling, for example advantage – *it's a great way to learn a foreign language,* disadvantage – *you need to have enough money to be able to travel.* Put students into pairs to discuss the questions. Share ideas as a class.

SPEAKING

1   Ask the students what is good and not so good about your school. Give some examples like *There is a great gym.* and *We only study one foreign language.* Put students together to make notes based on the questions. Encourage students to think of other aspects that they could talk about in their presentation, for example, a name for the school, what technology there is and how it is used, how students are tested and marked.

2   Ask each pair or group to present their perfect school. They should practise first and decide who will say what. Make sure that the students who need more support deal with the easier questions, for example questions 1–4. The class should vote on which school they think is best.

COOLER

Write *school* on the board. Ask students to make a word from the letters in *school* without changing the order of the letters (*cool*). Write these words on the board for students to do the same: *biology* (*big*), *technology* (*ten*), *science* (*since*), *homework* (*how*), *dictionary* (*diary*), *superlative* (*plate*). Put students into small groups to think of more words where you can do this then give the words to other groups to try.

VOCABULARY *take*

1 What does *take* mean in this sentence?

I'm 15 now, and I'm back at school because I need to take exams.

2 Now look at the mind map. Match the meanings of *take* a–g to these words.
EP

exams

photos/pictures

a train

take

an umbrella

medicine

(the second) turning

a subject

a	carry	**e**	go along
b	make	**f**	use
c	do	**g**	catch
d	study		

40 🔊 Listen and check. Then repeat.

3 Write an example sentence for each meaning of *take*.

4 Complete the questions with the correct form of the words from Exercise 2 and then answer them.

1 When did you last take an _____ out with you in the rain?
2 Which _____ do I need take to get to the park from here? The one on the left or the one on the right?
3 What extra _____ would you like to take at school ?
4 Have you taken any _____ today with your new camera? How many?
5 When was the first time you took a _____ to go somewhere? Were you on holiday?
6 Do you usually take _____ when you are ill?
7 How do you feel when you take an _____ at the end of the school year?

5 In pairs, compare your answers.

LISTENING

41 🔊 **1** Listen to the *What's New* section on a morning radio show. A boy called Ethan is talking about his experience of schooling. What phrase does Ethan use for the education he had on the trip?

41 🔊 **2** Listen again. Are the sentences right (✓) or wrong (✗)?

1 There are four people in Ethan's family.
2 Ethan's mum left her job because she wanted to see the world.
3 Ruth and Ethan were homeschooled before they went travelling.
4 Ethan's parents didn't tell anyone else about their plans.
5 Ruth and Ethan's parents helped with the 'world schooling'.
6 Ruth and Ethan do a lot of different things when they are travelling.
7 Ethan's parents wanted him to go back to school.
8 Ethan says he works harder at school than he did when he was world schooled.

3 In pairs, discuss the questions.

1 Would you like to be 'world schooled'?
2 Would your parents be good teachers?
3 Which parts of the world would you like to visit?
4 What would you miss about your school?

SPEAKING

1 In pairs, or a small group, use the questions to describe your perfect school. Make notes about what you discuss.

1 Where is the school?
2 What lessons do you have?
3 How many students are there?
4 Who are the teachers?
5 Do you have homework?
6 How many lessons do you have in a day/week?
7 How long are the school days/holidays?
8 Do you wear a uniform?
9 What's the food like?
10 Do you sleep there?
11 What makes your school better than other schools?

2 Now tell the rest of the class about your perfect school. Take turns in your group to speak.

6 FAVOURITE THINGS

 ABOUT YOU

Do you have a favourite thing? What is it?
Where did you get it?
Why is it special?
What do you like about it?

VOCABULARY AND LISTENING

Materials

1 Look at the photos below. Match the materials in the box to the photos A–J.

cotton	glass	gold	leather
metal	paper	plastic	silver
wood	wool		

🔊 42 Listen and check. Then repeat.

2 What are the things in the photos made of? Talk about the photos with your partner.

> The headphones are made of plastic.

3 Look at the examples. Which word is a noun and which is an adjective?

> The box is made of wood. It's a wooden box.

4 Work with your partner. Use the materials as adjectives to describe and find the things in the photo.

> They're cotton T-shirts.   Photo B

5 In pairs, look around the classroom and at what people are wearing. Find as many things as you can that are made from the materials in Exercise 1. Say what they are.

🔊 43 **6** Cam is doing a project for school. He asks three people in the street about their favourite things. Listen to the recording. Which thing was a present?

🔊 43 **7** Listen again and complete the table.

	Speaker 1	Speaker 2	Speaker 3
What is the thing?			
Who does it belong to?			
What is it made of?			

6 FAVOURITE THINGS

Unit Overview

TOPIC	Things
VOCABULARY AND LISTENING	Materials
	Asking people's about their favourite things
GRAMMAR	Possession
PRONUNCIATION	Weak forms: *a* and *of*
READING	Special Memories
VOCABULARY	Adjectives for describing objects
LISTENING	A conversation about people's belongings
WRITING	Adjective order
EXAM TASKS	Listening Part 5

Resources

GRAMMAR REFERENCE AND PRACTICE: SB page 152; TB page 265

PREPARE FOR THE EXAM: SB page on TB page 248; TB page 258

WORKBOOK: pages 24–27

PHOTOCOPIABLE WORKSHEETS: Grammar worksheet Unit 6; Vocabulary worksheet Unit 6

TEST GENERATOR: Unit test 6

ABOUT YOU

Tell students about your favourite thing, making sure you include answers to the four questions. Then have students answer the questions in pairs. Share ideas as a class.

VOCABULARY AND LISTENING

Materials

1 Put some objects on the desk and give the students one minute to look at them. Then cover them up and see how many objects and materials they name, e.g. *a plastic ruler.*

Ask students to name the objects in the photos. Then students match the materials to the photos.

Answers

The answers are recorded for students to check and then repeat.
A plastic **B** cotton **C** gold **D** wool **E** metal **F** leather **G** glass **H** wood **I** paper **J** silver

---

2 Put students into pairs to say what the things are made of. Write the construction on the board to help students.

_____ *is/are made of* _____.

Check as a class. Ask students to write down the materials in order of how expensive they are (*paper first and gold last*) and then compare with a partner.

Answers

A The headphones are made of plastic.
B The T-shirts are made of cotton.
C The ring is made of gold.
D The gloves are made of wool.
E The coin is made of metal.
F The jacket is made of leather.
G The bowl is made of glass.
H The box is made of wood.
I The cat is made of paper.
J The necklace is made of silver.

3 Ask students to identify the word class. Then ask students for the difference between *gold* and *golden* as adjectives (*gold is the material, golden is the colour or something associated with gold*).

Answers

wood is a noun; *wooden* is an adjective

4 Tell students that all of the words can be adjectives or nouns except for *wood*. Put students into pairs to use the materials as adjectives. Check as a class.

Answers

A They're plastic headphones.	**F** It's a leather jacket.
B They're cotton T-shirts.	**G** It's a glass bowl.
C It's a gold ring.	**H** It's a wooden box.
D They're wool gloves.	**I** It's a paper cat.
E It's a metal coin.	**J** It's a silver necklace.

5 You could turn this into a game by asking students to first look around the room carefully then close their eyes. They should describe what is in the room with their eyes still shut. Then students can open their eyes to check.

6 Ask students what is happening in the photo and what objects they can see. Ask students if they have ever done a project like this. Pre-teach (or demonstrate!) **origami.** Play the recording and have students say what was a present. Check as a class.

Answers

the origami birds

7 Play the recording again and students complete the table. Check as a class. Ask, 'Which is the nicest thing?'. As an extension activity, students imagine that a friend or relative is answering the same questions. In pairs, students answer as if they were their friend or relative.

Answers

Speaker 1: earrings, her mum, silver
Speaker 2: elephant, his dad, wood
Speaker 3: origami birds, her parents, paper

» AUDIOSCRIPT TB PAGE 290

GRAMMAR — Possession

1 Ask students to look at the pictures and for each one ask, 'Is there one or more than one boy?'. Have students match the sentences to the pictures as a class.

Answers
1 B 2 A

2 Have students look at the photos and ask, 'So if there is only one person, what do we write?'. Ask one student to write the answer on the board, *brother's*. If there is more than one person … ?' Ask the student to write the answer on the board, *brothers'*.

Answers
Sentence 1 has *'s* because there is one person.
Sentence 2 has *s'* because there is more than one person.

MIXED ABILITY
Some students will have problems with the difference between *'s* and *s'* because they are pronounced the same. Tell students to use different-coloured marker pens to mark the difference as this may make it easier for them to see and remember the forms.

3 Have students complete the sentences. Check as a class and have students tell you how they know whether who they belong to is singular or plural. For example, in question 1, 'them' shows that there is more than one sister.

Answers
1 sisters' 2 brother's 3 children's 4 dogs'

4 Take a pen from someone in the class and ask '(Julio), is this my pen or yours?'. Elicit the reply *It's not your pen, it's mine.* Write the question and answer on the board and say that *my* and *your* are determiners – they go before nouns, and *yours* and *mine* are pronouns – they are used instead of nouns. Students mark the sentences. Check as a class.

Answers
1 They're not (mine), they're my sister's.
2 Oh and what are (theirs)? Your dad's for example.

5 Students complete the table. Check as a class. Then ask students to close their eyes. Describe something on their desk or something they are wearing and ask who it belongs to. Students reply. For example:
'I can see a blue jacket. Is it Silvia's?'
No, it's not hers, it's Michaela's.

Answers
Pronouns: mine, yours, his, hers, ours, theirs

>> GRAMMAR REFERENCE AND PRACTICE ANSWER KEY TB PAGE 265

6 Have students describe the pictures and say what the difference is. (*The person with a football has a lot of friends in picture A but only one friend in picture B.*) Students match the sentences and pictures.

Answers
1 A 2 B

7 Demonstrate on the board with an example: *It's not _____, it doesn't belong to them.* (*theirs*) Have students complete the sentences. Check answers as a class.

Answers
1 his 2 theirs 3 ours 4 mine 5 yours 6 hers

8 Demonstrate on the board with an example: *My game is good but your is better.* (~~your~~ *yours*) Have students correct the sentences. Check answers as a class.

Answers
1 You can read your favourite **books** there.
2 My **friend's** name's Ben.
3 The bus stop is just five **minutes'** walk from my house.
4 Bring your computer because **mine** is broken.
5 My bedroom is bigger than **theirs**.

>> GRAMMAR WORKSHEET UNIT 6

ə PRONUNCIATION | Weak forms: *a* and *of*

🔊 44

9 Tell students to listen and notice how the words *a* and *of* have the sounds /ə/ and /əv/. They sound weaker than the other words. Play the recording again. Students repeat, clapping on the 'strong' words. Have students add three more sentences with the same rhythm and structure. For example:
Mike's a friend of ours.
That's a dream of mine.
The girls are fans of theirs.

10 Give some examples of things your family has and ask students who they belong to:
'A box of paints.'
Is it your daughter's?
'No, it's my wife's. She likes painting.'
In pairs, students choose and describe three things.
As an extension activity, have students choose one thing they talked about and write a paragraph based on the questions in Exercise 10.

Possible answer
My father has a cotton T-shirt from the 2018 World Cup in Russia. He went to a Brazil game and bought it at the stadium. His T-shirt is special because he really enjoyed his trip to Russia. I want a T-shirt like that!

COOLER
Tell students, 'I am something or somebody. You ask me questions to see what or who I am. I can only answer "yes" or "no".'
Are you alive?
'No.'
Can we see you in this room?
'Yes.'
Are you made of metal?
'Yes.'
Can we speak with you?
'Yes.'
Are you a phone?
'Yes!'
When the students understand, they play in pairs.

GRAMMAR Possession

1 Look at the pictures. Match sentences 1 and 2 to pictures A and B.

1 It's my brother's dog.
2 It's my brothers' dog.

2 Look at sentences 1 and 2 in Exercise 1. Which sentence has 's and which sentence has s'? Why?

3 Complete the sentences. Use the word in brackets in the singular or plural and 's or s'.

1 That's my _____ (sister) car. My dad bought them one to share last year.
2 I don't have a computer, but I use my _____ (brother) when I need to. I lend him my camera when he needs it because he hasn't got a good one.
3 My little sister loves going to the _____ (child) disco. It's specially for little kids and there are games and activities.
4 Don't put any cake on those plates! I use them for the _____ (dog) food. They don't like the bowls from the pet shop.

4 Look at the words in purple in the two examples from the listening. Underline the determiners and circle the pronouns.

1 They're not mine. They're my sister's.
2 Oh and what are theirs? Your dad's for example.

5 Now complete the table.

Determiners	Pronouns
my	mine
your	
his	
her	
our	
their	

>> GRAMMAR REFERENCE AND PRACTICE PAGE 152

6 Look at the pictures and decide who the football player is. Match sentences 1 and 2 to pictures A and B.

1 He's a friend of theirs.
2 He's a friend of hers.

7 Complete the sentences with the correct word.

1 That's not Robert's book, it's Paula's. Robert lost _____ yesterday.
2 My parents had a holiday on a boat last summer. I think it belonged to a friend of _____.
3 A cat plays in our garden sometimes, but it's not _____. We've got a dog.
4 You can't use my brother's football. But you can borrow _____ if you like. I got it for my birthday.
5 Are you looking for your hat? I saw Paul's in the garden, but I don't know where _____ is.
6 Sally is so good at art. That picture is _____.

8 Correct the mistakes in the sentences.

1 You can read your favourite book's there.
2 My friends name's Ben.
3 The bus stop is just five minutes walk from my house.
4 Bring your computer because my is broken.
5 My bedroom is bigger than their.

PRONUNCIATION | Weak forms: a and of

9 Listen and repeat.

She's a friend of mine.
He's a friend of hers.
They're friends of ours.
Is he a friend of yours?

10 Think of three things that are special and belong to different people in your family. In pairs, tell each other about them. Use the questions to help you.

1 What are they? What are they made of?
2 Who do they belong to?
3 Where did they come from?
4 Why are they special?
5 What else can you say about them?

READING

1 In pairs, tell your partner about a special present someone gave you. What was it?

2 Anja and Pete wrote about special memories in their online school magazine. Look at objects A–F. What present did Anja get? What present did Pete get?

HILL CREST ACADEMY

Special Memories

45

ANJA, AGE 13

My special memory is from when I was three years old. We were staying with my grandparents at their house in the country. They lived in an old wooden house. I remember the house was always cold and it was near a forest. When it was time for bed, Grandma took me upstairs to read me a story. On my bed there was a lovely wool blanket. It was really colourful. I remember touching it and it was so, so soft. 'It's yours. I made it for you,' my grandma said. I still have the blanket on my bed at home. It looks really small there, but I remember when I was younger it seemed so big!

PETE, AGE 14

My special memory isn't from very long ago. I was opening presents on my 13th birthday. My older brother gave me a large box. It was very hard. What could it be? I opened it and felt inside. I'm blind, so I needed to touch everything because I can't see. It was smooth and round. I remember thinking 'It's a leather football' and feeling upset. I can't play football because I can't see the ball. I picked it up. It felt quite heavy, and it made a noise. My brother told me it was a special football for blind people. There are little metal balls inside that make a noise when someone kicks or throws it. Perfect! Now I play football all the time.

3 Read the article again and answer the questions.

1 What was Anja's grandparents' house like?
2 When did Anja first see the blanket?
3 What was it like?
4 Why do you think Anja remembers it as big when in fact it's quite small?
5 Who was Pete's present from?
6 What did it feel like?
7 Why did he feel sad when he first felt the present?
8 What happened when he took it out of the box and why?

💬 TALKING POINTS

Anja's memory is from when she was three years old. What's your earliest memory?

Pete's memory is of his special football. What other special things can help someone like Pete?

VOCABULARY   Adjectives for describing objects

1 Match the words in the box to photos A–F.

EP

colourful	hard	heavy	large
little	lovely	old	pretty
round	small	smooth	soft

 Listen and check.

2 In pairs, describe the objects in the photos. Use the adjectives from Exercise 1 and others you know.

3 Take turns to describe something in the classroom to your partner for them to guess what it is. Use the words from Exercise 1 to help you.

It's large, smooth and colourful. It's made of paper and it's on the wall.

A map?

Yes.

38   UNIT 6

READING

WARMER

Write this recipe for a magic drink on the board:

A cup of horse's milk

Six birds' eggs

The hair of a friend of mine

A crocodile's skin

Two sleepers' dreams

Two things of yours

Ask students what they think this drink can do, for example, drink it and you can fly.

Then have students make their own magic drinks and put them in pairs to tell one another about them.

BACKGROUND INFORMATION

Only about five percent of people who have problems with their vision are completely blind. The Paralympics include different classifications of visual impairment and the football competition is a five-a-side match. The ball has a noise-making device so players can follow it. There are a number of other specially-modified products and services which can help the blind in everyday life. These include Braille displays on computers, where software converts text into Braille; over 100 radio-reading services where presenters read from a range of reading materials; tactile paving to help blind people move around outside; some currencies, such as the Canadian dollar, having banknotes which have Braille-like dots to indicate the different denominations.

1. Tell students about a present you got. For example: 'Two years ago my sister gave me a machine which makes ice-cream. I love ice-cream so I use it a lot!' Put students into pairs to describe their presents. Share ideas as a class.

2. Ask students if their school has an online magazine and if it does, what is in it, and if it doesn't, what could be in it. Have students name the objects. Give students a time limit to read the article and say what presents Anja and Pete got. Check answers as a class.

   Answers

   Anja: a blanket (D)
   Pete: a football for blind people (E)

3. Ask students, 'Whose memory is the earliest?' (*Anja's*). Tell students to read and answer the questions. Check answers as a class. Ask, 'Whose memory is the most interesting?'

   Answers

   1 It was an old, wooden house and it was always cold.
   2 When she was three years old and staying at her grandparents' house.
   3 It was beautiful, colourful and soft.
   4 Because she was small, the blanket seemed big to her.
   5 It was from his older brother.
   6 It felt round, hard and smooth (and quite heavy).
   7 Because he can't see and so can't play football.
   8 The ball made a noise because it had small metal balls inside.

FAST FINISHERS

Fast finishers write down the presents which they think Anja's grandmother gave her on each of her birthdays when she was four, five and six. When the other students have finished, fast finishers can tell their ideas to the rest of the class and see if the other students like the presents.

🔊 45 The Reading text is recorded for students to listen, read and check their answers.

💬 **TALKING POINTS**

Tell students your earliest memory. Put students into small groups to discuss theirs. Then ask students to tell you things that could help blind people. These could be objects, like the football, or services, like mobile phone apps giving useful information to blind people. Write the ideas on the board and read out the Background Information box if necessary. Then have students discuss the ideas and add others in their groups. Share ideas as a class.

VOCABULARY Adjectives for describing objects

1. Tell students to match the adjectives to the photos. Play the recording for students to listen, check and repeat. Concept-check the meaning of the adjectives. For example: 'The shape of an apple or the sun' (*round*), 'An elephant is this.' (*large, heavy*), 'How a baby's skin feels' (*smooth*).

🔊 46 **Answers**

The answers are recorded for students to check and then repeat.
A hard, heavy, old
B hard
C little, lovely, pretty, small
D colourful, lovely, pretty, soft
E hard, heavy, round, smooth
F round, small, smooth

2. Students should describe an object and their partner should say which one it is. Ask some students to describe the objects.

   Possible answers

   A It's a bell. It looks heavy. I think they used them in schools years ago.
   B It's a large box. It's made of plastic or wood and it looks hard.
   C It's a small wooden house and it looks old. It looks like a doll's house.
   D It's a blanket. It's really colourful and it looks soft too. I think it's lovely.
   E It's a football. Footballs are hard and round.
   F These are little metal balls. They are round and very smooth.

3. Demonstrate with some examples:

   'It's large and soft and it's on the floor.' (*rug*)

   'They're hard and heavy and you are all sitting next to one.' (*desks*)

   Students do the same in pairs and then as a class.

>> **VOCABULARY WORKSHEET UNIT 6**

PREPARE FOR THE EXAM

A2 KEY FOR SCHOOLS Listening Part 5

🔊 47 **1** Briefly review what students need to do in this part of the exam and if necessary read out the A2 Key for Schools box on TB page 30.

Tell students to read the background information about who is speaking and why carefully so they understand the context. They should also read the task and make sure they understand the connection between the five items and eight options. Students should be careful not to write down the first thing they hear as speakers may correct themselves and give the real answer.

Have students describe the photo and ask, 'What are they doing?' (*looking in boxes*). Ask students to read the task and ask, 'Who are speaking?' (*Carmen and Murat*) and 'Who do all these things belong to?' (*her relatives*). Play the recording for students to complete the task.

🔊 47 **2** Play the recording again for students to check their answers. Check answers as a class.

> **Answers**
> 1 A 2 H 3 B 4 D 5 F

» **AUDIOSCRIPT TB PAGE 290**

 WRITING

 PREPARE TO WRITE
Adjective order

GET READY Books closed. If you are able, show students a virtual tour of a famous museum like the Egyptian Museum in Cairo. Ask students, 'What museums do you know?' 'What do they have inside?'

Books open, ask students to read the notice from the museum and say what two things you should send to the museum (*an email, a photo*). Ask, 'What do you have to tell the museum?' (*what the object looks like, why it is special*). Students then read Ben's email and say what his favourite thing is. Check as a class.

Ask 'Why do we say *big wooden box* but not *wooden big box*?' and explain that there is an order of adjectives before a noun. Put the categories up on the board and give an example of each (see Answers).

Tell students to find the adjectives in Ben's email and the texts on page 38 and put them in the table. Check as a class.

> **Answers**
> Opinion: beautiful, lovely
> Size: small, little
> Physical quality: smooth
> Shape: round
> Age: old
> Colour: red
> Material: silver, wooden, wool, metal

PLAN Tell students to write notes answering the three questions. Ask students to include in their notes pairs of adjectives in the right order, for example:

wonderful, old ⎫
lovely, colourful ⎬ painting
small, modern ⎭

WRITE Students draw the picture of their object first, as this will help them describe it. They could use a photo if they are doing this as homework. Tell students to use Ben's email as a model when they write.

IMPROVE Students check one another's work. They underline the adjectives and check the order is correct. They should also check for other mistakes. Students then imagine that they are the director of the museum, read all the emails and decide which object to put in the exhibition.

> **Model answer**
> I've got an interesting object for you. It's a 1966 paper poster of The Beatles, a fantastic old pop group. It's from my uncle's house and I found it in his bedroom.
> From
> Ben

MIXED ABILITY

Give students a less demanding writing task. Write this answer on the board and ask students to find mistakes with the grammar done in this unit and the order of adjectives and rewrite it (see Answers above for the correct version).

I've got an interesting object for your. It's a paper 1966 poster of The Beatles, an old fantastic pop group. It's from mine uncles' house and I found it in her bedroom.

By

Ben

Students may be able to write their own emails after this.

COOLER

Read out a list of adjectives and one noun. Students put the adjectives in the right order and draw a picture of it. For example:

wooden house old frightening tiny → frightening, tiny, old, wooden house

cheese and tomato delicious pizza round → delicious, round, cheese and tomato pizza

green thing little strange plastic → strange, little, green, plastic thing

If you have space, arrange students into groups of seven (some of the students can have two words if the number is smaller). Give six students an adjective from the six different categories, for example *triangular, interesting, new, paper, large, blue* and give the seventh student a noun, for example *hat*. Students must line up in the correct order (*interesting, large, triangular, new, blue, paper hat*).

LISTENING

PREPARE FOR THE EXAM

Listening Part 5

1 For each question, choose the correct answer. You will hear Carmen talking to Murat about some things she has found in her grandparents' house. Who does each thing belong to?

Things		People
0 clock	*E*	**A** aunt
1 computer	☐	**B** brother
2 hat	☐	**C** cousin
3 toy bear	☐	**D** father
4 painting	☐	**E** grandfather
5 jacket	☐	**F** grandmother
		G mother
		H uncle

2 Listen again and check your answers.

WRITING

PREPARE TO WRITE

Adjective order

GET READY

THE CITY MUSEUM

Have you got a favourite thing or something from the past you want to tell us about? Send us an email. Describe the object and say why it's special for you and attach a photo if you have one.

Email: citymuseumfavobs@museum.uk

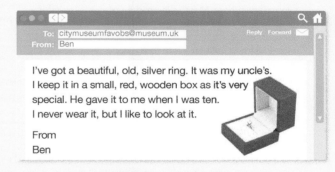

To: citymuseumfavobs@museum.uk
From: Ben

I've got a beautiful, old, silver ring. It was my uncle's. I keep it in a small, red, wooden box as it's very special. He gave it to me when I was ten. I never wear it, but I like to look at it.

From
Ben

Read the notice from the museum and then read Ben's email reply. What's his favourite thing?

Put the adjectives from the email in the correct column in the table.

Adjective order						
Opinion (pretty)	Size (big)	Physical quality (hard)	Shape (square)	Age (new)	Colour (blue)	Material (gold)

Find three more examples of pairs of adjectives in the texts on page 38 and add them to the table.

PLAN You are going to write to the museum about something special. Use these questions to plan your email.

What is it?   Where/who did it come from?   What does it look like?

Plan your email to the museum.

What groups of adjectives can you use to describe your object? What order do they go in?

WRITE Write an email to the museum. Use Ben's email to help you. Write about 35 words. Draw a picture of the object.

IMPROVE In pairs, read each other's email. Check for mistakes with adjectives. Rewrite your emails.

CULTURE

SECONDARY SCHOOL IN THE UK

1 Discuss the questions with your partner.

1 Do you like going to school?
2 Why? / Why not?
3 At what age do people start secondary school in your country?

2 Work with a partner. What do you know about secondary schools in the UK? Discuss your ideas. Read the web page. Were any of your ideas mentioned?

The secondary school system in the UK

From the age of 11 to 16, children go to secondary school. Most take children of all abilities and are called comprehensive schools. But there are also grammar schools, where children take an exam to enter, especially in Northern Ireland. In Scotland, secondary schools are called high schools or academies. When they are 14, all children choose the subjects they want to study at GCSE (or National 5 exams in Scotland). These are national exams you take at 16. Everyone has to do English and maths. Students also choose four or more additional subjects from a list. This includes subjects like languages and sciences but also photography and drama.

The school year

The school year goes from September to July in England and Wales, August to June in Scotland and September to June in Northern Ireland. There are three terms and short holidays in the middle of each term. The Christmas and Easter holidays are usually two weeks, and the summer holiday is six weeks, or two months in Northern Ireland.

The school day

The school day at secondary schools goes from about 8.45 am to 3.30 pm. There's a break in the morning and another for lunch. Most British school students have to wear a uniform. Each school has its own colours for the uniforms.

Sixth form / S5 and S6

When students are 17 and 18, they take more exams. In Scotland, these exams are called Highers in the first year and Advanced Highers in the second year. In the rest of the UK, students go into the sixth form to study four subjects at AS level in their first year and three of these at A level in the second year. You need to pass these high-level exams to go to university.

3 Read the web page again and complete the table.

 TALKING POINTS

In groups, compare the UK secondary school system with your own.

Types of public secondary schools in the UK

1 _____ schools – These schools take children of all abilities.
2 _____ schools – Children need to pass an exam to get in these schools.
3 _____ schools or academies – These are secondary schools in Scotland.

Secondary school	England and Wales	Northern Ireland	Scotland
National exams at age 16	GCSEs	4 _____	National 5 exams
National exams at age 17	AS levels	AS levels	5 _____
National exams at age 18	6 _____	A levels	Advanced Highers
School year starts	September	7 _____	August
School year finishes	8 _____	June	June

CULTURE

Learning Objectives

- The students learn about the secondary school system in the UK and what type of after-school activities schools provide.
- In the project stage, students design a web page for their school including a description, photos and newsletter.

Vocabulary

comprehensive schools   grammar schools   high schools
academies

Resources

CULTURE VIDEO AND CULTURE VIDEO WORKSHEET: High school in the US

BACKGROUND INFORMATION

The education system in England and Wales is divided into pre-school (ages 3–4), primary education (ages 4–11), secondary education (ages 11–16), sixth form (ages 16–18) and tertiary education (ages 18+). Over 90% of pupils go to state schools, where the education is free, and they follow a national curriculum which standardises subjects, syllabuses and assessment. Confusingly, old and prestigious independent schools like Eton are called public schools, although they are not in the state system.

WARMER

Write these anagrams of school subjects on the board. Do the first one as an example and then see which student can find the rest first.

ismuc (*music*), loigybo (*biology*), ythoisr (*history*), hglesni (*English*), aoghregyp (*geography*), tyechismr (*chemistry*), semaatthicm (*mathematics*), aylsipch unctieaod – 2 words (*physical education*)

Ask students which of these subjects they enjoy the most and why.

1   Books closed, put students into pairs and ask them to write down reasons why children go to school, not just educational, for example, to learn how to communicate and cooperate with people of the same age. Ask students for their ideas and write them on the board.

Books open, ask students to discuss the questions in the book. Share ideas as a class. If students don't like going to school, make the discussion constructive rather than negative by looking at what would make their experience more positive, for example if it was easier to get to school or there was a greater range of sports to do. Ask students, 'What is the best age for children to start learning and to start going to school?' (This might not be the same age.)

2   Ask students 'What countries are in the UK?' (*England, Scotland, Wales and Northern Ireland*) and 'Is the secondary school system the same in all these countries?' (*It is very similar but there are some differences.*). Arrange students into pairs to discuss what else they know about secondary schools in the UK. They then check with the web page. Point out that *GCSE* stands for *General Certificate of Secondary Education*. Ask students to say what the students are wearing in the photo (*school uniform*). Ask, 'Would you like to wear a uniform like this?' and 'What do you think is the purpose of a school uniform?'.

3   Go through the table so students know what kind of information they need to fill each gap, for example, 1, 2 and 3 will be types of school. Tell students to read the web page more carefully and complete the table. Check as a class. Ask students if there is any information missing which they would like to know more about, for example what the exam for grammar schools is like.

Answers

1 comprehensive   **2** grammar   **3** High   **4** GCSEs   **5** Highers
6 A levels   **7** September   **8** July

FAST FINISHERS

Tell fast finishers to write down advantages and disadvantages of exams while the other students are finishing. For example: advantage – they motivate students to study hard; disadvantage – they can cause stress. When everyone has finished, collect these ideas and put them on the board. You could then have a class discussion about whether exams are a good idea and what an alternative could be.

🔊 The Reading text is recorded for students to listen, read
48   and check their answers.

💬 TALKING POINTS

Put students into groups and ask them to compare their secondary school system with the UK's according to these categories: age students start and finish; different types of schools; subjects studied; types of exam and when they are; length of school year and holidays; dress code. If necessary, give students some useful language:

We go to secondary school at the age of …

We don't have three terms, we have …

We have national exams when we are …

Students should discuss the advantages and disadvantages of their school system compared to the UK, for example in their country they may have longer summer holidays but they may study on Saturdays. Tell each group to present their information to the rest of the class. To avoid repetition in the presentations, ask each group to focus on one difference, for example on exams.

4 Pre-teach **charity** (money, food or help that is given to people or things that need it, or an organisation which does this), and ask students to give some examples from their own country. Give students a time limit to read the website and say if the school is similar to theirs and, if so, in what ways. Then give students time to read the website more carefully and answer the questions. Check as a class.

Explain that Save the Children helps vulnerable children all over the world and it started its work in 1919 by feeding children starving after the First World War in Europe. Explain that the National Theatre is a major state-funded theatre in London. Ask students what information they think the Parents and Teachers parts of the website contain, for example, parents may be able to see examples of students' work.

> **Answers**
>
> **1** 18 **2** for the charity Save the Children **3** no **4** four
> **5** trainers **6** the National Theatre

MIXED ABILITY

Make the open questions into statements and write them on the board for weaker students. Tell students to say whether the statements are true or false and to say why the false statements are wrong and correct them.

1 Students leave Woodedge School when they are 18. (*True*)

2 Students need to bring money on November 13th to buy hats. (*False – The money is for charity*)

3 same question

4 Each student can buy four tickets for the concert. (*True*)

5 Students must wear trainers for the football competition. (*True*)

6 On 30th November all students go to the theatre. (*False – only Year 11 students*)

50

5 Books closed, tell students they are going to listen to a student from the school, Aleesha. Ask what questions they would like to ask her, for example, 'What year are you in?' and 'What's your favourite subject?'. Books open, students check if their questions are the same as in the book.

Play the recording twice for students to answer the questions. Ask students what they would make for Charity Day. As an extension activity, have students work in pairs. One student asks the questions and the other answers them as Aleesha. The students could add two more questions which 'Aleesha' will answer using her imagination.

> **Answers**
>
> **1** 1,200 **2** She is Asian. **3** 3.00 pm
> **4** What's in the news; money **5** hot food and sandwiches
> **6** She has a card. (Her parents put money into an online account which she accesses with the card.)
> **7** singing and badminton **8** cakes

» **AUDIOSCRIPT TB PAGE 291**

---

6 Put students into pairs to discuss how their school compares to Woodedge school on each of the different criteria. Students should say in which areas one school is better, for example, their school may have more interesting after-school clubs. Share ideas as a class. Ask students what their school or Woodedge could change to make it a better place to learn and spend time, for example, school lunches could be healthier.

PROJECT *A school web page*

Tell students that they have to make a web page for their school. This could be a completely new web page if the school doesn't have one in English or a new version. Ask students who it is useful for (*parents, new students, etc.*) and what kind of information and pictures it could contain. If students have access to mobile devices, tell them to look at some school websites in their country and the UK to get some ideas. Arrange students into groups. They could do this project in class or do it as homework, collecting information individually, then putting it together and checking it in class. Students should use the Woodedge website as a model and include some photos or artwork. (They may need to take some photos for this and they could even make a short video.) Students could make their web page as a real web page or turn it into a poster. In class, students should present and compare their web pages. Decide which web page has got the best content and which one has got the most attractive presentation.

PROJECT EXTENSION

Tell students to do a survey of school websites and find out how they compare according to the criteria in Exercise 6. Students could choose school websites in the UK or a range of schools in other countries (if they are in English). If students put 'school website' into a search engine they will be directed to websites of schools in English. Students should work in groups with everyone in the group responsible for finding and getting the information about one website. Students then put their information together and make a presentation to the class. The class can decide which sounds the most interesting school to study in.

 CULTURE VIDEO: High school in the US

04 When students have completed the lesson, they can watch the video and complete the worksheet.

COOLER

Students think of five crazy activities for an alternative school sports day. Give some ideas like underwater badminton and hotdog eating (speed and quantity).

4 Read the information on the Woodedge Secondary School website. Is this school similar to your school? Answer the questions.

Woodedge
Secondary School

Parents   Teachers   Students

Welcome to the Woodedge School website. We are a comprehensive school for girls and boys aged 11–18. Our children come from many different cultures and backgrounds. We are a popular school and children who come here do very well in their exams. As well as excellent teaching, we offer many interesting after-school clubs, including sports, drama and dance.

School Diary

Important dates for November

Friday 13th: **Charity Day** Can everyone please bring £1.00. This is a non-uniform day. Wear your own clothes, but no hats, please, and don't colour your hair. There will be things for sale, so bring in some extra money. All the money we make will go to the charity Save the Children.

Friday 20th: **Autumn concert** Tickets £3.00 on sale now – maximum four per student.

Tuesday 24th: **Years 7–10 Girls' indoor football competition** Sports Hall – trainers only, please.

Monday 30th: **Year 11 school trip to the National Theatre**

1 At what age do students leave Woodedge School?
2 Why do students need to bring money to school on 13th November?
3 Do students have to wear their school uniform on 13th November?
4 How many tickets can each student buy for the concert?
5 What must students wear for the football competition?
6 Where are Year 11 students going on 30th November?

5 Listen to Aleesha talking about Woodedge School. Answer the questions.

1 How many pupils are there at Woodedge?
2 What is Aleesha's cultural background?
3 What time does school finish?
4 What do students learn about in PDT?
5 What kind of food can you get at lunchtime?
6 How does Aleesha pay for her lunch?
7 What after-school clubs is she doing this term?
8 What is she making for Charity Day?

6 Compare Woodedge School with your own. Talk to your partner about these things.

- after-school clubs
- how long the day is
- mix of cultures
- number of students
- school concerts
- special days (like Charity Day)
- school lunches
- school trips

PROJECT   *A school web page*

Design a web page for your school. Include this information:

- a description of the school
- photos of your friends and the building
- a newsletter with school events for one month

Present your web page to the class.

▶ **04** NOW WATCH THE CULTURE VIDEO   **SECONDARY SCHOOL IN THE UK   41**

7 ADVENTURE HOLIDAYS

 ABOUT YOU

▶ **05 Watch the video and discuss the questions.**
What adventure holiday would you like to go on?
How would you like to get/travel there?
Who would you like to travel with?

VOCABULARY AND LISTENING

Holiday activities

1 **What activities can you do on adventure holidays? Match the words in the box to photos A–J.**

> camping   diving   hiking   horse riding
> kite surfing   mountain biking   paddle boarding
> sailing   waterskiing   zip wiring

🔊 **Listen and check. Then repeat.**
51

🔊 **2** **Listen to Tara and her friend Dan talking about their adventure holiday. Which activities from Exercise 1 do they <u>not</u> mention?**
52

🔊 **3** **Listen again. Complete the table with Tara's and Dan's holiday activities.**
52

Monday	Tuesday	Wednesday	Thursday	Friday

4 **Complete the sentences with the verbs in the box.**

> get back   get lost   getting on
> getting to   getting up

1 Tara's _____ the airport by car.
2 Tara and Dan have to _____ from the mountains to the activity centre alone.
3 Tara and Dan are _____ a bus at 5 am in the morning.
4 Tara and Dan are _____ early on Monday morning.
5 Dan hopes he doesn't _____ in the mountains.

5 **In pairs, ask and answer the questions.**

1 What time do you get up in the morning?
2 When was the last time you got lost?
3 How do you get to school?
4 How did you get back home from your last holiday?
5 When did you last get on a train?

✅ PREPARE FOR THE EXAM

Speaking Part 2

6 **Work with a partner. Talk together about the adventure activities in Exercise 1. Do you like these activities? Say why or why not.**

7 **In pairs, ask and answer the questions.**

Do you think:
- going sailing is dangerous?
- going camping is boring?
- going kite surfing is difficult?
- going paddle boarding is amazing?
- going horse riding is exciting?
- going mountain biking is hard?

8 **In pairs, ask and answer the questions.**

1 Which of these adventure activities do you like best? Why?
2 Do you like doing activities on the water? Why?
3 Is it better to do adventure activities when the weather is rainy or cold? Why? / Why not?
4 Do you prefer doing activities on your own or with other people? Why?

42 UNIT 7

7 ADVENTURE HOLIDAYS

Unit Overview

TOPIC	Holidays, travel and adventure
VOCABULARY	Holiday activities
AND LISTENING	A conversation about an adventure holiday
GRAMMAR	Present continuous for future
PRONUNCIATION	Sentence stress: present continuous
READING	Brecon Beacons adventure weekend
VOCABULARY	Things to take on an adventure holiday
LISTENING	A talk about an adventure holiday
SPEAKING	Talking about an adventure holiday
EXAM TASKS	Speaking Part 2; Listening Part 2

Resources

GRAMMAR REFERENCE AND PRACTICE: SB page 153; TB page 265

PREPARE FOR THE EXAM: SB pages on TB pages 250–251 and 245; TB pages 259 and 256

WORKBOOK: pages 28–31

VIDEO AND VIDEO WORKSHEET: Adventures!

PHOTOCOPIABLE WORKSHEETS: Grammar worksheet Unit 7; Vocabulary worksheet Unit 7

TEST GENERATOR: Unit test 7; Term test 1

WARMER

Put students into large groups. Tell them that they are going on an adventure holiday. You choose a pattern for things students can take with them, for example things beginning with D, things that are the same colour, things that have been in Units 1–6. One student begins, for example, (if the pattern is words beginning with D), *I'm taking my dog*. The next student continues, *I'm taking a dictionary*. The other students can challenge the student if they think the thing is not relevant to an adventure holiday and ask them to explain, for example: *Why are you taking a dictionary? The holiday is in a different country.* If students can't answer the challenge or think of a thing they are out of the game. Students continue until there is a winner.

ⓘ ABOUT YOU

▶ 05 You can begin the class and introduce the topic of the unit by showing the video and asking students to complete the video worksheet. Then, read the questions in the *About you* box and students exchange ideas in pairs.

VOCABULARY AND LISTENING

Holiday activities

1 Tell students to look at the photos and see if they can name any of the activities before the matching task. Check as a class. Concept-check some of the vocabulary, for example: 'Walking in hills and the country' (*hiking*). Ask students if they have ever done any of these activities.

🔊 51 **Answers**

The answers are recorded for students to check and then repeat.
A horse riding B camping C kite surfing D mountain biking
E diving F sailing G waterskiing H paddle boarding
I zip wiring J hiking

🔊 52 2 Play the recording and have students tick the activities as they hear them mentioned. Then ask them to identify the activities not mentioned.

Answers

diving, waterskiing

🔊 52 3 Play the recording again and tell students to fill in the plan. Remind them that they will not hear the days of the week in order. Check answers as a class. Ask some general comprehension questions after the students fill in the table, for example, 'Where is the holiday?' (*in the Pyrenees*) and 'Who is taking a musical instrument?' (*Tara, a guitar*)

Answers

Monday: hiking
Tuesday: sailing, horse riding
Wednesday: zip wiring
Thursday: mountain biking, paddle boarding
Friday: kite surfing

MIXED ABILITY

For weaker students, pause the recording after each activity and ask: 'What is that activity?' and 'When is it?'.

» AUDIOSCRIPT TB PAGE 291

4 Ask students what phrases they know with *get* (for example, *get on/off* and *get married* are A2). Have students complete the sentences. Check as a class.

Answers

1 getting to 2 get back 3 getting on 4 getting up 5 get lost

5 Have students discuss the questions in pairs. Ask students to report back to the class about their partners. As a variation, write the questions on the board (or dictate them) with gaps for the *get* phrases. Students fill in the gaps then answer the questions.

CONTINUED ON PAGE 82

A2 KEY FOR SCHOOLS Speaking Part 2

6 Briefly review what students need to do in this part of the exam and if necessary read out the A2 Key for Schools box on TB page 38.

Tell students to listen to each question carefully and give a full answer. Even if the question is a *yes/no* question, like *Do you think going camping is boring?*, students need to answer in detail. Teach students polite phrases for asking for repetition, for example, *Sorry, could you repeat that please?*, as students will not lose marks if they ask the examiner or their partner to say the question again. (Examiners cannot rephrase questions in Part 2 but they can repeat them.)

Put students into pairs to discuss what they like and don't like about each activity. Share ideas as a class.

7 Tell students to take turns asking and answering the questions in pairs. Share ideas as a class.

8 Have students discuss the questions in pairs. For extra practice, have students then repeat the activity in different pairs. Monitor and collect examples of mistakes and good use of language for feedback.

GRAMMAR Present continuous for future

1 Ask, 'Are the examples referring to the past, present or future?' (*future*) and 'Are they about making plans or just thinking what to do?' (*making plans*). Ask students to do the analysis task. Make sure that in the example sentence, *When are we going mountain biking ...* , students do not confuse *be going to* and the present continuous for the future. If necessary explain, that the present continuous for the future is used for definite arrangements which are going to happen in the foreseeable future. If it is a long-term plan, we use the *be going to* future form: *One day I am living am going to live in a castle.* At this level it is too early to teach students the difference between the two future forms.

Answers
1 now and the future 2 the future 3 usually

>> GRAMMAR REFERENCE AND PRACTICE ANSWER KEY TB PAGE 265

2 Ask students, 'What do you call a book where you write down your plans?' (*a diary*), 'Who are Bella's friends?' (*Gina and Anna*) and 'How is she getting to Anna's party?' (*by train*). Tell students to write down Bella's plans. Check answers as a class. Then tell students to cover up the diary, ask questions and see if students can remember what Bella is doing. For example: 'Silvia, is Bella going mountain biking with her father?' (*No, she's going mountain biking with her mother.*)

Answers
On Saturday she's going diving with Gina at 10.30. She isn't going home for lunch at 12.30. She's riding her new bike to her grandpa's at 3 pm. She's catching the train to Anna's party at 6.30 pm.
On Sunday she's going mountain biking with her mum at 9 am. She's doing her homework at 11 o'clock. She isn't cleaning her bedroom at 2 pm. She's watching the football game at 2 pm.

3 Books closed, write these two questions on the board and ask students what the difference is. *What time do you get up?* (everyday routine) *What time are you getting up?* (a plan for one time in the future) Books open, students correct the sentences. Check answers as a class.

Answers
1 Taylor Swift **is singing** at the football stadium next Saturday.
2 We**'re meeting** at 3 pm tomorrow at the bus station.
3 I'm very excited that you're **coming** to visit next summer.
4 **Are you bringing** any money with you this evening?
5 I**'m not visiting** my grandparents this weekend.

FAST FINISHERS
Fast finishers write down a reason to explain what is happening in each sentence. For example: **1** Taylor needs a stadium because she has a lot of fans.

>> GRAMMAR WORKSHEET UNIT 7

ə PRONUNCIATION
Sentence stress: present continuous

4 Tell students to read the sentences and predict which parts are stressed. Play the recording to check. Elicit which types of words are stressed and which aren't.

🔊 Answers
53

The answers are recorded for students to check and then repeat.
1 We're **going kite surfing** next **week**.
2 Are you **going mountain biking** in the **summer**?
3 They **aren't buying a paddle board** this **weekend**.
4 He's **going camping** next **month**.
5 Is she **coming horse riding** with us this **evening**?
6 He **isn't going hiking** during the **holidays.**

5 Have students work in pairs, say the sentences and check one another.

6 If possible, show some YouTube clips of exciting places for adventure holidays in your country and abroad, e.g. Kamchatka (a mountainous region in Russia) and Krabi (a resort for climbing and water sports in Thailand). Ask students what activities they could do in each place. For example, hiking and climbing in Kamchatka. Arrange students into pairs. They should choose a place and write a schedule with at least one different activity per day.

7 Put pairs together to compare their adventure weeks. Demonstrate and make sure that questions and answers are in the present continuous: 'Diego, what are you doing on Monday?' (*On Monday morning, we're flying to Santiago.*). Students then make a new schedule, combining the best activities, and present this to the whole class.

COOLER
Tell students to write down a plan for a terrible weekend. For example, *Saturday 9 am Visit the dentist*. Then put students into pairs to use the present continuous to ask and answer questions about their terrible weekends. Share ideas as a class and see which one is the worst.

GRAMMAR | Present continuous for future

1 Look at the examples. Then choose the correct words to complete the sentences below.

We're **getting on** a bus at five o'clock in the morning!
I'm **not taking** my keyboard with me next week.
When **are** we **going** mountain biking and paddle boarding?

1 We can use the present continuous to talk about *now / the future / now and the future*.
2 The three example sentences are about *now / the future*.
3 We *usually / never* use a time word with the present continuous for the future.

≫ **GRAMMAR REFERENCE AND PRACTICE PAGE 153**

2 Look at Bella's diary for this weekend. Write her plans using the present continuous and mention the day and time for each activity. Is there anything she isn't doing?

She isn't cleaning her room at 2 pm on Sunday.

Saturday:
- 10.30 Go diving with Gina.
- ~~12.30 Go home for lunch.~~
- 15.00 Ride my new bike to Grandpa's.
- 18.30 Take the train to Anna's party!!

Sunday:
- 09.00 Go mountain biking with Mum.
- 11.00 Do my homework.
- ~~14.00 Clean my bedroom.~~
- 14.00 Watch the football game.

3 Correct the mistakes in the sentences.

1 Taylor Swift sings at the football stadium next Saturday.
2 We meet at 3 pm tomorrow, at the bus station.
3 I'm very excited that you come to visit next summer.
4 Do you bring any money with you this evening?
5 I don't visit my grandparents next weekend.

PRONUNCIATION

Sentence stress: present continuous

4 Look at the sentences. Decide which words in each sentence are stressed and underline them.

1 We're going kite surfing next week.
2 Are you going mountain biking in the summer?
3 They aren't buying a paddle board this weekend.
4 He's going camping next month.
5 Is she coming horse riding with us this evening?
6 He isn't going hiking during the holidays.

◁)) **Listen and check. Then repeat.**
53

5 In pairs, take turns to read out your sentences from Exercise 2.

6 In pairs, write a list of all the activities you'd like to do on an adventure week. Where would you like to go? Now plan your week. Choose at least one activity for each day.

7 Work with another pair. Use the present continuous to ask and answer questions about each other's adventure weeks.

What are you doing on Tuesday?

On Tuesday, we're …

Choose the best activities from your group to make a perfect week. Tell the class.

This is our perfect adventure week on the Black Sea. On Monday morning, we're learning how to waterski and then in the afternoon we're …

READING

1 Look at the photo on the leaflet and answer the questions.

1 What kind of place are the students going to on their adventure weekend?
2 What activities do you think people can do here?

2 Read the leaflet from the school quickly and check your answers to the two questions in Exercise 1.

3 Read the leaflet again and answer the questions.

1 What can the weather be like in the Brecon Beacons?
2 Where can parents find information on what students should bring?
3 Why should students not take too much in their bags?
4 What's the reason for the length of the walk?
5 How many nights are students spending in their tents?
6 How are they getting to Wales?

VOCABULARY | Things to take on an adventure holiday

 1 Match the words from the kit list to photos A–L.

🔊 **55** Listen and check. Then repeat.

2 Read the kit list again. Which of the things on the list do the students need for:

wet weather?	eating and drinking?
sunny weather?	sleeping?
cold weather?	keeping clean?
having fun?	not getting lost?

💬 TALKING POINTS

Do you like the idea of an adventure weekend with the school? Why / why not?
Do you like hiking? Why / why not?
Do you like camping? Why / why not?
What else would you like to do on an adventure weekend?

Brecon Beacons adventure weekend

🔊 54

Students are going to the Brecon Beacons in Wales for our adventure weekend in May this year. The Brecon Beacons are mountains and the weather there can be sunny one minute and raining or foggy and cold the next. Please make sure that your son or daughter brings the right clothes. See the kit list below.

It's important students don't bring too many clothes because each group is going to carry everything they need for camping and cooking.

There are lots of different walks in the mountains. We know that some students don't walk very much, so our walk over the two days is only 25 km long.

● Students spend Saturday and Sunday hiking.
● Students camp for one night, on Saturday.
● Students sleep in tents in groups of three or four.

We are travelling to the Brecon Beacons by bus. The bus leaves from the school on Saturday at 6 am and returns on Sunday at 8 pm.

Please contact Mr Jones at the school if you have any questions or would like more information.

KIT LIST

CLOTHES
● walking boots
● waterproof trousers and jacket
● walking socks
● underwear
● T-shirts
● pyjamas
● sweaters
● trainers (for the evening)
● walking trousers (not jeans!)

KIT FOR EACH GROUP
● tent
● map and compass
● food

OTHER KIT
● backpack
● towel
● sleeping bag
● torch
● wash bag
● first-aid kit
● plate, bowl, mug, knife, fork, spoon
● water bottle

YOU MAY ALSO WANT:
● warm hat or sun hat
● gloves
● sun cream
● sunglasses
● playing cards
● snacks

WARMER

Ask students to give a score from 1 to 5 to each of the activities in Exercise 1 on page 42; 1 = very boring, 5 = very interesting. In pairs, they then compare and discuss the scores. Demonstrate in front of the class with one of the stronger students: *Mrs Sanchez, what do you think about zip wiring?* 'I gave it 4. It's interesting but may be dangerous! Do you agree?'

BACKGROUND INFORMATION

The Brecon Beacons is a mountain range in South Wales and the highest mountain is Pen y Fan (886 metres). The name Brecon Beacons probably comes from the tradition of lighting beacons (fires) on mountain tops to warn of danger or celebrate special events. Apart from its natural beauty, the Brecon Beacons is of major geological and historical interest with its minerals and castles. Because of the mountains and changeable weather, the Brecon Beacons is not easy terrain for hiking and the UK armed forces use this area for special training.

1 Ask students to look at the photo and tell them that this is in Wales. Have students tell you what else they know about Wales, for example, the capital is Cardiff, the flag has a dragon on it. Ask students to discuss the questions. Share ideas as a class.

2 Pre-teach **kit** (a set of things, such as tools or clothes, used for a particular purpose or activity). Give students a time limit to read the text and check their answers. Check as a class.

Answers

1 mountains 2 hiking and camping

3 Ask students, 'When are they going?', (*May*) 'How long will the hike be?' (*25 km*) and 'Who is organising this trip?' (*Mr Jones*). Have students read the text again and answer the questions in the book. Check as a class. Ask students to tell you any questions they would like to ask Mr Jones, for example, *How much will the trip cost?*. As an extension activity, you could put students into pairs. One student is Mr Jones and answers the other student's questions.

Answers

1 It can change very quickly. It can be sunny one minute and raining or foggy and cold the next.
2 On the Kit list
3 Because they are going to carry their bags and everything they need for camping and cooking.
4 It's because some students don't walk very much – so it's quite short.
5 One night
6 They are getting there by bus.

FAST FINISHERS

Fast finishers underline all the words on the kit list which they don't know and ask other fast finishers what they mean or look them up in a dictionary.

◁)) The Reading text is recorded for students to listen, read
54 and check their answers.

1 Tell students to look at the photos and see if they can name any of the objects before they match them to the words. Play the recording for students to check.

Concept-check some of the words, for example: 'You look at these if you are lost' (*map and compass*), 'You eat these to give you energy' (*snacks*) and 'You camp in this' (*tent*). Tell students to cover up the text and then say what the photos are.

◁))
55
Answers

The answers are recorded for students to check and then repeat.
A backpack B compass and map C first-aid kit
D sleeping bag E snacks F sun cream G tent H torch
I trainers J washbag K walking boots
L waterproof trousers and jacket

2 Have students read the list again and say what the various objects are for. Check answers as a class.

Possible answers

wet weather: waterproof trousers and jacket
sunny weather: sun hat, sun cream, sunglasses, T-shirts
cold weather: sweaters, warm hat, gloves
having fun: playing cards
eating and drinking: food, plate/bowl/mug/knife/fork/spoon, water bottle, snacks
sleeping: pyjamas, tent, sleeping bag
keeping clean: wash bag
not getting lost: map and compass, torch

TALKING POINTS

Ask students, 'Have you ever been on an overnight school trip?' and 'What would be good places in our/your country to visit?'. Put students into groups to discuss the questions in the book. Share ideas as a class. As an extension task, in groups students could make a plan of the weekend, saying what they are doing when and present this to the class.

≫ **VOCABULARY WORKSHEET UNIT 7**

LISTENING

1 Books closed, write down four dates which are important to you, for example: 15th March, 22nd May, 30th June, 1st September. The students must say the dates and guess why they are important (for example: my birthday, Cup Final day, start of the summer holiday, first day back at school). Books open, arrange students into pairs to say the dates. Students then write and say four dates for their partner to write down.

Answers

The seventeenth of August
The twenty-first of November
The third of February
Students' own answers

2 Ask students, 'What activity can you see in the photo?' (*kayaking*). Have students read the information sheet and predict the kind of information as a class.

Answers

1 a date 2 a number 3 a word describing a place
4 an amount in pounds 5 a phone number

 PREPARE FOR THE EXAM

A2 KEY FOR SCHOOLS
Listening Part 2

In this part, students listen to someone speaking and write down one word or a number or a date or a time in each of five gaps to complete a set of notes. One of the words is spelled out. Spelling is not penalised if the word is recognisable unless it is a very common word or the word is spelled out in the recording.

Tip Tell students that they have time to read the notes before they listen. They should think carefully about what the missing word might be, for example is it a time, a place, an amount of money? Students should write numbers as numbers, not words, so they don't make a mistake with spelling. The answer can only be one word or a number or a date or a time.

🔊 56 3 Play the recording twice for students to complete the notes. Check as a class. Ask students if they would be interested in this adventure holiday.

Answers

1 28th July 2 16 3 river 4 345 5 05371 255946

≫ AUDIOSCRIPT TB PAGE 292

≫ PREPARE FOR THE EXAM TEACHING NOTES AND ANSWER KEY TB PAGE 256

MIXED ABILITY

Weaker students often have problems listening to numbers, which are important in this exam task. Give students extra practice by writing pairs of numbers on the board. For example:

8th July / 28th July

16 / 60

345 / 354

05371 / 05361

Students copy the numbers. You say a number and students have to circle that number.

SPEAKING

1 Ask students if they would prefer to go on an adventure holiday with their parents or with their friends. Give students a time limit to read and answer the questions. Stronger students could answer the questions, book closed, just by listening. Check answers as a class. Ask some more comprehension questions, for example, 'Where's the horse riding?' (*near the beach*), 'Does Dad want to go mountain biking?' (*no*).

Answers

1 They're going kayaking in the morning and horse riding in the afternoon.
2 He's going waterskiing with Laura's mum.
3 She's sleeping late.

2 Say to the class, 'Let's watch an English film this weekend.' Elicit that *Let's* is used for making suggestions, it is short for *Let us* and it is followed by the base form. Tell students to find this and the other suggestions and responses in the text – the phrases in blue. Check as a class. Tell students to repeat the phrases. Ask students what forms follow these phrases: *How about* (+ -*ing*), *I'd prefer* (+ *to*-infinitive), *Would you like* (+ *to*-infinitive), *Why don't you* (+ base form), *I'd love* (+ *to*-infinitive), *I'm not that interested in* (+ -*ing*).

Answers

a Let's, How about, I'd prefer, Would you like to, Why don't you
b That's a great idea, I'd love to, Good idea
c I'm not that interested in, I'd prefer to
d It's a shame

🔊 57 3 Have students listen to then practise the conversation in pairs. Books closed, see if they can do it without the text.

4 Ask students some basic comprehension questions about the programme, for example 'When is the climbing?' (*Saturday afternoon*) and 'What can you do if you don't like zip wiring?' (*mountain biking*). Tell students to circle the activities they prefer.

5 Put students into pairs to discuss their plans and try and get the other person to do what they want. Ask some pairs to act out the conversation at the front of the class.

COOLER

Get students to line up according to their birthday, the earliest to the left and the latest to the right. To do this, they need to ask everyone, 'When's your birthday?' When students have lined up, check that the order is correct by having students say their birthday.

LISTENING

1 Work in pairs. How do you say these dates?

17th August
21st November
3rd February

Write down four other dates. In pairs, say them for your partner to write down.

2 Read the information sheet about the adventure holiday. What kind of information are you going to listen for?

✓ PREPARE FOR THE EXAM

Listening Part 2

3 For each question, write the correct answer in the gap. Write one word or a number or a date or a time.

🔊 56

You will hear a teacher telling students about an adventure holiday.

Exciting New

Adventure Holiday

Name: *Across the Water*

Start date: **(1)** _____

Number of student places: **(2)** _____

Place: **Close to a (3)** _____

Cost: **(4) £** _____

For more information, phone:
(5) _____

» **PREPARE FOR THE EXAM PAGE 129**

SPEAKING

1 Laura is on an adventure holiday with her parents. Read the conversation and answer the questions.

1. What are Laura and her dad going to do on Saturday morning and Saturday afternoon?
2. What's Laura's dad going to do on Sunday morning?
3. What's Laura going to do on Sunday morning?

Dad: Let's go waterskiing on Saturday morning, Laura.
Laura: I'm not that interested in waterskiing, Dad. How about mountain biking?
Dad: I'd prefer to go kayaking or something like that.
Laura: Kayaking! That's a great idea!
Dad: What shall we do in the afternoon? Would you like to go horse riding?
Laura: I'd love to. Where is it?
Dad: It's near the beach. It's a shame about the waterskiing. I wanted to do that. Never mind.
Laura: Why don't you go on Sunday morning with Mum, and I can sleep late?
Dad: Good idea. So, on Saturday we're going kayaking in the morning and …
Laura: … we're going horse riding in the afternoon!

2 Look at the words in the conversation.

Which phrases are used:
a to make suggestions   c to disagree
b to agree   d to express regret

🔊 57 **3** Listen to the conversation. Then practise it in pairs.

4 Read the programme for an adventure weekend. Circle the activities you want to do.

GOLDEN SANDS BEACH

Come and join us this weekend!

SATURDAY	SUNDAY
MORNING surfing OR waterskiing	**MORNING** zip wiring OR mountain biking
AFTERNOON climbing OR hiking	**AFTERNOON** tennis OR beach volleyball
EVENING barbecue OR night walk and picnic in the forest	**Write your name on the list or speak to John.**

5 In pairs, talk about your weekend choices. Use Exercise 1 to help you.

Make suggestions, agree and disagree, depending on what you are planning for the weekend.
Can you get your partner to change their mind?

8 LIFE IN THE FUTURE

Homes of the future

ABOUT YOU

In pairs, look at the words. Imagine it's the year 2040. Describe what these things are like.

books   cars   computers   homes
planes   smartphones   televisions

VOCABULARY AND LISTENING

Furniture and household appliances

1 Match the definitions 1–12 to the words in the box.

> air conditioning   barbecue
> bin   bookcase   drawer
> fridge   heating   lights   roof
> seat   stairs   washing machine

1 This keeps your food cold.
2 This makes your clothes clean.
3 This keeps you cool.
4 This is a place for things you like to read.
5 This keeps the rain out of your home.
6 This is for cooking food outside.
7 These take you from one floor to another.
8 You put clothes and small things in it.
9 These make it easier to see when it's dark.
10 This is for sitting on.
11 This keeps your home warm.
12 You put things you don't want in this.

 Listen and check. Then repeat. **58**

2 In pairs, answer the questions about the words in Exercise 1.

1 Which things need electricity to work?
2 Which things are furniture?
3 Where in a home do you usually find each thing?

3 Look at these actions. Write *H* (using my hands) or *T* (using technology) next to each one. In pairs, compare your answers. Discuss the technology you use for actions you marked *T*.

> open your front door   turn off the TV
> turn on the computer   lock the car
> turn on the lights   close the windows
> close the garage door

4 Listen to a radio interview about homes of the future. What furniture do they talk about? **59**

5 Listen again. Number the information in the order you hear it. **59**

☐ **a** changing the temperature, music and lights in different rooms
☐ **b** changes to the outside of buildings
☐ **c** having a computer as part of a table
☐ **d** homes of the future looking different from homes of today
☐ **e** using smartphones to turn washing machines on and off

6 In pairs, discuss which things in your house you would like to control using your hands and which you would like to control without touching anything.

8 LIFE IN THE FUTURE

Unit Overview

TOPIC	The future
VOCABULARY AND LISTENING	Furniture and household appliances
	An interview about homes of the future
GRAMMAR	Future with *will*, *may* and *might*
PRONUNCIATION	*will* and *won't*
READING	What will you put in your time capsule?
VOCABULARY	Words with two meanings
LISTENING	Five short conversations
WRITING	*too*, *also*, *as well*
EXAM TASKS	Reading Part 4; Listening Part 4

Resources

GRAMMAR REFERENCE AND PRACTICE: SB page 154; TB page 265

PREPARE FOR THE EXAM: SB pages on TB pages 240 and 247;
TB pages 254 and 257

WORKBOOK: pages 32–35

VIDEO AND VIDEO WORKSHEET: Time capsule

PHOTOCOPIABLE WORKSHEETS: Grammar worksheet Unit 8;
Vocabulary worksheet Unit 8

TEST GENERATOR: Unit test 8

WARMER

Write *furniture* in large widely spaced letters horizontally on the board. Ask one student to come up and write a word vertically using one of the letters. For example:

```
C
O
M
P
F U R N I T U R E
T
E
R
```

Ask another student to add another word horizontally using one of the letters. Continue adding words vertically and horizontally until the board is a giant crossword. Then rub out all the words and see if the students can remember them.

ABOUT YOU

Say to students, 'It is 2040. How old are you?', 'What job do you have?' and 'Where do you live?'. Then put students into small groups to imagine what the things in the book are like. As feedback ask students, 'What things have changed the most?' and 'Can you think of any completely new things that we have in 2040?'.

VOCABULARY AND LISTENING

Furniture and household appliances

1 Books closed, ask students, 'What rooms are there in a home?'. Then have students tell you what things are usually in each room, for example, kitchen – cooker and sink. Tell students to look back at page 24 if they can't remember. Books open, students match the words to the definitions.

Play the recording for students to check. Tell students to cover up the definitions and have them look at the words and remember the definition or think of a new one.

Answers (58)

The answers are recorded for students to check and then repeat.
1 fridge 2 washing machine 3 air conditioning 4 bookcase
5 roof 6 barbecue 7 stairs 8 drawer 9 lights 10 seat
11 heating 12 bin

2 Have students answer the questions in pairs. Check answers as a class.

Answers

1 air conditioning, fridge, heating, lights, washing machine
2 bookcase, drawer, seat 3 Students' own answers

FAST FINISHERS

Fast finishers look back at the work on order of adjectives on page 39 and think of two words to go with as many of the words in Exercise 1 as possible, for example, *expensive new air conditioning, old white fridge*.

3 Demonstrate by asking students 'How do you cook a pizza? Using your hands or using technology?' (*using technology*), 'Which technology?' (*you put it in the oven*) and 'How do you eat a pizza?' (*using your hands*). Pre-teach **(light) switch** and **remote control** by showing them in the classroom. Have students mark the actions and then compare and discuss in pairs. Check answers as a class.

Possible answers

open your front door – H
turn on the computer – T (using the switch)
turn on the lights – T (using a light switch)
close the garage door – H/T (using my hands or a remote control)
turn off the TV – T (using the switch or a remote control)
lock the car – H/T (using my hands or a remote control)
close the windows – H

 4 Tell students that they are going to hear a professor talk about homes of the future. Ask students, 'What questions do you want to ask the professor?'. Elicit questions and possible answers. Have students listen and write down the furniture. Check as a class.

Answers

seat, bookcase, table, drawer

CONTINUED ON PAGE 90

5 Have students reorder the information before they listen again and check. Ask students to give you more information about the information they have reordered, for example, 'changing the temperature, music and lights in different rooms' already happens in Bill Gates' house. Ask students if there are any predictions which they don't believe or don't want to happen.

Answers

a 2 b 5 c 4 d 1 e 3

>> **AUDIOSCRIPT TB PAGE 292**

6 Tell students to look at Exercise 3 and then say other things that happen at home, for example, feed the cat, have a shower, make a cake. Put students into pairs to discuss how they want these things to be done. Share ideas as a class.

GRAMMAR | Future with *will*

1 Tell students to read the examples. Write these two sentences on the board:

Jason is meeting Susie at six o'clock tomorrow.

Homes will be very different in the future.

Ask the students 'Are they about the past, present or future?' (*future*), 'We studied the first future form on page 43. When do we use it?' (*for plans and arrangements*), 'Is *will* the same?' (*no*) and 'Why not?' (*It is a prediction, not a plan; we can't be sure.*).

2 Have students complete the rules. Check as a class. You can also tell students the following: *will* is the most common way of talking about the future; *shall* for a future meaning is now very rare, except in suggestions (*Shall we go …?*); the contraction *'ll* is mainly used after pronouns, *it'll be difficult.*

Answers

1 in the future 2 often use 3 without 4 do not use 5 after 6 don't use

>> **GRAMMAR REFERENCE AND PRACTICE ANSWER KEY TB PAGE 265**

3 Have students complete the sentences. Check answers as a class. Ask students if they agree with the speaker in questions 3 and 4.

Answers

1 won't be 2 will arrive 3 will use 4 Will people live

Future with *may* and *might*

4 Books closed, write the examples on the board without *may* and *might* and have students complete them from memory. Tell students to open their books and check.

5 Have students complete the rules. Check answers as a class. Tell students to give an example for each rule, for example (1), *I may study English at university.*

Answers

1 possible 2 often use 3 without 'to' 4 do not use 5 after 6 don't use

>> **GRAMMAR REFERENCE AND PRACTICE ANSWER KEY TB PAGE 265**

6 Have students put the words in order to complete the sentences. Check answers as a class.

Answers

1 I may do 2 might technology help 3 may not be able 4 might not want

7 Have students correct the sentences. Check answers as a class.

Answers

1 A few other friends **will/may/might** come to my house later.
2 I met a new friend and I think you **may/might/will** like her.
3 It **won't** rain this evening.
4 I'm not sure but the book **may/might** be on your kitchen table.
5 I'**ll/will** meet you in the skatepark later.

>> **GRAMMAR WORKSHEET UNIT 8**

PRONUNCIATION | *will* and *won't*

8 Books closed, students listen and write down the four sentences. Books open, they check, then listen and repeat.

MIXED ABILITY

Students who have weaker pronunciation probably have two problems – the rounded /w/ sound and the 'dark' /l/ sound in the contraction *'ll*. For /w/, exaggerate the rounding of the lips when you drill *will* and *won't*. For *'ll*, ask students to compare the two /l/ sounds in *little*, the second is the sound in *'ll*, the tongue being curled up further back in the mouth.

9 Put students into pairs to talk about their ideas from the *About you* box using the future forms. Demonstrate with a stronger student at the front of the class. 'Do you think everyone will have a personal plane?' (*They may do but it still might be very expensive.*). Share ideas as a class.

10 Tell students to read the sentences and decide if and when they think the things might happen.

11 Put students into small groups to decide their answers to Exercise 10. Share ideas as a class. As an extension activity, you could ask students to make a graph of what percentage of the class think each thing will, might and won't happen. Students ask everyone in the class, work out what percentage of students fit into each category and make a graph. (There are many online tools for doing this and producing different kinds of graphs.)

COOLER

Write these tongue-twisters on the board and get students to repeat them.

Wayne won't want to walk to work in wet, windy weather.

What will we wear on Wednesday when we welcome the winners?

We'll wash your watch with warm water while you wait.

Then get students to make their own tongue-twister using the /w/ sound.

GRAMMAR | Future with *will*

1 Look at these examples from the interview.

I think they'll (will) be very different from today's homes.
You won't (will not) have to use your hands to do it.
Will it work for the heating and the lights too?

2 Choose the correct words to complete the rules.

> **1** We use **will** when we think something is going to happen *now / in the future*.
> **2** We *often use / don't use* 'think' before **will**.
> **3** After **will**, we use the infinitive *without / with* 'to'.
> **4** We *use / do not use* third person 's' with **will**.
> **5** To make a negative, we put 'not' *before / after* **will**.
> **6** To make a question with **will**, we *use / don't use* the auxiliary 'do'.

>> GRAMMAR REFERENCE AND PRACTICE PAGE 154

3 Complete the sentences with the correct form of *will*.

1 My phone isn't working very well. It _____ (not be) possible to text you later.
2 I think my sister _____ (arrive) late because she missed her train.
3 People _____ (use) different new technology, not only their smartphones.
4 _____ (people / live) on the moon in the future? I don't think so, do you?

Future with *may* and *might*

4 Look at these examples from the interview.

Seats, bookcases and things like that might not look very different.
But you may have a table or drawer with a computer inside it.
Might our homes look different on the outside, too?

5 Choose the correct words to complete the rules

> **1** We use *may*, *might* when we think something is *possible / definitely going to happen* in the future.
> **2** We *often use / don't use* 'think' before *may*, *might*.
> **3** After *may* and *might*, we use the infinitive *without 'to' / with 'to'*.
> **4** We *use / do not use* third person 's' with *may* and *might*.
> **5** To make a negative, we put 'not' *before / after* *may* and *might*.
> **6** To make a question with *may*, *might*, we *use / don't use* the auxiliary 'do'.

>> GRAMMAR REFERENCE AND PRACTICE PAGE 154

6 Put the words in brackets in the correct order to complete the sentences.

1 Next summer, _____ (do / I / may) an online course on ICT. I'm not sure yet.
2 How _____ (help / might / technology) ill people in their homes?
3 We _____ (be able / not / may) to see you tomorrow. We're very busy.
4 I _____ (not / might / want) robots in my house.

7 Correct the mistakes in the sentences.

1 A few other friends come to my house later.
2 I met a new friend, and I think you can like her.
3 It don't rain this evening. The weather app on my phone says sunshine all day.
4 I'm not sure, but the book will be on your kitchen table.
5 I meet you in the skatepark later. I've got nothing else to do today.

ꝋ PRONUNCIATION | *will* and *won't*

8 Listen and repeat.

Houses will be smaller.
I'll live in a big house.
People won't use door keys.
I won't walk anywhere.

9 Work with a partner. Use *will*, *won't*, *may*, *may not*, *might*, *might not* to talk about your ideas from *About you* at the beginning of this unit.

10 Read the sentences. Do you think these things will happen in the future? When?

1 People will live under the sea.
2 During the summer, there might not be any ice at the North Pole.
3 Space travel will get cheaper and might even cost the same as a plane ticket.
4 People may travel to Mars and live there.
5 There will be cars without drivers.
6 People might be able to communicate with technology by just thinking.
7 Most people will live to be 100 and their bodies won't get old.

11 In groups of three, discuss your answers. Use *will*, *won't*, *may*, *may not*, *might*, *might not*.

> I think people might live under the sea in the future. What do you think?

WHAT WILL YOU PUT IN YOUR TIME CAPSULE?

A

There is a little bag on the moon with a time capsule inside it. The capsule is tiny, about the size of a small **(1)** _____ . At the top, it says: 'Goodwill messages from around the world brought to the moon by the astronauts of Apollo 11.' The Apollo 11 Astronauts **(2)** _____ it there in 1969. There are 73 messages from **(3)** _____ countries written on the time capsule in very small letters. Each one is smaller than a human hair. The messages are to anyone who **(4)** _____ the time capsule in the future. Who will that be? Who **(5)** _____ where those people will come from? They might come from Earth, but they might be from **(6)** _____ else in the solar system.

B

Harold Davisson had a shop in Seward, Nebraska in the USA. He thought it was important for his children and grandchildren to touch and see real things, not just to read about them in books. So he decided to build the biggest time capsule in the world. He put more than 5,000 real objects inside, including clothes and even a new car and buried it on 4th July 1975 in front of his shop. Then he heard there was another time capsule bigger than his, so he put a second time capsule on top of the first one. His grandchildren will open them both on 4th July 2025. They know some of the things they will find, but they might find things Harold didn't tell them about!

READING

1. Look at the photos of the time capsules. What do you think a time capsule is? Do you think time capsules are a good idea? Why / Why not?

2. Read both texts quickly. Choose the best title for each text.

   1 Two are better than one   2 Out of this world

✓ PREPARE FOR THE EXAM

Reading Part 4

3. Read text A. For each question, choose the correct answer for each gap.

	A	**B**	**C**
1	money	coin	pence
2	arrived	travelled	left
3	usual	different	available
4	finds	looks	learns
5	understands	thinks	knows
6	everywhere	nowhere	somewhere

» **PREPARE FOR THE EXAM PAGE 124**

4. Read the texts again and answer the questions.

   Which time capsule, A or B
   1 is older?
   2 is under the ground?
   3 might people open first?
   4 is smaller?
   5 is for someone's family?
   6 has something for people to read?

5. Discuss with your partner. Which time capsule do you think will be the most interesting for the people who will open it? Why?

💬 TALKING POINTS

▶ 06 Watch the video and ask and answer the questions in groups.

What will you put in your time capsule to show people in the future what life is like today?

What eight things will you put in your group time capsule? Say why.

WARMER

Tell students you are from the year 2099. Get them to ask you questions about the world in 2099, for example, *Do people still watch TV?*. Write some categories on the board, for example *houses*, *food*, *school*, *work*, *towns*, to give them ideas for questions. Once students understand, they continue the activity in pairs.

BACKGROUND INFORMATION

One of the earliest time capsules was the Detroit Century Box, created on 31st December 1900 and opened on 31st December 2000. It was filled with photographs and letters from people who lived in Detroit. There are several capsules in space. The time capsules on the Voyager 1 and 2 spacecrafts each have a record with sounds, images and music representing life on Earth.

1 Have students discuss when and where they would travel in time. Books open, put students into pairs to describe the photos and discuss the questions.

2 Pre-teach **solar system** (the sun and the group of planets that move around it) and **bury** (to put something into a hole in the ground and cover it). Give students a time limit to read and choose the titles. Check as a class. Explain that *out of this world* is also an idiom meaning 'extremely good'.

Answers
1 B 2 A

A2 KEY FOR SCHOOLS
Reading Part 4

In this part, students have to read a cloze text with six missing words. There are six multiple-choice questions with A, B and C options. The main focus is on vocabulary but one or two of the missing words could be grammar words, for example parts of phrasal verbs or pronouns.

Tip Tell students first to read the text quickly to get an idea of what it is about. As they read they should think about the grammar and meaning of the missing words. For grammar, students should think about the word class, for example noun or verb, and form, for example singular or plural; for meaning, which word matches the context of the sentence and whole text. Then students should do each multiple-choice question in turn, making sure that their answer fits grammatically and make sense.

3 Give students a time limit to do the task. Check as a class.

Answers
1 B 2 C 3 B 4 A 5 C 6 C

>> **PREPARE FOR THE EXAM TEACHING NOTES AND ANSWER KEY TB PAGE 254**

MIXED ABILITY

Do the first question together to demonstrate the strategy. 'There is *a* before the gap so what does this tell us about the word?' (*It is a noun, singular and countable.*), 'Which of the three words is singular and countable?' (*coin*) and 'Why are the others wrong?' (*money is uncountable, pence is plural*). Continue with more questions if necessary.

4 Ask students, 'Which time capsule is in Space?' (*A*). Have students read and answer the questions. Check answers as a class. Ask students, 'What do you think Harold's children will do with all the objects?'.

Answers
1 A 2 B 3 B 4 A 5 B 6 A

🔊 61 The Reading text is recorded for students to listen, read and check their answers.

5 Tell students to discuss what is interesting about each of the capsules before they decide which is the most interesting. See if all the class agree on which is the most interesting time capsule.

💬 TALKING POINTS

▶ 06 Show the video and ask students to complete the video worksheet. Then, read the questions in the *Talking points* box and students answer the questions.

Tell students that you will put an apple, a shoe and a joke in your time capsule. Get them to guess why and then give them your reasons: an apple because people in the future probably won't eat real food, there will be food tablets; a shoe because it will show how tall people were (people will probably be much taller in the future); a joke so people can see what was funny for us.

Each student makes a list of three things for the time capsule. Then, in groups of four, they choose eight things and explain why their objects are important. Each group presents their time capsule to the class.

VOCABULARY — Words with two meanings

1 Ask students to read the two sentences in the book. Say, 'In which sentence does *letter* mean the same as *message*?' (*the second*). Write *hello* in tiny letters on the board. Ask, 'Why is this difficult to read?' (*the letters are tiny*). Have students tell you the two meanings of the word.

Answers

letter = message
letter = alphabet symbol

2 Check that the students know both meanings of each word by asking questions, for example 'What is a small clock?' (*watch*) and 'An apple is a … of fruit.' (*kind*)

Answers

book: something you read or to reserve
kind: to be nice to people or another word for *type* or *sort*
picture: something you draw or another word for *photo*
ring: to make a phone call to someone or something you wear on your finger
watch: a small clock you wear or to look at something continuously e.g. a film

FAST FINISHERS

Fast finishers think of as many words as they can which have two meanings and write example sentences to show the meanings. Examples: *light* (not heavy or not dark), *may* (modal verb or month), *right* (correct or not left), *second* (unit of time or ordinal number).

3 Tell students to go to page 136 and complete the sentences. Check as a class.

Answers

1 ring 2 picture 3 kind 4 watch 5 book 6 kind 7 ring
8 book 9 picture 10 watch

>> VOCABULARY WORKSHEET UNIT 8

LISTENING

1 Have students read the task. Ask how many people are speaking in each question.

Answers

One person: questions 2 and 3
Two people: questions 1, 4 and 5

 PREPARE FOR THE EXAM

A2 KEY FOR SCHOOLS
Listening Part 4

In this part, students listen to a mixture of monologues and dialogues on different topics. There are five different situations and five multiple-choice questions. The questions test the main idea or point.

Tip Tell students first to read each question carefully so they understand what the situation is: who is speaking and why. Tell students to underline key words in the questions and answers to help them focus on them as they listen.

 2 Play the recording twice then check as a class.

Answers

1 A 2 A 3 B 4 A 5 B

>> AUDIOSCRIPT TB PAGE 293

>> PREPARE FOR THE EXAM TEACHING NOTES AND ANSWER KEY TB PAGE 257

WRITING

PREPARE TO WRITE
too, also, as well

GET READY Books closed, explain that we have a time capsule from some children in 1965. Ask students to guess three things that are in the capsule and why they are there, for example, a school book from 1965 (to show what children studied then). Say that there is also a letter in the capsule. Ask students to write down three things they think the letter says.

Books open, they read Liliana's letter and check their ideas. They then answer the questions in the book. Check answers as a class.

Then draw students' attention to the words in blue and have students complete the sentences. Check answers as a class.

Answers

Liliana makes five predictions.
None of them are true now. Students' own answers about whether they think they will be true in a few years.
1 the end 2 the end 3 has

PLAN If students need help with ideas, write some categories on the board and ask them to think of two ideas for each. For example:

- *Transport: travel by bicycle / no private cars*
- *School: old people study / children teach them*
- *Free time: a lot more / fast food not popular*
- *Home: live under the sea / 100-floor flats*

Students should choose about five predictions.

WRITE Tell students to use *will* (*not*) for predictions and the linking words.

IMPROVE Students then correct each other's writing and make suggestions for improvements.

Model answer

Hello,
I'm writing this in 2020. I think in 2070 there will be no cars and we will travel by bicycle. Also old people will study at school and they might go to university as well. A lot of people will live under the sea but there will be big 100-floor flats too. Life will be great!
Are my predictions true?
Maria

COOLER

Put students in small groups and give each group a dice (or write numbers on a sugar cube). Tell them what the numbers on the dice mean: 1 and 2 = *will*, 3 and 4 = *might*, 5 and 6 = *will not*. Students take it in turns to ask a question about the future (their future or the future generally), roll the dice and say the prediction. For example:

Will I go to university? – 4 – I might go to university.

VOCABULARY Words with two meanings

1 Some English words have two meanings. Read the sentences. What are the two meanings of *letter*?

There are 73 messages written on the time capsule in tiny letters.
Some people wrote letters to people in the future and put them inside their time capsules.

2 Each word in the box has two meanings. What are they?

book	kind	picture	ring	watch

3 » Go to page 136.

LISTENING

1 Read the five questions and the possible answers. In which questions will you hear one person speaking, and in which questions will you hear two people speaking?

PREPARE FOR THE EXAM

Listening Part 4

2 For each question, choose the correct answer.

🔊 **1** You will hear two friends talking about technology.
 62 What do they think they will use in the future?
   A smartphones
   B smart watches
   C smart glasses

2 You will hear a teacher talking about an activity students are doing in class. What does she say?
   A They will finish the project in groups.
   B They will complete the project at home.
   C They will write the project on a computer.

3 You will hear a boy talking about his shopping trip. What did he buy?
   A something to wear
   B something to read
   C something to eat

4 You will hear a daughter talking to her father about a new computer he is buying for her. What does she like best about the computer?
   A the software
   B the colour
   C the size

5 You will hear a boy talking to his mother about the weather for his holiday. What will the weather be like tomorrow?
   A It'll be wet.
   B It'll be cloudy.
   C It'll be sunny.

» PREPARE FOR THE EXAM PAGE 131

WRITING

PREPARE TO WRITE
too, also, as well

GET READY More than 50 years ago, some children buried a time capsule in their town. In a few years, people in the town will open it. Read one of the letters in it. How many predictions does Liliana make? How many of them are true now or will be true in a few years?

> Hello,
>
> I'm writing this in 1965. Here are my predictions for 2025. There will be cities under the sea and there might be cities on Mars, too. There may not be any teachers because robots will teach the students. Most doctors will be robots as well. Also, I think there will be cars that drive themselves.
>
> Are my predictions true?
>
> Liliana

Look at the words in blue.

We use *too*, *as well* and *also* to add more information to our writing.

Choose the correct options to complete the sentences.

1 *Too* comes at *the beginning / the middle / the end* of a sentence.
2 *As well* comes at *the beginning / the middle / the end* of a sentence.
3 At the beginning of a sentence, *also has / doesn't have* a comma (,) after it.

PLAN You are going to write a letter for a time capsule for your own town. Plan your ideas. What do you think the world will be like in 50 years?

WRITE Write your letter. Use Liliana's letter to help you and all your ideas.

Write about 60 words. Use *also, too* and *as well* to join your ideas.

IMPROVE In pairs, read each other's letters. Check for mistakes and try to make your letters better.

LIFE SKILLS COMMUNICATION

HAVING A GOOD CONVERSATION

 LIFE SKILLS

To have good conversation, you should remember that:
- when only one person talks and the other listens, it is not a conversation!
- some people are quiet, some people like talking more.
- a good conversation includes everyone.

Good conversations

Imagine you have to spend an hour with a student you don't know from another class. Maybe you're going to take a test, or you're waiting to see the head teacher. For some people, it's a difficult situation because you don't know the person very well. For other people, it's easy to start a conversation and say, for example, *How are you?* or *Are you nervous?*

Talking to an older person can be even more difficult. For example, your parents' friends or aunts, uncles or grandparents. Sometimes they ask all the questions and you only answer! The best way to manage this is to think of questions to ask the other person. People like to talk about their experiences and to give an opinion about things.

Group conversations are also difficult to manage sometimes, but there are some easy ways to make sure everyone speaks, including yourself! If you are a person who can talk easily, then think about the others in the group. If you notice one person is not speaking, then ask them a question. A simple *And you?* or *Why?* Or show interest – *Really?*

When you are in a group and everyone is talking at the same time, it is sometimes hard to interrupt, especially if you think this is not a polite thing to do. When you want to give your own opinion politely, you can use *Excuse me, can I say something?* Then other people know you have something to say.

We can all learn to have good conversations.

 64

---

1 Are these statements true (*T*) or false (*F*) for you? In pairs, compare your ideas.

> I talk more than I listen.

> I'm quiet, so I don't want to talk.

> I prefer to talk in pairs than in groups.

> I like to hear different opinions.

 63 **2** Listen to the conversations and answer the questions.

Conversation 1 Does the conversation include everyone?
Conversation 2 Is the girl, Poppy, polite?
Conversation 3 How does the boy stop his grandmother's questions?

3 Read the text above and tick (✓) the best sentence.

The text explains how to …
a speak more clearly.
b improve your conversation skills.
c ask questions.
d make more friends.

50 LIFE SKILLS

LIFE SKILLS

Learning Objectives

- The students learn that we can all improve our conversation skills and a good conversation includes everyone.
- In the project stage, students make a time capsule that will be opened in two years' time and present it to the rest of the class.

Vocabulary

answer ask give make show speak

BACKGROUND INFORMATION

Small talk, often used with people you don't know well or at the start of a longer conversation, may seem trivial or meaningless but it is actually an important kind of conversation with a strong inter-personal function. There are three typical situations in which small talk takes place. The first is at the start of a conversation when people don't know one another well or are unsure of their intentions. Among other things, this establishes the relationship between the speakers, for example what they have in common, and is an introduction to the main part of the conversation. The second role of small talk is at the end of the conversation to avoid the conversation ending abruptly and one person feeling rejected. The third role is to fill silences. In many cultures, people feel awkward during silences and small talk avoids gaps in the conversation. The content of small talk is less important than its function and some topics are more appropriate than others in certain cultures. For example, in regions where the weather is variable, like the UK, the weather is a common and appropriate topic for small talk because it is easy to discuss and there is no chance of offending the listener. Linguists have also found gender differences in small talk. For example, women are more likely to pay one another compliments than men.

WARMER

A silent conversation. Arrange students into pairs. Each student has a piece of paper and writes the first line of a conversation. They then pass it to their partner. Their partner continues the conversation with a new line and passes the paper back. Continue until the students have a dialogue of ten lines or give a time limit. Students then read out the conversations to the rest of the class. Ask students, 'What is the difference between this and a real conversation?' and 'Why is it more effective to speak?'.

🔅 LIFE SKILLS
HAVING A GOOD CONVERSATION

Tell students to read the information and check vocabulary as necessary. Invite students to say if they agree or disagree with any of the points in the text and to give their reasons. Encourage open-class discussion and help students make connections between their contributions.

1 Tell students to decide if the statements are true or false for them. Put students into pairs to compare their ideas.

🔊 63 2 Books closed. Put students into pairs and ask them to remember who their last conversation was with, what they discussed and what their role was. For example, I talked with my sister about a film we had both seen. She liked it but I disagreed with her. You could ask students to repeat these conversations as a role-play in front of the class.

Books open, ask students to read the questions and underline the key words, for example, include everyone in Conversation 1. Play the recording for students to answer the questions. Play the recording a second time for students to check as a class. Ask students more questions about the conversations.

Conversation 1: 'What are they discussing?' (whether to get the bus or walk), 'What do they decide?' (to get the bus)

Conversation 2: 'What subject do they need to do a project for?' (science), 'What are their three ideas for a project?' (a poster, a presentation, a model)

Conversation 3: 'What is the boy's grandmother asking him about?' (his education)

Answers

Conversation 1 Yes   Conversation 2 Yes
Conversation 3 He asks her a question.

≫ AUDIOSCRIPT TB PAGE 293

3 Ask students to look at the pictures and ask, 'Where are the teenagers?' (on the stairs) and 'What's the difference between the pictures?' (in the first picture the girl is separate from the group of boys talking; in the second picture she is the centre of attention and everyone is involved). Give students time to read the text and answer the question. Check as a class.

Answer
b

FAST FINISHERS

Tell fast finishers to imagine they are at a party and meet someone they don't know at all or don't know very well. Tell them to write down questions which they could ask this person to get the conversation going. For example: Do you know (name of friend) as well? Those jeans are great! Where did you get them?

4   Books closed, read out the beginning of each sentence and have students complete them (orally or in writing) with their own answers. Books open, tell students to read the text again and match the sentence halves. Check as a class.

Answers

1 c 2 a 3 d 4 b

5   Books closed, demonstrate with some examples on the board using verbs from the word box.

You need to _____ sure everyone speaks in the conversation. (make)

If you're not sure what to do, _____ a question. (ask)

Books open, have students complete the sentences then check with the text. Check as a class.

Answers

1 speak 2 answer 3 show 4 make 5 ask 6 give

MIXED ABILITY

With weaker students, do this the other way round. First get students to underline examples of these verbs in the text and then tell students to do the exercise.

🔊 The Reading text is recorded for students to listen, read
64 and check their answers.

6   Put students in pairs to give examples of both situations. Give your own examples first to demonstrate, for example, 'My friend was telling me about his holiday in Italy and I preferred to listen because what he was saying was really interesting.' and 'Everyone was saying they loved the film but I wanted to tell everyone that I didn't like it.' Ask students to share their examples with the rest of the class.

🔊 7 Ask questions to see what students can remember about
65   the texts about time capsules on page 48. 'How big is the time capsule on the moon?' (*the size of a small coin*) and 'When will Harold Davisson's family open his time capsule?' (*2025*). Tell students to listen and write down the country and object. Check as a class.

Answers

Russia, a doll

🔊 8 Tell students to listen again and answer the questions.
65   Check as a class. Ask students, 'If you chose one object from your country for a time capsule, what would it be?' and 'If you chose one object from another country, which country and object would it be?'.

Answers

1 Brazil 2 It isn't special 3 history 4 pizza 5 five

🔊 9 Tell students to listen again and tick the expressions they
65   hear. Check as a class and have students repeat them. Stronger students may be able to add some expressions, for example, helping others to speak, *Is that okay?*, interrupting politely, *Yes, but…*

Answers

Tick all except: Really? Come on! and Pardon?

≫ **AUDIOSCRIPT TB PAGE 294**

10 Tell students to complete the conversation. Check as a class. Have students repeat the conversation in groups of three.

Answers

1 What about you 2 Why 3 Excuse me / Can I say something

PROJECT *A time capsule*

Put students into groups to discuss the questions. Tell students to use the tips in Exercise 4 and the useful language in Exercise 9 during their conversation. When you give feedback, give examples of when students have done this, for example interrupted politely with *Excuse me?* Each group draws their time capsule and presents it to the class.

PROJECT EXTENSION

Tell students to imagine that they are school students who open this time capsule not in two years' time but two hundred years' time! They should have a conversation about what they think the things are in the time capsule and give their opinions about why people used them. Demonstrate:

A: *This small plastic thing might be a communication device.*

B: *I'm not sure because the screen is so small and …*

C: *Can I say something?*

Monitor and give feedback as you did before.

COOLER

Ask six students to come to the front of the class. Ask one student from the rest of the class to ask them a question, for example, *Will people still go to school in the future?* The six students take it in turns to say one word which makes and continues a reply to the question until they have made a sentence. For example:

Student 1:   *I*

Student 2:   *think*

Student 3:   *that*

Student 4:   *most*

Student 5:   *people*

Student 6:   *will*

Student 1:   *still*

Student 2:   *go*

Student 3:   *to*

Student 4:   *school.*

If the answer breaks down, for example there is a grammar mistake or a student takes too long to think of a word to continue the sentence, replace that student with another student and tell the other students to ask a new question. Keep changing the students at the front of the class and have the class ask new questions.

4 Read the text again and match the two halves of the sentences.

1 To start a conversation with someone you don't know well
2 To have a good conversation with someone
3 To help quiet people to speak
4 To give your opinion when other people are talking

a you should ask him/her questions as well as answer.
b you should interrupt politely.
c you can ask how they feel.
d you can ask them a question.

5 Complete the sentences with a verb from the box. Find the verb in the text to check your answers.

answer	ask	give
make	show	speak

1 You should always _____ in English in the class.
2 I couldn't _____ a question in the test because it was very difficult.
3 I wanted to _____ interest in his life, so I asked him about his hometown.
4 Please _____ sure you bring a calculator to class tomorrow.
5 Can I _____ a question? What time does the bus leave?
6 At the end of the video, you should _____ your opinion.

6 Do you prefer to listen or to speak? Tell your partner about a time when you preferred to listen and a time when you wanted to speak.

7 🔊 65 In Newton school, the students are working on a time capsule project. Each group has to choose a country and an object from that country to include in the capsule. Listen to the conversation. Which country and which object does the group choose?

8 🔊 65 Listen again and answer the questions.

1 Which country is good at football?
2 Why isn't a football a good object to choose?
3 What did the children study about Russia last term?
4 What object do they think about for Italy?
5 How many other dolls are there in Laura's Russian doll?

9 🔊 65 Listen again and tick the expressions you hear.

> ⓘ **USEFUL LANGUAGE**
>
> | Helping others to speak | Interrupting politely |
> |-------------------------|-----------------------|
> | Do we all agree? | Excuse me |
> | What about you? | Can I say something? |
> | Come on! | Pardon? |
> | Why? | |

10 Complete the conversation with some of the phrases from the *Useful language* box.

Ali: I think we should choose a small country. (1) _____, Jamie?
Jamie: I'm not sure. Maybe a big country is better.
Ali: (2) _____?
Jamie: Because people in the future will know more about a big country.
Lily: (3) _____? I think it's better to choose a country with interesting history.
Ali: Sorry, Lily. We didn't ask your opinion.
Lily: Thanks, Ali. Then we can choose an object from its history.
Jamie: Good idea.

PROJECT
A time capsule

You are going to make a time capsule that you will open in two years' time.

- Work in small groups.
- In your group discuss these questions:
  - What will you make the time capsule with: a box, a bag, a tin?
  - How will you decorate it? Will you write anything on it?
  - Where will you keep it? Remember, in two years you are going to open it.
  - What will you put in it?

Draw your time capsule and present it to the rest of the class.

HAVING A GOOD CONVERSATION 51

REVIEW 2 UNITS 5–8

VOCABULARY

1 Use the correct form of *get*, *go* or *take* to complete the sentences.

1 At our school, we _____ exams at the end of every term.
2 Last summer, we _____ paddle boarding when we were on holiday. It was amazing!
3 I _____ back from school at about 5.30 every day.
4 My friends _____ sailing this afternoon at the activity centre.
5 Our flight was at 6.00 in the morning, so we _____ up at 3.00.
6 _____ the third turning on the left after the supermarket. That's the quickest way to my house.
7 My friends _____ lost in the mountains, but another hiker found them.
8 Next year, we can _____ another language and another science subject.
9 I think I prefer _____ kite surfing to waterskiing.

2 Put the words in the correct column.

air conditioning	bookcase	compass
cotton	first-aid kit	fridge	gold
heating	leather	map	metal
plastic	roof	silver	sleeping bag
stairs	tent	torch

Materials	Home	Adventure

3 Match the school subjects in the box to the pictures 1–10.

biology	chemistry	drama
foreign languages	geography	history
ICT	maths	PE	physics

1 _____ 2 _____ 3 _____

4 _____ 5 _____ 6 _____ 7 _____ 8 _____ 9 _____ 10 _____

GRAMMAR

1 Choose the correct words to complete the sentences.

1 She is very *good* / *well* at climbing.
2 You have to bring a pencil and an *art's* / *art* book.
3 We *meet* / *are meeting* at 5 pm tomorrow.
4 How was *you* / *your* dinner yesterday?

Correct the mistakes in these sentences.

5 I went to the beach and swam with parents, then we flew a kite.
6 I want to be a friend of him because he is funny.
7 I going to Mexico to visit Manuela, a friend.
8 We are meeting at the park at two o'clock because before that I going to the dentist's.

2 Put the words in brackets in the correct order to make sentences.

1 _____ (will / brother / study / My) drama when he's older.
2 _____ (It / not / might / snow) tomorrow.
3 _____ (may / We / not / get) lost if we follow the path.
4 _____ (visit / you / Will) your grandparents at the weekend?
5 What time _____ (will / get / they) back?
6 _____ (I / take / may / not) my camera on the school trip.
7 _____ (might / People / share) cars in the future.
8 What _____ (we / will / learn) in today's English lesson?

3 Complete the sentences with the correct adverb form of the adjective in brackets.

1 Please write your name _____ (clear) on the exam paper.
2 Our team didn't win on Saturday. I played _____ (bad) of all!
3 You have to speak _____ (loud) than that. No one can hear you.
4 Usain Bolt ran _____ (fast) of all the runners in the 2016 Olympic Games.
5 Our new television works _____ (good).
6 My dad had an accident last year. Now he drives _____ (careful) than before.
7 My baby brother smiles _____ (happy) of all the babies I know.
8 Fred usually gets up _____ (early) than his twin brother.

Overview

VOCABULARY	School subjects; *take*; materials; adjectives for describing objects; holiday activities; things to take on an adventure holiday; furniture and household appliances; words with two meanings
GRAMMAR	Comparative and superlative adverbs; possession; present continuous for future; future with *will, may* and *might*
EXAM TASKS	Reading Part 4; Speaking Part 2; Listening Part 4

Resources

PHOTOCOPIABLE WORKSHEETS: Grammar worksheets Units 5–8; Vocabulary worksheets Units 5–8; Review game Units 5–8; Literature worksheet; Speaking worksheet; Writing worksheet

WARMER

Write these on the board and ask students to tell you which one is different and why (there may be alternative answers).

biology drama diving science (*diving* because it is not a school subject)

badly well easily quickly (*well* because it is an irregular adverb)

shirt cotton silver paper (*shirt* because it does not describe an object)

mine there his hers (*there* because it is not related to possession)

horse riding, kite surfing, zip wiring, camping (*camping* because it is only one word)

may, do, might, will (*do* because it is not a modal verb)

VOCABULARY

1 Ask students to tell you the three forms of *go* (*go–went–gone*), *get* (*get–got–got*) and *take* (*take–took–taken*) and then have them complete the sentences. Check as a class.

Answers

1 take 2 went 3 get 4 are going 5 got 6 Take 7 got 8 take 9 going

2 Concept-check some of the words, for example, 'this keeps a house warm' (*heating*), 'shirts are often made from this material' (*cotton*) and 'it stops rain coming in your house' (*roof*). Tell students to put the words in the correct category. Check as a class.

Answers

Materials: cotton, gold, leather, metal, plastic, silver
Home: air conditioning, bookcase, fridge, heating, roof, stairs
Adventure: compass, first-aid kit, map, sleeping bag, tent, torch

3 Ask students what each of the pictures shows, for example, 1 is a soldier, 2 is a tennis racket and ball. Tell students to match the school subjects to the pictures. Check as a class. As an extension activity, ask students to draw more pictures representing school subjects. Students then work in groups, show one another the pictures and say what the subject is.

Answers

1 history 2 PE 3 biology 4 physics 5 chemistry 6 ICT 7 foreign languages 8 maths 9 geography 10 drama

GRAMMAR

1 Tell students to complete sentences 1–4 in Exercise 1 and correct sentences 5–8. Check as a class.

Answers

1 good 2 art 3 are meeting 4 your
5 I went to the beach and swam with **my** parents then we flew a kite.
6 I want to be **a friend of his / his friend** because he's funny.
7 I **am/'m** going to Mexico to visit Manuela, a friend.
8 We are meeting at the park at two o'clock because before that I **am/'m** going to the dentist's.

MIXED ABILITY

For questions 1 to 4, guide weaker students towards the right answer.

Question 1: 'Do we need an adjective or adverb here?' (*an adjective*), 'Which word is an adjective?'

Question 2: 'What kind of nouns do we use the possessive s with?' (*people*), 'So is art's right?' (*no*)

Question 3: 'Is this about the past or the future?' (*the future*), 'What tense can we use for future plans?' (*the present continuous*)

Question 4: 'Do we need a possessive pronoun here?' (*yes*), 'Which word is a possessive pronoun?' (*your*)

2 Briefly review the form of modal verbs: they go before the main verb in statements (*They might know ~~might~~*); they act as auxiliaries in questions (*Will you go?*); they are followed by the base form (*will ~~to~~ go*). Ask students to put the words in brackets in the right order to complete the sentences. Check as a class.

Answers

1 My brother will study
2 It might not snow
3 We may not get
4 Will you visit
5 will they get
6 I may not take
7 People might share
8 will we learn

CONTINUED ON PAGE 102

3 Briefly review how to form adverbs from adjectives and the form of comparative and superlative adverbs: add -ly to make an adjective into a simple adverb (careful<u>ly</u>); add more to make a comparative adverb (more carefully); add the + most to make a superlative adverb (the most carefully). Remind students that good and bad are irregular and elicit the forms (good–well–best; bad–worse–worst). Ask students to complete the sentences with the correct adverb forms. Check as a class.

Answers

1 clearly 2 the worst 3 louder / more loudly 4 the fastest
5 well 6 more carefully 7 the most happily 8 earlier

 **PREPARE FOR THE EXAM**

A2 KEY FOR SCHOOLS Reading Part 4

1 Briefly review what students need to do in this part of the exam and if necessary read out the task description and tip on TB page 93. Ask students what they know about Bill Gates. Give students time to read the text. Ask some basic questions about it, for example, 'When was Bill Gates born?' (28th October, 1955) 'What's his wife's name?' (Melinda).

Tell students to cover up the answers and go through the gaps with them and see if they can work out what kind of word would be suitable. For example, 1 must be a verb and the rest of the sentence shows he was a very good student so it could be loved. Then give students time to look at the answer choices and complete the task. Check as a class.

You could give students more information about the Bill and Melinda Gates Foundation. This is one of the biggest private foundations in the world and it has funded a wide range of social, health and educational programmes in the USA and abroad. For example, it makes a large financial contribution to the World Health Organization and it gives scholarships to students outside the UK to study at Cambridge University.

Answers

1 B 2 A 3 B 4 C 5 A 6 C

FAST FINISHERS

Tell fast finishers to write down three things they would do if they were the richest person in the world, for example, start a space tourism company. When the other students have finished, fast finishers can present their ideas to the rest of the class and the other students can decide which is the best way to spend a lot of money.

🔊 The Reading text is recorded for students to listen, read
66 and check their answers.

A2 KEY FOR SCHOOLS Speaking Part 2

2 Briefly review what students need to do in this part of the exam and if necessary read out the task description and tip on TB page 82. Go through each of the pictures and ask students to say what kind of home it is. Concept-check the meaning of the adjectives in question 2: 'you feel relaxed there' (comfortable), 'not safe' (dangerous), 'different from other places' (unusual), 'not easy' (difficult), 'pleasant and enjoyable' (fun). Put students in pairs.

Give them time to read the questions then tell them to take turns to answer them. Remind students to use the conversation strategies they learned on pages 50 and 51. Give feedback at the end then arrange students into new pairs to repeat the activity. Ask students to share their opinions on the questions as a class.

A2 KEY FOR SCHOOLS Listening Part 4

🔊 3 Briefly review what students need to do in this part of
67 the exam and if necessary read out the task description and tip on TB page 94. Give students time to read the questions and then ask questions about them to check that students know what to listen for.

Question 1: 'What are the teacher and students preparing for?' (a school trip)

Question 2: 'What subject are they talking about?' (history)

Question 3: 'Is the mother unhappy with her son for one thing or different things?' (different things), 'How do you know?' (the question says most unhappy)

Question 4: 'Where did the friends go to?' (a sports centre)

Question 5: 'Which answer is about good weather?' (C)

Play the recording twice for students to answer the questions. Check as a class. Ask some more questions about the recording, for example, 'What does the teacher say about the backpacks?' (don't put too much in them), 'Did it take the girl a long time to finish her homework?' (yes), 'What did the boy have for breakfast?' (toast), 'Who didn't bring tennis shoes?' (the girl) and 'What are they going to do in question five?' (go hiking).

Answers

1 A 2 C 3 C 4 B 5 A

≫ **AUDIOSCRIPT TB PAGE 294**

COOLER

Put students into groups. Give each group a different set of ten words or expressions from Units 5–8 (or let them choose their own). Tell students they must make a story using these words and expressions. The story should also include at least one comparative or superlative adverb and at least one future form, either the present continuous or will, may or might. Give students a time limit to think of the story, make notes and decide who is going to say which part of the story. Then have each group present their story to the class. The other students listen and write down which words and expressions from Units 5–8 were used and check that examples of the grammar were included. At the end the class can vote for the most interesting story.

Reading Part 4

1 For each question, choose the correct answer.

Bill Gates

Bill Gates was born on 28th October 1955. He **(1)** _____ reading as a child and did very well in maths and science at school. He went to Harvard University to study law in 1973, but he **(2)** _____ more time on computers than in the classroom. In 1975, he left university without **(3)** _____ his studies and started Microsoft with his friend Paul Allen. Microsoft grew quickly to **(4)** _____ one of the biggest companies in the world and soon Bill Gates was one of the world's richest men. In 1994, he married Melinda French in Hawaii. Six years **(5)** _____, he and his wife started the Bill and Melinda Gates Foundation because they wanted to do good things with their money. This company **(6)** _____ people all over the world with health and education.

1	**A** wanted	**B** enjoyed	**C** hoped
2	**A** spent	**B** made	**C** took
3	**A** closing	**B** finishing	**C** testing
4	**A** go	**B** happen	**C** become
5	**A** later	**B** soon	**C** next
6	**A** sees	**B** gives	**C** helps

Speaking Part 2

2 Work with a partner. You are going to talk about the six homes in the pictures. Discuss these questions with your partner. Take turns to speak.

Section 1
1 Do you like these different homes? Why / Why not?
2 Do you think
- sleeping in a tent is comfortable?
- staying on a mountain is dangerous?
- living near water is unusual?
- making a home from a bus is difficult?
- sleeping in a tree house is fun?

Section 2
3 Which is better? A small home or a large home? Why?
4 Which is better? A home on land or on the water? Why?
5 Which is better? A home you can move or a home that stays in one place? Why?

Listening Part 4

3 For each question, choose the correct answer.

1 You will hear a teacher talking to students about a school trip. What do they need to bring?
   A some snacks
   B a torch
   C their walking boots

2 You will hear a girl talking about her history homework. What does she say about it?
   A She didn't understand it.
   B She didn't finish it.
   C She didn't have her book.

3 You will hear a woman talking to her son. What is she most unhappy about?
   A He didn't eat his breakfast.
   B He missed the bus.
   C He got up late.

4 You will hear two friends talking about a visit to the sports centre. What did they do there?
   A They had a snack.
   B They played tennis.
   C They went swimming.

5 You will hear a man talking to his daughter. What's the weather like at the moment?
   A It's raining.
   B It's windy.
   C It's sunny.

54 UNIT 9

ABOUT YOU

How many sports can you name?
Which ones do you do at your school?
Do you play video games?
Which are your favourites?

VOCABULARY AND **READING**

Sports and activities

1 Match the words in the box to photos A–O.

badminton	board game
card game	climbing	cricket
dance class	diving	fishing
fitness class	golf	karate	puzzle
skateboarding	skiing	video game

🔊 Listen and check. Then repeat.
68

2 Look at the photos in Exercise 1 again. In pairs, decide which activities need special equipment or a sports kit.

3 Write about your favourite sport or activity, using the ideas below.

> number of players
> sports kit special equipment
> how you play who wins

4 Read Max's message and the climbing club rules. Answer the questions.

1 What sort of club is Cool Zone?
2 What does Max want his friend to do?
3 Can you climb? If not, would you like to learn?
4 What sports clubs are there in your school or local area? Do you belong to any of them?

I belong to Cool Zone climbing club now! You don't have to be a member to climb there, but it's cheaper if you are. Why don't you become a member too? It's really easy to join. I just had to fill in a form and agree to the club rules. I didn't have to bring a photo – they took one of me there and made my membership card. Max

COOL ZONE
Climbing Centre Rules 🔊 69

1 You must show your membership card every time you come.

2 You must not lend your membership card to anyone else.

3 You do not have to bring your own climbing shoes.

4 You must not talk to people when they are climbing.

5 You must not take photos or record videos.

6 If you are under 12, you must climb with an adult.

7 You must climb with a partner if you are a beginner.

8 You do not have to book if you come on a weekday.

9 You must not stand under people when they are climbing.

10 If you have an accident, you must tell a member of staff.

Unit Overview

TOPIC	Sports and leisure
VOCABULARY	Sports and activities
AND READING	Cool Zone Climbing Centre Rules
GRAMMAR	*must, mustn't, have to* and *don't have to*
PRONUNCIATION	*must* and *mustn't*
VOCABULARY	Sports vocabulary; Suffix *-er*
READING	What are eSports?
LISTENING	A conversation about eSports and mind sports
SPEAKING	Talking about eSports
EXAM TASKS	Reading Part 3

Resources

GRAMMAR REFERENCE AND PRACTICE: SB page 155; TB page 265

PREPARE FOR THE EXAM: SB page on TB page 239; TB page 253

WORKBOOK: pages 36–39

VIDEO AND VIDEO WORKSHEET: Games

PHOTOCOPIABLE WORKSHEETS: Grammar worksheet Unit 9; Vocabulary worksheet Unit 9

TEST GENERATOR: Unit test 9

WARMER

Write the word *skateboarding* on the board. Underneath write *great* and *breaking*, showing that the letters come from *skateboarding*. In groups, give students three minutes to find as many words as they can from the word.

⑦ ABOUT YOU

Write the alphabet on the board. Give students three minutes to try and write a sport which matches each letter (e.g. Athletics, Basketball, Cycling, etc.). Then have students answer the questions in small groups. Share ideas as a class. Ask students, 'What sports and activities do you do to keep fit or relax?'.

VOCABULARY AND READING

Sports and activities

1 Books closed. Elicit some of the vocabulary, for example, 'You do this on a mountain in winter.' (*skiing*), 'Monopoly is an example.' (*board game*), 'This is one way you can get into a swimming pool.' (*diving*).

Books open. Ask students to cover the word box and see how many activities they can name in the photos. Then they look at the word box and do the matching. Play the recording for students to check. Ask, 'Which of these activities can help you get fit?', 'Which are sports?' and 'Which can you do sitting down?'.

🔊 Answers
68

The answers are recorded for students to check and then repeat.

A board game **B** golf **C** climbing **D** cricket **E** dance class
F karate **G** badminton **H** fishing **I** diving **J** skiing
K skateboarding **L** card game **M** puzzle **N** fitness class
O video game

2 Ask, 'What equipment do you need for cycling?' (*a bike and a helmet*) and 'What sports kit do you need for football?' (*shorts and a football shirt*). Tell students to do the same for the photos. Help with any vocabulary students don't know, like *shuttlecock*. Check answers as a class and write the new words on the board.

Possible answers

Badminton – racket and shuttlecock
Board game – board and counters, dice
Card game – cards
Climbing – ropes, special shoes
Cricket – bat, ball
Dance class – special shoes
Diving – swimsuit, goggles
Fishing – rod
Fitness class – sports clothes
Golf – clubs and ball
Karate – special clothes
Puzzle – pencil or pen
Skateboarding – skateboard
Skiing – skis, boots, warm clothes
Video games – games console

FAST FINISHERS

Draw a table on the board with these headings: *Games, Team sports, Water sports, Racket sports, Winter sports, Others*. Fast finishers classify the activities in Exercise 1 and see how many words they can add. The rest of the class can join in when they have finished.

Possible answers

Games: board game, card game, video game, chess
Team sports: cricket, basketball, football, hockey, rugby, volleyball
Water sports: diving, sailing, surfing, swimming
Racket sports: badminton, table tennis, tennis
Winter sports: skiing, ice skating, snowboarding
Others: climbing, dance class, fishing, fitness classes, golf, karate, puzzle, skateboarding, cycling, running

3 As a model, tell students about your own favourite sport or activity. Try to include words from Exercise 2. Put students into pairs to tell each other about their own favourite things. Then have students write about them. Ask some students to read what they have written about their sport or activity to the class. Have the rest of the class ask them questions like, 'How long have you done this?' 'Where do you do it?'.

CONTINUED ON PAGE 106

Possible answer

My favourite sport is hockey. There are six players on each team and they wear helmets. You need a hockey stick and puck to play. The team that scores the most goals wins.

4 Ask students which of the sports in Exercise 1 could be dangerous. Tell students to look at the photo of a climbing club and ask, 'Why can climbing be dangerous?'. (Remind students that the *b* in *clim(b)* is silent and if necessary tell them to look back at the words with silent letters on page 20.) Ask students what rules a climbing centre might have, for example, *Do not use mobile phones when you climb*. Give students two minutes to read the message and rules and see which of their rules are mentioned. Then have students read the text again and answer the questions. Check answers as a class.

Answers

1 a climbing club 2 join the club
3 and 4 Students' own answers

🔊 The Reading text is recorded for students to listen, read
69 and check their answers.

GRAMMAR | *must, mustn't, have to, don't have to*

1 Pre-teach **necessary** (something you need to do, like go to school). Give a list of things. Students say if they are necessary or not: *drink* (yes), *eat chocolate* (no), *sleep* (yes), *travel by taxi* (no). Have students underline the examples and match the sentences. Check answers as a class.

Answers

1, 2 c 3 a 4 b

2 Have students underline the main verbs and say what the form is. Tell students what the past tenses of *must*, *have to* and *don't have to* are.

Answers

infinitive without *to*

>> **GRAMMAR REFERENCE AND PRACTICE ANSWER KEY TB PAGE 265**

3 Tell students to re-read the climbing club rules and answer the questions. Check answers as a class.

Answers

1 No 2 No 3 No 4 Yes 5 No 6 No

MIXED ABILITY

Weaker students may have problems understanding the difference between *have to* and *don't have to* so give another example. Draw a barred window on the board with a face behind it. Say, 'Fred is in prison. Can he get up when he wants?' (*no*). Say and write on the board, 'Fred has to get up at six o'clock.'. Ask, 'Is it all right to stay in bed?' (*no*). Say and write on the board, 'He mustn't stay in bed.'. Say, 'There are other people in prison. Does Fred need to see them?' (*yes*). 'Does he need to be friends with them?' (*no*). Say and write on the board, 'Fred has to see other people but he doesn't have to be friends with them.'.

4 Do the first sentence together. 'Is it OK to eat in class?' (*no*), 'So what form do we need?' (*mustn't*). Tell students to rewrite the sentences. Check answers as a class.

Answers

1 You mustn't chew gum or bring food into the class.
2 You mustn't talk while the teacher is talking.
3 You don't have to wear special clothes.
4 You must put your phone on silent during the lesson.
5 You mustn't leave a class before the end.
6 You mustn't wear street shoes inside the dance studio.
7 You don't have to call if you need to miss a class.
8 You must take off all jewellery before class.

5 Tell students to look again at the past forms of *must* and *have to* in Exercise 2. Pre-teach **goggles** (glasses you wear when you swim or dive). Check that students know that this exercise is now about the past: 'When was the competition?' (*last week*), 'So can we use *must*?' (*no*). Tell students to write the sentences. Check as a class.

Answers

1 They had to arrive at the pool at 8.30 am.
2 They had to wear a swimming hat.
3 They didn't have to wear goggles.
4 They had to bring sandwiches for lunch.
5 They didn't have to stay until 6 pm.

6 Give example activities to help the students make their lists, for example *housework*, *helping people*, *shopping*. Students compare lists by asking one another in pairs. To demonstrate, get students to ask you questions: *Did you have to mark any tests?* 'Yes, I did. I had to check your progress.'. Share ideas as a class.

7 Have students correct the sentences. Check as a class.

Answers

1 The skatepark is free – we **don't have** to pay anything.
2 You **have** to bring your pencil case to the next lesson. / You must ~~to~~ bring your pencil case to the next lesson.
3 We **don't have to** bring food to the party – Jake's mum is making everything.
4 When I was younger I **had to** live far away from my grandparents.
5 Dad says I **don't have to** help him on Saturday, so I can come to your house!

>> **GRAMMAR WORKSHEET UNIT 9**

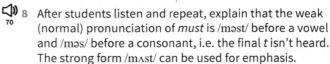

PRONUNCIATION | *must* and *mustn't*

🔊 8 After students listen and repeat, explain that the weak
70 (normal) pronunciation of *must* is /məst/ before a vowel and /məs/ before a consonant, i.e. the final *t* isn't heard. The strong form /mʌst/ can be used for emphasis.

🔊 9 Have students listen and put a tick if they hear *must*
71 and a cross if they hear *mustn't*. Check as a class. Tell students to listen again and repeat the sentences.

Answers

1 ✓ 2 ✓ 3 ✗ 4 ✓ 5 ✗ 6 ✓ 7 ✗

>> **AUDIOSCRIPT TB PAGE 294**

10 Put students into pairs and tell them to go to page 137. They choose a sport and a name for their club and write rules using the modal verbs. Then put pairs together into small groups to tell one another about their club.

COOLER

Get students to tell you all the words for activities they have learned in this unit. Write them on the board. Individually, students write down the three most difficult, the three most dangerous and the three most expensive.

GRAMMAR *must, mustn't, have to, don't have to*

1 <u>Underline</u> the examples of *must*, *must not*, *have to* and *don't have to* in the club rules on page 54. Match sentences 1–4 to meanings a–c. Use one of the meanings twice.

1 You must do this.
2 You have to do this.
3 You mustn't (must not) do this.
4 You don't have to do this.

a Do not do this.
b It's not necessary to do this.
c It's necessary to do this.

2 <u>Underline</u> the main verb after *must* and *have to*. Is it the infinitive with *to* or without *to*?

> The past of *must* and *have to* is *had to*.
> I had to fill in a form.
>
> The past of *don't have to* is *didn't have to*.
> I didn't have to bring in a photo.

>> **GRAMMAR REFERENCE AND PRACTICE PAGE 155**

3 Read the climbing club rules again and answer the questions.

1 Is it OK for your friend to use your membership card?
2 Can you chat to your friends while climbing?
3 Can you take photos in the club?
4 Is it OK to climb alone if you are 14?
5 Is it necessary to book if you go on a Monday?
6 Can you stand under people when they are climbing?

4 Read the dance class rules. Rewrite them using *must*, *mustn't* and *don't have to*.

1 Don't chew gum or bring food into the class.
2 Don't talk while the teacher is talking.
3 Special clothes are not necessary.
4 Put your phone on silent during the lesson.
5 Don't leave a class before the end.
6 Don't wear street shoes inside the dance studio.
7 It's not necessary to call if you need to miss a class.
8 Take off all jewellery before class.

5 Last week, there was a swimming competition. Write sentences about what people had to do and what they didn't have to do.

0 Cost: £5 to enter the competition.
They had to pay £5 to enter the competition.

1 Arrive at the pool at 8.30 am.

2 Wear a swimming hat.

3 You can wear goggles if you want, but it's not necessary.

4 Bring sandwiches for lunch.

5 Last race at 6 pm. Not necessary to stay until 6 pm.

6 Think of eight things you had to / didn't have to do last week. Then ask and answer with a partner.

> I had to clean my room.

> I had to finish my geography project.

> Did you have to … ?

> Yes, I did.

7 Correct the mistakes in the sentences.

1 The skatepark is free – we haven't to pay anything.
2 You must to bring your pencil case to the next lesson.
3 We mustn't bring food to the party – Jake's mum is making everything.
4 When I was younger, I must live far away from my grandparents.
5 Dad says I mustn't help him on Saturday, so I can come to your house!

⊝ PRONUNCIATION | *must* and *mustn't*

8 Listen and repeat.

You must listen carefully. /məs/
You mustn't speak now. /mʌsnt/

9 For each sentence, put a (✓) if you hear *must* and a (✗) if you hear *mustn't*.

1 ....   2 ....   3 ....
4 ....   5 ....   6 ....
7 ....

Listen again and repeat.

10 >> Work with a partner. Go to page 137.

SPORTS, GAMES AND ACTIVITIES 55

READING

1 Look at the photos. What do you think is happening? Who do you think the people in the photos are? Read the article quickly to check your ideas.

Playing a good video game is an exciting experience. Games are full of light, sound, action and surprises, and this makes them fun to watch as well as to play. Because of this, more and more people are taking part in eSports. This is the short name for electronic sports – playing video games against other people in competitions. There are huge tournaments all over the world, where big crowds watch matches on giant screens, and millions more watch online.

Just like many normal sports, eSports players usually play in teams, and have fans who follow them through every competition. Prizes for important eSports competitions are very large, and eSports champions can earn more than £1 million a year. That makes it sound like a great job, but in fact it's not easy to be a winner. Players have to practise for up to 14 hours a day, so they don't get much rest. The games they play change often and there are always new things to learn.

ESports stars are not well known in the way that some football stars are. However, some top eSports players now work for real football teams. For example, Koen Weijland, a professional player of the football video game FIFA, is part of Ajax, a famous Dutch football team. As a little boy he wanted to be a footballer and was a big fan of Ajax, so for him this is like a dream come true. And who knows, maybe one day, eSports stars like him will be as famous as today's top footballers.

PREPARE FOR THE EXAM

Reading Part 3

2 For each question, choose the correct answer.

1 What does the writer say about eSports in the first paragraph?
   A They are more fun to watch than to play.
   B They are becoming more popular.
   C Most people don't understand them.

2 What is hard for top eSports players?
   A They don't have a lot of free time.
   B They don't make much money.
   C They get bored of playing video games.

3 What is the writer doing in the third paragraph?
   A explaining why eSports stars are not famous
   B showing how eSports and normal sports can come together
   C describing the daily life of an eSports star

4 What is a 'dream come true' for Koen Weijland?
   A meeting some famous footballers
   B winning a video game competition
   C working for his favourite football team

5 What is the best title for this article?
   A Are eSports a good thing?
   B The history of eSports
   C What are eSports?

3 In small groups, ask and answer the questions.

1 Do you play video games? If yes, which ones?
2 Would you like to watch an eSports competition? Why / Why not?
3 Do you know any eSports stars?
4 Do you think eSports is a good name for these competitions? Why / Why not?

56 UNIT 9

WARMER

Arrange students into groups. Ask them to write six crazy rules for their country using *must (not)* and *(not) have to*. Give some examples:

Everyone must go to bed before nine o'clock.

Children don't have to go to school.

You must not eat vegetables at the weekend.

Ask groups to present their rules to the rest of the class. The other students can vote on which rule is the craziest.

BACKGROUND INFORMATION

The first video game competition was in 1972 in the USA with a game called Spacewar played on home computers. There have been online competitions from the 1990s but professional eSports developed from about 2005. There is controversy over whether eSports are real sports and sometimes they are classed as mind sports, like board games. Exhibition eSport events were held at the 2018 Winter Olympics in South Korea, where eSports are particularly popular.

1 Write *hiking, chess, Counter-Strike* (or another video game popular with your students), *fishing* on the board. Ask students to say which of these are sports and why or why not. Put students into pairs to describe the photos on the page. Share ideas as a class. Give students a time limit to read the article and check their ideas.

PREPARE FOR THE EXAM

A2 KEY FOR SCHOOLS Reading Part 3

2 Briefly review what students need to do in this part of the exam and if necessary read out the A2 Key for Schools box on TB page 65.

Tell students to first read the text quickly to get an idea of what it is about. Then they should read each question carefully and be careful to check whether the possible answers are positive or negative. Tell students not to leave any questions unanswered but to guess if necessary as they won't lose marks for wrong answers. In this situation they should try and work out which of the answers is definitely wrong as then they are only guessing between two rather than three options.

Do the first question together. 'Look at answer A. Does the text say eSports are fun?' (*yes*), 'Does the text say it is better to watch than play them?' (*No, it says they are fun to watch and to play.*), 'Look at answer B. Does the text say eSports are becoming more popular?' (*yes*), 'What phrase means the same as *more popular*?' (*more and more people*), 'So is B the answer?' (*yes*). Tell students to read and answer the other questions. Check answers as a class.

As a variation, write the five questions on the board and have students answer them without looking at the options. Students should then compare their answers to the three options and choose the one which is closest.

After checking the answers, ask some extra comprehension questions: 'Are all eSports team sports?' (*no*), 'What make eSports difficult?' (*You have to practise a lot and the games change a lot.*) and 'Is Koen famous?' (*not yet*).

Answers
1 B 2 A 3 B 4 C 5 C

FAST FINISHERS

Tell fast finishers to write down new words beginning with *e-* and what they could mean, for example *eFriend* (someone you only know online), *eWaste* (to waste time online), *e-xcited* (excited because of something online). Have fast finishers tell the rest of the class their new words. The class can vote on which is the best or silliest word.

◁)) The Reading text is recorded for students to listen, read
72 and check their answers.

» PREPARE FOR THE EXAM TEACHING NOTES AND ANSWER KEY TB PAGE 253

3 Ask students, 'Which game did Koen play?' (*FIFA*) See if anyone knows about or plays this game. (It is the best-selling video sports game franchise in the world.) Have students name some other popular video games. Put students into groups to discuss the questions. Share ideas as a class. Ask students, 'Is it more difficult to be an eSports star than a sports star?' and 'Which eSport do you think you would be good at?'.

As an extension activity, tell students to work in groups and think of a new eSport and make a PowerPoint presentation (or a poster) about it. Students must describe what the eSport is and how you play it. (It could be based on one of the video games they have just discussed or something completely different.) They should give the rules and say why it will be popular. Students then listen to one another's presentations and vote for one eSport to go into the eOlympics.

1 Books closed. Read out the definitions and see if students can give you the words. Books open. Tell students to find the words they have trouble with in the article and match them to the definitions. Check as a class. Tell students that after *take part* you need the preposition *in* and give an example: 'In Unit 1 Grace and Daniel wanted to take part in the Duke of Edinburgh's Award.'.

Answers
1 f   2 d   3 b   4 e   5 a   6 c

2 Elicit the words: 'This person comes first in a competition' (*winner*), 'Someone on a sports team' (*player*) and 'Lionel Messi is a famous one' (*footballer*). Tell students to find the words and say what they mean using the words *win*, *play* and *football*. Explain the spelling rules to students.

Answers
winner – someone who wins
player – someone who plays
footballer – someone who plays football

3 Tell students to add *-er* to the words. Check as a class. Tell students to work in pairs and for each of these people say the name of someone they know or someone famous, for example, *Mrs Sanchez is a cleaner in our school.*

Answers
cleaner, climber, dancer, diver, golfer, photographer, runner, singer, skier, swimmer, teacher, worker

---

MIXED ABILITY

For students who have problems with spelling, use word games to make them familiar with the rules and common spellings of sounds. For example, to practise the consonant + vowel + consonant spelling, have students write one letter down, then add another letter in steps underneath until they make a word ending *-er*. For example:

s	r
sw	ru
swi	run
swim	runn
swimm	runne
swimme	runner
swimmer	

---

4 Have students make five sentences. Put them into pairs to compare their sentences. Have some students share their sentences with the class. To make this into a game, write the words from Exercise 1 spaced out on the left side of the board. Then write the words from Exercise 3 spaced out on the right side of the board. Give one student a ball. She throws the ball at the left side of the board and then at the right. The student has to make a sentence with the two words her balls came closest to. Repeat with different students.

≫ **VOCABULARY WORKSHEET UNIT 9**

LISTENING

 1 Tell students to look at the photo and ask, 'What kind of sport is this?' (*a mind sport*) Ask students what they think the game in the photo might be. Ask students to read the words in the box, say which ones are eSports, which ones are mind sports and which they think will be in the conversation. Play the recording for students to check their ideas.

Answers
You hear all of them except medal, prize and tournament.

2 Tell students to read the sentences and say whether they are right or wrong. Play the recording for students to check their answers. Ask them to correct the sentences that are wrong.

Answers
1 ✓
2 ✗ Dad doesn't think it's a good idea to have mind sports in the Olympics.
3 ✗ Lily says you have to use your brain too.
4 ✓
5 ✗ Lily says the Olympics are more famous.
6 ✓
7 ✗ Dad disagrees.

≫ **AUDIOSCRIPT TB PAGE 295**

TALKING POINTS

 Show the video and ask students to complete the video worksheet. Then, read the questions in the *Talking points* box and students answer the questions.

SPEAKING

1 Put students into groups to discuss the sentences. Monitor and encourage students to use the useful language. Share ideas as a class.

As an extension activity, get students to design their own puzzles for a minds sports competition.

Give an example of a number puzzle and a word puzzle:

Give the next number: 2, 5, 9, 14, 20, ? (27: start by adding 3, then add 1 more than the previous number each time)

Find a word for a part of the body. Put one letter on the start and one on the end to make a new word for a part of the body. (*heart*)

Then put students into groups to think of five more puzzles. Groups test their puzzles on another group.

COOLER

Write these puzzles on the board.

What turns everything around but does not move? (*a mirror*)

What are two things you cannot eat for dinner? (*breakfast and lunch*)

What is in the middle of nowhere? (*h, the letter*)

Is an old hundred-dollar bill (use your own currency) *better than a new one?* (*Yes, it is 99 dollars better.*)

VOCABULARY Sports vocabulary; Suffix -er

1 Find these words in the article, then match them to the definitions.

1 take part
2 tournament
3 fan
4 prize
5 champion
6 professional

a This person or team comes first in a competition.
b This person loves a sports star or team.
c This describes a person who earns money for something most people do as a hobby.
d This is a competition that includes several matches or games.
e You sometimes get this if you do well in a competition.
f This means to join other people in an activity.

2 Find these words in the text: *winner*, *player*, *footballer*. What do they mean?

> We can add *-er* to some verbs and nouns to make a person. If the spelling is vowel + consonant + vowel, you must double the last letter before adding *-er*.
> *win – winner*
> If the word already ends in e, add *-r*

3 Make people from these words.

clean   climb   dance   dive
golf   photograph   run   sing
ski   swim   teach   work

4 Make some sentences using at least one word from Exercise 1 and at least one word from Exercise 3. In pairs, compare your sentences.

> There were lots of photographers at the sports tournament.

1 You will hear a girl called Lily talking to her dad about eSports and mind sports. Which of these words do you think you will hear? Listen once and tick the ones you hear.

board games   body   brain
card games   chess competition
equipment   football   medal   prize
Olympics   tournament   video games

2 Read the sentences, then listen again. Decide if each sentence is right (✓) or wrong (✗).

1 Lily explains to Dad what eSports are.
2 Dad thinks it's a good idea to have mind sports in the Olympics.
3 Lily says fitness is the most important thing for sportspeople.
4 Dad agrees that thinking is important in sport.
5 Lily says some chess competitions are more famous than the Olympics.
6 Dad and Lily both think that Olympic medals are special.
7 Dad and Lily both think that chess will be in the Olympics one day.

TALKING POINTS

07 Watch the video and ask and answer the questions.
What board games do you have at home?
How often do you play board games?
Do you like playing chess? Are you good at it?
Do you think that games like chess should be in the Olympics? Why? / Why not?

SPEAKING

1 In small groups, talk about the sentences. Say if you agree with them or if you don't and say why. Use the phrases in the box to help you.

1 eSports are not sports because you don't have to be fit to do them.
2 It's a good idea to have eSports in the Olympics.
3 Thinking and using your brain is important in every sport.
4 Mind sports will be in the Olympics in ten years' time.

I think / I don't think …	That's true.
I agree / I don't agree …	I'm not sure.
I suppose so …	Maybe
I see!	

10 USEFUL WEBSITES

VOCABULARY AND READING

Relationships

1 Read the problems on the website. In pairs, discuss the problems and think of some advice for each person.

? ABOUT YOU

Do your friends or family ever have problems? What kind?

What do you do when you have a problem? Who do you talk to? Do you often try to find advice online?

TEEN TROUBLES

Got a problem and not sure who to ask for advice? Write to us and we will help! When you see this , click to hear some advice from Dr Mandy, our top teen expert!

I go to dance lessons with some close friends of mine. The teacher moved me to a higher-level group, but she says my friends have to stay in the lower level. I'm worried about moving to a new class without them. I'll really miss seeing them! What should I do?
Andrea, 13

 I am homeschooled and I don't spend much time with people my age. I am friends with some of my neighbours, and I have old friends from primary school, but they often forget to invite me when they go out. I have penfriends as well, but it's not the same as seeing people.
Ben, 15

My best friend won't stop copying me! I love wearing bright clothes and looking different from everyone else. But last month my friend started buying all the same things as me. Now we look exactly the same as each other!
Katy, 14

2 Listen to Dr Mandy giving three pieces of advice to the teenagers. Write the correct name beside each number.

1 _____   2 _____   3 _____

3 Listen again and make notes about the advice for each person. Was any of the advice the same as yours?

4 Match the people 1–10 to the descriptions a–j.

(EP)
1 guest
2 old friend
3 neighbour
4 close friend
5 member
6 contact
7 best friend
8 classmate
9 penfriend
10 relative

a You live near this person.
b This person is a visitor in your home.
c You have this person's details in your phone or online.
d This person belongs to a group or club.
e You like this person very much and you know each other well.
f You met this person a long time ago.
g This person is part of your family.
h This is your one special friend.
i You study with this person.
j You don't meet this person, but you write to them.

Listen and check. Then repeat.

5 In pairs, ask and answer the questions. Then write three more questions.

1 How many contacts do you have online?
2 Are you friendly with your neighbours?
3 How many of your relatives live near you?
4 Who do you miss when you go away on holiday?

6 With a different partner, ask and answer your new questions together.

10 USEFUL WEBSITES

Unit Overview

TOPIC	The internet
VOCABULARY AND READING	Relationships
	Teen troubles
PRONUNCIATION	gh
GRAMMAR	Verb patterns: gerunds and infinitives
READING	Six great websites for teenagers
VOCABULARY	Internet nouns and verbs
LISTENING	Young app developers talk about their work
WRITING	An email
EXAM TASKS	Reading Part 4; Writing Part 6

Resources

GRAMMAR REFERENCE AND PRACTICE: SB page 156; TB page 266

PREPARE FOR THE EXAM: SB pages on TB pages 240 and 242; TB pages 254 and 255

WORKBOOK: pages 40–43

PHOTOCOPIABLE WORKSHEETS: Grammar worksheet Unit 10; Vocabulary worksheet Unit 10

TEST GENERATOR: Unit test 10

WARMER

Word association. Write the word *winter* in the middle of the board and get students to tell you words and phrases associated with winter, for example, *cold, snow, my birthday, skiing*, and write them on the board.

Arrange students into pairs. You say a word and they have two minutes to write down associations. Example words: *teenager, the Olympics, English.*

Then join pairs to make groups of four and ask them to explain their associations. For example: *teenager – problems, because we have got a lot of them!*

⑦ ABOUT YOU

Books closed. Ask students to give you examples of problems, for example, bad marks at school, noisy neighbours, difficult decisions. Books open. Put students into groups to discuss problems. Then ask students for different ways of dealing with problems and list them on the board. Ask students which way works best and worst in each situation.

VOCABULARY AND READING

Relationships

1 Pre-teach **troubles** (troubles are problems you have). Have students read the problems. Ask some comprehension questions, for example, 'What sport does Andrea do?' (*dancing*), 'How does Ben feel?' (*lonely*) and 'Is Katy pleased with her friend?' (*no*). Then put students in pairs to discuss the problems and think of some advice for each person. Remind students that *advice* is

uncountable; we say *some advice* or *a piece of advice*. Share ideas as a class.

🔊 74 The Reading text is recorded for students to listen, read and check their answers.

🔊 75 2 Play the recording for students to match the name to each piece of advice.

Answers
1 Ben 2 Katy 3 Andrea

🔊 75 3 Have students listen again and make notes. Remind students that notes are not full sentences, just the important information. Ask students if Mandy's advice was the same as theirs and if they agree with her. As an extension activity, ask students to write a reply from one of the teenagers to Mandy, saying if they agree with her advice and why or why not.

>> **AUDIOSCRIPT TB PAGE 295**

MIXED ABILITY

Some students will need more guidance on making notes. Play the first piece of advice again and show these notes on the board:

studying alone isn't easy

think about joining some clubs

remember to wait for people to call you

Say, 'These notes about advice are not very good. Why?' Explain or elicit the reasons.

studying alone isn't easy – this is not advice

think about joining some clubs – this could be written more simply, e.g. *join clubs*

remember to wait for people to call you – wrong information, the opposite is true

Play the other two pieces of advice for students to make their own notes individually. In pairs, students compare them – first as notes and then with their advice in Exercise 1.

4 Books closed. Ask students to make a list of the last ten people they wrote or spoke to, for example *Mario, Mrs Robinson, Dad*, etc. They should then categorise these people by relationship, for example *friends, relatives, teachers*. Books open. Students do the matching task. Play the recording for students to check.

Tell students to cover up the people with their hand, read the description and say who it is. Ask students to give you an example about how they know or met each of these people, for example, *When it was my birthday last month I had a party and there were eight guests.*

🔊 76 #### Answers
The answers are recorded for students to check and then repeat.
1 b 2 f 3 a 4 e 5 d 6 c 7 h 8 i 9 j 10 g

CONTINUED ON PAGE 114

5   To demonstrate, get students to ask you the questions. Reply in full sentences:

Student: *How many contacts do you have online?*

Teacher: *I've got a lot, but most of them are not really close friends.*

Put students into pairs to answer the questions and then write additional questions.

6   Put students into new pairs to ask and answer the questions they wrote in Exercise 5. Have some students ask their questions to the whole class.

 PRONUNCIATION | *gh*

 7   Write this sentence on the board and see if any of the students can pronounce it correctly: *I th__ought__ my n__eigh__bour on the r__igh__t had __eigh__t da__ugh__ters.* Ask how many different sounds for vowel + *gh* there are (*three*).

Play the recording for students to listen to the different sounds. Have students try to put the words into the correct column.

Play the recording for students to check their answers. Play the recording again for students to repeat.

Elicit from students that in all these examples, except *enough*, the rule is that *gh* is silent after a vowel. Tell students to think of other words which could go in each column, for example /aɪ/ light, /eɪ/ weigh, /ʌf/ tough, /ɔː/ ought.

Answers

The answers are recorded for students to check and then repeat.
/aɪ/ night: bright, flight, right
/eɪ/ eight: neighbour, straight
/ʌf/ rough: enough
/ɔː/ bought: caught, daughter, thought

GRAMMAR | Verb patterns: gerunds and infinitives

1   Tell students that when a verb is followed by another verb, the second verb can be either a *to*-infinitive or a gerund (*-ing* form). They just have to learn which verbs take an infinitive and which take a gerund. There is sometimes a subtle difference between the infinitive and the gerund; compare *I tried __to warn__ Jack but he was out* and *I tried __warning__ Jack but he did it anyway*, but this is beyond the level. Have students read the examples then complete the rules. Check as a class.

Answers

1 about, at, for   2 try, decide, forget   3 stop, miss

2   Tell students to read the sentences and tell you the form.

Answers

verb + *-ing*

>> **GRAMMAR REFERENCE AND PRACTICE ANSWER KEY TB PAGE 266**

3   Tell students to look back at Exercise 1 to help them choose the correct form. Check answers as a class.

Answers

1 to buy   2 Waiting   3 carrying   4 to be   5 Swimming
6 sitting   7 running   8 to get / getting   9 getting   10 Saving

FAST FINISHERS

Fast finishers think of three sentences beginning *I'm thinking of …* , for example *I'm thinking of changing my phone* and compare with other fast finishers.

4   Tell students to correct the sentences. Check answers as a class. As a variation, have students close their books and read out the sentences for students to correct.

Answers

1   I hope **to** see you very soon and I hope that you like my mobile phone.
2   I want **to** write about my life.
3   I like **to play/playing** computer games best.
4   You can get to my house **by** taking the number 6 bus.
5   I think it's better to finish **studying** before we go out.
6   Would you mind **coming** with me to the shops?

5   To demonstrate write an example on the board:

I'm worried about _____ a lot of money. (*spending*)

Tell students to complete the sentences. Check answers as a class.

Answers

1 to make   2 Eating   3 to improve   4 Watching   5 playing
6 Passing   7 to come   8 Chatting   9 going   10 Spending

6   Tell students that you have a problem. They must listen and write down the infinitives and gerunds: 'It's my best friend's birthday soon and I'm thinking of __getting__ her a present. It's difficult __to decide__ what __to buy__ because she's got everything. I don't want __to give__ her money because she won't want __to take__ it. I don't mind __spending__ about 30 dollars. Have you got any advice?'

Students must give you advice, for example *Take her to a nice café.*

Arrange students into groups to do the same thing with a problem from Exercise 5 or a new one.

Each group then writes the most interesting problem and advice down and puts it on the classroom wall. Students go round all the problems and write some extra advice underneath.

>> **GRAMMAR WORKSHEET UNIT 10**

COOLER

Write on the board *Friendship is …* and give some examples with gerunds to finish the sentence, for example, *doing things together* and *being there when your friend needs you*. Get some more examples from the class. Arrange students into pairs. You give them a sentence starter and they have two minutes to think of ways of ending the sentence using gerunds.

Example sentence starters: Love is … , Happiness is … , My idea of a perfect weekend is …

🔊 **7** Listen to the words and repeat them. Then
77 put them into the correct column.

bright	caught	daughter
enough	flight	neighbour
right	straight	thought

/aɪ/	/eɪ/	/ʌf/	/ɔ:/
night	**eight**	**rough**	**bought**

🔊 Listen and check. Then repeat.
78

GRAMMAR **Verb patterns: gerunds and infinitives**

1 Look at the example sentences. Then complete
the rules about verb patterns.

I'm worried about moving to a new class.
You'll get better at dancing.
Thank you for writing to the website.

Try to talk to her about how you feel.
If you decide to do this, you can give her advice.
They often forget to invite me when they go out.

My best friend won't stop copying me.
I'll really miss seeing them.

1 We use the **gerund** (*-ing* form) after
prepositions: _about_, _____, _____
(also *by, of, with*, etc.)
2 We use the **infinitive** + *to* after some verbs:
try, _____, _____ (also *choose,
learn, hope, plan, need, want*)
3 We can use the **gerund** after some verbs:
stop, _____ (also *finish, don't mind*)
4 We can use either the **gerund** or the **infinitive**
after these verbs: *start, begin, enjoy, like,
love, prefer*.

2 Look at three more examples. What form do we
use when the verb is the subject of a sentence?

Studying alone isn't easy.
Leaving your friends behind is difficult.
Waiting for them to contact you first isn't always
a good idea.

» **GRAMMAR REFERENCE AND PRACTICE PAGE 156**

3 Choose the correct form of the verb. In one
sentence, both forms are possible.

1 My friend decided *buy* / *to buy* a new pair
of sunglasses.
2 *Wait*/ *Waiting* for people makes me angry.
3 I helped the teacher by *carry* / *carrying*
her books.
4 One day, I hope *to be* / *being* a doctor.
5 *Swim* / *Swimming* in the sea on a hot day
is lovely.
6 I don't mind *to sit* / *sitting* by the window.
7 I think *to run* / *running* is the best kind of
exercise.
8 Everyone loves *to get* / *getting* presents!
9 I'm thinking of *get* / *getting* a new poster for
my room.
10 *Saving* / *Save* a bit of pocket money every
week is a really good idea.

4 Correct the mistakes in the sentences.

👁 1 I hope see you very soon, and I hope that you
like my mobile phone.
2 I want write about my life.
3 I like play computer games best.
4 You can get to my house taking the number
6 bus.
5 I think it's better to finish study before we go out.
6 Would you mind come with me to the shops?

5 Complete each sentence with a verb from the box
in the gerund or infinitive.

chat	come	eat	go	improve
pass	play	spend	watch	make

1 We need _____ a cake, but we don't know
how to do it.
2 _____ chocolate isn't very good for you.
3 I need _____ the marks I get in maths. Mine
are terrible.
4 _____ TV late at night makes you tired the
next day.
5 I'm angry with my neighbour for _____ his
music really late at night.
6 _____ my exam is very important to me.
7 Jack didn't want _____ to my party.
8 _____ with friends is really good fun.
9 My best friend spends all her free time _____
to the shops with the new girl in our class.
10 _____ a lot of time indoors is quite boring.

6 In groups of three, each person writes a few
sentences about a problem. Listen to each other's
problems and give advice. Who has the most
interesting problem? Who gives the best advice?

1 Tick (✓) the things you use websites and apps for.

- playing games
- watching videos
- chatting to friends
- finding information
- doing schoolwork
- reading articles
- listening to music
- sharing photos, stories, etc.

2 What are your three favourite websites or apps? In pairs, compare your answers.

3 Read what the people say. Which of the activities in Exercise 1 do they want to do?

1 I'm working on a project about the human body at the moment and I'm interested in learning about animals. I like having fun online too.

2 I'm hoping to become a writer one day. I'd like to put my stories online and discuss ideas with people my age.

3 I like to know what is happening in the world. I'm also interested in music and would like to learn more about my favourite stars.

I'm interested in nature and wildlife and want to learn about ways to help the planet. I like making short films and want to share them with others. **4**

4 Read about six websites and decide which is best for each person. In pairs, compare your answers.

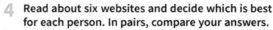

SIX GREAT WEBSITES FOR TEENAGERS

A EcoCentral

This **site** is all about looking after the Earth. There are facts about different animals as well as information about forests, deserts and oceans. You can **upload** your own videos onto the site for everyone to see.

B TeenPress

This is one of the best sites on **the web** for teenagers who love writing. You can share your work with others, and there is a **message board** where you can chat about things that are important to you.

C ChannelTwenty

On this site, you can watch a daily news programme and **search** for information about big news stories. There are also videos on different subjects, articles about famous bands, games and competitions. The app is free and works on all kinds of smartphones.

D ScienceZone

There's lots of information on this site about maths, chemistry and biology. You can 'visit' some of the world's most famous museums and watch wildlife via webcams. There are also some very cool games, such as *Save the Planet*.

E Tune-in

There are millions of songs on this site for you to **download** or listen to online. You can **save** your favourite songs in your own list. If you're in a band, you can **record** your music and upload it. The website is large, but the **menu** is easy to use. The app that goes with it is excellent.

F Inside-the-cover

Finding out about your favourite writers is easy on this site. There are lots of interesting articles and information about the latest books. You can read **blogs** by well-known writers and **post** questions and messages to them. There are **links** to other sites too.

60　UNIT 10

WARMER

Give students two minutes to write down things they love and things they hate. For example, *I love singing in the shower. I hate getting up early.* They then compare their answers in pairs before sharing ideas with the class.

BACKGROUND INFORMATION

The internet is a network which connects computers so that they can communicate with one another. The World Wide Web is a way, not the only way, of accessing information through the internet. A British research scientist, Tim Berners-Lee, developed the Web in the 1980s and he thought of the name World Wide Web. The first users of the Web were researchers and scientists but early websites included the webcomic *Doctor Fun*, *WWW Useless Pages* and *Pizza Hut*.

An app is usually used to mean a computer program designed to run on a mobile device like a smartphone rather than a desktop computer or a web browser. One of the first apps was a game called *Snake* in 1998.

1 Write your favourite websites or apps (they don't need to be English language ones) on the board and ask students to say what they know about each one, for example it is for listening to music, and if they use it themselves. Make sure students remember how to pronounce website addresses (from page 12). Tell students to tick what they use websites or apps for. They could add other categories if they need to, for example *downloading films*.

2 Students make their own list of their three favourite websites or apps. Arrange students into pairs. They should describe what the websites are and why they like them. Then they should go through each website function in Exercise 1 and say if they like doing these kinds of thing. For example: *I don't like playing games much but I know a great site for playing chess, it's …*

3 Demonstrate with an example on the board:

I know a lot of people and I can't phone them all, so this is great for finding out what's going on with everyone. (*chatting to friends*)

Students then match each text to the activities in Exercise 1. Check answers as a class.

Answers

1 reading articles, finding information, playing games
2 sharing stories, chatting to other people
3 reading articles, listening to music, finding information
4 reading articles, finding information, sharing and watching videos

4 Ask students if they know about any websites which would be interesting for each person. Then tell students to read about the websites and match them to the people. You could do the first one together. 'Are any of these websites about the human body, animals and fun things to do online?' (*D – biology, wildlife, cool games*)

Students should underline the key words and phrases in Exercise 3 and the corresponding ones in the websites which give the answer. They compare their answers in pairs. Check answers as a class. Ask students which website would be most interesting for them.

As an extension activity, ask students if they know a website which would be useful for the following people: a foreigner who has just moved to your country; a teenager who is looking for a part-time job; a parent with six children; an elderly person who has just learned to use a computer. If students don't know of any websites for this, they could do some research on the internet at home and tell the rest of the class in the next lesson.

Answers

1 D   2 B   3 C   4 A

FAST FINISHERS

Write these comments from teenagers on the board and have students match them to the websites.

I've just got an answer to my question from J. K. Rowling! (*Inside-the-Cover*)

I've now got almost 100 pieces of music on my play list! (*Tune-in*)

I've just read your poem and I love it! (*TeenPress*)

It felt like the lion was in my bedroom! (*ScienceZone*)

I can't believe that Bruce Willis is President! (*Channel Twenty*)

I never knew that Russia has the most forests! (*EcoCentral*)

As a class activity, you could ask students to give more information about each comment, for example, what question the teenager wrote to Rowling and what her answer was.

🔊 79 The Reading text is recorded for students to listen, read and check their answers.

1 Tell students to look at the blue words in the texts and decide if they are nouns or verbs. They then match the nouns with the meanings 1–6 and complete sentences 7–12 with the verbs. Check answers as a class.

Answers
The answers are recorded for students to check and then repeat.
1 the web 2 message board 3 link 4 site 5 blog 6 menu
7 record 8 search 9 post 10 upload 11 download 12 save

>> **VOCABULARY WORKSHEET UNIT 10**

PREPARE FOR THE EXAM

A2 KEY FOR SCHOOLS Reading Part 4

2 Briefly review what students need to do in this part of the exam and if necessary read out the A2 Key for Schools box on TB page 93.

Remind students that the three words will be similar to each other but used in different ways. Students should read the words around the gap very carefully and may need to think about grammar to get the right answer. For example, in number 2, only B and C go after the preposition *on* and only C makes sense.

Give students a time limit to read the text and then ask, 'What is Catherine's website for?' (*making friends*) Tell students to read the text again and choose the answers. Check answers as a class. Ask students if they would like to use MeetMe.com.

Answers
1A 2C 3B 4A 5B 6C

 **LISTENING**

 1 Play the recording for students to match the speakers to the kind of app. Check answers as a class.

Answers
Speaker 1 – c
Speaker 2 – a
Speaker 3 – b

 2 Play the recording again for students to complete the table. Check answers as a class.

Answers
Speaker 1: 11, 99p, 100, play a physics game
Speaker 2: 15, £1.50, 30, make a list of your jobs
Speaker 3: 12, free, 70, learn about geography, do quizzes, test yourself

>> **AUDIOSCRIPT TB PAGE 295**

 WRITING

PREPARE FOR THE EXAM

A2 KEY FOR SCHOOLS
Writing Part 6

In this part, students have to write a note or email of at least 25 words. They are given the context and three content points to cover.

Tip Students must read the task carefully as they must cover all three of the content points in their answer.

 PREPARE TO WRITE
Writing Part 6 An email

GET READY Tell students to re-read the description of the websites and pay attention to how the sentences start. Check answers as a class.

Answers
1 *here is / There are …* is used seven times to start sentences.
2 *You can …* is used five times to start sentences.
3 *This …* is used twice to start sentences.
Other ways: *On this site …* , *The app/website is …* , *The app that …* , *If …* , *Finding out …*

PLAN Students identify the three content points and make notes.

WRITE Tell students they can use the website descriptions in Reading Exercise **4** to help them.

IMPROVE Write these sentences on the board and ask students to find the mistakes.

There is many photos of animals. (*There ~~is~~ are*)

To search for information is easy. (*~~To search~~ Searching*)

Students then check their own and their partner's work.

Model answer
Dear Sal,
My favourite website is DC Comics. It's about Superman and other super heroes. You can get information about the characters and there are games too. I like it because I love Superman!
Dan

MIXED ABILITY
Write a frame for the email on the board. Weaker students can then fill in the gaps.
My favourite website is _____. This is about _____.
You can _____. I like it because _____.

>> **PREPARE FOR THE EXAM TEACHING NOTES AND ANSWER KEY TB PAGE 255**

COOLER
Give students a quiz on vocabulary from Units 6–10. Read the definitions and they must write down the word.
1 A surface which is not rough. (*smooth*, Unit 6)
2 A small light you carry in your hand. (*torch*, Unit 7)
3 This keeps the rain out of your home. (*roof*, Unit 8)
4 You put things you don't want in this. (*bin*, Unit 8)
5 A game you play on a table. (*board game*, Unit 9)
6 Someone who lives next to you. (*neighbour*, Unit 10)

VOCABULARY — Internet nouns and verbs

1 Look at the words in the texts on page 60. Find six nouns and six verbs.

Match the nouns to definitions 1–6.

1 This is all the pages online that you can visit.
2 You can write things here for others to read and reply to.
3 If you click on these, they take you to another website.
4 This is another way of saying 'website'.
5 These are online diaries.
6 You look at this list to choose which part of a website to visit.

Use the verbs to complete the sentences.

7 You can _____ a short voice message and then share it with friends.
8 You can _____ for information online by typing a word into a box.
9 You can _____ a message or question on the internet for others to read.
10 You can _____ a file from your computer onto a website.
11 You can _____ a file from the internet to your computer.
12 You can _____ a document or other file on your computer so you don't lose it.

🔊 **Listen and check. Then repeat.**
80

✓ PREPARE FOR THE EXAM

Reading Part 4

2 For each question, choose the correct answer.

Catherine Cook

Catherine Cook was only 15 when she started myYearbook.com. She had the idea of creating a new **(1)** _____ to help people find friends. She also had lots of great ideas about how to make myYearbook.com different from everything else on the **(2)** _____ .

myYearbook.com is now called MeetMe.com. When you join, you fill in a form and **(3)** _____ a photo of yourself to the site. After that, you can start **(4)** _____ for friends to add. It's not difficult to explore the site and **(5)** _____ people. You can play games, post **(6)** _____ , do quizzes and more. It's available on the web and as an app.

1 **A** website	**B** computer	**C** file
2 **A** information	**B** link	**C** internet
3 **A** record	**B** upload	**C** copy
4 **A** searching	**B** finding	**C** missing
5 **A** talk	**B** contact	**C** speak
6 **A** screens	**B** menus	**C** messages

LISTENING

🔊 **1** Listen to three young app developers talking about their work. Match each speaker to what the app they made helps you do.
81

Speaker 1	**a** use your time well
Speaker 2	**b** learn things
Speaker 3	**c** play games

🔊 **2** Listen again and complete the table.
81

	Speaker		
	1	2	3
How old was each person when they wrote their first app?			
How much is it?			
How many people download it per week?			
What can you do on the app?			

WRITING

✎ PREPARE TO WRITE

Writing Part 6   An email

GET READY Count how many times these phrases are used to start sentences in the texts in Reading Exercise 4. Then find three other ways of starting sentences in the texts.

1 There is / There are …
2 You can …
3 This …

PLAN You are going to reply to this email from your penfriend.

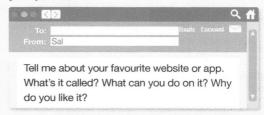

To:
From: Sal

Tell me about your favourite website or app. What's it called? What can you do on it? Why do you like it?

Make notes to help you answer each question.

✓ **WRITE** Write your email. Use the descriptions of the websites in Reading Exercise 4 to help you. Try to begin each sentence with a different phrase.

Begin *Dear Sal*, and end with your name.

IMPROVE In pairs, read each other's emails. Check that you both included all the information from your plan and that you started each sentence with a different phrase.

≫ **PREPARE FOR THE EXAM PAGE 126**

CULTURE

THE BEAUTIFUL GAME

1 Discuss the questions with your partner.

1 Do you like playing or watching football?
2 Do many girls and women play football in your country?
3 Do you ever watch girls or women playing football on TV or live?

2 What can you see in the photos? Read the text and check your ideas. Match the photos A–D to the paragraphs 1–4.

A SPORT FOR ALL ?

1 In 1920, there was a match between two women's football teams at Everton's football ground in Liverpool. Around 53,000 people went to watch it! Just a few years earlier, during the First World War, many men were fighting abroad. This meant there were no football players and no important games. People loved the sport and wanted to watch it, so women started to play. Some of the best players, such as Lily Parr, are still famous today. She became famous when she was only 14 and scored 43 goals in one season.

2 A year later, in 1921, the Football Association (FA) decided to stop women's football because they thought it was not a sport that women should play for payment. Fifty years later, in 1971, women could finally play football as a profession and not just as a hobby. However, it wasn't until 1993 that the English FA recognised international women's football. After that, women could play in competitions with other countries.

3 Nowadays, nearly three million girls and women play football in the UK, and there are 100,000 registered players who can play official tournaments. There are only about 200 professional players, and many have to do other work to earn enough money, but you can often see women's football on television. They sometimes play in really famous places, such as Wembley Stadium in London.

4 In schools, girls and boys play football in the playground – there are teams with both boy and girl players. Recently, all-girl teams are playing against all-boy teams. So football is really a sport for everyone!

62 CULTURE

CULTURE

Learning Objectives

- The students learn about the history and development of women's football and about different types of football.
- In the project stage, students find out about the history of a sport in their country and make a presentation about it for the class.

Vocabulary

ground games profession tournaments stadium playground

Resources

CULTURE VIDEO AND CULTURE VIDEO WORKSHEET: Football

BACKGROUND INFORMATION

The first men's football World Cup was in 1930 and the first women's World Cup was in 1991 in China. In 1988 the Federation of International Football Associations (FIFA) organised an international women's tournament in China and the success of this led to the first World Cup three years later, although it was officially a World Championship rather than World Cup. In this first World Cup the USA beat Norway 2:1 in the final in front of 65,000 fans. For the first time in a FIFA competition there were six female referees (women have also gone on to referee professional men's matches). Like the men's competition, the Women's World Cup is held every four years and there is a qualification stage. The USA has won the most World Cups and two players, Miraildes Maciel Mota of Brazil and Homare Sawa of Japan, have played in six World Cups, a record not matched by any men.

The success of the Women's World Cup shows that there is greater participation by women in sport and appreciation of their performances but unfortunately there is still gender inequality. For example, the modern Olympics began in 1896 but it was not until London 2012 that women competed in every sport (including football). While there has always been a marathon race (42 kilometres) for men, up to the Moscow Olympics in 1980, the furthest that female athletes could race was 3000 metres! Wages and prize money have also been an issue with men typically receiving far more money than women in the same sport. For example, the men's professional golf tour in the USA offers more than five times the prize money of the women's tour. There are exceptions, for example from 2007 the Wimbledon and French Open tennis championships started to offer equal prize money to men and women, but the reality is that in many sports women have to earn money in other ways even if they are at the very top of their sport. Media interest in women's sports is probably the key to gender inequality (in the UK only about 20% of sport on television is women's sport) and the good news is that social networking is giving sports women a wider audience.

WARMER

Tell students this story.

'A father and his son are driving home when the car suddenly goes off the road and crashes. The son is quickly taken to hospital because he needs an operation. The surgeon comes into the room, sees him and screams, "My son, my son!" Who is the surgeon?' (*the boy's mother*)

After students tell you the answer, tell them that people often take a long time to work it out. Ask students what this says abut our attitude to women.

1. Books closed. Ask students to find out, on mobile devices or by asking one another, which of these countries has not hosted a men's or women's World Cup: Australia, England, Italy, South Africa, the USA, Uruguay (*Australia*). Books open. Put students into pairs to discuss the questions. Share ideas as a class. Ask students to think of a country which has never hosted the World Cup but deserves to and explain why.

2. Ask students, 'Why do you think football is so popular around the world?'. Tell students to describe the photos. Give students a time limit to read the text and match the photos to the paragraphs. Check as a class. Ask students which men's football teams are popular in their country and whether they also have a women's team, for example Manchester City has both a men's and women's team. Ask students to name some players that they particularly like or don't like.

Answers

1 B   2 C   3 A   4 D

FAST FINISHERS

Tell fast finishers to think of three new rules or changes to the rules to make football games more interesting, for example, you get two points for scoring a goal with your head.

3 Have students read the text again and answer the questions. Check as a class.

Answers

1 53,000 **2** because the men were fighting abroad
3 because the FA decided to stop women's football
4 in 1993 **5** no **6** no

MIXED ABILITY

Tell weaker students which paragraph to look in for each answer.

Question 1 – paragraph 1

Question 2 – paragraph 1

Question 3 – paragraph 2

Question 4 – paragraph 2

Question 5 – paragraph 3

Question 6 – paragraph 4

4 Tell students to match the words to the definitions. Check as a class. Elicit or explain the differences between the words in 1 and 2: a **ground** is the area on which people play; a **stadium** is the playing area and the building around it; a **playground** is where children play at school; a **game** is a match between two teams but a **tournament** is a series of matches between different teams. Ask students which is the best stadium they know.

Answers

1 ground, stadium, playground **2** games, tournaments
3 profession

🔊 **82** The Reading text is recorded for students to listen, read and check their answers.

📃 TALKING POINTS

Books closed. Read out a list of sports and activities and ask students to put them in three columns: more popular with men, more popular with women, popular with both. Include football in the list. Students compare their answers in pairs. Books open. Students discuss the questions. Share ideas as a class. Ask students how schools can encourage both boys and girls to do sports.

🔊 **83 5** Ask students if they know about any other types of football, for example beach football. (You can tell students that the first FIFA Beach Football World Cup was held in 1995 and won by Brazil.) Put students into pairs and ask them to try and complete the table with their own ideas. You will probably need to tell students that futsal is a type of five-a-side football played indoors on a hard surface. Play the recording and then check as a class. Ask students which of these types of football they would like to watch or try.

Answers

1 1920 **2** indoor **3** Spain **4** 1993 **5** indoor
6 10 (5 in each team) **7** Brazil

» **AUDIOSCRIPT TB PAGE 296**

PROJECT *The history of a sport*

Tell students that they are going to find out about the history of a sport in their country and present this to the class. Tell students that it could be an international sport which is played everywhere, like football, or it could be specific to their country, for example Sambo, a martial art similar to judo, in Russia. Put students into groups and have them decide which sport they want to find out about. It's a good idea for groups to tell you their sport at this point so that you can make sure there is a variety of sports. Each group should decide who is going to get which information. Students could get information from the internet, reference books or just by asking other people (if they have friends who do this sport). Students can get the information out of class but they should design the poster with text, pictures and photos in class. Each group should practise before they actually give the presentation to the whole class. There should be time at the end of each presentation for comments or questions. Give the class feedback on the content and language of the presentations.

PROJECT EXTENSION

Tell students to make a questionnaire about all the sports presented and give that questionnaire to another class. Put students into groups to think about what questions should be included. Put some examples on the board:

Which of these sports do you do?

Which of these sports do you watch?

Do you think both men and women can do this sport?

As a class, decide on the best questions. Divide the questions up so that each group makes a different set. Put all the questions together and then have students give the questionnaire to the other class. Students report back the results.

▶ **CULTURE VIDEO:** Football
08 When students have completed the lesson, they can watch the video and complete the worksheet.

COOLER

Arrange students into small circles. One student says a sport or activity, the next says another sport or activity beginning with the last letter of the first word, and so on, around the circle. For example, hockey – yoga – athletics – skiing. If nobody can think of a sport beginning with the last letter, they could try with the second to last (for example, skiing – netball). See which group can make the longest chain of words.

3 **Read the text again and answer the questions.**

1 How many people went to watch the women's football match in Liverpool in 1920?
2 Why did many women start playing football during the First World War?
3 Why did women stop playing football after 1921?
4 When did the Football Association in England allow women to play in international competitions?
5 Do professional women players receive a lot of money nowadays?
6 Do boys and girls always play in separate football teams?

4 **Match the highlighted words in the text to the definitions.**

1 three words for a place or places where people can play football
2 two words for football competitions
3 one word that means 'job'

 TALKING POINTS

Are some sports in your country only for girls or only for boys?
Which ones are played only by girls or only by boys?

5 **Look at the table about different types of football. In pairs, try to complete the gaps.**

	When people first played it	Number of players	Indoors or outdoors	Where people play it most
Table football	1	Usually two or four	Indoors	Europe and the USA
Futsal	1930	ten (five in each team)	2	South America and 3 ....
FIFA video game	4	Maximum 8	5	All over the world
Football for the blind	1920s	6	Both indoors and outdoors	7 ....

🔊 **Listen and check. Complete the information you didn't know.**
83

PROJECT *The history of a sport*

Find out about the history of a sport in your country. Make a poster to present the information to the class. Use pictures and photos to make the poster more interesting. Include information about:

• when and where it started
• who plays the sport: only men, only women or both
• some famous teams or players
• what competitions there are for this sport

Present your poster to the class.

11 CITY LIVING

 ABOUT YOU

What are the three biggest cities in your country?
What are they famous for?
What's good or bad about living in cities?

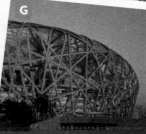

VOCABULARY AND LISTENING

Places in a city

1 Think about what can you do at the places in the box. Write five questions. Then test your partner.

café	church	hospital	library
museum	park	police station	
post office	restaurant	shop	
sports centre	theatre	train station	
university			

> Where do you go to buy a stamp?

> A post office. What do you use a bridge for?

2 Match the words in the box to photos A–L.

EP

art gallery	cathedral	embassy
fountain	mosque	old town	palace
shopping area	skyscraper	stadium
statue	temple	

 Listen and check.
84

3 In pairs, talk about the city where you live, or your capital city. What things from Exercises 1 and 2 does it have? What are their names?

4 What countries are these cities in? Which are capital cities? What are they famous for?

Beijing	Cairo	London	Madrid
Mexico City	Mumbai	New Delhi	
New York	Paris	Rio de Janeiro	
Rome	San Francisco	Tokyo	

5 Listen to the quiz. Match the questions to the names of the cities.
85

Question 1	Mumbai
Question 2	Tokyo
Question 3	Rio de Janeiro
Question 4	Paris
Question 5	New York
Question 6	Beijing

6 Read the sentences and write the name of the city. Then listen again and check.
85

1 It's the largest city in the world.
2 Every year, there's a big carnival here.
3 Lots of films are made here.
4 The city has a lot of bridges.
5 The Olympic Games were in this city in 2016.
6 It has a statue that's known around the world.
7 It's the second-biggest city in China.
8 Its most famous cathedral is on an island.

64 UNIT 11

11 CITY LIVING

Unit Overview

TOPIC	The city
VOCABULARY	Places in a city
AND LISTENING	World cities quiz
GRAMMAR	Determiners
PRONUNCIATION	*the*
READING	Signs, notices and messages
VOCABULARY	Uncountable nouns
LISTENING	Six short conversations
SPEAKING	Making requests in different situations
EXAM TASKS	Reading Part 1

Resources

GRAMMAR REFERENCE AND PRACTICE: SB page 157; TB page 266

PREPARE FOR THE EXAM: SB page on TB pages 236–237;
TB page 252

WORKBOOK: pages 44–47

VIDEO AND VIDEO WORKSHEET: Favourite cities

PHOTOCOPIABLE WORKSHEETS: Grammar worksheet Unit 11;
Vocabulary worksheet Unit 11

TEST GENERATOR: Unit test 11

WARMER

Write the word CITY on the board. Tell students to make a new word by changing two letters, for example, CATS. Have students do the same with CATS, for example, PETS. Put students into pairs and give them three minutes to continue this. The pair which has made the most words is the winner.

⑦ ABOUT YOU

Have students answer the questions in pairs then share ideas as a class.

BACKGROUND INFORMATION

Since 1950 there has been massive growth in the number of people living in cities. For example, in Spain the city population has increased from about 50% to 80% of the total population; in Venezuela, from 45% to 95%.

Mythical cities include El Dorado, a city of gold and treasure said to be in South America; Vineta, which angry gods sank to the bottom of the Baltic sea; Biringan in the Philippines, where the creatures who live there can take human shape; Gotham City, home of Batman.

The Monopoly game was originally based in Atlantic City in the USA. There are now versions for cities in more than 100 countries.

Cities in Space may be far in the future but some people take the idea seriously. The UAE government are building a prototype Space city on Earth before they build the real thing on Mars.

VOCABULARY AND LISTENING

Places in a city

1 Demonstrate the activity by asking your own questions, for example 'Where can you book a table?' (*a restaurant*). Students write five questions individually, then they get into pairs to ask each other.

2 Elicit some of the words, for example, 'a very tall building' (*skyscraper*). Have students match the words to the photos. Check answers as a class.

84

Answers

The answers are recorded for students to check and then repeat.
A statue B skyscraper C shopping area D old town
E art gallery F mosque G stadium H fountain I embassy
J temple K palace L cathedral

3 Put students into pairs to talk about their city or capital city. Have some students tell the whole class.

4 To demonstrate, ask where other cities are and why they are famous, for example, Santiago (*Chile – it is surrounded by mountains*). Put students into pairs to tell one another about the cities in the box. Check answers and ask students what else they know about the cities.

Answers

Cities in capital letters are capital cities.
BEIJING – China CAIRO – Egypt LONDON – the UK
MADRID – Spain MEXICO CITY – Mexico Mumbai – India
NEW DELHI – India New York – the USA PARIS – France
Rio de Janeiro – Brazil ROME – Italy San Francisco – the USA
TOKYO – Japan
Students' own answers

FAST FINISHERS

Fast finishers find out the language and currency of each country, for example, China – Chinese, the yuan.

85
5 Read out this text: 'This is a very old city. Two thousand years ago people spoke Latin here. It has some very old temples and famous churches. Which city is it?' (*Rome*).

Play the recording for students to listen and match the questions to the cities. Check answers as a class.

Answers

Question 1 – Beijing Question 2 – Paris
Question 3 – New York Question 4 – Rio de Janeiro
Question 5 – Tokyo Question 6 – Mumbai

6 Tell students to read the sentences and write the name of the city. Play the recording again for students to check. Ask students which of these cities they would like to visit.

Answers

1 Tokyo 2 Rio de Janeiro 3 Mumbai 4 Paris
5 Rio de Janeiro 6 New York 7 Beijing 8 Paris

>> **AUDIOSCRIPT TB PAGE 296**

GRAMMAR | Determiners

1 Books closed. Say, 'This is a city in England. The city has a famous football team and was the home of the best pop group in the world, The Beatles. Which city is it?' (*Liverpool*). Then say, 'First, I said <u>a</u> city and then <u>the</u> city. Why?' (*First you say a, then you say the when you say the word again.*), 'Did I say best pop group or <u>the</u> best pop group?' (*the best*) and 'Why?' (*We use the with superlatives.*). Tell students to read the sentences and complete the rules. Check answers as a class.

> **Answers**
> We use *a/an* to introduce something for the first time.
> We use *the* to talk about something already mentioned.

2 Fill in the first gap together. Ask, 'Why is it <u>a</u> great holiday?' (*Rosa talks about the holiday for the first time.*). You can also tell students that *a/an* is common before nouns used in descriptions, as in gap 10. Students then work alone. Afterwards, in pairs, the students should explain their answers to each other. Check answers as a class.

> **Answers**
> 1 a 2 the 3 a 4 an 5 the 6 the 7 the 8 the 9 a 10 a

PRONUNCIATION | *the*

🔊 **3** Play the recording for the students to listen and repeat. Ask if they can work out the rule. Check that they know what a vowel and a consonant are. Ask, 'Are /e/ and /əʊ/ vowel sounds or consonant sounds?' (*vowel sounds*) and 'And /p/ and /z/?' (*consonant sounds*). Tell students there may also be a linking sound similar to /j/ between /ði:/ and the following vowel sound, e.g. the oldest = /ði:jəʊldɪst/.

> **Answers**
> /ði:/ before a vowel sound
> /ðə/ before a consonant sound

4 Demonstrate with *the embassy* /ði:/ and *the Trevi Fountain* /ðə/. Have students put the words in the table. Play the recording for students to check and repeat.

🔊 **Answers**
87
> *The answers are recorded for students to check and then repeat.*
> /ði:/ the apple, the Arctic, the Earth, the Indian Ocean, the orange, the umbrella
> /ðə/ the dog, the North Sea, the River Nile, the Statue of Liberty

5 Tell students to underline the examples and complete the rules. Check answers as a class. Elicit the meaning of *other* (*as well as the thing or person already mentioned*). Tell students that *all* and *both* are followed by plural verbs, *another* by a singular verb, *other* + singular noun by a singular verb and *other* + plural noun by a plural verb. Write examples on the board:

All the cities <u>are</u> beautiful.

Both cities <u>are</u> beautiful.

Another famous city <u>is</u> Granada.

The other famous city <u>is</u> Granada.

Other famous cities <u>are</u> Granada and Seville.

> **Answers**
> We use *both* to talk about two things.
> We use *all* to talk about a total number of things.
> *Another* means 'one more'.

>> **GRAMMAR REFERENCE AND PRACTICE ANSWER KEY TB PAGE 266**

6 Books closed. Ask, 'What is the biggest island in the world?' (*Australia*). 'What is its capital city?' (*Canberra*) and 'Do you know any other cities there?'.

Books open. Students see if they named the cities in the text. They then complete the text individually. Check answers as a class. Ask students which city, Sydney, Cairns or Melbourne, they would prefer to visit.

> **Answers**
> 1 All 2 both 3 Other 4 both 5 Another 6 all 7 another 8 other

> **MIXED ABILITY**
> For students who need more support, go through each gap in the text with them. For example, (1) 'Does this mean every tourist?' (*yes*), 'Which determiner means *every*?' (*all*); (2) 'How many places are mentioned?' (*two*) and 'Which determiner means *two*?' (*both*).

7 Tell students to correct the sentences. Check answers as a class.

> **Answers**
> 1 It's **the** biggest museum in my town.
> 2 It's not boring like **other** computer games.
> 3 The T-shirts **both cost** £15.
> 4 This phone has **a** very good screen and camera.
> 5 I went to **the** park and I played football with my friends.
> 6 We went on holiday to ~~the~~ Edinburgh.

>> **GRAMMAR WORKSHEET UNIT 11**

8 Ask students what information they could include in a city description; Exercise 6 on page 64 gives some ideas. For example: where it is, how many people live there, interesting places, transport, culture, why it is famous. Students choose three cities and make notes for each one. They shouldn't include the name of the city in the description but they should give a choice of four cities to guess from. Put the pairs into groups of four. Students read out their descriptions for the other pair to guess the cities.

> **COOLER**
> Write these questions on the board. Students complete them with *a* or *the* and then answer them.
> 1 Is _____ city usually smaller than _____ town? (*a, a; no, bigger*)
> 2 What is _____ highest capital city in the world? (*the; La Paz, Bolivia*)
> 3 Name _____ city which has _____ different name today from its name in the past. (*a, a; many examples: Smyrna/Izmir, New Amsterdam / New York, Bombay/Mumbai*)
> 4 Moscow has _____ famous square. What is the name of _____ square? (*a, the; Red Square*)

GRAMMAR · Determiners

1 Read the sentences in Exercise 6 on page 64 again and <u>underline</u> all the examples of *a/an* and *the*. Choose the correct word to complete the rules.

> We use ***the*** / ***a/an*** to introduce something for the first time.
> We use ***the*** / ***a/an*** to talk about something already mentioned; with superlatives; if there is only one in the world; in front of *first, second*, etc.

2 Complete the email with *the* or *a/an*.

> To: Camilla
> From: Rosa
> Reply Forward
>
> I'm having **(1)** _____ great holiday in Rome with my family! Today we visited **(2)** _____ Colosseum, and we went to **(3)** _____ fantastic museum called MAXXI. Afterwards, my brother and I each had **(4)** _____ ice cream in **(5)** _____ city centre. We both said it was **(6)** _____ best ice cream in **(7)** _____ world! Tomorrow, we're going to see **(8)** _____ Trevi Fountain and also **(9)** _____ palace – but I can't remember which one. Rome is **(10)** _____ really wonderful city!

◑ PRONUNCIATION · *the*

🔊 3 Listen and repeat. When do we say /ðiː/ and when do we say /ðə/?

/ðiː/ **the**	/ðə/ **the**
the oldest	the youngest
the east	the north
the Atlantic Ocean	the Pacific Ocean
the Olympic Games	the World Cup

4 Put the words into the correct column in the table.

the apple	the Arctic
the dog	the Earth
the Indian Ocean	the North Sea
the orange	the River Nile
the Statue of Liberty	the umbrella

🔊 Listen and check. Then repeat.

5 Read the examples below and <u>underline</u> all the examples of *all, both, other* and *another*. Choose the correct word to complete the rules.

All the questions are about cities.
Are you all ready?
The city has both beaches and museums.
Central Park and Times Square are both popular.
There are many other great places to visit.
The other famous thing here is the statue of Jesus.
There's another beautiful church in the city.

> We use ***all*** / ***both*** to talk about two things.
> We use ***all*** / ***both*** to talk about a total number of things.
> ***Another*** / ***Other*** means 'one more'.

》 GRAMMAR REFERENCE AND PRACTICE PAGE 157

6 Complete the text about Australian cities with *all, both, other* and *another*. Use each word twice.

Australian cities have a lot to offer visitors to the country. **(1)** _____ visitors to Australia should go to Sydney. It's the largest and oldest city in the country, and **(2)** _____ the Opera House and Harbour Bridge are important world-famous monuments. **(3)** _____ popular cities are Perth, Brisbane and Cairns.

Cairns is in Queensland, in the northeast of Australia. From this city, you can enjoy **(4)** _____ the rainforest and the ocean, including the Great Barrier Reef. **(5)** _____ thing you can do in Cairns is learn **(6)** _____ about the culture of the Aboriginal people of Australia.

Melbourne is **(7)** _____ great Australian city. It has excellent museums and also a modern arts centre. Phillip Island is not far from Melbourne, and you can see koalas, penguins, kangaroos and many **(8)** _____ animals here.

7 Correct the mistakes in the sentences.

👁 1 It's a biggest museum in my town.
2 It's not boring like others computer games.
3 The T-shirts cost both £15.
4 This phone has very good screen and camera.
5 I went to park and I played football with my friends.
6 We went on holiday to the Edinburgh.

8 In pairs, write a city quiz.

- Choose three cities.
- Write some notes about each one.
- Describe the cities to another pair of students.
- Can they guess your cities? Can you guess theirs?

1 Look at the signs, notices and messages. For 1–4, where would you see them? For 5 and 6, where is the writer? Match each sign to a place in the box.

at school in a shop by a river
at a train station in a café on a website

1 Wildlife Safari Park
Open March to October
Under 16s £12.50 Adults £25.00
Click here to book!

2 Boat Trips
10 am and 2 pm
Trips take 3 hours
ⓘ Full details available from Tourist Information Office

3 Jeans for All
Need a bigger or smaller pair?
Ask the assistant

4 Left Luggage
We open early and close late
Large bag – £6.00 Small bag – £3.00

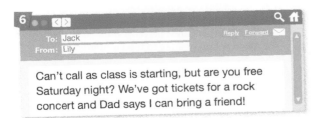

5 Tilly – we're all waiting for you at the Silver Fish Café. The film starts soon! Shall we wait here for you or meet you at the cinema?

6
To: Jack
From: Lily
Reply Forward

Can't call as class is starting, but are you free Saturday night? We've got tickets for a rock concert and Dad says I can bring a friend!

 PREPARE FOR THE EXAM

Reading Part 1

2 For questions 1–6, choose the correct answer. In pairs, compare your answers and say why you chose the answer you did.

1 A Children cannot come here without an adult.
  B It's not possible to see the animals all year.
  C Summer prices are lower than winter ones.
2 A There's one trip in the morning and another in the afternoon.
  B Go online to get more information about the boat trips.
  C One of the boat trips is longer than the other.
3 A Some of these jeans aren't available in all sizes.
  B The assistant can tell you which size looks best.
  C Staff here can help you find the right size.
4 A You can leave your suitcases here.
  B You must arrive early to leave your bag.
  C If you have two bags, you get a discount on the smaller one.
5 What must Tilly do now?
  A Go to the cinema as quickly as possible.
  B Let her friends know what to do next.
  C Stay where she is until her friends arrive.
6 Why did Lily write this message?
  A to give Jack some bad news about the concert on Saturday
  B to tell Jack to get a ticket for the concert
  C to invite Jack to a concert

» **PREPARE FOR THE EXAM PAGE 120**

 TALKING POINTS

▶ 09 Watch the video and ask and answer the questions.
What's your favourite city?
Why do you like it there?
Is there anything you don't like about it?
What places in your city do you go to regularly and why?

66 **UNIT 11**

1 Books closed. Draw a box on the board. In the box write, *Wet paint!* Ask, 'What is this?' (*a notice/sign*), 'Where would you see it?' (*on a seat in a park, a door in school*) and 'Why is it there?' (*to warn you that you can get paint on your clothes*).

Write some of the places in Exercise 1 on the board and ask students what sign or notice they might see there. For example: by a river (*Do not swim!*).

Books open. Students answer the questions. Check answers as a class. Ask some comprehension questions, for example, 'What time is the first boat trip?' (*10 am*) and 'Where are Tilly's friends waiting?' (*at the Silver Fish Café*).

Answers

1 on a website 2 by a river 3 in a shop 4 at a train station
5 in a café 6 at school

PREPARE FOR THE EXAM

A2 KEY FOR SCHOOLS
Reading Part 1

In this part, students have to read six short texts and answer a three-option multiple-choice question about each one. The texts are not connected and they could be emails, online messages or notices. The questions test what the overall meaning of the texts are.

Tip Tell students to look for the sentence that says the same thing as the text, but in different words. For example, the sentence might say 'big towns' but the text may talk about 'cities'. They shouldn't choose a notice just because it has the same words as the sentence. They should think about the meaning.

2 Demonstrate the strategy with students. Tell students to read the first text. Ask, 'What three things does this tell a visitor to the safari park?' (*when it is open, how much it costs, how to book*). Say, 'Look at answer A. Does the sign say children must go with an adult?' (*no*), 'Look at answer B. Does the sign say the safari park is closed in some months?', (*yes*) 'Look at answer C. Does the sign say that there are different prices in summer and winter?' (*no*) and 'So which is the correct answer?' (*B*). Tell students to answer the other questions themselves then check with a partner. Check answers as a class.

Ask students if they have ever been to a safari park or taken a boat trip and what it was like. As an extension activity, have students work in pairs, choose one of the texts and write questions about it. For example, text 2:

Is the trip on a river or lake?

How much does a ticket cost?

Can I get a ticket online?

Put pairs together to take turns asking and answering the questions. For example:

Student A: *Is the trip on a river or lake?*

Student B: *There are two different trips, both around the lake.*

Answers

1 B 2 A 3 C 4 A 5 B 6 C

FAST FINISHERS

Fast finishers calculate how much it would cost for their family to go to the safari park and leave two large bags and a small bag at the railway station while they are there.

» **PREPARE FOR THE EXAM TEACHING NOTES AND ANSWER KEY TB PAGE 252**

TALKING POINTS

09 You can give more information about the topic of the unit by showing the video and asking students to complete the video worksheet. Then, read the questions in the *Talking points* box and students answer questions in pairs. For extra speaking practice, ask students, 'How will cities change in the future?' and write on the board different factors, for example transport, homes, shops, for students to think about when they answer.

1 Books closed. Ask, 'What music do you like?' and get some answers. Tell students that *music* is an uncountable noun so we can't say *What musics … .* Ask students to give you examples of other uncountable nouns. Books open. Students see if the nouns they said are in the box in Exercise 1. Concept-check some of the countable and uncountable words, making sure that students use *a/an* in the answer if it is a countable noun. For example: 'People who work in a company' (*staff*) and 'It is metal and you buy things with it' (*a coin*).

Have students complete the table. Check answers as a class. Elicit that the determiners *a, few* and *many* are not used with uncountable nouns; *much* is generally used in negatives and questions and *a lot of* in statements. Write these examples on the board:

It hasn't got <u>many</u> big cities. Does it have <u>many</u> big cities? There are <u>a lot of</u> big cities.

There isn't <u>much</u> bread. Do you have <u>much</u> bread? There's <u>a lot of</u> bread.

> **Answers**
> 1 furniture 2 homework 3 news 4 traffic 5 money 6 food
> 7 electricity 8 information 9 wildlife 10 staff 11 luggage
> 12 jewellery

2 Demonstrate with an example on the board:

fruit/orange   How many _____ do you eat a week?

Ask, 'After *many* do we need a countable or uncountable noun?' (*countable*), 'Which of the nouns is countable?' (*orange*) and 'Do we need to change the form of *orange*?' (*Yes, make it plural, oranges.*). Have students complete the sentences. Check answers as a class.

Books closed. Read out one of either the countable or uncountable nouns from Exercise 1 and have students tell you the matching noun.

> **Answers**
> 1 furniture 2 projects 3 article 4 traffic 5 coin 6 food
> 7 electricity 8 information 9 animals 10 staff 11 suitcase
> 12 jewellery

3 Put students into pairs and tell them to turn to page 137. One student chooses an uncountable noun from Exercise 3 and the other student asks a question about it beginning *How many …?*.

>> **VOCABULARY WORKSHEET UNIT 11**

1 Pre-teach **bowling** (mime the action) and **cloakroom** (a place where you leave your coat). Ask about picture A: 'Where is the boy?' (*at a shop*) and 'Why do you think he is speaking to the woman?' (*He wants to buy something.*). Arrange the students into pairs to describe the other picture.

Have students read the conversations and say which conversations pictures A and B show.

> **Answers**
> A 6 B 4

2 Get students to categorise the phrases into questions and replies before they complete the conversations.

Questions: *Can you tell me, Could I, Could you, Do you mind if I, Is it OK if I*

Replies: *I'd like to, I'm afraid not, I'm sorry but, No problem, Of course, Sure, That's fine*

Play the recording for students to listen and check. Put students into pairs to act out the conversations. Tell students that with a polite request, often the pitch starts high and the intonation rises at the end.

> **Answers**
> 1 I'd like to 2 I'm sorry, but 3 Could you 4 No problem
> 5 Is it OK if I 6 I'm afraid not 7 Do you mind if I 8 That's fine
> 9 Can you tell me 10 Sure 11 Could I 12 Of course

> **MIXED ABILITY**
>
> Give weaker students more help with the meaning of the phrases in the box in Exercise 2. Write sentences on the board and have students change them in different ways, making them more polite, using the phrases. For example:
> I need some fresh air. – Do you mind if I open the window?, Could you open the window, please?
> Yes, I can help you. – Of course., Sure.

1 To make it more fun, give each pair a dice. They write down six places and number them 1–6. Then they write down six requests and number them 1–6. They throw the dice twice. The first number is the place, the second number is the request. Students make a conversation using the phrases in Exercise 2.

> **Possible answer**
> (place) at the zoo / (request) feeding the lion
> A: Excuse me, do you mind if I give the lion some ice cream?
> B: Sure, but our lion only likes banana ice cream.

2 Each pair acts out their conversations while the other students listen and try to guess what the place is.

> **COOLER**
>
> Ask students to close their eyes. Say, 'You are at home in your kitchen. Go to your fridge. Open the door. What do you see inside? Open your eyes and write down everything you see.'
>
> Students make a list using determiners, for example *some cheese, a lot of tomatoes.*

VOCABULARY Uncountable nouns

1 Complete the table. Match the uncountable nouns in the box to the countable nouns in the table.

(EP)

electricity	food	~~furniture~~
homework	information	
jewellery	luggage	money
news	staff	traffic	wildlife

Countable	Uncountable
1 desk	*furniture*
2 project	
3 article	
4 car	
5 coin	
6 meal	
7 battery	
8 details	
9 animals	
10 shop assistant	
11 suitcase	
12 necklace	

2 Complete the sentences with the countable or uncountable form of the words in the table in Exercise 1.

1 I haven't got much _____ in my room – just a bed and a chair.
2 I've got two science _____ to finish this weekend!
3 There's an interesting _____ about Rihanna in this magazine.
4 There's too much _____ on the streets in my town.
5 Have you got a 50p _____? I need it for the drinks machine.
6 Mum prepared a lot of _____ for our picnic.
7 Dad says my new radio doesn't use much _____.
8 You can find all the _____ you need about the competition on the website.
9 The number of _____ in Africa is going down.
10 I couldn't find a member of _____ to help me.
11 I took a really small _____ when I went on holiday.
12 My sister gave me a lovely piece of _____ for my birthday.

3 ≫ Work with a partner. Go to page 137.

LISTENING

1 Read the six conversations. Which conversations do pictures A and B show?

1 **A:** Hi. Can I help you?
  B: (1) _____ go bowling this afternoon.
  A: Ah, **(2)** _____ we're closing in ten minutes. Come back tomorrow morning.
  B: Oh, OK. Thanks.
2 **A:** Excuse me. **(3)** _____ open the door for me?
  B: (4) _____. There you are.
  A: Thanks!
3 **A: (5)** _____ leave my guitar here while I go round the museum?
  B: (6) _____. You need to put it in the cloakroom. It's over there, next to the shop.
  A: Thank you.
4 **A:** Excuse me. **(7)** _____ open the window? It's really hot in here.
  B: (8) _____. I'm hot too!
5 **A:** Excuse me. **(9)** _____ the way to the skatepark?
  B: (10) _____. Walk along this road for about 100 metres, then turn left. You'll see the park on your right.
  A: Great! Thanks very much.
6 **A:** Excuse me. **(11)** _____ have a can of lemonade, please?
  B: (12) _____. That's £1.50, please.

2 Complete the conversations with the phrases from the box.

Can you tell me	Could I
Could you	Do you mind if I
I'd like to	I'm afraid not
I'm sorry, but	Is it OK if I
No problem	Of course
Sure	That's fine

3 Listen and check. In pairs, practise the conversations.
89

SPEAKING

1 In pairs, write three new conversations. For each conversation choose:

- a different place – shop / café / park / tourist information office, etc.
- a different request – something to eat / drink / a ticket / help / advice / directions, etc.

2 Role-play your conversations for the class for them to guess where you are.

12 FILMS

 ABOUT YOU

How often do you go to the cinema?
What's your favourite film? Who is in it? What is it about? Why do you like it?

VOCABULARY AND READING

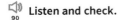

Types of film

1 Match the types of film in the box to the pictures A–I.

EP

action film	adventure film	animated film
comedy	drama	horror film	musical
science-fiction film	thriller	

🔊 90 Listen and check.

2 In groups, answer the questions.

1. Name an example of each type of movie in Exercise 1.
2. Which is your favourite type of film?
3. What's the worst film you've ever seen? Why didn't you like it?

3 Read the blog about the 'tricks' movie companies use to make their films into hits. Match the 'tricks' a–e to paragraphs 1–5.

a. Make a movie that might win a prize.
b. Make a film that has a story or characters that the audience knows and likes.
c. Advertise the movie well.
d. Use actors who are really famous.
e. Make a film which people will write or talk about.

4 Read the blog again. Are the sentences right (✓) or wrong (✗)?

1. Great acting is the most important aspect of a good film.
2. It costs film companies a lot of money to use famous actors.
3. People only use reviews in papers to decide which film to watch.
4. The job of a famous actor includes telling the public how good the film is.
5. Awards can make more people go to see a movie.

5 In pairs, look at the points in Exercise 3 again and discuss what is most important to you when choosing a film to see.

WHAT MAKES A MOVIE A HIT? 🔊 91

We all know a good film when we see it. It has a great story, excellent photography and wonderful acting. But what makes a good movie into a big hit? This is a question that filmmakers are always asking themselves! Of course, there is no perfect answer. However, movie companies have a few tricks which help make their films become as successful as possible.

1
Some stars have fans who will go and see any movie they are in. Unfortunately, not all movies that have big stars in them are successful, and using famous actors can be expensive!

2
There are lots of movies which come from books, comics, computer games or TV shows. Just think of Harry Potter, Wonder Woman, X-Men, Star Wars, etc. People already love these, so they can't wait to see the film.

3
People often check to see what newspapers or websites are saying about a film before they go and see it. Also, people who love a movie will tell their friends how good it is.

4
This is really important. As well as posters and trailers, most big films will now have a website that gives extra information about the film. Also, when a new film comes out, the stars of the movie usually travel around the world and give interviews to get people interested in the film.

5
Awards like the Oscars and the Golden Globes let people know which films are good to watch. A movie that gets an award often becomes much more popular than before.

12 FILMS

Unit Overview

TOPIC	Films and cinema
VOCABULARY	Types of film
AND READING	What makes a movie a hit?
GRAMMAR	Relative pronouns *who, which, that*
PRONUNCIATION	Spelling and syllables
READING	Showing today at Star Cinema
VOCABULARY	Conjunctions
LISTENING	A conversation about going to the cinema
WRITING	An invitation to the cinema
EXAM TASKS	Reading Part 2; Listening Part 3

Resources

GRAMMAR REFERENCE AND PRACTICE: SB page 158; TB page 266

PREPARE FOR THE EXAM: SB pages on TB page 238 and 246; TB pages 253 and 257

WORKBOOK: pages 48–51

PHOTOCOPIABLE WORKSHEETS: Grammar worksheet Unit 12; Vocabulary worksheet Unit 12

TEST GENERATOR: Unit test 12

WARMER

To revise words from Unit 11, write anagrams of (some of) these places on the board: *library, stadium, cathedral, mosque, museum, theatre, palace, temple, statue, sports centre.* Tell students that they are places in a town or city with the letters mixed up. Do the first one together: *rbyrail → library.* Then students work individually, with books closed, to see who can finish first. Let weaker students look back at Unit 11. You can give the first letter of each word if they need it.

⑦ ABOUT YOU

Books closed, show some film clips and ask the class if these look like interesting films and why. Alternatively, ask students, 'When was the last time you went to the cinema?', 'What did you see?' and 'Did you like it?'. Books open. Students answer the questions in pairs. Share ideas as a class.

VOCABULARY AND READING

Types of film

BACKGROUND INFORMATION

The Oscars, or Academy Awards, are a set of 24 different awards. The Oscar ceremony was first held in 1929 in Hollywood and now it is shown live in over 200 countries. Three films have won 11 Oscars: *Ben-Hur* (1959), *Titanic* (1997) and *The Lord of the Rings: The Return of the King* (2003). The youngest winner of a competitive Oscar was Tatum O'Neal, aged ten. The Golden Globes are awards for both films and television shows. Meryl Streep has won the most Golden Globes, eight.

1 Have students match the types of film to the pictures. Play the audio for students to check and repeat. Name some films which your students will know and have students say the type of film, for example, *Beauty and the Beast* (animated film), *La La Land* (musical), *A Cambio de Nada* (drama).

🔊 Answers
90
The answers are recorded for students to check and then repeat.
A comedy B adventure film C animated film D action film
E drama F science-fiction film G thriller H musical
I horror film

2 Put students into groups to discuss the questions. Share ideas as a class. Ask students, 'Which types of film are most popular in your country?' and 'Do people prefer to watch films from your country or foreign films?'.

3 Pre-teach **hit** (a thing that is very popular and successful). Ask students to look at the title of the blog and give different answers to that question.

Pre-teach **trick** (an effective or quick way of doing something) and **trailer** (short parts of a film or television programme which are shown in order to advertise it). Have students match the tricks to the paragraphs. Check answers as a class.

Answers
1 d 2 b 3 e 4 c 5 a

FAST FINISHERS

Have fast finishers think of more films based on books like the ones in paragraph 2. Ask them to write down two films which were worse than the books and two films which were better than the books. Fast finishers can then tell the class when they have finished the matching exercise and see if they agree.

4 Write these sentences on the board and have students say whether they are right or wrong based on the text and why.

A good movie is a big hit. (Wrong – filmmakers need to make a good movie into a big hit.)

Harry Potter was a book before it was a film. (Right – the film came from the book.)

Tell students to read the text again, decide whether the sentences in the book are right or wrong and correct the wrong sentences. Check answers as a class and have students tell you where they found the answer.

Answers
1 ✗ – a great story and excellent photography are also important 2 ✓ 3 ✗ – they also use reviews on websites
4 ✓ 5 ✓

🔊 The Reading text is recorded for students to listen, read
91 and check their answers.

5 Put students into pairs to discuss. Ask students if there are any other things which are important, for example, if you can download the film and watch it online.

1 Explain that *who*, *which* and *that* are relative pronouns and that we use them when we want to give more information about people and things. They also combine information into one sentence. Show this with the first example from the blog:

This is a question. Filmmakers always ask themselves this!

This is a question <u>that</u> filmmakers are always asking themselves!

Have students underline the other examples in the blog and complete the sentences. Check answers as a class.

Answers

1 who / that 2 that / which

» **GRAMMAR REFERENCE AND PRACTICE ANSWER KEY TB PAGE 266**

2 Write an example on the board:

I know someone _____ won an Oscar.

Ask, 'Is the information about a person or a thing?' (*a person*) and 'So which words can we use?' (*who/that*). Have students complete the sentences. Check answers as a class.

Answers

1 which / that 2 who / that 3 which / that 4 who / that
5 which / that 6 who / that

┌───┐
MIXED ABILITY

Weaker students will mix up *who* and *which*. Give them extra practice in this. Read out a list of nouns and have students put them next to *who* or *which*.

who: David, the children, her sister, a friend, our neighbours, anyone

which: the mouse, my scarf, news, a language, Tom's bag, some milk
└───┘

3 Books closed. Ask, 'How are cinemas changing?' Books open. Have students look at the photos, describe them and give more ideas about the future of the cinema. Pre-teach **bean bag** (a soft seat consisting of a large cloth bag filled with dried beans or something similar) and **hot tub** (a large, usually wooden, container full of hot water in which more than one person can sit). Have students complete the text. Check answers as a class.

Answers

1 who 2 that 3 which 4 that 5 that

4 Ask students to look at the photo at the bottom right of the page and ask, 'What kind of cinema is this?' (*IMAX*) and 'Have you ever been to one?'. Tell students to match the sentence halves. Check answers as a class. Then tell students to join them with *who* or *which*. Check answers as a class. Ask, 'Do you think all films will be 3-D in the future?' and 'What about 4-D or 5-D?'.

Answers

1 f IMAX cinemas are popular with people who like 3-D films.
2 c The cinemas have special seats which move, and sometimes you'll feel wind or water during the film.
3 d It's not possible for children who are under 13 to go in alone.
4 a You need to wear special glasses which let you see in 3-D.
5 e Some IMAX cinemas have screens which are as tall as four double decker buses – about 16 metres.
6 b There's a 3-D film called *Bugs!* which shows you the world of rainforest insects.

5 Have students correct the mistakes. Check as a class.

Answers

1 My favourite colour is blue so I bought a mobile phone **which/that** was blue.
2 There are two windows **which/that** don't close very well.
3 He told me about something interesting **which/that** happened in the film.
4 I want to sell a TV **which/that** is two years old.
5 It's a music concert **which/that** is going to be in Sao Paulo.
6 There are some great books **which/that** can help you learn English.

» **GRAMMAR WORKSHEET UNIT 12**

 PRONUNCIATION | **Spelling and syllables**

🔊 6 Books closed. Write, don't say, the English town name
92   *Loughborough* on the board. Ask, 'How many letters are in the word?' (*12*) 'How do you pronounce it?' See if any students get close to /ˈlʌfbrə/. Ask 'How many syllables are there?' (*2*)

Books open. Explain the task and play the recording, pausing it after each word to give the students time to think and write. Check answers as a class.

Answers

action – 6 letters, 2 syllables
adventure – 9 letters, 3 syllables
because – 7 letters, 2 syllables
children – 8 letters, 2 syllables
chocolate – 9 letters, 2 syllables
cinema – 6 letters, 3 syllables
dictionary – 10 letters, 3 syllables
different – 9 letters, 2 syllables
horror – 6 letters, 2 syllables
interesting – 11 letters, 3 syllables
medicine – 8 letters, 2 syllables
photography – 11 letters, 4 syllables
sometimes – 9 letters, 2 syllables
where – 5 letters, 1 syllable
which – 5 letters, 1 syllable
while – 5 letters, 1 syllable
who – 3 letters, 1 syllable

7 Put students into small groups and tell them to go to page 137 and read the task. Students design their own cinema then one person from each group presents their ideas to the rest of the class.

┌───┐
COOLER

Put students in pairs and ask them to make a sentence using as many of the words in the box in Exercise 6 as they can. The sentence which uses the most words from the box and is grammatical and makes sense is the winner. For example: The <u>horror</u> film <u>which</u> we saw at the <u>cinema</u> was <u>interesting</u> <u>because</u> of the actors <u>who</u> were in it. (six words)
└───┘

Relative pronouns *who, which, that*

1 Find and <u>underline</u> the examples of *who*, *which* and *that* in the blog post.

Choose two words to complete each sentence.
1 We use *who* / *that* / *which* when we talk about people.
2 We use *who* / *that* / *which* when we talk about things.

>> **GRAMMAR REFERENCE AND PRACTICE PAGE 158**

2 Choose the correct answer for each sentence. Write *A* (*who/that*) or *B* (*which/that*).

1 I like films _____ make me laugh.
2 I have a friend _____ watches two movies a day during the holidays.
3 There's a cinema near my home _____ is over 100 years old.
4 I know a person _____ knows Jaden Smith.
5 I can't remember the name of the film _____ was on TV last night.
6 There are quite a lot of actors _____ can speak two or more languages.

3 Choose the correct words to complete the text.

Cinemas of the future?

In the past, people **(1)** *who* / *which* wanted to see a film had to go to the cinema. That's not true any more, and these days many cinemas can't find enough customers **(2)** *which* / *that* are happy to pay their high ticket prices. That's why some cinemas are starting to try different ideas. There are cinemas **(3)** *which* / *who* have giant beds instead of seats, and one in Malaysia **(4)** *who* / *that* has bean bags. Others have sofas, dining tables or even hot tubs! Some cinemas even show '4D' films. These are 3D films with special effects **(5)** *who* / *that* happen in the cinema at the same time as in the film. These can be rain, wind, smoke and smells. The seats also move around, so you really feel like you are in the movie!

4 Match the two halves of the sentences and join them with *who* or *which*.

1 IMAX cinemas are popular with people
2 The cinemas have special seats
3 It's not possible for children
4 You need to wear special glasses
5 Some IMAX cinemas have screens
6 There's a 3-D film called *Bugs*!

a _____ let you see in 3D.
b _____ shows you the world of rainforest insects.
c _____ move, and sometimes you feel wind or water during the film.
d _____ are under 13 to go in alone.
e _____ are as tall as four double-decker buses – about 16 metres.
f _____ like 3-D films.

5 Correct the mistakes in the sentences.

1 My favourite colour is blue, so I bought a mobile phone who was blue.
2 There are two windows don't close very well.
3 He told me about something interesting happened in the film.
4 I want to sell a TV who is two years old.
5 It's a music concert it's going to be in São Paulo.
6 There are some great books can help you learn English.

PRONUNCIATION | Spelling and syllables

6 Listen and repeat the words. How many letters does each word have? How many syllables?

action	adventure	because
children	chocolate	cinema
dictionary	different	horror
interesting	medicine	
photography	sometimes	where
which	while	who

action – 6 letters, 2 syllables

7 >> Work in small groups. Go to page 137.

Showing today at STAR ★ CINEMA

A The Drake Adventures

Tom Drake is on holiday with his family, visiting various European cities. He doesn't enjoy sightseeing or museums, so he is really bored and can't wait to go home. But things change when the family visits a castle, where Tom sees two men steal a painting. He is in big trouble when the men come after him. Things get really exciting when Tom finds out who the men are and what their real reason for stealing the painting is.

B Body Swap

Hannah and her brother Chris were good friends when they were little, but now they hate each other. Everyone thinks Hannah is really cool, but no one wants to be Chris's friend, and she says she won't help him. Then, one morning, they wake up in each other's bodies. They have to learn to understand each other better, or they'll stay this way forever. This film will make you laugh till you cry!

C Game, Set and Match

Carly James is a brilliant young tennis player, but has lots of problems in her life. She's not close to her parents because they're often away on business, and she doesn't find schoolwork easy. But while she's preparing for a big competition, she starts working with a new coach. It seems he is the one person who really understands her. He knows that she can be a big star if she listens to him and works hard. Finally, things start to improve for Carly, but can she do well in the competition?

GAME SET MATCH

READING

1 Read about the films on the cinema web page. What type of film do you think each one is?

✓ PREPARE FOR THE EXAM

Reading Part 2

2 For each question, choose the correct answer. Write *A* for *The Drake Adventures*, *B* for *Body Swap* or *C* for *Game, Set, Match*.

1 Which film is about someone who is in danger?
2 Which film is about someone who gets the help she needs?
3 Which film is about someone who isn't very popular?
4 Which film is about someone who might win a prize?
5 Which film is about someone who learns why something happened?
6 Which film is about someone who is happier after meeting someone new?
7 Which film is about someone who doesn't like a family member?

💬 TALKING POINTS

Which of these films would you like to see? Why?
Do you prefer watching films at home or at the cinema? Why?

VOCABULARY — Conjunctions

Conjunctions are words that join parts of sentences together.

I enjoy films. I don't like going to the cinema.
I enjoy films, but I don't like going to the cinema.
I want to go shopping. I haven't got any clothes.
I want to go shopping because I haven't got any clothes.
I'm having a party on my birthday.
I'm visiting my family on my birthday.
I'm having a party and I'm visiting my family on my birthday.

EP These words can also be conjunctions:

if	or	so	that
when	where	while	

WARMER

Write these instructions on the board or dictate them:

Find somebody who …

has a birthday soon.

can count to ten in more than three languages.

has an interesting pet.

went to bed late.

needs a new phone.

saw a film yesterday.

Students have ten minutes to find as many answers as possible by asking each other. They then share their information as a class.

1 Ask, 'Where do you find out what films are on at the cinema?' and elicit the cinema's web page. Pre-teach **come after** (try to get), **forever** (for all time in the future) and **swap** (to give something to someone and get something from them in return). Tell students that a *game* and a *set* are part of the scoring system of tennis and that the umpire says *game, set, match* when there is a winner. However, *game, set, match* is used more generally to mean that someone is the winner in a situation.

Give students a time limit to read about the films and write down the type of each film. Check answers as a class.

Answers

A thriller/action **B** comedy **C** drama

 **PREPARE FOR THE EXAM**

A2 KEY FOR SCHOOLS Reading Part 2

2 Briefly review what students need to do in this part of the exam and if necessary read out the A2 Key for Schools box on TB page 41.

Tell students to read each word in the questions carefully. For example, in question 7 it says a *member of her family* so you know it is about only one person. This is why text C is not the right answer, because it says *Carly is not close to her parents*, two people.

Ask students some comprehension questions, for example, 'Where does Emily's adventure begin?' (*in a castle*), 'How can Chris and Hannah get their bodies back?' (*They have to learn to understand each other better.*) and 'What is Carly training for?' (*a tennis competition*). Have students match the questions in the exam task to the film. Check answers as a class.

As an extension activity, give students two imaginary 'lines' from the films and ask them to guess which film they came from: 'One day you will be a champion!' (*Game, Set, Match*) and 'I'm not going to the cinema with him!' (*Body Swap*). In groups, students should make up six lines from the films for other groups to guess which film they are from. Strong students could make up mini-dialogues.

Answers

1 A **2** C **3** B **4** C **5** A **6** C **7** B

FAST FINISHERS

Fast finishers use relative pronouns to write explanations of these nouns from the text.

museum (a place which has old statues, paintings and other things)

friend (somebody who you like and spend time with)

tennis (a sport that two people play with a small ball)

parents (people who have children and look after them)

star (somebody who is famous)

coach (a person that trains people to do sport)

When the other students have finished, fast finishers can read their sentences to the rest of the class for them to say the word.

🔊 **93** The Reading text is recorded for students to listen, read and check their answers.

💬 **TALKING POINTS**

Ask, 'How do you think these films finish?' Have students give you versions with happy endings and sad endings. For example, *The Drake Adventures*: Emily finds out that the men are not really criminals and that they are taking back the painting which somebody stole from them and sold to the museum; *Game, Set, Match*: Carly is just about to win the tennis competition but she hurts her foot, loses the match and can never play again.

Put students into pairs to discuss the questions in the book. Ask students to tell you the advantages and disadvantages of watching films at home and at the cinema. For example, at home you can watch a film at any time on your laptop; at the cinema there is a big screen.

VOCABULARY Conjunctions

1 Books closed. Write on the board: 'Is it more interesting to watch a film **or** read a book?' and discuss briefly. Point out *or* in the question and explain that it is a conjunction – a word which joins sentences or parts of a sentence. Compare the question on the board with 'Is it better to watch a film? Is it better to read a book?'.

Elicit other conjunctions students know, *but* and *and*, and ask for example sentences. Tell students to read the information on page 70, find the conjunctions in the web page and then match the two halves of the sentences on page 71.

Answers

1 b **2** c **3** e **4** a **5** d **6** g **7** f

2 Students complete the sentences then compare in groups.

>> **VOCABULARY WORKSHEET UNIT 12**

LISTENING

 PREPARE FOR THE EXAM

A2 KEY FOR SCHOOLS
Listening Part 3

In this part, students have to listen to a dialogue and answer five three-option multiple-choice questions. They need to listen for specific information, for example dates and prices, as well as feelings and opinions. The answers will come from both speakers.

Tip Often all three options are mentioned so students should be careful to choose the correct one. Tell students that they will hear the recording twice so they shouldn't worry if they miss an answer the first time.

1 Put students in groups and ask, 'What is a great way to celebrate a birthday? Have you got any ideas? Make a list together.'. Give some examples, like go to a café or visit the circus, to start them off. Share ideas as a class and decide which group has the best way to celebrate.

Tell the class that a boy called Finley is going to celebrate his birthday at the Star Cinema and he is calling his friend Ana to invite her. Play the recording and have students answer the questions individually.

2 Put students in pairs to compare answers. Play the recording again and have students check their answers. If necessary, stop the recording after each question so students can check the answers one at a time. Ask who changed their answers, which ones and why. (Students might find it easier to explain if they can look at the audioscript.)

Answers
1 B 2 C 3 C 4 C 5 A

MIXED ABILITY
Students who are weak at listening may understand a text when they see it written down but cannot understand it when it is read as connected speech. To help learners, take phrases from the audioscript, write them on the board and show how they might be changed in connected speech. For example:

it'll have to be Saturday – the /h/ in *have* may not be pronounced and *to* is probably the weak form /tə/.

Are we going to see – *Are* may be reduced to /ə/ and *going to* could become /ɡɒnə/

Mum will come and get us in the car – *come an(d)* may be linked together and the /d/ not pronounced; *get us in* may also be linked together.

>> **AUDIOSCRIPT TB PAGE 297**

>> **PREPARE FOR THE EXAM TEACHING NOTES AND ANSWER KEY TB PAGE 257**

WRITING

✏ **PREPARE TO WRITE**
An invitation to the cinema

GET READY Books closed. Ask, 'What is the best cinema where you live?', 'How do you get there?' and 'How much do tickets cost?'. Books open. Have students look at the poster and ask them if they have seen either the old or the new version of *Ghostbusters*. Tell students to read the email and answer the questions. Ask, 'Why do you think they made a new *Ghostbusters* film?' and 'Are the original films usually better?'.

Answers
1 Leo 2 *Ghostbusters* 3 On Saturday at 6.45

Have students match the prepositions to their function.

Answers
a at b on c on d at e to

Call out some days, times, places, etc. for students to supply the correct preposition. For example, 'Monday' (*on*), 'three o'clock' (*at*), etc.

PLAN Books closed. Ask, 'When you are inviting someone to see a film, what do you need to think about?'. Brainstorm answers and then, with books open, compare them with the bullet points. Students then plan their invitation individually.

WRITE Remind students to think about prepositions and to try to use the grammar and vocabulary studied in this unit.

IMPROVE Tell the students to underline all the relative pronouns, conjunctions and prepositions in their invitation. They read it through again as a final check. Then they swap letters and check each other's work, paying particular attention to the words underlined.

Model answer
Hi Sasha,
We're going to Worldclass Cinema tomorrow afternoon at 3 o'clock. Would you like to come with us? We want to see a new film, *Old Times*. It's about two old people who want to build a time machine which can take them back to their school days. It sounds cool! We're meeting at Claudio's flat at 14.30 and we're going to walk there. I hope you can come!
Marina

COOLER
Students play Bingo to revise the new words. Get them to draw a six-square grid in their books. Elicit the new words from this unit and make a list on the board. Students should fill in each square in their grid with a word from the list.

Read out words from the list in random order or give definitions. If students have that word in their grid, they cross it off. The first student to cross off all six squares is the winner.

After you have demonstrated with the whole class, students play in small groups.

1 Find and <u>underline</u> all the conjunctions on the cinema web page. Study the sentences carefully, then match the two halves of the sentences below.

1 My friends and I go to the cinema if
2 My friend says that
3 I like eating popcorn while
4 We usually sit at the back, where
5 I don't like it when
6 I could have a party for my birthday or
7 The film was very scary, so

a we get the best view of the screen.
b we have enough money and there is a good film on.
c the Harry Potter books are better than the films.
d people talk during the film.
e I'm watching a film in the cinema.
f I didn't stay till the end.
g we could go to the cinema.

2 Complete the sentences so that they are true for you. Then, in groups, compare your answers.

I often listen to music while I'm _____
I'd like to live in a place where _____
In the future, I am sure that _____
I'm happiest when _____
I only get angry if _____
This weekend, I'll _____ or
_____

LISTENING

 PREPARE FOR THE EXAM

Listening Part 3

1 For each question, choose the correct answer. You will hear Finley inviting a friend to the cinema.
94

1 What day will they go to the cinema?
  A Friday
  B Saturday
  C Sunday
2 What does Ana say about *Body Swap*?
  A It's a bit too short.
  B It's got famous actors in it.
  C It's popular with her friends.
3 What time does the film begin?
  A 6.10   B 6.30   C 6.45
4 How much are the tickets?
  A £5.00   B £7.50   C £10.00
5 How will they get home?
  A They'll get a lift.
  B They'll walk.
  C They'll get the bus.

2 In pairs, compare your answers. Then listen again to check your answers.
94

 PREPARE FOR THE EXAM PAGE 130

WRITING

PREPARE TO WRITE
An invitation to the cinema

GET READY Read the invitation to the cinema in the email and answer the questions.

1 Who is Jake inviting?
2 What film does he want to see?
3 When does he want to go?

Look at the prepositions. **Which preposition do we use with:**

a times?   b days?   c streets?
d places where you do something?
e if you are moving to a place?

To: Leo
From: Jake

Reply Forward

Hi Leo,

Would you like **to** come to the cinema with me and a few friends **on** Saturday? We want to see *Ghostbusters*. It's about a group of women who try to find ghosts **in** New York. It sounds really good! It's on **at** Galaxy Cinema and it starts **at** 6.45 pm. We're meeting **at** the bus stop **on** Friar Road **at** 6 pm. Let me know if you can come!

Jake

PLAN Plan your own invitation to the cinema. Make notes.

- What day are you going?
- Which film are you going to see?
- What's it about?
- What time does it start?
- Which cinema are you going to?
- How are you getting there?

WRITE Write your invitation. Begin with *Hi/ Dear* and your friend's name. End with your name. Use some relative pronouns, conjunctions and prepositions in your invitation. Write 50–80 words.

IMPROVE In pairs, read each other's invitations. Check for mistakes with relative pronouns, prepositions and conjunctions.

LIFE SKILLS CREATIVITY AND INNOVATION

BRAINSTORMING

1 When do you need ideas from other people? Tick the sentences that are true for you.

to do projects at school
to decide what to wear in the morning
to make a room more attractive for a party
to do homework
to buy a present for a friend

In pairs, compare your answers.

2 Think of an example where you worked with other people to get ideas and tell the class.

> Last term, we had a science project. We had to think of an experiment to do in groups.

3 Read the text and match groups A–D to the brainstorm techniques 1–4.

 LIFE SKILLS

Brainstorming is a way to think of different ideas:
• to solve a problem
• to create something
• to plan something

Brainstorming is thinking of lots of ideas in a group or individually. If more people take part, then there are more ideas.

How and what can we brainstorm?

1 Mind map

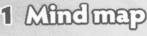

location
restaurants
buildings — (The best city)
monuments
shops

2 Lists

School trip to the mountains			
Food	Drink	Clothes	Equipment
sandwiches	water	warm	backpack
biscuits	juice	sweater	whistle
		boots	

3 Cards

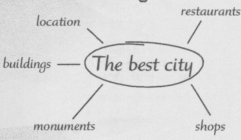

Name for our school pet

Max   Archie   Leo   Fluffly

Tilly   Jack   Tucker

4 Image circles

palm trees   TV
shells
hamburgers   console

LIFE SKILLS

Learning Objectives

- The students learn what brainstorming is and how it can be useful in solving problems, being creative and making plans.
- In the project stage, students use a brainstorming technique to make a poster for a young filmmakers' competition.

BACKGROUND INFORMATION

The brain is at the centre of the nervous system and it is the most complex organ in the body. The brain of humans is very large compared to other animals and it needs about 20% of the blood and oxygen processed in our bodies. If you are thinking hard, that percentage might rise to 50%. The length of blood vessels in our brain is about four times the distance around the world.

The basic function of the brain is to control and coordinate our physical and cognitive activity by collecting information from sense organs, like the eyes, and processing information based on past experiences. Almost all animals, even worms, can change their behaviour based on experience and this reflects changes in the brain. Neuroscience is the field which researches the brain and the nervous system generally and thanks to technological developments neuroscientists have been able to carry out experiments showing what happens where in the brain.

There are different, but connected, types of learning and memory that the brain relies on. First, working memory is the ability of the brain to store information about what is happening now. A lot of information can be collected in working memory but storage is only temporary and the information is forgotten unless it is activated in another way. Episodic memory is the ability to remember details of an event and this information may never be forgotten. Semantic memory is the ability to remember facts and relationships. Instrumental learning changes behaviour based on positive and negative experiences. Motor learning relies on repetition to make our actions automatic. All these types of brain activity may be used when we approach a task, especially complex tasks.

The brain never stops changing and there are ways that we can keep it active and healthy. As with any organ of the body, using your brain is the most effective way of keeping it healthy. Brainstorming is one way of exercising the brain. There is also a link between physical exercise and the brain because exercise increases blood flow to the brain and makes connections between nerve cells. We should also try to improve our diet and avoid stress.

WARMER

Write these sets of words in two columns, with the words in each column mixed up, on the board (or dictate each group of words separately) and have students match the words to make compound nouns.

brain	storm
head	ache
tooth	paste
pop	corn
sun	bathe
film	maker
baby	sit
fire	works
bed	room
card	board

Check as a class. Then put students into groups and give them a time limit to write down more compounds. See which group has the most.

LIFE SKILLS

BRAINSTORMING

Tell students to read the information and check vocabulary as necessary. Invite students to say if they agree or disagree with any of the points in the text and to give their reasons. Encourage open-class discussion and help students make connections between their contributions.

1 Books closed, ask students to write down situations when they need ideas from other people. Give some examples: when you are planning a trip, when you have a personal problem and don't know what to do. Books open, have students see if any of their situations are mentioned in Exercise 1. Tell students to tick the sentences that are true for them. Put students in pairs to compare and discuss. Ask students to tell you in which situations it is most important to get other people's ideas.

2 Put students in small groups to tell one another about a situation when they worked with other people to get ideas. Ask some students to tell the whole class.

3 Ask, 'Do you do brainstorming by yourself or in a group?' (*both*) and 'Is a small group better than a big group?' (*yes*). Ask students to describe the pictures and say how they are connected to brainstorming. Tell students to match the paragraphs to the brainstorming techniques. Check as a class. Ask students what they would write in the empty circles in the Image circles if the topic was free time.

Answers
1 C   2 A   3 D   4 B

FAST FINISHERS

Tell fast finishers to add more lines to the mind map, for example, museums, good schools, clean environment, and then two more headings to the lists, for example, Route and Teachers.

4 Tell students to read the texts again and answer the questions.

Answers

1 no, only the secretary
2 in lists under different headings
3 one or two words
4 no, some students drew pictures
5 the topic
6 yes
7 cards
8 They put them in groups and then chose the best overall idea.

5 Put students into pairs to discuss which brainstorming idea they think is best. Check ideas as a class. As feedback, collect ideas from the class and write the advantages and disadvantages of each method on the board, for example, a mind map is good because it is very visual but some of the ideas might be more important than others and the mind map doesn't really show this.

🔊 **95** The Reading text is recorded for students to listen, read and check their answers.

🔊 **96** **6** Ask students how each brainstorming method could be used to plan a party. For example, you could use cards to write down important things to think about for the party. Students then listen and identify the brainstorming method on the recording. Check as a class.

Answer

a mind map

🔊 **96** **7** Tell students to listen again and answer the questions. Check as a class. As an extension activity, ask students to draw the mind map for the party (school party in the middle with lines for food, drink, theme and date). Have students imagine they are planning a school party. Put them in groups to brainstorm ideas using this mind map.

Answers

1 food, drink, theme, date
2 (Any two of) under the sea, pirates, cinema, Roman times
3 Japanese, French, Spanish
4 five
5 decorations

🔊 **96** **8** Tell students to choose the correct option. Put students into pairs to check with one another. Play the recording again for students to listen again and check.

As an extension activity, have students role play the conversation in groups of four as if they were discussing the same ideas but using a different brainstorming technique, for example lists.

Answers

1 Shall we, first 2 Why don't we 3 Then 4 Let's
5 What about 6 Next

>> AUDIOSCRIPT TB PAGE 297

MIXED ABILITY

Go through each question with weaker students.

Question 1: 'Do we use *Do* or *Shall* for suggestions?' (*Shall*), 'Which means *at the beginning – first* or *firstly*?'

Question 2: 'Which phrase introduces a question?'

Question 3: 'Which is an adverb – *then* or *last*?'

Question 4: 'Is this a question?' (*no*)

Question 5: 'Is there a verb in this sentence?' (*no*), 'So can we use a modal verb?' (*no*)

Question 6: 'Which is an adverb – *next* or *after*?'

PROJECT *An advertisement*

Ask students if they have ever taken part in a competition and if so what kind of competition it was, what they had to do and whether there was a prize. Tell students there is a competition to come up with an idea for a film and make a poster for it. They need to brainstorm ideas. Tell students to look back at page 68 for some ideas about the types of film they could make. Put students into small groups and tell them to decide on a brainstorming technique, brainstorm ideas, choose the best ones, then make the poster. Tell students they could use more than one brainstorming technique. Each group then presents their ideas to the rest of the class, who decide which poster would win the competition. Then ask groups how well their brainstorming technique(s) worked and how they could have organised this better.

PROJECT EXTENSION

Tell students to imagine that they are directors at the film school. The directors have noticed that there are not enough female filmmakers. Put students into small groups to brainstorm ways of encouraging more women to become filmmakers. Each group can present their ideas and answer questions from the rest of the class.

COOLER

Put students into small groups. Tell students this story and ask them to use a brainstorming technique to find solutions to this problem.

'A man went to a toothpaste company and told them he could increase their profits by 10% immediately. He said that if the company gave him 1 million dollars he would tell them to do something. After this, without spending any money or reducing the quality of their toothpaste, their profits would increase by 10%. The company agreed, the man told them what to do, and their profits increased 10%. What did he tell them to do?' (*To increase the size of the hole in the toothpaste tube by 10%.*).

Ask students if they have similar puzzles. Students could present their puzzles for the groups to brainstorm solutions.

4 Read the texts again and answer the questions.

GROUP A

1 Did all the students write down their ideas?
2 How did they organise their ideas?

GROUP B

3 What did the students write in the circles?
4 Did all the students write in the circles?

GROUP C

5 What did the students write in the middle circle?
6 Did they learn new information?

GROUP D

7 What did the students use to show their ideas?
8 What did they do with ideas that were the same?

5 In pairs, discuss which brainstorming idea you think is best and explain why.

 6 Listen to four students planning a school party. Which brainstorming method do they use?

Group A

We chose one person in our group to be the secretary, who wrote down the ideas. We put the ideas in lists in different columns. When we had lots of ideas, we numbered them in order of importance. Then, we crossed out the ideas we didn't like so much. In the end, we planned a fantastic event!

Group B

In my group, we drew lots and lots of circles on the page. Then, we took turns to put an idea in each bubble or circle. We didn't write sentences. Instead, we wrote one or two words which expressed our idea, although some people drew a picture. Some of the ideas were crazy, but it was fun to see things that other people thought were important.

Group C

We decided to draw a circle in the middle of the page and write the topic in the centre. Then, we drew lines which connected the middle circle to the other circles. Each of the circles contained ideas about a different part of the topic. It was good because everyone knew different pieces of information, like names or places, so when we finished, we had a lot to write about.

Group D

Each person in the class wrote one idea on a card. Then, we put all the cards on the board at the back of the room. We put the cards that had the same ideas together in groups on the board and then we voted to decide on the best one.

 7 Listen again and answer the questions.

1 What are the topics they mention first?
2 List two of the themes the students suggest.
3 Which nationalities do they mention?
4 How many topics do they have at the end?
5 What is the name of the final topic they mention?

8 Choose the correct options.

> **(!) USEFUL LANGUAGE**
>
> 1 *Do we / Shall we* all write down a list of suggestions *first / firstly*?
> 2 *Why don't we / We think to* make a mind map?
> 3 *Then / Last*, what about the other circles?
> 4 *What about / Let's* start with the theme.
> 5 *Shall we / How about* different nationalities?
> 6 *Next / After*, we'll have to choose decorations.

Listen again and check.

PROJECT *An advertisement*

You see this advertisement for a competition and decide to take part.

YOUNG FILMMAKERS

COMPETITION

Have you got an idea for a new film?
Make a poster with the title, names of the actors and a scene from the film. Write a short description of the scene you choose.
The winners will spend a day at the film school, learning to use cameras and create special effects.

- Work in small groups.
- Read the situation.
- Decide which brainstorming technique you are going to use.
- Brainstorm ideas.
- Choose the best ideas and make a poster for the competition.
- Present your poster and explain your film idea to another group or to the class.

BRAINSTORMING 73

VOCABULARY

1 Match the words 1–8 to a–h to make compound nouns. Use each word once only.

1	shopping	a	class
2	card	b	film
3	old	c	game
4	fitness	d	board
5	art	e	assistant
6	action	f	area
7	message	g	gallery
8	shop	h	town

2 Find the odd word out in each set. Say why it does not fit.

0 blog   link   (prize)   site

'Prize' is the odd one out. The others are all about the internet.

1 traffic   stadium   cricket   fan

2 horror   skier   musical   adventure

3 embassy   mosque   temple   cathedral

4 guest   member   statue   relative

5 climber   diver   runner   golfer

6 board game   puzzle   video game   badminton

7 skyscraper   tournament   champion   professional

3 Write the missing letters to complete the word in each sentence.

1 Ben loves all kinds of sport. He's starting k _ _ _ _ _ _ lessons on Saturday.

2 I was really sad when my mum was in hospital. I m _ _ _ _ _ _ her a lot.

3 Do you have a c _ _ _ _ _ _ _ _ at the school? Then I can phone and ask for that person.

4 I don't want to play cards. Let's do a p _ _ _ _ _ _ instead.

5 My favourite type of film is a c _ _ _ _ _ _ because they always make me laugh.

6 It didn't take a long time to u _ _ _ _ _ _ all the photos to my blog.

7 I found a great new website for teens. You don't have to pay. It's free to j _ _ _ _.

8 I got my mum a necklace for her birthday as I know she loves j _ _ _ _ _ _ _ _ _ _.

GRAMMAR

1 Choose the correct words to complete the sentences.

1 My dad *hadn't / didn't have* to work yesterday.

2 I'm happy with your idea about *go / going* shopping.

3 I think that I lost it on *the / a* sofa in the living room.

4 I bought three shirts *who / which* cost £10, £17 and £25.

Correct the mistakes in these sentences.

5 Oh, and we must forget to take our video and camera.

6 I will try call to you on Wednesday.

7 Where can I find an information about the bus times?

8 My favourite meal is pizza. I love it, especially the pizza who my mum cooks!

2 Put the words in the correct order to make sentences.

1 lots / I / to / listening / of / kinds / of / enjoy / music / different / .

2 for / contact / Could / to / school / you / try / the / me / ?

3 anyone / speak / exam / mustn't / to / before / Students / the / .

4 I / this / is / than / interesting / think / film / the / one / more / other / .

5 helping / the / I / with / mind / activities / don't / tomorrow / you / sports/ .

6 worried / was / about / another / Frank / dance / joining / class / .

7 caught / bus / outside / hospital / that / Elsa / stops / the / the / .

3 Complete the sentences with the correct form of the verbs in brackets.

1 I might stop _____ (have) piano lessons next year.

2 My best friend hopes _____ (take part) in the cricket match on Saturday.

3 We decided _____ (visit) the art gallery first.

4 I forgot _____ (do) my maths homework last night.

5 My mum really misses _____ (see) my brother now that he's at university in the USA.

6 You need _____ (write) your names on this list before we start.

7 I didn't enjoy _____ (watch) that horror film last night.

Overview

VOCABULARY	Sports and activities; sports vocabulary; relationships; internet nouns and verbs; places in a city; uncountable nouns; types of film; conjunctions
GRAMMAR	*must, mustn't, have to* and *don't have to*; verb patterns: gerunds and infinitives; determiners; relative pronouns *who, which, that*
EXAM TASKS	Reading Part 1; Listening Part 3

Resources

PHOTOCOPIABLE WORKSHEETS: Grammar worksheets Units 9–12; Vocabulary worksheets Units 9–12; Review game Units 9–12; Literature worksheet; Speaking worksheet; Writing worksheet

WARMER

Put students into pairs. Tell them to look through Units 9–12 and find three words from each unit. Each pair needs to make sentences with relative pronouns defining these words, for example:

This is a game which you can play on a table. (board game)

This is somebody who lives next to you. (neighbour)

Put pairs together and have them test one another.

VOCABULARY

1 Books closed, say the first half of a compound noun and have students complete it, for example: book(*case*), lap(*top*), bath(*room*). Students could then do this in groups, taking it in turns to say the first part of a compound noun. Books open, have students match the words to make compound nouns. Check as a class.

> **Answers**
>
> 1 f 2 c 3 h 4 a 5 g 6 b 7 d 8 e

2 Tell students to find the odd word out and explain why. Check as a class. See if students can think of alternative answers, for example, *fan* is the odd one out in 1 because *fan* can refer to a person and the others are things.

> **Answers**
>
> 1 *traffic* is the odd one out. The others are all about sport.
> 2 *skier* is the odd one out. The others are all types of film.
> 3 *embassy* is the odd one out. It is the only one that isn't a religious building.
> 4 *statue* is the odd one out. The others are all people.
> 5 *diver* is the odd one out. The others are all people who do land sports.
> 6 *badminton* is the odd one out. It's the only sport.
> 7 skyscraper is the odd one out. The others are all sports-related.

MIXED ABILITY

Concept-check any of the words which you think weaker learners might not remember before you do the exercise. For example, 'a very tall building' (*skyscraper*), 'you can get a visa from here' (*embassy*), 'a type of film with a lot of singing and dancing' (*musical*).

3 Have students write the missing letters. Check as a class. You could do this exercise orally, books closed, with stronger students.

> **Answers**
>
> 1 karate 2 missed 3 contact 4 puzzle 5 comedy 6 upload
> 7 join 8 jewellery

GRAMMAR

1 Tell students to complete sentences 1–4 in Exercise 1 and correct sentences 5–8. Check as a class.

> **Answers**
>
> 1 didn't have 2 going 3 the 4 which
> 5 Oh, and we **mustn't** forget / must **remember** to take our video and camera.
> 6 I will try **to** call you on Wednesday.
> 7 Where can I find ~~an~~ information / **some** information about the bus times?
> 8 My favourite meal is pizza. I love it, especially the pizza **which** my mum cooks.

2 Ask students to reorder the words to make sentences. Check as a class.

> **Answers**
>
> 1 I enjoy listening to lots of different kinds of music.
> 2 Could you try to contact the school for me?
> 3 Students mustn't speak to anyone before the exam.
> 4 I think this film is more interesting than the other one. / I think the other film is more interesting than this one.
> 5 I don't mind helping you with the sports activities tomorrow.
> 6 Frank was worried about joining another dance class.
> 7 Elsa caught the bus that stops outside the hospital.

3 Have students complete the sentences with the correct form of the verbs. Check as a class.

> **Answers**
>
> 1 having 2 to take part 3 to visit 4 to do 5 seeing
> 6 to write 7 watching

A2 KEY FOR SCHOOLS Reading Part 1

1 Books closed. Ask students to remember and write down an example of a short notice, email or message which they have seen or written recently (they could translate it into English if it was in their first language – help them with this if necessary.) Put students into pairs. They should show their text to one another, explain what it means and give any extra information about it. For example:

Student A: *Diana sent me an SMS. It said, 'Can we meet at 6 not 7?'*

Student B: *Why did she send you the message?*

Student A: *We are going to the cinema but the film begins at 6.30 not 7.30.*

Student B: *What did you answer?*

Student A: *I wrote back, 'Sure! No problem.'*

Have some students read out their texts and talk about them in front of the class.

Briefly review what students need to do in this part of the exam and if necessary read out the A2 Key for Schools box on TB page 129. Ask questions about each text before students read the questions.

Where does Ben want to go? (*the cinema*)

How much does the skateboard cost? (*20 pounds*)

Why can't Penny phone her aunt? (*her battery is low*)

Are all pizzas the same price? (*no*)

What did Andy forget? (*his umbrella*)

Can anyone go to the dance classes? (*yes*)

Give students time to read the questions and then do the task. Check as a class.

Ask students some follow-up discussion questions about the texts:

When was the last time you missed a bus or train? What happened?

Is there anything you want to sell?

When was the last time you got a pizza?

When was the last time you forgot something important?

Can you dance? If not, would you like to learn?

Answers

1 A 2 A 3 C 4 C 5 B 6 A

FAST FINISHERS

Tell fast finishers to write a text message from Jim to Ben. Say that they must write exactly ten words.

For example:

Ben

No problem, see you outside the ticket office.

Jim

A2 KEY FOR SCHOOLS Listening Part 3

🔊 2 Briefly review what students need to do in this part of the
97 exam and if necessary read out A2 Key for Schools box on TB page 138. Ask students if there is a sports centre near them, how often they go there and what activities

it offers. Give students time to read the situation and questions and then ask questions to check that students know what to listen for.

Does Serena like the new sports centre? (*yes*)

Can you give an example of a board game? (*possible answer: Scrabble*)

Why do you think Ed might want to contact the games club? (*possible answer: He needs some information about a team he wants to join*)

Is the sports centre open at the weekends? (*yes*)

Where do people usually climb? (*at a climbing wall or in the mountains*)

Play the recording twice for students to answer the questions. Check as a class.

As an extension activity ask students to think which activities would be appropriate for the following teenagers:

Mario: quite fit but lazy, doesn't like team sports

Marina: not very strong but likes to test herself

Gemma: hasn't exercised for a long time and needs motivation

Sebastian: likes to do sport with other people but doesn't have much time

Leo: spends all his time on computer games so is not very fit

Answers

1 B 2 A 3 B 4 A 5 C

» AUDIOSCRIPT TB PAGE 298

COOLER

Write some or all of these sentences on the board (or dictate them). Tell students to correct the mistakes and explain why they are wrong. With weaker students you could underline the vocabulary or grammar which is wrong.

Monopoly is an example of a card game. (*card – board*)

We must to leave in ten minutes. (*must to leave*)

You don't have to be late for the exam. (*don't have to – mustn't*)

The diver got to the top of the mountain. (*diver – climber*)

A closed friend is a very good friend. (*closed*)

Don't forget doing your homework. (*doing – to do*)

I posted for some information for my project. (*posted – searched*)

We saw a match at the palace. (*palace – stadium*)

I need other pen. (*other – another*)

Is there many traffic today? (*many – much*)

The comedy was really frightening! (*comedy – horror film or frightening – funny*)

I saw a film what was great. (*what – which/that*)

If I get home, I always play with my sister. (*If – When*)

You could also include sentences where the vocabulary and grammar is correct.

✓ PREPARE FOR THE EXAM

Reading Part 1

1 Jim

> I missed the bus! Don't wait for me. My mum can give me a lift later, so I'll meet you after the film.
>
> Ben

2
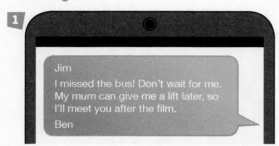

Skateboard for sale

- Needs wheels
- £20
- Nearly new
- Small size

Diana 09863567

3 John

> I forgot Aunt Sandra's address! My battery's low, so please phone her to say I'm coming, and text me Aunt Sandra's address. Thanks!
>
> Penny.

4

Pizzas

**Starting at £6
Buy two, get one free
6 pm–9 pm only**

5

Clare

> I left my umbrella in the bookshop. Can you pick it up for me? I'll let them know you're coming.
>
> Andy.

6

Dance Classes

Mondays and Fridays
All levels and ages
Discounts available

0131–6006655

---

1 For each question, choose the correct answer.

1 **A** Ben wants Jim to go to the cinema without him.
    B Ben will catch the next bus.
    C Ben is meeting his mum at the cinema.

2 **A** There is something missing from the skateboard.
    B The skateboard is several years old.
    C The skateboard is too small for Diana.

3 **A** Penny asks John to send a text to Aunt Sandra.
    B Penny wants to call Aunt Sandra.
    C Penny needs to get Aunt Sandra's address.

4 **A** All pizzas are free in the evening.
    B Two pizzas cost the same as one.
    C The cheapest pizzas cost £6.

5 **A** Andy tells Clare that he found her umbrella in the bookshop.
    B Andy will contact the bookshop to tell them Clare will collect his umbrella.
    C Andy dropped his umbrella and wants Clare to find it for him.

6 **A** There are classes twice a week.
    B All classes are full price at the moment.
    C The classes are for adults only.

Listening Part 3

2 For these questions, choose the correct answer.

🔊 **97** You will hear Serena talking to her friend Ed about the new sports centre.

1 What does Serena like best about the new sports centre?
    A she can take fitness classes.
    B she can play racket sports.
    C she can go climbing.

2 The sports centre closes
    A at the same time every day.
    B later on Saturdays and Sundays.
    C earlier in the holidays.

3 Serena thinks Ed will like climbing because
    A he already knows the teacher.
    B he doesn't like team sports.
    C he's got a strong body.

4 Ed likes board games because
    A they make him think.
    B he doesn't have to move around.
    C he can't play them at school.

5 Ed can contact the games club
    A by text.
    B by letter.
    C by email.

13 LIFE EXPERIENCES

The Great Outdoors:
10 things to do before you're 16

Have you ever climbed a tree or kayaked down a river?
No, you haven't? Well, now's the time to do it!

Start with these ten activities. Download the app and tick the activities off as you do them. You can do them in any order and at any time. When you have finished these ten, click on another section, *Animals, People* or *Sport,* and download ten more. Compare your activities with your friends.

❯ Off you go! No time to lose.

(?) ABOUT YOU
List as many outdoors activities that you can think of.
Which ones do you like doing?
Which ones don't you like doing?

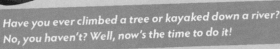
VOCABULARY AND READING

Outdoor activities

1 Match the phrases in the box to the pictures on the website A–J.

(EP)

camp under the stars	climb a tree	explore a cave
kayak down a river	look for fossils	pick wild fruit
play in the snow	record birdsong	track wild animals
try rock climbing		

 Listen, check and repeat.

2 Listen to Juan talking to his friend Susanna about the activities on the website. Which activities would Juan like to do?

3 Listen again and complete the table about Susanna. Which activities are new for Susanna and which are not new?

Activity								
New								
Not new								
When?								
Where?								

4 Look at the table. In pairs, ask and answer the questions.

1 Which of the outdoor activities on the website do you like doing or would you like to do? Why?
2 Which ones don't you like doing or wouldn't you like to do? Why?

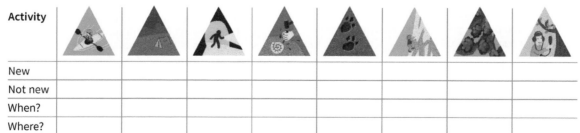

76 UNIT 13

13 LIFE EXPERIENCES

Unit Overview

TOPIC	Activities and achievements
VOCABULARY AND READING	Outdoor activities
	The Great Outdoors: 10 things to do before you're 16
GRAMMAR	Present perfect with *ever* and *never*
PRONUNCIATION	Past participles
READING	Life quiz
VOCABULARY	Past participles
LISTENING	An interview with an explorer
SPEAKING	Doing your own Life quiz
EXAM TASKS	Reading Part 5

Resources

GRAMMAR REFERENCE AND PRACTICE: SB page 159; TB page 266

PREPARE FOR THE EXAM: SB page on TB page 241; TB page 254

WORKBOOK: pages 52–55

VIDEO AND VIDEO WORKSHEET: Life experiences

PHOTOCOPIABLE WORKSHEETS: Grammar worksheet Unit 13; Vocabulary worksheet Unit 13

TEST GENERATOR: Unit test 13

WARMER

Pretend to be someone from space who visits Earth for the first time. You have a lot of questions! Demonstrate with one of the students. For example:

Teacher:	*Who are you?*
Student:	*I'm a student.*
Teacher:	*What's a student?*
Student:	*Someone who learns things, like English.*
Teacher:	*What's English?*

When students understand, arrange them in pairs to do the same. Encourage them to use relative pronouns when explaining things.

ⓘ ABOUT YOU

Books closed. Write these activities on the board: *picnicking, skiing, sun-bathing, gardening.* Ask, 'What do they have in common?' and elicit that you do them outdoors. Books open. Students answer the questions in pairs. Share ideas as a class. Ask, 'Which outdoors activities can you can only do in good weather?' (for example, *sunbathing*) and 'Which outdoors activities can you do without spending a lot of money?' (for example, *running*).

VOCABULARY AND READING

Outdoor activities

1 Books closed. Tell students to write down five things that they would like to do before they are 16, for example, ride an elephant, do the Key for Schools exam. Books open. Tell students to see if anything on their list is on

the website. Explain that *the outdoors* means the place where you do things outside. Ask, 'Is this the complete list of activities?' (*no*), 'Can you explore a cave before you kayak down a river?' (*yes*) and 'When do you need to start?' (*now*).

Have students match the words to the pictures. Check answers as a class. Ask students which of these activities they have already done. Play the recording for students to check and repeat. Then ask students to cover up their answers, say a verb and have students complete the activity, for example, *look* (*for fossils*). Do the same with the nouns: *wild animals* (*track*).

◁)) 99 Answers

The answers are recorded for students to check and then repeat.
A kayak down a river **B** climb a tree **C** camp under the stars **D** play in the snow **E** explore a cave **F** look for fossils **G** track wild animals **H** try rock climbing **I** pick wild fruit **J** record birdsong

FAST FINISHERS

Tell fast finishers to write different nouns that can go with each of the verbs, for example, *camp* (*next to a river*), *climb* (*a mountain*), *pick* (*mushrooms*).

◁)) 98 The Reading text is recorded for students to listen, read and check their answers.

◁)) 100 2 Tell students that they are going to listen to two friends, Juan and Susanna, discussing the activities on the website. Ask students to listen and tick the activities Juan wants to do. Check answers as a class.

Answers

kayak down a river, look for fossils

◁)) 100 3 Play the recording again and have students complete the table about Susanna. Check answers as a class.

Ask some general comprehension questions about the recording, for example, 'Who found the website?' (*Juan*), 'Why hasn't Susanna explored a cave?' (*She doesn't like going underground.*) and 'Where did she go climbing?' (*on a climbing wall*). Ask, 'Which activity do you think Susanna enjoyed the most?' 'Do you think climbing on a climbing wall is a real outdoors activity?'

Answers

New: explore a cave, look for fossils, track wild animals
Not new: kayak down a river, climb a tree, camp under the stars, play in the snow, try rock climbing, record birdsong, pick wild fruit
When?/Where?: kayak down a river – last year in Spain
camp under the stars – last summer in Scotland
try rock climbing – a few weeks ago at school
pick wild fruit – yesterday in grandma's garden
record bird song – last week at school

≫ **AUDIOSCRIPT TB PAGE 298**

CONTINUED ON PAGE 150

4 Tell students to number the activities according to the order that they would do them, so they write 1 next to the activity they want to do first. Put students into pairs to discuss the questions. Share ideas as a class and see which are the most popular outdoor activities. Ask students to think of good places near where they live to do each of these activities, for example: It would be fun to kayak down the river Ebro.

GRAMMAR Present perfect with *ever* and *never*

1 Books closed. Ask a student, 'Did you walk home from school yesterday?'. If 'no', ask 'Have you ever walked home?' (If the first answer was 'yes', ask a different student.). Write the two questions on the board. Ask, 'In the first question, am I asking about a specific time in the past?' (*yes*), 'So what tense is it?' (*past simple*) and 'Is the second question about a specific time?' (*No, it's asking about any time in the past.*). Explain that in this case we use the present perfect and *ever*. Books open. Have students read and then complete the rules. Check answers as a class.

Answers

1 past 2 past 3 can't 4 ever 5 never

>> **GRAMMAR REFERENCE AND PRACTICE ANSWER KEY TB PAGE 266**

MIXED ABILITY

The form and meaning of the present perfect will be challenging for weaker students so extend the presentation and provide more practice. In the presentation, explain that *ever* means 'in your life' and *never* has the meaning 'not ever'. Also point out that for regular verbs, the past participle is the same as the past simple form but the students should be careful about spelling rules (*travel – travelled, worry – worried*, etc.). For practice, download the song *Brighton in the Rain* to play in class or show it on YouTube. The song begins 'I've never been to Athens and I've never been to Rome' and every line has the present perfect with *never*. *Brighton in the Rain* is so ideal for teaching the present perfect that online you can find many worksheets to go with it. It is an authentic song and it has both regular and irregular verbs, so you will have to present both together.

2 Demonstrate with an example on the board:

They / pick / three apples. (*They have picked three apples.*)

Tell students to make sentences and questions. Check answers as a class. Then ask students to make the sentences into questions and the questions into positive and negative sentences.

Answers

1 My mum has visited a safari park.
2 I've never camped in the winter.
3 Have you ever picked fruit from a tree?
4 Has Kris ever climbed a mountain?
5 We've never returned to the amazing campsite in the woods.
6 My little sisters have played in snow.

3 Tell students to correct the sentences. Check answers as a class. Point out that with the superlative, as in sentences 2 and 4, we often use the present perfect and give more examples, for example, *It's the highest mountain I've ever climbed*.

Answers

1 I've never tried sleeping under the stars before.
2 These are the best apples I've ever picked.
3 My mother has never **played** the piano.
4 And it is in a forest. The best place I've **ever** visited.
5 No, I've **never** failed an exam.

>> **GRAMMAR WORKSHEET UNIT 13**

♂ PRONUNCIATION Past participles

🔊 101 **4** Play the recording and pause after the first two words. Ask, 'Is the *-ed* in *camped* an extra syllable? (*no*) and 'Is the *-ed* in *recorded* an extra syllable?' (*yes*).

Play the rest of the recording and have students complete the table. Then play the recording for students to listen, check and repeat. Elicit the rule: you pronounce *-ed* as an extra syllable when the word ends in a /t/ or /d/ sound. You can also tell students how *-ed* is pronounced: /d/ for verbs which end with a voiced sound other than /d/; /t/ for those which end in an unvoiced sound other than /t/; /ɪd/ for verbs which end in a /t/ or /d/ sound. As an extension activity, give students a time limit and tell them to add the past participle of as many verbs as they can to each column, for example, camped – *opened, walked*; recorded – *visited, needed*. For the verbs under *camped* students could add how the *-ed* is pronounced (*opened* = /d/ *walked* = /t/).

🔊 102 **Answers**

The answers are recorded for students to check and then repeat.
camped: climbed, explored, finished, jumped, played, tidied, tried
recorded: collected, ended, hated, painted, wanted

5 Ask students to add two more questions of their own. Drill the questions first, making sure that the students use the correct *-ed* pronunciation, and the short answers. Students then ask and answer the questions in pairs. Tell them to give additional information in their answers, for example *Have you ever camped under the stars? Yes, I have. I camped with my friends in a forest last year.* As feedback, have students report back their partner's answers to the class, for example, *Maria's never kayaked down a river but she's always wanted to climb Mount Elbrus!*

COOLER

Put students into groups. They make five present perfect sentences about themselves or people they know, for example, *I have never walked home from school.* Four sentences should be true and one false. Students take it in turns to say their sentences and the other students should guess which is false.

GRAMMAR | Present perfect with *ever* and *never*

1 Read the statements and questions. Then, choose the correct words to complete the rules.

Statements	Questions	Short answers
I've picked wild fruit. I've never tracked wild animals.	Have you ever kayaked down a river? Have you ever climbed a tree?	Yes, I have. No, I haven't.

1 We use **have** or **has** and the *present / past* participle of the main verb to form the present perfect.
2 We use the **present perfect** to talk about experiences in the *past / present / future*.
3 We *can / can't* use words like *last week* or *ago* with the present perfect.
4 We use *never / ever* in present perfect questions about people's experiences.
5 We use *never / ever* in present perfect statements about people's experiences.

>> **GRAMMAR REFERENCE AND PRACTICE PAGE 159**

2 Make sentences and questions in the present perfect.

1 My mum / visit / a safari park.
2 I / never camp / in the winter.
3 you / ever pick / fruit from a tree?
4 Kris / ever climb / a mountain?
5 We / never return / to the amazing campsite in the woods.
6 My little sisters / play / in snow.

3 Correct the mistakes in the sentences.

1 I never try sleeping under the stars before.
2 These are the best apples I ever picked.
3 My mother has never play the piano.
4 And it is in a forest. The best place I never visited.
5 No, I've ever failed an exam.

∂ PRONUNCIATION | Past participles

🔊 **4** Listen to the past participles and decide in which words we say *-ed* as an extra syllable.

Write these verbs as past participles in the correct column.

climb	collect	end	explore
finish	hate	jump	paint
play	tidy	try	want

camped	recorded

🔊 Listen and check. Then repeat.

5 Make questions about the activities on the website on page 76 using the present perfect. Then, in pairs, ask and answer them.

> Have you ever played in the snow?

> Yes, I have.

> Have you ever explored a cave?

> No, I haven't.

LIFE EXPERIENCES 77

READING

✓ PREPARE FOR THE EXAM

Reading Part 5

1 Read the introduction to the quiz. For each question, write the correct answer.
Write ONE word for each gap.

To: Nina
From: Marco
Reply Forward ✉

Hi Nina

Have **(0)** ___*a*___ look at this quiz. I found it **(1)** _____ the internet and thought you'd like to see it. It's about people's different life experiences, both good **(2)** _____ bad. Don't worry! I did the quiz and there are quite a **(3)** _____ things I haven't done. Some things are more fun **(4)** _____ others – for example who wants to ride a horse? However, I read that it's important to have different kinds of life experiences because they help us learn **(5)** _____ the world. Let **(6)** _____ know what you think.

Marco.

» **PREPARE FOR THE EXAM PAGE 125**

2 Match the questions in the Life Quiz to photos A–L.

3 Answer the questions in the Life Quiz. In pairs, compare your answers. Are your answers the same or different?

Life Quiz

🔊 103

1 Have you ever **swum** with sharks?

2 Have you ever **broken** anything valuable?

3 Have you ever **met** a famous person?

4 Have you ever **had** a bad dream?

5 Have you ever **eaten** Korean food?

6 Have you ever **been** in a film?

7 Have you ever **made** fresh pasta?

8 Have you ever **slept** in a tent?

9 Have you ever **grown** vegetables to eat?

10 Have you ever **ridden** a horse?

11 Have you ever **flown** in a plane?

12 Have you ever **sent** a message in a bottle?

💬 TALKING POINTS

▶ 10 Watch the video and ask and answer the questions.

What's the most amazing thing you've ever done?

What's the most interesting place you've ever visited?

What's the most unusual thing you've ever done?

Have you swum with dolphins?

Have you ridden a camel?

Have you eaten a frog?

78 UNIT 13

WARMER

Write on the board, or dictate, these sentences. Students should discuss if they are true or false. (They could find the answers on their mobile devices or in reference books.)

1 It has never snowed in Australia. (*False – it often snows in the mountains.*)

2 No one has ever travelled to Mars. (*True – only unmanned space craft have travelled to Mars.*)

3 A teenager has never climbed Mount Everest. (*False – Jordan Romero was the first teenager to do this – he was 13 years old.*)

4 Nobody has ever walked from London to Paris. (*True – it's impossible – there is a sea between them.*)

5 An animal has never learned English. (*True – apes have learned some words.*)

 PREPARE FOR THE EXAM

A2 KEY FOR SCHOOLS
Reading Part 5

In this part, students have to read a short text, either an email or a message, and complete it with six words. These words are grammar words like prepositions, pronouns and determiners.

Tip Tell students to first read the text quickly to get an idea of what it is about. Then they should look at each gap and read the sentence around it carefully. Tell students to think of one word which completes the sentence grammatically. They should not think of content words like nouns and adjectives because they will not be the answer. If the gap is difficult they should go through the grammatical categories and think about the grammar of the missing word, for example: Do I need a preposition? If yes, which preposition? If no, do I need a pronoun?

1 Ask students to read the email and then ask some comprehension questions, for example, 'Who found this quiz?' (*Marco*) and 'What is the quiz about?' (*people's different life experiences*). Tell students to look at the example. Ask, 'Why is the answer a?' (*There needs to be an article before the noun look.*).

Do the first question together. Ask, 'What grammar word do we need before a noun?' (*a determiner or a preposition*), 'Is there an article here?' (*yes, the*) and 'So what preposition do we need before *the internet*?' (*on*). Tell students to complete the rest of the email. Check as a class and have students explain, in their first language if necessary, why they chose each answer. Ask students if they agree with Marco that different kinds of life experiences help us learn about the world and, if so, to give examples.

Answers

1 on 2 and 3 few 4 than 5 about 6 me

FAST FINISHERS

Put fast finishers together and have them write a short reply from Nina to Marco. Check the replies. Then choose one of the texts and write it on the board with gaps for grammatical words. The rest of the class should complete the email using the same strategy they used in Exercise 1.

For example:

Hi Marco

Thanks a lot _____ (for) the email! This quiz is _____ (a) great idea and I will do it tomorrow. See _____ (you) soon!

Nina

>> PREPARE FOR THE EXAM TEACHING NOTES AND ANSWER KEY TB PAGE 254

2 Books closed, put students into pairs to think of six questions that could be in the life quiz. Tell students that the questions must be in the present perfect and give some examples, for example, *Have you ever walked on a frozen lake or river?* or *Have you ever stayed in a terrible hotel?*. Books open, ask students to describe each photo. Then tell students to match them to the questions. Check as a class.

Answers

1 E 2 F 3 H 4 L 5 B 6 J 7 C 8 A 9 K 10 I 11 G 12 D

3 Have students answer the questions themselves. See which student has done the most things and ask which is the most difficult thing to do. Drill all the questions and point out that there is usually linking in *you ever* so it is pronounced /juːˈwevə/. Have students ask one another the questions and compare their answers. Encourage students to use follow-up questions and demonstrate. For example:

Teacher: *Fernando, have you ever swum with sharks?*

Student: *No, I haven't. Have you?*

Teacher: *No, I haven't and I don't want to because I'm afraid of them!*

As feedback, ask students to report back on their partners' answers.

Books closed, ask students to remember as many of the twelve questions as they can. Books open, students check.

🔊 The Reading text is recorded for students to listen, read
103 and check their answers.

💬 **TALKING POINTS**

▶ Pre-teach **camel** (a large animal that lives in the desert and
10 has one or two raised parts on its back) and **frog** (a small animal with long back legs for jumping that lives in or near water). Show the video and ask students to complete the video worksheet. Then, read the questions in the *Talking points* box and have students answer the questions. Share ideas as a class.

1 Go through the verbs and have students say the past simple form. Ask students, 'What tense are the questions in the quiz?' (*present perfect*) and 'So what forms are the main verbs?' (*past participles*). Match the first as an example then students work individually. Tell them that these are all irregular verbs. Drill all three forms. As an extension activity, read out some other irregular verbs and have students write down the three forms, for example: *forget / forgot / forgotten, wear / wore / worn, do / did / done, lose / lost / lost.*

Answers

be / was / been (6)
break / broke / broken (2)
eat / ate / eaten (5)
fly / flew / flown (11)
grow / grew / grown (9)
have / had / had (4)
make / made / made (7)
meet / met / met (3)
ride / rode / ridden (10)
send / sent / sent (12)
sleep / slept / slept (8)
swim / swam / swum (1)

2 Put students in pairs to choose photos and make sentences about them in the present perfect. As feedback, ask some students to share their sentences with the class.

3 Write on the board: 'What is the most exciting thing you have ever done?'. Give your own example, for example, 'I've ridden on the back of a motorbike on a mountain road.' Put students into small groups to ask one another. As a class, share ideas and decide which student has done the most exciting thing. Then ask, 'What is the most boring thing you have ever done?' and get some answers.

>> **VOCABULARY WORKSHEET UNIT 13**

LISTENING

BACKGROUND INFORMATION

The Tour d'Afrique from the north to the south of Africa is one of the longest cycle races in the world. It takes place from January to May each year and both professional and amateur cyclists take part. Although the start is always in Cairo and the finish is always in Cape Town, the exact distance and number of countries visited varies each year. A typical race covers around 12,000 kilometres and goes through ten countries. The route is divided into about 100 stages where competitors need to cover between 40 and 200 kilometres in a day but there are also rest days.

1 Ask students, 'How many different countries have you been to?' and 'What do you call somebody who likes to go to places other people haven't visited?' (*an explorer*). Tell students they are going to listen to an interview with an explorer. Ask students, 'Which places would you like to explore?'.

Play the recording and ask students to name the three places Christina talks about. Check as a class.

Answers

Brazil / Brazilian rainforest
North Pole
Africa

 2 Play the recording again and have students complete and answer the questions. Check as a class. Ask students which of these trips sounds the most interesting and what kind of preparation Christina would need to make for them.

Answers

1 got lost on any of your travels? Yes, in the Brazilian rainforests.
2 She was looking for insects.
3 That she got lost in the rainforest.
4 wanted to come home early from a trip? No, she hasn't.
5 She was skiing.
6 She wrote in a diary.
7 She will be with other people, not alone.
8 She will cycle / ride a bike.
9 It'll take four months.

MIXED ABILITY

Write the answers to the questions in a different order on the board. Weaker students can then match the answers to the questions.

>> **AUDIOSCRIPT TB PAGE 299**

SPEAKING

1 Put students into pairs and tell them to write down eight life experiences, some positive and some negative. Give examples, such as, learn to ride a bike and fail a test. Tell each pair to choose six of the experiences and make them into present perfect questions. Combine pairs into small groups and have them choose eight of the questions. Each student then writes the eight questions down. Give students a time limit to go round the class asking their questions to different students. Then tell students to go back to their original groups and report back on the answers to their questions. Using the phrases from the box, students then tell the whole class about the answers to their quiz.

COOLER

Arrange the chairs in a circle in the middle of the room. There should be one chair fewer than the number of students. So, 19 chairs if you have 20 students in your class. Tell the students to walk around the chairs. You read out a list of verbs. When students hear an irregular verb, they should sit down. For example:

open, try, live, work, move, share, do – sit down

One student will not have a chair so they are out of the game. Students who try and sit down at the wrong word are also out of the game. Keep taking away a chair and continue in the same way until there is a winner. You can make the activity shorter by having fewer chairs so several students will be out of the game at each stage.

VOCABULARY · Past participles

1 What is the past simple form of each verb in the box?

EP Now, match each verb to a past participle in the quiz.

> be break eat fly grow have
> make meet ride send sleep swim

2 In pairs, take turns to name a photo from the Life Quiz and make a true statement about it.

> Picture I

> I've ridden a horse. Picture A

> I've never slept in a tent. I like sleeping inside.

3 In groups, ask and answer questions about the most exciting thing each of you has done. Tell the class.

LISTENING

1 Listen to the radio show. Jim is talking to Christina Wells, an explorer. Which three parts of the world does she talk about?
104

2 Listen again. Complete the questions about each trip. Then in pairs, answer the questions.
104

Trip 1
1 Complete Jim's question to Christina: Have you ever
    ?
2 What was she doing in the rainforest?
3 What information did she not want to share with people?

Trip 2
4 Complete Jim's question to Christina: Have you ever
    ?
5 How was she travelling to the North Pole?
6 What did she do to help her think more clearly?

Trip 3
7 What is different for Christina about this trip?
8 How will she travel?
9 How long will it take?

SPEAKING

1 Now, you're going to write your own Life Quiz.

a In pairs, think of other life experiences you think are important. They can be good or bad.

b In pairs, write six questions beginning *Have you ever …*

c In small groups, read each other's questions and choose eight questions you think are the best.

d Individually, write the eight questions for the Life Quiz on a piece of paper. Make sure there is room to write answers for at least two students.

e Ask your questions to at least two other students in the class. Don't ask students from your group.

f In your original group, discuss the answers students gave you to the eight questions.

g Report back to the class about the results of the Life Quiz. Use the phrases in the box to help you.

> We asked … students.
> Some of the students we asked have …
> Most of the students we asked have …
> Most of the students we asked haven't …
> None of the students we asked have …
> All of the students we asked have …

14 SPENDING MONEY

ABOUT YOU

Do you like shopping? Why? / Why not?
What shops do you go to the most?

VOCABULARY AND READING

Shops

1 Match the shop words in the box to the photos A–L.

> bakery   bookshop   butcher's
> café   chemist's   clothes shop
> department store   market
> newsagent's   shoe shop
> sweet shop   supermarket

🔊 105 Listen and check. Then repeat.

2 Where can you buy these things? Choose from the shops in Exercise 1. Sometimes, there is more than one possibility.

> apples   bread   burgers
> chocolates   dictionary
> magazines   sandwich   socks
> sun cream   tea towels   trainers

3 In pairs, think of at least two more things you can buy in each shop.

4 Read the advertisements in a magazine. What kind of shops are they?

5 Where can you ...

1 surf the internet?
2 buy something to wash your hands with?
3 buy something for a lower price than usual?
4 have some free food?
5 pick up something you bought online?

6 Read the advertisements again and answer the questions.

1 What is the date of the magazine?
2 When does each shop open?

YORK TIMES 🔊 106
21st March

📖 Reading Time
16 Old Road

Are you a reader? Then this is the place for you. Choose something from the shelves. Then relax, have a coffee and read.
Comfortable sofas and free wi-fi.

Doors open **6th March**

Something Special
52 Main Street

Do you like sweets and chocolates? Come and choose from the hundreds we have in our shop.
You can even try before you buy!
Opening 20th March.

One Foot After Another
13 River Avenue

We've got everything you need for your feet. There's something for everyone in our store. Walking boots on sale.
Our first day is 3rd April.

Shop and Try
www.shopandtry.net

All the latest fashions in clothes.
Order online, collect from our shop in York.
Try your jeans, jumpers and dresses on in store.
Make sure they're right for you!

Open from **24th March**

Brown's Chemist's
30 Grove Street
As well as medicines, get soap and make-up here.
Everything you need for baby too.
Free coffee.

Opening **19th March**

14 SPENDING MONEY

Unit Overview

TOPIC	Shopping and money
VOCABULARY AND READING	Shops
	York Times
GRAMMAR	Present perfect with *just, yet* and *already*
PRONUNCIATION	Intonation: questions and statements
READING	Pocket money
VOCABULARY	Units of measurement and money
LISTENING	A conversation about a birthday picnic
WRITING	An email
EXAM TASKS	Writing Part 6

Resources

GRAMMAR REFERENCE AND PRACTICE: SB page 160; TB page 266
PREPARE FOR THE EXAM: SB page on TB page 242; TB page 255
WORKBOOK: pages 56–59
PHOTOCOPIABLE WORKSHEETS: Grammar worksheet Unit 14;
Vocabulary worksheet Unit 14
TEST GENERATOR: Unit test 14; Term test 2

WARMER

Write these verbs from Unit 13 on the board, well spaced out: *be*, *break*, *eat*, *fly*, *grow*, *have*, *make*, *meet*, *ride*, *send*, *swim*. Bring in a ball, or improvise with some paper screwed up into a ball. Arrange students into two teams, lined up facing the board. The first student in team A throws the ball at a verb. The first student in B must ask a *Have you ever ... ?* question using the verb closest to where the ball hits the board, for example, *Have you ever sent an email to the wrong person?*. One of the students in team A must answer. The second students in the line do the same, team B throwing the ball. Teams get a point for asking a grammatically correct question and for giving a grammatically correct answer. Continue until all the students have played and add up the points.

⑦ ABOUT YOU

Ask students, 'What was the last thing you bought?' and 'Where did you buy it?'. Then they answer the questions in pairs. They may already know some vocabulary for shops but if they don't they should say the name of the shop. Share ideas as a class. Ask, 'Do you prefer to go to shops or shop online?'

Shops

1 Ask students to name what is in each picture, for example, *In picture A there are some sweets. In picture B there is a green sign.* Then ask students to match the words to the photos.

Play the recording for students to check and repeat.

Point out the apostrophe and *s* with *butcher's* and *newsagent's* and say you sometimes see *chemist's* too.

Answers

The answers are recorded for students to check and then repeat.
A sweet shop B chemist's C department store D café
E shoe shop F supermarket G bookshop H clothes shop
I market J butcher's K newsagent's L bakery

2 Ask students, 'Where can you buy tablets and medicine?' (a chemist's, a supermarket). Tell students to write down where you can buy each thing. Share ideas as a class. Ask students, 'Do you prefer to buy things from supermarkets and department stores or go to smaller shops?'

Possible answers

apples – market, supermarket
bread – bakery, supermarket
burgers – butcher's, supermarket
chocolates – sweet shop, department store, supermarket
dictionary – bookshop
magazines – newsagent's, bookshop, supermarket
sandwich – café, bakery, supermarket
socks – clothes shop, department store, market, supermarket
sun cream – chemist's, department store, supermarket
tea towels – department store, market, supermarket
trainers – shoe shop, department store, market, supermarket

3 Put students into pairs and tell them to write down at least two more things you can buy at each shop. Share ideas as a class.

Possible answers

bakery: cakes, buns
bookshop: school books, reading books
butcher's: beef, chicken
café: tea, cakes
chemist's: face cream, medicine
clothes shop: T-shirts, jeans
department store: hats, furniture
market: fruit, vegetables
newsagent's: newspapers, pens
shoe shop: sandals, shoes
sweet shop: soft drinks, sweets
supermarket: flowers, food

4 Books closed, pre-teach **advertisement** (show some examples from YouTube or a magazine) and ask students if they have a favourite (they could find it on their mobile devices or just describe it). Books open, tell students to read the advertisements and say what the shops are. Check as a class.

Answers

Reading Time – bookshop with a café
Something Special – sweet shop
One Foot After Another – shoe shop
Shop and Try – clothes shop
Brown's Chemist's – chemist's

5 Ask students, 'Where can you get something for your six-month-old sister?' (*Brown's Chemist's*). Tell students to read the advertisements again and answer the questions. Check as a class.

CONTINUED ON PAGE 158

6 Tell students to answer the questions. Check as a class.

106 The Reading text is recorded for students to listen, read and check their answers.

GRAMMAR Present perfect with *just, yet* and *already*

1 Ask students which shops are open now and which will open soon. Tell students to match sentences a and b to the two shops. Check as a class.

2 Tell students to read the examples in Exercise 1 again and then match the sentence halves to complete the rules. Check as a class. Point out the word order: *already* and *just* come after *have* and before the main verb; *yet* goes at the end of the sentence.

MIXED ABILITY

Weaker students may benefit from a more visual presentation. Bring three cans of soft drink into the lesson. Two should be unopened and one finished. Put them on your table. Ask students to gather round you. Open one can and say 'I've just opened the can.' Get students to repeat this after you and write it on the board. Show the empty can and say 'I've already finished this.' Get students to repeat this after you and write it on the board. Open the last can, drink some and say 'I've just opened the can but I haven't finished it yet.' Get students to repeat this after you and write it on the board. Go to the half-empty can and ask, 'Have I finished it yet?' (*no*) Elicit *You haven't finished it yet.* Ask, 'Have I already opened it?' (*yes*) Take the empty can and ask, 'Have I just drunk it?' (*no*). Students then complete the rules in Exercise 2.

» **GRAMMAR REFERENCE AND PRACTICE ANSWER KEY TB PAGE 266**

3 Books closed, arrange students into pairs. Ask them to write eight things which you need for a camping trip (students could look back at the kit list on page 44). Books open, they compare with the picture and shopping list. Ask the students 'How many things has Carla already bought?' (*seven*) and 'How many hasn't she bought yet?' (*five*). Students then make sentences saying what she has already bought and what she hasn't bought yet. Check as a class. Ask students in which shops she could buy the things she still needs.

4 Give your own examples first, for example, 'I've just asked Sandra a question.' and 'I've just remembered something important.'. Tell students to write down six things then compare their lists with a partner. Share ideas as a class. Ask students to report back about their partner, for example, *Pedro has just learned a new word.*

5 Demonstrate with an example on the board:

Max just has been to the shop. (just has been – has just been.)

Tell students to correct the mistakes in the sentences. Check as a class.

» **GRAMMAR WORKSHEET UNIT 14**

ə PRONUNCIATION

Intonation: questions and statements

107 6 The purpose of this pronunciation exercise is to prepare students for Exercise 7. Students listen to the recording and repeat. Elicit that *yes/no* questions usually have a rising intonation and that statements have a falling intonation. If students have problems hearing the difference between a rising and falling intonation, hum the sentences, not saying the words, as that can make the intonation more obvious. Students can then hum the intonation patterns themselves as a first stage before saying the sentences with words.

7 Books closed, demonstrate by writing a short list of your own routine on the board and get students to ask you questions about your day so far with *yet* and *already*. For example, 'Have you prepared your lessons for tomorrow yet?' Books open, students make their lists and then ask each other questions. Monitor and make sure that students are using a rising intonation on the questions and a falling intonation on the answers.

COOLER

Tell students to stand up. Tell them to sit down if what you say is true about them today. Say some sentences with the present perfect, *yet* and *already*, for example:

Sit down if

… you've sent a text today.

… you've drunk some coffee.

… your mum has phoned you.

… you've already watched a video.

… your best friend has said 'Hello' to you.

… you haven't been to a shop yet.

The last person standing is the winner.

GRAMMAR — Present perfect with *just, yet, already*

1 The date of the magazine is 21st March. Which shops are open and which shops will be open soon?

Reading Time (6th March). It has already opened.
Something Special (20th March). It has just opened.
One Foot After Another (3rd April). It hasn't opened yet.
Has One Foot After Another opened yet? No, it hasn't.

Choose the correct sentence, a or b, for these two shops. Today is 21st March.

Shop and Try opens on 24th March.
Brown's Chemist's opened on 19th March.

a It hasn't opened yet.
b It has just opened.

2 Study the examples in Exercise 1. Then match 1–4 with a–d to make sentences about the present perfect.

1 To talk about something which happened a very short time ago,
2 To talk about something which we expect to happen in the future,
3 To talk about something which happened not long ago, or sooner than someone expected,
4 To ask about something which we expect to happen in the future,

a we use the present perfect negative with *yet*.
b we use present perfect questions with *yet*.
c we use the present perfect with *already*.
d we use the present perfect with *just*.

» GRAMMAR REFERENCE AND PRACTICE PAGE 160

3 Look at the things in the picture that Carla has just bought for a camping trip. Then, look at her shopping list. Answer the questions using *yet* and *already*.

1 Which things has she already bought?
2 Which things hasn't she bought yet?

4 Write a list of six things you've just done. In pairs, compare your lists.

I've just opened my book.

5 Correct the mistakes in the sentences.

👁 **1** You already borrow my book for a week.
2 I've just bought a new smartphone, but I didn't put music on it yet.
3 I just see a football match with my father.
4 I already have bought something to eat.
5 Are you still looking for your keys? If you don't find them yet, I think they are in your bag.

⊖ PRONUNCIATION

Intonation: questions and statements

🔊 **6** Listen and repeat.
107

Has your brother arrived yet?
Yes, he's just arrived.
Has your sister arrived yet?
Yes, she's already arrived.

7 Make a list of ten things you do every day. In pairs, ask and answer questions about today.

Have you done your homework yet?

Yes, I've already done my homework.

Have you used the computer yet?

Yes, I've just used the computer.

Shopping List:

pillow	☐	water bottle	☐
blanket	☐	hat	☐
socks	☐	gloves	☐
biscuits	☐	T-shirt	☐
boots	☐	scarf	☐
toothbrush	☐	fruit	☐

SPENDING MONEY 81

POCKET MONEY

Did you know?

1. Most teenagers receive pocket money every week. But not everyone gets the same amount of money. Have you asked your friends how much they get? You might be surprised. And if you're a girl you'll be amazed to learn that boys often get more than girls of the same age!

2. Teenagers up to the age of about 15 in the UK have about £5 a week in pocket money. But in Italy, France and Spain, the same age group gets about €9, which is a bit more. In the US, pocket money is called 'an allowance'. Most teenagers get an allowance of about $30, which is more than £20 or €25.

3. Quite a lot of teenagers do. They have to do things in the house, like washing-up and cleaning and then they get their pocket money. If they don't do the jobs, they don't get the money. Some teenagers have part-time jobs too, which means they have more than their pocket money to spend each week.

4. You might be surprised at the answer. Teenagers in the UK spend more of their money on food than on clothes. Is that true for you too? Teens do more shopping online than before and online clothes shopping is cheaper. So perhaps this is one reason they don't spend so much on clothes.

5. Some parents do! They only let them buy some things. Other parents want their teens to save all their pocket money and spend it on something big in the future, or not spend it at all.

TALKING POINTS

What was the most surprising thing for you in the article?

READING

1 In pairs, ask and answer the questions.

1 What is pocket money?
2 Do you get pocket money?
3 How much do you get a week?
4 Do you spend more of your pocket money on food or clothes?

2 Read the article quickly. Match the question to the correct paragraph.

a So what happens in different countries?
b Do teens have to work for their pocket money?
c Do parents tell teens what to spend pocket money on?
d What do teenagers spend their money on?
e Do all teenagers get pocket money?

3 Answer the questions about the article.

1 What's the difference between the pocket money girls get and the pocket money boys get?
2 Where do teenagers get more pocket money, the USA, the UK or Italy, France and Spain?
3 What is pocket money called in the USA?
4 What do some teens have to do before they get their pocket money?
5 How do some teenagers add to their pocket money?
6 What do some parents want their children to do with their pocket money?

VOCABULARY — Units of measurement and money

1 Complete the sentences using words from the box.

centimetres	dollars and cents	euros and cents
grams	kilograms	kilometres	litres
metres	millilitres	pounds and pence

1 You buy food in _____ or _____.
2 You buy drink in _____ or _____.
3 You use _____, _____ and _____ to buy things.
4 You find out how far away something is in _____, _____ and _____.

2 Work with a partner and decide how you say the amounts.

| 260 g | €15.34 | 700 ml | 55 cm | 2.5 l |
| 37 p | £19.99 | 6 kg | 62 c | $27 | 1.65 m |

Listen and check. Then repeat.

3 Complete the descriptions for photos 1–4 with the words in the box.

| a pair of | a set of | a slice of | a variety of |

1 _____ pizza

3 _____ cups

2 _____ sunglasses

4 _____ drinks

READING

WARMER

Students write down everything they've eaten today. In pairs they ask each other questions in the present perfect to see if they've eaten the same: *Have you had any chocolate?* They then compare lists to see who is the healthiest and who has eaten the most.

1 Point to your pocket and ask, 'What is this?'. Then put students into pairs to discuss the questions. Share ideas as a class. Students may feel uncomfortable answering question 3 so tell them to skip it if necessary.

2 Ask, 'What are the teenagers doing in the photographs?' (*saving money, doing housework*). Give students a time limit to match the questions to the paragraphs. Check as a class. Ask students to convert the different currencies into their own currency as this will make the pocket money figures more meaningful. Ask students if teenagers should only get pocket money if they do jobs around the house.

Answers
1 e 2 a 3 b 4 d 5 c

3 Ask students, 'How much pocket money does a Spanish teenager get every month?' (*about €36 = €9 × 4*) and 'Why do teenagers buy clothes online?' (*It's cheaper.*). Tell students to answer the questions in the book. Check as a class. Ask students, 'What do your parents let you spend your pocket money on?' and 'What don't they let you spend money on?'.

Answers
1 Girls don't get as much as boys.
2 They get the most in the US.
3 It is called an allowance.
4 They have to do jobs around the house.
5 They have part-time jobs.
6 They want them to save it to spend on something big in the future, or not spend it at all.

🔊 **108** The Reading text is recorded for students to listen, read and check their answers.

FAST FINISHERS

Tell fast finishers to think of three things that they would like to save up their pocket money to buy, for example, a new phone, a holiday to the seaside. They could calculate how many weeks it would take them to save this money.

💬 TALKING POINTS

Ask students, 'Why do you think boys often get more pocket money than girls?'. Put students into pairs to discuss their reactions to the article. Share ideas as a class. Ask students, 'Do you think your parents got pocket money?' and 'If so, what did they spend it on?'. If students don't know, they could ask their parents and report back in the next lesson.

VOCABULARY Units of measurement and money

BACKGROUND INFORMATION

In Britain, there are some units of measurement, called imperial units, not widely used in other countries. For example, often distances are given in miles (1 mile = 1.6 kilometres) and people say their weight in stones and pounds (1 stone = 6.4 kilograms). Britain also has the oldest currency in use, the pound, dating back to the 8th century.

There are about 180 different currencies in the world but about 22 are dollar currencies, for example the Canadian dollar and Singapore dollar.

1 Books closed, take a ruler and ask students, 'What is this?' (*a ruler*), 'What is it for?' (*It's for measuring things.*) and 'How?' (*in centimetres and millimetres*). Ask students if they know any more words like these. Books open, tell students to complete the sentences. Check as a class. Point out that in American English some of these words end in *-er* rather than *-re*, so are spelt *meter, milliliter, kilometer*, etc. Point out that *kilogram* is often shortened to *kilo*.

Answers
1 kilograms or grams
2 litres or millilitres
3 dollars and cents, euros and cents and pounds and pence
4 centimetres, metres and kilometres

2 Go through the pronunciation of numbers, especially prices, by writing some on the board and getting students to say them aloud. Then put students into pairs to say the amounts. Play the recording for students to check and repeat. Point out that the British usually write and say *p* not *pence*. Then ask the students to find out how much these things are and say the amounts: the price of a cinema ticket; the distance to the nearest airport; how many litres of water you need to drink a day; how much a pound is worth in your money.

🔊 **109** #### Answers
The answers are recorded for students to check and then repeat.
Two hundred and sixty grams
Fifteen euros and thirty-four cents
Seven hundred millilitres
Fifty-five centimetres
Two point five litres or two and a half litres
Thirty-seven pence
Nineteen pounds, ninety-nine pence
Six kilograms
Sixty-two cents
Twenty-seven dollars
One metre sixty-five centimetres or one point six five metres

3 Tell students that a common pattern is noun *of* noun and give as examples *a loaf of bread* and *a pair of trousers*. Tell students to complete the descriptions. Check as a class.

Answers
1 a slice of pizza
2 a pair of sunglasses
3 a set of cups
4 a variety of drinks

4 Ask students what other nouns could go with the first nouns, for example, *a slice of bread, a pair of scissors, a set of paints, a variety of snacks*. Tell students to complete the sentences. Check as a class.

> **Answers**
> 1 a pair of 2 a variety of 3 a slice of 4 a set of

> **MIXED ABILITY**
>
> Ask weaker students whether these words are followed by singular, plural or uncountable nouns:
>
> *slice* (a thin section) + uncountable
>
> *bit* (a small part) + uncountable
>
> *pair* (two things, or something with two parts) + plural
>
> *set* (a group of similar things) + plural
>
> *variety* (different things) + plural
>
> To show the meaning, ask students to think of more combinations for each word, for example *set + books, clothes, friends*; *bit + time, bread, money*; *slice + bread, cheese*; *pair + trousers, shoes*.

>> **VOCABULARY WORKSHEET UNIT 14**

LISTENING

1 Books closed, ask students to line up according to their birthday, January on the left and December on the right. They do this by asking one another *When's your birthday?*. Books open, put students into pairs to discuss what they like to eat on their birthdays. Share ideas as a class.

 2 Give students some time to read the task. Then play the recording and ask them to tick what David and Lana have already got for the picnic. (They should put the ticks on the left of the words, as they will have to write the quantity after each word when they listen again in Exercise 3.) Check as a class.

> **Answers**
>
> They have already got pizzas, crisps, apples and a blanket. (David has got her present but Lana hasn't yet.)

 3 Play the recording again and ask students to note down 'how much' next to each item on the list. Check as a class.

> **Answers**
>
> pizzas – 3 = 24 slices
> crisps – 4 big bags
> apples – 1.5 kilos
> lemonade – 3 litres
> fruit juice – 2 litres
> water – 1 litre

>> **AUDIOSCRIPT TB PAGE 299**

4 Ask students to read the conversation in pairs and then answer the questions. Check as a class. Point out that we can use *if not* (and the positive *if so*) instead of repeating a clause. For example: *We can meet at 6 p.m. If we can't meet at 6 p.m., 7 p.m. will be all right. / If not, 7 p.m. will be all right.*

> **Answers**
>
> 1 I could … , I can … if you like 2 If not

5 Put students into pairs and have them read aloud the conversation in Exercise 4. Then tell them to write two conversations and practise them. As feedback, have some pairs perform their conversations for the class.

WRITING

✎ **PREPARE TO WRITE**
Writing Part 6 An email

A2 KEY FOR SCHOOLS Writing Part 6

Briefly review what students need to do in this part of the exam and if necessary read out the A2 Key for Schools box on TB page 118.

Tell students to look back at the email they wrote on SB page 61. Tell students to leave time to check their email for spelling, punctuation, grammar and vocabulary mistakes.

GET READY Dictate a list of punctuation marks, including full stops, capital letters, apostrophes and question marks, to students to write down as symbols. Students then correct the note and compare with each other before you check the answer.

> **Answer**
>
> Dear Dad,
> Lana and I need to get some things for Pia's party. Please can you take us to the supermarket this morning? Thanks! See you later.
> David

PLAN Students read the task and make notes.

WRITE Students expand their notes into sentences. Remind them that they need to pay attention to the tenses in the prompts because they will normally use the same tenses in their reply.

IMPROVE Students pass their notes to one another to check that they have covered all three content points and that there are no mistakes.

> **Model answer**
>
> Hi Sam,
> I have just bought a set of Lego for my sister because she loves it. I got it from the supermarket near my house.
> Best,
> Cecilia

> **COOLER**
>
> Send students this text message (or write it on the board). They must send it back to you with the correct spelling and punctuation (or write it in their books).
>
> *happy new year ru coming 2 the party 2nite*
>
> *i need 2 know*
>
> *cu soon*
>
> > **Answers**
> >
> > Happy New Year! Are you coming to the party tonight?
> > I need to know.
> > See you soon.

4 Complete the sentences with the words from Exercise 3.

1 I've just bought _____ shoes. Do you like them?
2 Let's have _____ music styles at the party. We can have rock, blues and rap.
3 Can you pass me the knife? I'll cut you _____ cake.
4 Our teacher has got _____ keys for the school.

LISTENING

1 Work in pairs. Tell your partner what you like to eat on your birthday.

🔊 110 **2** David and Lana are planning a birthday picnic for their friend Pia. Listen and tick (✓) the things they have already got.

Things for Pia's Picnic

- pizzas ● fruit juice
- crisps ● water
- apples

Plus

- cake ● blanket
- lemonade ● presents!

🔊 110 **3** Listen again. Look at the list in Exercise 2. How much of each food and drink have they got or do they want?

4 Read the next part of Lana and David's conversation and answer the questions.

Lana: Hey, just a minute, we forgot about music. We haven't chosen the music yet. We can't have a party without music. What shall we do?
David: I <u>could</u> bring my guitar, I suppose.
Lana: Yes, and <u>I can</u> text everyone who's coming, <u>if you like</u>, and ask them to bring instruments, too. Right. Is that all?
David: Oh, I nearly forgot. The biscuits! I'll try and make them this afternoon. <u>If not</u>, I'll make them in the morning.
Lana: OK.

1 Which two <u>underlined</u> phrases make offers and suggestions?
2 Which <u>underlined</u> phrase says what the situation will be when something does not happen?

5 In pairs, write conversations. Use the ideas below and the conversation in Exercise 4 to help you. Then, in pairs, practise the conversations.

1 You're planning a day out at the beach with your friend. You forgot about the food.
2 You're planning a visit to a new shopping centre. You forgot how you're going to get there.

WRITING

✏ PREPARE TO WRITE

Writing Part 6 An email

GET READY Read the note from David to his dad. Correct the punctuation. Add full stops, capital letters, apostrophes and question marks.

> dear dad
>
> Lana and i need to get some things for pias party please can you take us to the supermarket this morning thanks see you later
>
> david

In pairs, compare your corrected notes.

PLAN You have just bought a birthday present for your sister. Write a message about it to your English friend Sam.
In your message

- say what you have bought for your sister
- say why you chose it
- say which shop you bought it in.

☑ **WRITE** 25 words or more. Make sure you include information about all three ideas in your answer. Think carefully about punctuation.

IMPROVE In pairs, read each other's notes and look for mistakes. Check that you have both included all the necessary information and that you used punctuation correctly.

CULTURE

SHOPPING AND MONEY

1 In pairs, discuss the questions.

   1 Where do you usually go shopping?

   2 Do you or your parents ever shop in markets?

2 Match the types of markets in the box to the photos A–D. How many objects can you name that you can buy in them? Do you have similar markets in your country?

> food market   clothes market
> antiques market   flower market

3 Read about three famous markets. Which one isn't a food market?

Amazing MARKETS

🔊 111

A You should definitely visit the Queen Victoria Market in Melbourne, Australia. The market started in the 1870s. Today, it's open every morning on Tuesdays and Thursdays to Sundays. There's also a night market on Wednesdays from 5 to 10 pm. There are more than 600 shops and stalls in the market. The fresh-food areas sell fruit and vegetables, cakes, fish and meat (including kangaroo and crocodile steaks!).

C St Lawrence Market in Toronto, Canada, started in 1803, but they built the buildings you can see today in 1904. The market is open Tuesday to Saturday from 8 am to early evening. You can buy many different things there from more than 100 stalls, especially fresh food and delicious homemade products. A fun thing to do is cookery classes in the Market Kitchen. Here, you can learn to make different dishes and take them home to eat! The farmers' market opens on Saturdays at 5 am, and local farmers come to sell meat, fruit, vegetables, eggs, etc.

84 **CULTURE**

CULTURE

Learning Objectives

- The students learn about famous markets, and markets and shopping in general.
- In the project stage, students find out about a famous market in their country and make a presentation about it for the class.

Vocabulary

stall steak jewellery jazz built home-made

Resources

CULTURE VIDEO AND CULTURE VIDEO WORKSHEET: Famous Markets

BACKGROUND INFORMATION

The first open-air markets probably developed in Persia in about 3000 BC and the Persian word *bazaar*, meaning an enclosed marketplace, spread into many languages. Bazaars were usually in major cities close to trade routes. They were important not only for the goods they sold but also as meeting places where travellers could get news and pass on information.

The Grand Bazaar at Istanbul is one of the oldest and most famous continuing markets in the world. Work on the bazaar started in 1455 and the first goods sold were textiles and jewels. The bazaar has gone through several stages of expansion and reconstruction and survived earthquakes and fires. Today it is one of the most popular tourist attractions in the world. About 25,000 people work there and there are between 250,000 and 400,000 visitors each day. The challenge of modern restoration is to keep the traditional attractions of the bazaar but make conditions better for those working and visiting there.

Another type of traditional market is the floating market, where goods are sold from boats on rivers. Floating markets are common in south Asia, where waterways were the centre of trade before road and rail systems developed, but many are now mainly tourist attractions. One of the most famous and well-visited is Damnoen Saduak floating market in Thailand, about 100 kilometres from Bangkok. The market is only open in the mornings, before the sun gets too hot, but at its peak hundreds of boats sell everything from fish to souvenirs. You can even have a Thai massage on some of the boats!

The biggest markets in the world are online now. eBay, an auction website where customers bid for a huge range of goods and services, was founded in California in 1995. The directors of the company became instant billionaires when eBay went public in 1998. The first thing sold was a broken laser pointer and eBay is famous for the strange things people have bought and sold there, including one Brussels sprout, a town in California, an aircraft carrier and a new species of sea urchin.

WARMER

Say 'I went to the shops and I bought some bread.' Ask another student to repeat the sentence but add one more thing they bought, for example, *I went to the shops and I bought some bread and a red T-shirt*. Tell another student to continue in the same way, for example, *I went to the shops and I bought some bread, a red T-shirt and two cans of cola*. Put students into large groups to do the same, continuing until one student can't remember. See which group can make the longest unbroken story.

1 Books closed. Ask students to write down as many different shops they can remember then tell them to check with page 80. Books open. Put students into pairs to discuss the questions. Share ideas as a class. Ask students, 'Do you ever argue with your parents about what to buy or not to buy?'.

2 Tell students to look at the photos, match them to the types of markets and then say what you can buy in them. Ask students to give an example of each type of market in their country. Ask students, 'Why do you think some people prefer to shop in a market outside rather than a supermarket or online?'.

Answers

Photo A – food market
Photo B – clothes market
Photo C – antiques market
Photo D – flower market
Students' own answers

3 Give students time to read and say which market isn't a food market. Check as a class. Ask students which market would be the most interesting for tourists.

Answer

Hell's Kitchen market

FAST FINISHERS

Tell fast finishers to write down ways that each market could get more customers. This could be marketing, competitions or special offers. For example:

Queen Victoria market – free kangaroo steak for anyone who can jump over a stall

Hell's Kitchen market – 25% discount in rain and 50% discount in snow

St Lawrence market – free coffee for anyone who arrives as the farmers' market opens

🔊
111
The Reading text is recorded for students to listen, read and check their answers.

4 Ask students, 'Which market is the newest?' (*Hell's Kitchen*). Have students read the text again and answer the questions. Check as a class. Ask students if people go to these markets mainly to shop or mainly just to look around.

Answers
1 A 2 B 3 B 4 A and C 5 C 6 A 7 A

5 Tell students to find the words that match the definitions. Check as a class. Ask students what they would like to learn to cook in St Lawrence market.

Answers
1 stall 2 steak 3 jewellery 4 jazz 5 built 6 home-made

MIXED ABILITY
Pre-teach these words to weaker students before Exercise 3. Exercise 5 then tests the students' retention of the vocabulary presented.

---

112 **6** Ask students if they have been to London and if so if they have visited any of the famous markets there. Ask students to listen and say which part of the market Alice liked most. Check as a class. Ask students which market she visited (*Camden Lock*). Ask students what else they would like to know about this market. Tell students that Camden Lock Market is centred on the banks of a canal (a *lock* is a gate in a canal which controls water levels; a *canal* is an artificial waterway). Tell them that when Camden Lock Market started in the 1970s, it was a market for craft goods but now the range of goods has expanded.

Answers
the clothes stalls

112 **7** See if students can say whether the sentences are right or wrong without listening again. Play the recording for students to check. Ask more questions about the recording: 'What two other places did she see in London?' (*Buckingham Palace and the Science Museum*), 'What colour was the handbag?' (*green*) and 'How much money did she have left at the end of the day?' (*five pounds*).

Answers
1 ✗ 2 ✓ 3 ✗ 4 ✗ 5 ✓ 6 ✓

» AUDIOSCRIPT TB PAGE 300

🗩 TALKING POINTS
Put students into pairs to discuss which market they would like to visit. Share ideas as a class. Ask if there are any other famous markets they would like to go to.

PROJECT *A market*
Tell students to say the names of famous markets in their country and write them on the board. Ask students what they already know about each one. Put students into small groups. (Make sure that the groups are different from the last project.) Tell them to choose different markets, for variety. As a variation, you could allow students to make up their own markets, perhaps unusual ones like an underwater market specialising in seafood, and describe them.

Have students organise their groups so each person is responsible for finding out about one area and finding pictures and photos. Students find out the information on the internet or in reference books and then report back to the group. The group decides what to put on the poster and then designs it including pictures and photos. Each group takes it in turns to present their poster to the class and answer questions. Leave feedback until you have heard all the presentations and make error correction anonymous so students don't feel embarrassed hearing their own mistakes.

PROJECT EXTENSION
Tell students to work in the same groups and design a website for the market they presented. First, they should see if the market already has a website. If it doesn't have one, students should decide what information the website should contain (they can base it on their poster presentations) and which student is responsible for that part of the website. If the market has a website, students should decide how to improve it. Students then make a plan of the website, either as a poster again or a Powerpoint presentation. Each group pins their presentation on the wall. Groups then go round the website plans and write comments and suggestions on them. If groups have the time and IT skills, they could actually make real websites.

---

11 ▶ **CULTURE VIDEO:** Famous Markets
When students have completed the lesson, they can watch the video and complete the worksheet.

COOLER
Put students into pairs, a market trader and a customer. The market trader is selling a carpet to the customer and they must negotiate a price. The market trader wants a high price (minimum $200), the customer wants a low price (maximum price $220). Let students negotiate – they can make up details such as the quality and condition of the carpet. The student with the best price, based on their minimum or maximum, wins. (If they can't reach an agreement in the time limit, they both lose!)

B Hell's Kitchen market is an outdoor street market in New York, USA. It only opens at weekends from 9 am to 5 pm, with nearly a hundred stalls on the streets – but if the weather is bad, there aren't so many people selling or buying. It started in 1976, and you can buy antiques, such as old furniture or clothes and jewellery. If you enjoy music, it is a great place to visit because there are often jazz concerts, and you can buy musical instruments there, as well. Local artists also show their paintings, sculptures and photos.

4 Read the text again and answer the questions.

Which market(s) ...
1 is sometimes open at 9 pm?
2 has fewer visitors if it is raining?
3 can you buy a guitar in?
4 is over 100 years old?
5 can you learn to cook in?
6 sells unusual meat?
7 is the biggest?

5 Find words in the text that match the definitions.

1 a kind of small shop (text A)   ....
2 a piece of meat (text A)   ....
3 rings, necklaces, etc. (text B)   ....
4 a kind of music (text B)   ....
5 constructed (text C)   ....
6 food that people prepare
  themselves (text C)   ....

🔊 **6** Listen to Alice talking to her friend Dan about a market
112 in London. Which part of the market did she like most?

🔊 **7** Listen again. Are these statements right (✓) or wrong (✗)?
112
1 Alice went to Camden Lock Market last Saturday.
2 Camden Lock Market is very big.
3 You can buy fresh fruit and vegetables in the market.
4 Alice ate pizza in the market.
5 Alice bought three T-shirts and a handbag.
6 Alice's friend Lisa likes Justin Bieber.

💬 **TALKING POINTS**
Which market would you like to visit:
Queen Victoria, Hell's Kitchen, St Lawrence
or Camden Lock? Explain why.

PROJECT *A market*

**Find out about a famous market in your
country. Make a poster to present the
information to the class. Use pictures
and photos to make the poster more
interesting. Include information about:**

• where it is
• when it is open
• what you can buy, see and do there.

Present your poster to the class.

▶ **11 NOW WATCH THE CULTURE VIDEO**   **SHOPPING AND MONEY** | 85

15 FREE TIME

? ABOUT YOU

How many hours of free time do you have per week?
Is this the right amount, too much or too little?

VOCABULARY AND LISTENING

Free-time activities

1 In pairs, match photos A–E to activities in the questionnaire. Which of the activities do you think are most popular in your class?
EP

Questionnaire

Activities	I do this	I'd like to try this	I'm not at all interested in this
chatting			
collecting			
cooking			
going out with friends			
going shopping			
listening to music			
making things			
photography			
playing an instrument			
playing computer games			
playing sport			
reading books			
singing, acting, dancing			
spending time online			
watching TV			

2 Do the questionnaire in your class. Walk around the room and ask people which activities they do in their free time, which they'd like to try and which they are not interested in. Write your results for each activity or hobby like this: ⫽⫽⫽ ⫽⫽

3 In small groups, look at all your results and write some sentences.

In our class, lots of / some / a few people already do these activities: _____, _____, _____.
In our class, lots of / some / a few people want to try these activities: _____, _____, _____.
In our class, no one likes these activities: _____, _____, _____.

Were you surprised by any of your results? Why?

15 FREE TIME

Unit Overview

TOPIC	Having fun
VOCABULARY AND LISTENING	Free-time activities
	Three young people talk about free-time activities
GRAMMAR	Present perfect with *for* and *since*
PRONUNCIATION	Weak forms
READING	My hobby – geocaching
VOCABULARY	Collocations about having fun
LISTENING	A girl talking about her unusual hobby
SPEAKING	An interview about an unusual hobby
EXAM TASKS	Reading Part 3

Resources

GRAMMAR REFERENCE AND PRACTICE: SB page 161; TB page 266
PREPARE FOR THE EXAM: SB page on TB page 239; TB page 253
WORKBOOK: pages 60–63
PHOTOCOPIABLE WORKSHEETS: Grammar worksheet Unit 15; Vocabulary worksheet Unit 15
TEST GENERATOR: Unit test 15

WARMER

On the board write some adjectives that describe how people feel, for example *happy, tired, hungry*. Elicit more from students. Ask a student, 'Why are you [adjective]?' and tell the student to answer with a sentence in the present perfect and *just* or *yet*. For example:

Teacher: *Why are you happy?*

Student: *I've just passed my maths test.*

Demonstrate with more examples, then arrange students into pairs to do the same.

⦿ ABOUT YOU

Books closed, tell students to write down how many hours a week they spend on: studying, sleeping, eating, housework, travelling and free time. (Students can add other categories.)

Books open, students answer the questions in pairs. Share ideas as a class. Ask students to go back to the list they wrote down and change the number of hours to make an ideal week. Students then compare their lists in pairs.

VOCABULARY AND LISTENING

Free-time activities

1 Books closed, arrange students into pairs. Ask them to write down as many free-time activities as they can in two minutes. Each activity must have a verb and a noun, for example, *reading books, listening to music*. Books open, students see if any of their ideas are in the photos. Ask them to describe the photos. If necessary, pre-teach **bowling** (a game in which you roll a large ball

along a wooden track in order to knock down bottle-shaped objects), **knit** (to make clothes using wool and two long needles to join the wool into rows) and **badge** (a piece of plastic, metal, etc. with words or pictures on it that you wear on your clothes for decoration). Then students match the photos to five of the activities in the questionnaire and discuss which activities in the questionnaire they enjoy. Ask students to predict in pairs which activities will be more popular with boys and which with girls and explain why. Check as a class.

Ask students questions about the photos, for example:

Photo A: 'Where are they?' (*a clothes shop*), 'What do they want to buy?' (*a shirt*) and 'Which shirt would you choose?'

Photo B: 'How do they feel?' (*excited*) and 'What game do you think they are playing?'

Photo C: 'Are they doing this inside or outside?' (*inside*)

Photo D: 'What do you think she is making?' and 'How long do you think it will take her to make it?'

Photo E: 'Can you read anything on any of these badges?' and 'Which of them do you like best?'

Answers

A going shopping **B** playing computer games
C going out with friends / playing sport **D** making things
E collecting
Students' own answers

2 Ask students to give you examples of some of the activities, for example: *going out with friends – going to a café, having a party; going shopping – the shops on page 80; making things – origami, models.* Then tell students to stand up and go around the classroom asking questions to the other students. Give students a time limit to do the survey and make sure that they ask full questions (for example, *Which activities do you do in your free time?*) and give full answers (*I do … and …*). Students could also ask follow-up questions for each activity students do, for example: (listening to music) *Where do you download music? How often do you go to concerts?* They should record the results as they ask the questions.

MIXED ABILITY

With weaker students, write the three questions on the board and drill them.

Which activities do you do in your free time?

Which activities would you like to try?

Which activities are you not interested in?

With stronger students, get them to add three more activities to the list and ask about them.

3 Put students into small groups. Tell them to add up their results and complete the sentences. Students compare the results with their predictions, see where they were right and wrong and discuss if anything was surprising. They could turn the results into a chart using Excel or just draw one. Ask some students to report back the results to the class.

◁)) 113 **4** Pre-teach **pin** (a type of badge, with a sharp point; people wear them on their jackets). Play the recording and ask students to write the activities below each speaker. Check as a class.

> **Answers**
> Owen – spending time online
> Kyle – collecting, playing sport
> Erin – playing an instrument, reading books, photography

◁)) 113 **5** See if the students know the answers before you play the recording again. For the wrong answers, ask students to correct the information. Check as a class. Ask students which person, Owen, Kyle or Erin, would be the most interesting person to have as a friend.

> **Answers**
> 1 ✓ 2 ✗ (you learn a lot from it) 3 ✓ 4 ✓ 5 ✓
> 6 ✗ (I use my dad's camera)

»» AUDIOSCRIPT TB PAGE 300

GRAMMAR   Present perfect with *for* and *since*

1 Ask students to guess which free-time activity you are talking about:

I've done it <u>for a long time</u>. You need water but you don't get wet. (*fishing*)

My friend Boris has played it <u>since he was a teenager</u>. It's the only time he can be a king. (*playing chess*)

We've only done it <u>for a year</u> but the fridge door is already full of them. (*collecting fridge magnets*)

My brother has played these <u>for a month</u> and no one has had much sleep since he started. (*playing the drums*)

Repeat the sentences for students to write down. Ask them to underline the phrases with *for* and *since*. Ask, 'What tense are these sentences with *for* and *since*?' (*present perfect*), 'Which says from when: *for* or *since*?' (*since*) and 'Does *for* say how long or how much?' (*how long*).

Tell students to read the sentences and complete the rules. Check as a class.

> **Answers**
> 1 for 2 since

»» GRAMMAR REFERENCE AND PRACTICE ANSWER KEY TB PAGE 266

2 Do the first two together. 'Is number 1 about a start date?' (*yes*) 'So we need …?' (*since*) and 'What about 2?' (*No, it's about how long.*). Tell students to complete the sentences. Check as a class. Then have students put the *since* time expressions in order, from the most distant (*I was three years old*) to the most recent (*yesterday*).

> **Answers**
> 1 since 2 for 3 since 4 for 5 since 6 since 7 for 8 since
> 9 for

FAST FINISHERS

Tell students to make new sentences which finish with the *since/for* part of the sentences. For example:

My brother has loved football since he was three years old.

We've been at school for four hours.

You could ask fast finishers to make some of the sentences true and some false. When the rest of the class have finished, fast finishers read out their sentences and the class guess if they are true.

3 Give an example on the board:

I've been in this room since … (*10.30 / the lesson started*).

Tell students to complete the sentences with their own ideas and then compare with a partner. Share ideas as a class.

4 Books closed. Write an example on the board:

We've collected badges since a long time. (*since* – *for*)

Books open. Tell students to correct the sentences. Check as a class. Have students explain what the mistakes were.

> **Answers**
> 1 It's been my hobby **since** I was ten years old.
> 2 I've needed one **for** a month.
> 3 I've had it **for** a year.
> 4 I've wanted to buy this T shirt **for** several weeks.
> 5 It has been open **for** one month.

»» GRAMMAR WORKSHEET UNIT 15

ə PRONUNCIATION | Weak forms

◁)) 114 **5** Students listen to the sentences and compare how the underlined words are said and how they are written. Play the recording again for students to listen and repeat. Elicit from students that function words like auxiliaries and prepositions have weak forms (write the transcription of the weak forms with schwa /ə/ on the board if students know phonetic script) and that these forms are usually used in sentences.

6 Demonstrate in front of the class with one of the stronger students. In pairs, students do the same.

7 Students use this information to write sentences about their partner. They then get into groups and read the sentences to each other. They should listen to what is said about them and check that their partner has remembered it correctly.

COOLER

Say to students, 'One, two, three, four' and get them to chant with you. Do the same thing adding *and*, 'One and two and three and four'. The rhythm in the chant will stay the same. You can show this by clicking your fingers on the numbers. Explain that this is because *and* is pronounced quickly, without any stress. If students know phonetic script, write the weak form of *and* /ən/ on the board. Continue the chant with students until they can do it on their own using the weak form.

🔊 **4** Listen to three young people talking about what they do in their free time.
113 Write the activity or activities from the questionnaire below each speaker.

Owen	Kyle	Erin

🔊 **5** Listen again. Are the sentences right (✓) or wrong (✗)?
113

1 Owen keeps his computer in his bedroom.
2 Owen thinks he uses his computer too much.
3 Kyle still collects pins and badges.

4 Kyle does two different sports.
5 Erin has got a new guitar.
6 Erin has her own camera.

GRAMMAR | Present perfect with *for* and *since*

1 Look at these examples. Then, complete the rules below with *for* or *since*.

I've had my own computer for three years.
I haven't bought any football cards for a long time.
I've played the guitar for two years.
I've had this guitar since January.
I've had one of them since I was ten.
My dad's had his camera since he was a teenager.

> **1** We use _____ with an amount of time, such as a number of hours / months / years.
> **2** We use _____ with the time when the action started, such as a day / date / age.

≫ **GRAMMAR REFERENCE AND PRACTICE PAGE 161**

2 Complete the sentences with *for* or *since*.

1 Jack's lived here _____ he was three years old.
2 Mum's been asleep _____ four hours.
3 I've been a member of the club _____ last month.
4 Sophie's had her new phone _____ three days.
5 We've had our puppy _____ 31st October.
6 The students have worked together _____ Monday.
7 You've been at this school _____ six months.
8 I've had a headache _____ yesterday.
9 They've known Jules _____ a long time.

3 Complete the sentences so they are true for you. In pairs, compare your answers.

1 I haven't read a comic since _____.
2 I haven't watched a cartoon for _____.
3 I've played _____ for _____.
4 I've been able to _____ since I was _____.
5 I've lived in my home since _____.
6 I've had this pen for _____.
7 I've known my best friend since _____.

4 Correct the mistakes in the sentences.

👁 **1** It's been my hobby from I was ten years old.
2 I've needed one since a month.
3 I've had it since a year.
4 I've wanted to buy this T-shirt since several weeks.
5 It has been open since one month.

ə **PRONUNCIATION** | **Weak forms**

🔊 **5** Listen to the sentences and
114 notice the pronunciation of the underlined words.

I've had this since I <u>was</u> three.
He's played basketball <u>for</u> two years.
I've just walked home <u>from</u> school.
They haven't been <u>to</u> your house since Saturday.
I've bought <u>some</u> nice shoes.

🔊 Listen again and repeat.
114

6 In pairs, ask and answer.

Do you have a hobby?

Yes → What is it?

No → What do you do in your free time?

How long have you enjoyed doing it?
Do you need anything special to do it?

Yes → What do you need?

No

Do you usually do it with other people?

7 Write sentences about your partner. In groups, read out your sentences. How much did your partner remember about you?

Andrei has done karate since he was seven. He has a special white jacket and trousers called a gi. He has a blue belt. He's had it for six months.

FREE TIME 87

1. Look at the photos and the title of the blog. What do you think geocaching is?
   Read the blog once to check your ideas.

MY HOBBY – geocaching
Blog post written by Lucy Barton, aged 14

I started geocaching because of my uncle – he's done it for years. Geocaching is a treasure hunt that you do with an app. The 'treasure' is a box called a cache that someone else has hidden. There are 2 million of these, all over the world! It's a really fun hobby and I'm so glad my uncle told me about it. We have a great time doing it together, but if he's busy I go with friends, or do it by myself.

The app takes you quite close to the cache, and then it gives you a puzzle to help you find exactly the right place. A lot of older people are geocachers, so some of the puzzles are difficult for me as they are about movies and TV shows that I haven't seen. But I don't really mind – I can always look them up on the internet!

It's a fantastic feeling when you find a cache! You have to open the box and put your name in the little book inside. Often, there are things in the cache as well. You can take something out to keep if you want to, but if you do that, you should always put something new inside for the next person.

Next year, I'm going to start using the paid version of the app. Then, I can make and hide my own caches! I'm also going to tell all my friends and family about geocaching. It's such a great way for everyone, from adults to little kids, to spend time together, enjoy themselves and get to know their local area.

✔ PREPARE FOR THE EXAM

Reading Part 3

2. Read the text again. For each question, choose the correct answer.

1 What do we learn about Lucy from the first paragraph?
   A She has done her hobby for longer than her uncle.
   B She didn't enjoy her hobby much at the beginning.
   C She doesn't always do her hobby with other people.

2 What does Lucy say about the puzzles?
   A They can be hard for her because she's young.
   B It's a shame so many of them are about films.
   C People shouldn't look online to find the answers.

3 What must you do when you find a box?
   A check how many people have already found it
   B leave something of yours for the next person
   C write down who you are in the little book

4 What does Lucy plan to do in the future?
   A spend more time geocaching in the city
   B get other people interested in geocaching
   C spend less money on going geocaching

5 What do we find out about geocaching from this article?
   A It's becoming more popular every year.
   B It takes a long time to learn how to do it.
   C It's a good hobby for people of all ages.

 TALKING POINTS

What makes geocaching a good hobby?
Would you like to try it?
Why / Why not?

WARMER

Draw this on the board and ask students what it is.

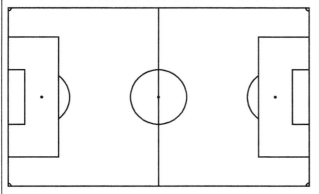

It's a football field!

Divide students into two teams. Team A attack from left to right. Team B attack from right to left.

Toss a coin to see who kicks off. They start in the middle. Ask a question to the team which kicks off. Examples: 'What is this [point to something in the room] in English?' and 'What is the past participle of [verb]?'.

If the team get the question right, they progress to the next line on the field; if they get it wrong the 'ball' passes to the other team.

While a team has the ball, keep asking questions until they get to the goal line (the furthest lines on the left and right) – this is a goal and the other team restarts the game from the centre.

Have a time limit for the game (not 90 minutes!) or the first to, say, five goals wins.

If you have a large class, get students to write a list of questions and answers, then split the class into groups to play with a referee to ask these questions.

If students don't like football, you can change this to tennis, hockey, etc.

BACKGROUND INFORMATION

Geocaching is a technological update of the much older game letterboxing. In letterboxing people also try and find boxes in public places and sign a log book to show they have found it. However, originally, the clues to finding the boxes were spread by word of mouth or written in special books. The hobby is called 'letterboxing' because people used to leave letters or postcards in the boxes for finders to post.

Geocaching became possible because GPS technology gives users the exact coordinates of a cache. The first cache was made in 2000 and was a black bucket containing among other things a can of beans. There is some controversy over geocaching. For example, some people think the caches are litter and they can be hidden in places which are dangerous to get to. However, there is at least one case of a geocache saving lives: in 2008 two hikers were lost in the snow in Oregon but found a geocache and were able to give their location to rescuers.

1 Ask students to look at the photos and ask, 'What do you think they're looking?', 'What do you think is in the box?' and 'What do you think the boy is writing down?'. Then ask students if they've heard of geocaching, /ˈdʒiː.əʊ.kæʃ.ɪŋ/, or can guess what it is (give students a hint that the prefix geo- also goes with geography). Give students a time limit to read and check their ideas.

✓ PREPARE FOR THE EXAM

A2 KEY FOR SCHOOLS Reading Part 3

2 Briefly review what students need to do in this part of the exam and if necessary read out the A2 Key for Schools box on TB page 65.

Point out that the questions test main ideas and details but they may also test opinion and feeling. They are in the order that the information is presented but the last question may be a general question about the whole text, for example 'What's the best title for this article?' or 'What is the writer doing in this text?'.

Tell students that they should read the questions carefully because they can also give a lot of information about the text, for example question 3 tells us that geocaching involves finding a box; question 4 tells us that Lucy talks about her future plans.

Ask students, 'Who wrote this?' (Lucy Barton), 'What do you need to go geocaching?' (an app) and 'How do you find a cache?' (You solve a puzzle.). Tell students to answer the questions in the book. Check as a class.

Answers

1 C 2 A 3 C 4 B 5 C

MIXED ABILITY

With weaker students go through some or all of the questions as a class. For example, Question 1: 'Where is the answer to this question?' (in the first paragraph), 'Who started geocaching, Lucy or her uncle?' (her uncle), 'So A is wrong. Does she like geocaching?' (Yes, she says it's fun.), 'Does she say she didn't like it at the beginning?' (no), 'So B is wrong. C is the answer then but what words does Lucy use to say she sometimes goes geocaching alone?' (by myself).

🔊 The Reading text is recorded for students to listen, read
115 and check their answers.

💬 TALKING POINTS

Ask students if they agree with Lucy that both children and adults would enjoy geocaching. Put students into small groups to discuss the questions in the book. Share ideas as a class. Ask students where they would hide a cache and what they would put inside it. You could also ask students to make a puzzle for other students to find where their geocache is.

VOCABULARY — Collocations about having fun

1 Books closed, write on the board.

I liked it.

This is good.

Ask students to think of more interesting ways of saying these, for example, *It was brilliant! It's super fun!.* Books open. Tell students to underline examples of the phrases in the blog. Check as a class.

Answers

a really fun hobby
I'm so glad
We have a great time
It's a fantastic feeling
It's such a great way

2 Demonstrate with an example on the board.

It _____ brilliant to see you yesterday. (was)

Tell students to complete the sentences in the book and remind them to change the form of the verb if necessary. Check as a class.

Answers

1 had **2** Spending **3** enjoys **4** spent, was **5** have
6 was/is, was/am **7** enjoyed

FAST FINISHERS

Tell fast finishers to go through the completed sentences and take as many words out as possible so that the sentence is still grammatical. They cannot make any changes to the rest of the sentence or add any words. For example:

1 I had a ~~wonderful time at the~~ party ~~last night~~.

2 Spending time with friends is my favourite ~~free-time~~ activity.

---

3 Go through the sentences completing them with your own examples. For example:

1 finished the 10-kilometre run last weekend.

2 my cousins in Barcelona.

3 I went bowling with some other teachers.

Tell students to complete the sentences with their own ideas and then compare with a partner. Encourage students to ask their partner follow-up questions about the sentences and demonstrate with yours, for example, 'What time did you run the 10 kilometres in?', 'How often do you see your cousins?' and 'Where did you go bowling?'. As feedback, ask some students to read out their sentences and see which are the most interesting.

>> **VOCABULARY WORKSHEET UNIT 15**

LISTENING

🔊 **1** Tell students to look at the photograph at the bottom left
116   of the page and say that this is beekeeping. Ask students why someone would want to do beekeeping. Pre-teach **hive** (a container like a box where bees live). Play the recording for students to listen and answer the questions.

Answers

She's speaking to her class. She's done her hobby for two years.

🔊 **2** See if students can answer the questions before the
116   second listening. Then play the recording again for students to check. Ask students how they think Libby would answer the questions in Exercise 3, for example, *It was a fantastic feeling when I saw all my bees around the hive.*

Answers

1 ✗ 2 ✗ 3 ✓ 4 ✓ 5 ✓ 6 ✗ 7 ✗

>> **AUDIOSCRIPT TB PAGE 301**

SPEAKING

1 Tell students to match the hobbies to the photographs. Ask some questions connected with the hobbies, for example:

Jewellery making: 'What jewellery would you like to make?'

Dog training: 'Who do you think gets fitter – the person or the dog?' and 'You can train dogs but are some animals impossible to train?'

Fencing: 'What skills do you need to do this well?' and 'Is it dangerous?'

Remote controlled vehicles: 'What type of vehicle would you like to own?'

Ask generally, 'Which of these hobbies is the most unusual?'.

Put students into pairs. Students must decide who is the journalist and who is answering the questions. (Weaker students will find it easier to answer the questions.) They should also decide what the unusual hobby is. Get some ideas from the class and write them on the board so pairs can choose. Tell the journalists to use the sentence beginnings in the box to help them.

2 Give students time to practise their interviews. Tell them to look back at Exercise 6 on page 87 for some ideas and remind them to use weak forms. Pairs then take it in turns to perform their interviews in front of the class. The rest of the class can ask questions to the person with the hobby once the interview is finished. You can then repeat the process with the journalists and interviewees swapping roles or putting students into new pairs.

COOLER

Arrange students into groups. Read out (some of) these questions about vocabulary from Units 11–15. To help weaker students, give them the first letter of each word.

1 The home of a princess. (*palace*, Unit 11)

2 Rings and necklaces, etc. (*jewellery*, Unit 11)

3 A type of film about future worlds and technologies. (*science-fiction*, Unit 12)

4 A rock with the shape of an animal or plant that died a long time in the past. (*fossil*, Unit 13)

5 You _____ a tree. (climb, Unit 13)

6 A shop where you can buy medicine. (*chemist's*, Unit 14)

7 It means a piece of pizza, bread, etc. (*slice*, Unit 14)

8 Talking in a friendly way face-to-face or online. (*chatting*, Unit 15)

VOCABULARY — Collocations about having fun

1 Look at the phrases in the box. Which ones are in the blog? **EP**

have	fun
	a great time
	a laugh
spend time	with a friend
	doing a hobby
be	glad
feel	happy
enjoy	yourself
	an activity

a(n)	fun	feeling
	brilliant	day out
	exciting	hobby
	fantastic	feeling

2 Complete the sentences with the correct form of *have*, *spend*, *be* or *enjoy*.

1 I _____ a wonderful time at the party last night.
2 _____ time with friends is my favourite free-time activity.
3 My brother _____ playing computer games more than anything else and is really good at them.
4 I _____ most of yesterday at the beach. It _____ a really fun day.
5 I always _____ fun when I see my cousins.
6 It _____ an amazing feeling to win the race! I _____ so glad I entered!
7 My dad and my brother went fishing and they really _____ themselves.

3 Complete the sentences so they are true for you. In pairs, compare your answers.

1 It was a fantastic feeling when I _____ .
2 I love spending time with _____ .
3 The last time I had a good time was when _____ .
4 I always enjoy myself when I _____ .
5 My idea of a fun day out is _____ .
6 I was really glad when _____ .

LISTENING

1 🔊 116 Listen to a girl talking about her hobby – beekeeping. Who is she speaking to? How long has she done her hobby?

2 🔊 116 Listen again and decide if the sentences are right (✓) or wrong (✗).

1 Libby got her bees as a birthday present.
2 Libby went on a beekeeping course with some other teenagers.
3 Libby loved beekeeping as soon as she tried it.
4 Libby does more for her bees in summer than in winter.
5 Libby thinks her bees know what she looks like.
6 Libby says it's good to have lots of bees in her hive.
7 Libby says collecting the honey is her favourite part of beekeeping.

SPEAKING

1 In pairs, prepare an interview. One of you is a journalist. The other has an unusual hobby. Use the examples of unusual hobbies in the box, or you can choose your own.

dog training   fencing   jewellery making
remote-controlled vehicles

In the interview, the journalists must ask at least five questions:

Tell me about…
How long have you…?
When did you…?
How do you feel about…?
Why did you…?
How did you get the idea to…?
Are you glad you…?

2 Practise your interview. Then, role-play your interview in front of the class.

16 LANGUAGES OF THE WORLD

How do you feel about learning English?
Is it a fun hobby?
Is it boring and not very useful?
Is it important for your future?

VOCABULARY AND LISTENING

Words to describe language learning

1 Complete the quiz with the words in the box.

EP

articles	exercises	guess	list	look up
meaning	mistakes	spell	topic	translate

What kind of language learner are you?

1 When do you use English outside the classroom?
- **A** to read (1) .... online
- **B** when I'm on holiday abroad
- **C** to watch English-language movies and TV shows
- **D** only when I'm doing homework

2 What do you do when you find a new word in a text?
- **A** (2) .... it .... in a dictionary
- **B** try to (3) .... what it means
- **C** ask my teacher to (4) .... it into my language
- **D** ask my little brother for the (5) ....

3 What's the best way to learn vocabulary?
- **A** from a (6) .... of words
- **B** by doing vocabulary (7) ....
- **C** by reading books and magazines
- **D** five minutes before a test

4 Which of these sentences do you agree with?
- **A** It's important to be able to (8) .... correctly.
- **B** Making (9) .... is an important part of learning.
- **C** Pronunciation doesn't matter as much as grammar.
- **D** I only learn if the (10) .... of the lesson is interesting.

2 Now do the quiz. Choose only one answer for each question. Turn to page 137 to see your results. Do you agree with them?

3 In pairs, compare your quiz results.

✓ PREPARE FOR THE EXAM

Listening Part 4

4 For each question, choose the correct answer. Read through the questions before you listen. 🔊 117

1 You will hear a boy called Danny talking to his friend. How did Danny improve his Spanish?
- **A** by writing to his penfriend
- **B** by practising online
- **C** by spending time in Spain

2 You will hear a teacher talking to her class. What does she want them to work harder on?
- **A** their grammar
- **B** their pronunciation
- **C** their vocabulary

3 You will hear two friends talking about some homework. Why hasn't the boy done his homework?
- **A** He forgot to make a note of it.
- **B** He wasn't at the lesson.
- **C** He wrote down the wrong thing.

4 You will hear a girl telling her mother about her new friend, Yumi. What languages does Yumi speak well?
- **A** English, Russian and Swedish
- **B** Swedish, Japanese and English
- **C** Japanese, Swedish and Russian

5 You will hear a boy giving a classmate some important news. How did he find out about the news?
- **A** from a family member
- **B** he heard from a teacher
- **C** the teacher told him

🔊 117 **5** In pairs, compare your answers. Then, listen again and check.

16 LANGUAGES OF THE WORLD

Unit Overview

TOPIC	Languages
VOCABULARY AND LISTENING	Words to describe language learning
	Five short conversations
GRAMMAR	Present perfect and past simple
READING	Languages of the world
VOCABULARY	Large numbers
PRONUNCIATION	Word stress in numbers
LISTENING	A talk about different languages
WRITING	Information about your English class
EXAM TASKS	Listening Part 4; Speaking Part 1

Resources

GRAMMAR REFERENCE AND PRACTICE: SB page 162; TB page 267

PREPARE FOR THE EXAM: SB pages on TB pages 247 and 249; TB pages 257 and 258

WORKBOOK: pages 64–67

VIDEO AND VIDEO WORKSHEET: Different languages

PHOTOCOPIABLE WORKSHEETS: Grammar worksheet Unit 16; Vocabulary worksheet Unit 16

TEST GENERATOR: Unit test 16

WARMER

Arrange students into groups. Give them two minutes to write down English words which have come into their language, for example *le camping* in French. See which group can find the most words. Afterwards ask students why their language has taken these English words and if this is a good thing.

 ABOUT YOU

Ask students, 'Do a lot of people in (your country) speak English?' and 'Why? / Why not?'. Put students into pairs to discuss the questions. Share ideas as a class. Ask students, 'How many hours a week do you think you should learn English in school?' and 'Would you like to learn another language as well as English?'.

 VOCABULARY AND **LISTENING**

Words to describe language learning

1 Books closed, ask students to think of some questions about learning English, for example *Have you ever sung a song in English?*. Books open, check the meaning of some of the words in the box, for example 'How do you spell dog?' (*D-O-G*) and 'You do this when you think you know something but don't know for sure.' (*guess*).

Say to students, 'All these words are about …?' (*language learning*). Tell them to look at the first item in the quiz and say, 'After *read* we need a …?' (*noun*) and 'Which noun in the list makes sense here?' (*articles*).

Pre-teach **abroad** (in a foreign country). Students complete the quiz then check as a class. Tell students to translate all the words in the box into their own language on a separate piece of paper and then translate them back to English. Ask students if they think this is a good way of learning and remembering vocabulary.

Answers

1 articles 2 look, up 3 guess 4 translate 5 meaning
6 list 7 exercises 8 spell 9 mistakes 10 topic

2 Have students do the quiz and then look at their results on page 137. Ask students if they agree with the results.

FAST FINISHERS

Tell fast finishers to add one more option to each of the questions, for example: Question 1 – (E) *to play computer games.* Then tell fast finishers to write the alternative options on the board. At the end of Exercise 3 you can ask students if they do any of these things.

3 In pairs, students compare their quiz results. Ask them, 'Do you think your English has improved much since the school year began?' and 'What do you need to work on most?'.

 PREPARE FOR THE EXAM

A2 KEY FOR SCHOOLS Listening Part 4

4 Briefly review what students need to do in this part of the exam and if necessary read out the A2 Key for Schools box on TB page 94.

117

Tell students to listen for words and phrases which signal that important information is coming or a contrast is being made, for example 'however' in question 2 and 'How do you know?' in question 5.

Give students time to read the questions carefully. Ask students a question about each question to check that they know what they are listening for. Question 1: 'What language is Danny learning?' (*Spanish*), Question 2: 'If the teacher said the present perfect, would the answer be A, B or C?' (*A*), Question 3: 'What problem does the boy have?' (*He hasn't done his homework.*), Question 4: 'Which language does Yumi definitely speak well?' (*Swedish – it is in all three options.*) and Question 5: 'What do you think the news could be about?' (*maybe a sports competition*). Play the recording for students to answer the questions in Exercise 4 individually.

5 Put students in pairs to compare answers. Play the recording again to check as a class. Ask students, 'Why is homework important?', 'What kind of homework is most useful for you to do?' and 'How else can you work on your English outside of class?'.

117

Answers

1 B 2 B 3 A 4 C 5 A

≫ AUDIOSCRIPT TB PAGE 301

GRAMMAR — Present perfect and past simple

1 This grammar has already been presented in the book but it is the first time the two tenses are contrasted. Write on the board:

I have known Alex for two years. He was a first-year student when I met him.

Ask students to name the underlined tenses. (*present perfect, past simple*)

Ask, 'Do I still know Alex?' (*yes*), 'So can the present perfect mean something not finished?' (*yes*), 'Is Alex a first-year student now?' (*no*) and 'So can the past simple mean something in the present?' (*no*).

Books open, tell students to mark the sentences present perfect or past simple. Check as a class.

> **Answers**
> **1** past simple **2** past simple **3** present perfect **4** past simple
> **5** present perfect **6** past simple

2 Books closed, elicit the rules from the students. Ask: 'Which tense goes with time words like *yesterday* and *ago*?' (*past simple*), 'Which tense goes with *never* and *yet*?' (*present perfect*), 'Which tense goes with something that started and finished in the past?' (*past simple*) and 'Which tense goes with something which finished in the past but is still important?' (*present perfect*). Books open, have students complete the rules. Check as a class.

> **Answers**
> **1 a** past simple **b** present perfect **2 a** present perfect
> **b** present perfect **c** past simple **d** present perfect

» **GRAMMAR REFERENCE AND PRACTICE ANSWER KEY TB PAGE 267**

3 Tell students to match the sentences to the different uses of the tenses. Check as a class.

> **Answers**
> **1** d **2** a **3** c **4** a **5** b **6** a **7** d **8** d **9** c

4 Books closed, students write down 'Hello' in as many languages as they can.

Books open, students read the text quickly and see if they had any languages which Susanna can't speak. Then tell students to complete the text. Check as a class. Ask students, 'Which language do you think was most difficult for Susanna to learn?' and 'What would you like to see or read about on her blog?'.

> **Answers**
> **1** has studied **2** was **3** learned **4** moved **5** studied **6** heard
> **7** decided **8** has written **9** has been **10** has had

> **MIXED ABILITY**
> Go through all the gaps and have students explain their choice of tense (in their first language if necessary) according to the rules in Exercise 2. For example: 1 *is present perfect because she probably hasn't stopped learning these languages*; 2, 3 and 4 *are past simple because they are facts which finished in the past.*

5 Write on the board:

He finished / has finished, *so it is my turn now.*

Ask students which tense is right and why (*has finished, rule 2d*). Tell students to complete the sentences in the book. Check as a class.

> **Answers**
> **1** watched **2** have already bought **3** have seen **4** watched
> **5** arrived **6** danced, ate

6 Tell students that we often answer a question with the present perfect when we talk about whether this has happened in general but we use the past simple to talk about a definite past situation or action. Write this example on the board for students:

Have you ever been to Rome?

Yes, I have. I went there last summer.

Have students complete the conversations. Check as a class.

> **Answers**
> **1 A:** Have you done **B:** finished
> **2 A:** did you go **B:** went, has lived
> **3 A:** Have you ever eaten **B:** had
> **4 A:** Did you enjoy **B:** have never seen, liked

7 Put students into pairs to write and practise four dialogues similar to those in Exercise 6. Monitor and make sure students are using the present perfect and past simple correctly. Have some pairs perform their dialogues at the front of the class. As a variation, you could ask students to expand the dialogues in Exercise 6 rather than make new ones.

» **GRAMMAR WORKSHEET UNIT 16**

> **COOLER**
> Read out sentences in the past simple and present perfect. If the sentence is true for them, students get up and swap chairs. Examples:
>
> You got up before seven o'clock.
>
> You have worked hard in this lesson.
>
> Your mum was born in a different town.
>
> Someone has said something nice to you today.
>
> Once students understand the activity, they can take it in turns to say sentences for other students to follow.

GRAMMAR — Present perfect and past simple

1 Look at the sentences from the recordings on page 90. Which are present perfect and which are past simple?

1 She lived in Sweden three years ago.
2 She learned Russian last year.
3 She's spoken Japanese since she was a baby.
4 Did you go to Spain in the holidays?
5 I've already finished mine.
6 The teacher gave it to us three days ago.

2 Complete the rules with *present perfect* or *past simple*.

1 We use the
   a _____ with words and phrases like *yesterday*, *ago*, *last year*, *in the holidays*.
   b _____ with words like *since*, *already*, *yet*, *just*, *ever*.

2 We use the
   a _____ to talk about an action that began in the past but continues into the present.
   b _____ to talk about someone's general life experiences.
   c _____ to talk about an action that finished in the past.
   d _____ to talk about an action that finished in the past, but the result is important or interesting now.

>> GRAMMAR REFERENCE AND PRACTICE PAGE 162

3 Match the sentences to uses a–d in part 2 of Exercise 2.

1 Have you done the German homework yet?
2 I've noticed you're all using a good level of vocabulary these days.
3 Did you meet anyone interesting?
4 I haven't missed any lessons this term.
5 She's lived all over the world!
6 She hasn't learned much English yet.
7 I've just heard some amazing news!
8 Our French teacher has won first prize in a competition!
9 We had a lesson with her this morning.

4 Complete the text with the present perfect or past simple form of the verbs in brackets.

An amazing language learner

Susanna Zaraysky **(1)** _____ (study) 11 languages (English, Russian, French, Spanish, Italian, Portuguese, Croatian, Ladino, Hebrew, Arabic and Hungarian) and speaks eight of them. Susanna **(2)** _____ (be) born in Russia and first **(3)** _____ (learn) English when she **(4)** _____ (move) to California. She **(5)** _____ (study) French and Spanish at school. Then, one day, she **(6)** _____ (hear) some tourists speaking in Italian and **(7)** _____ (decide) to learn that language. Portuguese came next and then all her other languages.
Susanna **(8)** _____ (write) several books and **(9)** _____ (be) on TV many times. She **(10)** _____ (have) a special interest in language and music for many years. On her blog, you'll find many interesting articles about this, as well as video clips and language-learning advice.

5 Choose the correct verb form to complete each sentence.

1 Yesterday, I *have watched / watched* a swimming competition with my brother.
2 I *already bought / have already bought* the tickets for the film tonight.
3 I'm in Melbourne, and I *saw / have seen* the beach and the sea.
4 My friend John *has watched / watched* the competition with me.
5 We *have arrived / arrived* home at eight o'clock in the evening.
6 It was a great party. We *have danced / danced* all night and *have eaten / ate* too much food!

6 Complete the conversations with the present perfect or past simple of the verbs in brackets.

1 **A:** _____ (do) your homework yet, Tania?
   B: Yes, I _____ (finish) it an hour ago.

2 **A:** Where _____ (you go) on holiday last summer, Robin?
   B: We _____ (go) to New York to visit my sister. She _____ (live) there since 2014.

3 **A:** _____ (you ever eat) curry?
   B: Yes, I _____ (have) some yesterday. Delicious!

4 **A:** _____ (you enjoy) the *Toy Story* films when you were little, Sergio?
   B: I _____ (never see) any of the *Toy Story* films. But I _____ (like) *Despicable Me*.

7 In pairs, make conversations. Ask a question in the present perfect, and answer in the simple past. Use the conversations in Exercise 6 for ideas.

Hallo   привет   مرحبا   Hallå

READING

1 **Look at questions 1–4. In pairs, discuss the questions. Then, read the texts quickly to check your answers.**

1. How many languages are there in the world?
2. What European language family does Polish belong to?
3. Which Asian language has the most speakers?
4. What are some common second languages in Africa?

2 **Read the texts again and answer the questions.**

1. What are the three biggest languages in the world? How many speakers do they have?
2. Which continent has the most languages?
3. Which country has the largest number of languages?
4. What is special about the Basque language?
5. What has happened to some of the languages of Australia and Oceania?

LANGUAGES *of the* WORLD

118

There are around 7,000 different languages in the world today. Languages that are similar to each other are in groups or 'families'. Some languages have a lot of speakers and others have very few. Many of the smaller languages have no writing, so when the last speaker dies, the language dies too.

Europe

Europe has 284 different languages. One language family here is Romance languages, which includes Spanish, Portuguese and Italian. Another is Slavic languages, such as Russian, Polish and Czech.

English belongs to the Germanic group, and is the third largest language in the world: 335 million people speak it as a first language and 505 million speak it as a second language. The Basque language from Spain and France is very unusual. It doesn't belong to any language family!

Asia

Asia has 2,303 languages. Chinese has a billion speakers – more than any other language in the world. Hindi is the world's fourth largest language, and Arabic comes fifth. Some parts of Asia have a very large number of languages.

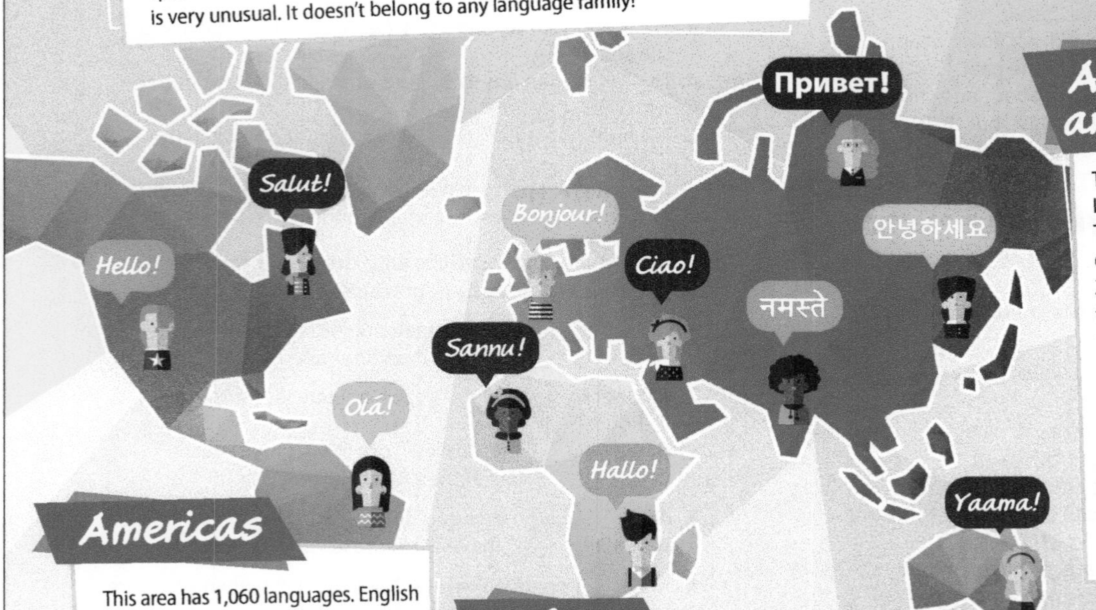
Привет!
Salut!
Bonjour!
안녕하세요
Hello!
Ciao!
नमस्ते
Sannu!
Olá!
Hallo!
Yaama!

Australia and Oceania

This area has 1,311 languages in total. The main language of Australia and New Zealand is English, but there are a lot of smaller languages too. Papua New Guinea has only around 8 million people, but it has 832 languages – more than any other country! Unfortunately, some Aboriginal languages are very small now and have only one or two speakers.

Americas

This area has 1,060 languages. English and Spanish have the most speakers on these continents. Spanish, with 406 million speakers, is the world's second-largest language. Portuguese is spoken in Brazil. While in Canada people speak mainly English and French. There are also many other native languages, for example Mam, a Mayan language, which people speak in parts of Mexico and Guatemala.

Africa

Human language probably began on this continent. There are 2,146 languages here. Many people in Africa can speak more than one language because, as well as their own language, they also speak English, French or Portuguese.

TALKING POINTS

12 Watch the video and discuss the questions.

What languages do you speak?
What languages are you studying?
What languages do your parents speak?

WARMER

Arrange students into groups. You say a country and students write the capital: 'Spain' (*Madrid*), 'Russia' (*Moscow*), 'Kenya' (*Nairobi*), 'Canada' (*Ottawa*), 'Mexico' (*Mexico City*), 'Chile' (*Santiago*), 'Norway' (*Oslo*), 'New Zealand' (*Wellington*), 'South Korea' (*Seoul*), 'India' (*New Delhi - not Delhi*). Give one point for the name and one point for correct spelling.

BACKGROUND INFORMATION

Fossil evidence suggests that modern humans evolved in Africa about 200,000 years ago. 50,000 years ago those humans started to leave Africa and spread to other continents. Between these periods we developed a system of language and this gave us a tremendous advantage over other animals, and other species of human-like apes, allowing us to spread over the globe very successfully. Why and how language evolved in humans is very controversial. For example, language may have evolved gradually or it may have appeared quite suddenly over a short space of time; there may be a natural language gene in humans not found in other animals or we may have developed language because of our need to interact and socialise.

Of course, there is no direct evidence of what this early language sounded like as it was a long time before people started to write down language. The earliest records we have of written language date to Sumerian tablets from about 3000 BC written in modern-day Iraq. However, we can use evidence from archaeology, anthropology and linguistics to give us some idea of how and why language developed. Archaeologists have found early human skulls and analysis shows that humans had bigger brains than other animals and at one stage our mouths and throats changed so we could produce a wide range of sounds. Anthropologists have studied how language is connected to culture – we know that humans painted on cave walls and produced other forms of art. Linguists have studied how remote tribes, for example those in Papua New Guinea, learn new languages, like English, they come into contact with and also how children learn their first language.

Once humans started separating and crossing the globe over many thousands of years, it was natural for a number of languages to emerge. For example, people would have needed new words to name objects which they hadn't seen before. Language families like Romance, Slavic and Turkic (spoken by peoples in Eurasia) probably reflect the main migration patterns as people settled, grouped and came into contact with a new environment.

The growth of different languages is now reversing because of globalisation. Smaller languages are dying out as the new generation prefers to learn languages such as English which are seen to offer more opportunities. On the one hand this is perhaps a natural process and the world might be a simpler place to live if everyone speaks a few major languages. On the other hand, language diversity is like biological diversity and the death of a language is like the death of a plant or animal species.

1 Students quickly read the text and see which countries from the Warmer are mentioned (*Spain, Russia, India, Canada, Mexico and New Zealand*). Put students into pairs to discuss the questions. Then give them a time limit to read and see if they were right. Check as a class.

Answers

1 7,000 2 Slavic 3 Chinese 4 English, French, Portuguese

2 Ask some oral questions first: 'Give an example of a Romance language.' (*Spanish, Portuguese, Italian, French*) and 'Where did language probably begin?' (*Africa*). Tell students to answer the questions in the book. Check as a class. Ask students, 'What information in the text surprised you most?'.

Answers

1 Chinese – a billion speakers; Spanish – 406 million speakers; English – 335 million speakers
2 Asia (2,303 languages)
3 Papua New Guinea – 832 languages
4 It does not belong to any language family.
5 They have become very small and have few speakers.

FAST FINISHERS

Write these language puzzles on the board for fast finishers to solve:

Which English word is most often pronounced incorrectly? (*incorrectly*)

What do you find twice in a lifetime, but once in every year. Twice in a week but never in a day? (*the letter e*)

Which word, if pronounced right, is wrong, but if pronounced wrong is right? (*wrong*)

What is unusual about this question: Was it a car or a cat I saw? (*it's a palindrome – it reads the same backwards.*)

🔊 118 The Reading text is recorded for students to listen, read and check their answers.

💬 **TALKING POINTS**

▶ 12 You can conclude this section by showing the video and asking students to complete the video worksheet. Then, read the questions in the *Talking points* box and students answer questions in pairs.

Ask students, 'Do you think there will be more or fewer languages in the future?', 'Why is English an international language?' and 'Could another language replace English as an international language?'.

A2 KEY FOR SCHOOLS Speaking Part 1

1 Briefly review what students need to do in this part of the exam and if necessary read out the A2 Key for Schools box on TB page 22.

In this part there are two phases. In phase 1 the examiner will ask each student factual information of a personal kind. In phase 2 the examiner will ask questions about two topics, for example, the student's family, school, hobbies, home, etc. The examiner will speak to both students but will ask each one different questions.

Tell students to answer in full sentences rather than just words or phrases. For example:

Examiner: Where do you come from?

Student: ~~Segovia~~ I live in Segovia, a very old town not far from Madrid.

Put students in pairs to take turns asking and answering the questions. Ask students, 'What would you like to do more of in English lessons? Less of?'.

VOCABULARY | Large numbers

1 Teach students the arithmetic signs of + (plus), − (minus), × (multiplied by), and ÷ (divided by) and read out some calculations for them to do, for example: 17 + 44 (*61*), 11 × 8 (*88*), 90 ÷ 6 (*15*). Tell students to match the numbers to the words. Check as a class.

Answers

176	one hundred and seventy-six
7,468	seven thousand, four hundred and sixty-eight
76,000,000	seventy-six million
7,000,000,000	seven billion

2 Tell students to underline and write out the large numbers. Check as a class.

Answers

Seven thousand. Two hundred and eighty-four. Three hundred and thirty-five million. Five hundred and five million, Two thousand three hundred and three. One thousand and sixty. Four hundred and six million. Two thousand one hundred and forty-six. One thousand three hundred and eleven. Eight million. Eight hundred and thirty-two.

 3 Play the recording and then put students into pairs to practise saying the numbers.

PRONUNCIATION | Word stress in numbers

4 Ask students, 'How many syllables are there in *language*?' (*two*) and 'Is the stress on the first or second syllable?' (*first*). Play the recording for students to listen, mark the stressed syllable and work out the rule. Check as a class.

Answers

thir<u>teen</u>, <u>thir</u>ty, fif<u>teen</u>, <u>fif</u>ty, eigh<u>teen</u>, <u>eigh</u>ty, nine<u>teen</u>, <u>nine</u>ty
For numbers 13–19 the stress is on *teen*. For twenty, thirty, forty, etc. the stress is on the first syllable.

5 Put students into pairs to practise saying the numbers.

---

6 Put students in pairs to take turns saying numbers from the text and what they refer to.

» **VOCABULARY WORKSHEET UNIT 16**

LISTENING

 1 Books closed, draw a rainbow on the board and ask students to name the colours in English (*red, orange, yellow, green, blue, indigo, violet*). Ask them to name all the colour words in their language. Do they know of any languages which have more or fewer words for colours?

Books open, students see if they know any of the answers already. Then play the recording. Check as a class.

Answers

1 12 in Russian and Greek; 11 in English
2 three (*one, two, many*)
3 They use one with their family, the other when they need to be polite.
4 They use *north/south/east/west*.
5 There are talking dictionaries and smartphone apps to help young people learn the language.

» **AUDIOSCRIPT TB PAGE 302**

WRITING

✎ PREPARE TO WRITE
Information about your English class

GET READY Write *i am an english teacher* on the board and ask 'What's the problem?' (*No capital letters for I and English and no full stop.*). Tell students to read Maria's text, and find examples of the capital letters.

PLAN Tell students to use the notes to plan a paragraph.

WRITE Tell the students to look back at Maria's paragraph as a model as they write.

IMPROVE Students pass their paragraphs to one another to check that they have included all the required information and have used capital letters correctly.

Model answer

I'm Artur and I'm from Sopot in Poland. Almost everyone in this class is Polish but there are two girls from Ukraine and a Lithuanian guy. We all speak Polish, and some English of course, but the Ukrainian and Lithuanian students know Russian too. I love listening to American rock music and one day I want to be in a band.

COOLER

Write this on the board: *I went to Oo on Ooo.* Tell students that o shows an unstressed syllable and O is a stressed one. They need to put in words that match the stress pattern, for example, *I went to POland on HOliday, I went to PEter's on SAturday.* Repeat with more sentences, for example: *I love Oo but I hate oOo.* (*lemons … tomatoes*)

PREPARE FOR THE EXAM

Speaking Part 1

1 **Ask and answer with a partner.**

1 Where do you come from?
2 What languages do people in your country speak?
3 Do you enjoy studying English?
4 Tell me something about what you do in your English lessons.

VOCABULARY   Large numbers

1 **Match the numbers to the words.**

176	seven billion
7,468	one hundred and seventy-six
76,000,000	seven thousand four hundred
7,000,000,000	and sixty-eight
	seventy-six million

2 **Find and <u>underline</u> all the big numbers in the text. Write them in words.**

3 **Listen and check. Then, in pairs, practise saying the numbers.** 119

PRONUNCIATION
Word stress in numbers

4 **Listen to the numbers and <u>underline</u> the stressed syllable. Can you make a rule about the stress in numbers?** 120

thirteen	thirty
fifteen	fifty
eighteen	eighty
nineteen	ninety

5 **Work in pairs. Practise saying the numbers.**

6 **Work in pairs. Student A, say a number from the text. Student B, close your book. Can you remember what the number refers to?**

Two hundred and eighty four.

That's the number of languages in Europe.

LISTENING

1 **You will hear a man giving some information about different languages. In pairs, discuss the possible answers.**

1 How many colour words are there in Russian and Greek? How many in English?
2 How many number words does the Pirahã language of Brazil have?
3 Some languages have two sets of vocabulary. Why?
4 Some languages have no words for *left*, *right*, *in front of* and *behind*. How do they say where things are?
5 How is modern technology helping small languages?

Listen and check. 121

WRITING

PREPARE TO WRITE
Information about your English class

GET READY **Read what a Spanish student wrote about her English class.**

> My name is María and I come from Spain. Most of the people in my English class are from Spain too, but one of my classmates is from China and two are from Ecuador. The languages people speak in my class are Spanish, Catalan, Chinese and English. I like speaking in English, but I find listening difficult. I plan to spend more time learning vocabulary in the future.

Look at how she uses capital letters. Find examples of these uses:

- after a full stop
- for people's names
- for countries
- for nationalities
- for languages
- for 'I'

PLAN **Plan a paragraph about your English class. Make notes about:**

- people's nationalities
- languages people speak
- languages people in the class are learning
- your likes, dislikes, plans about learning English.

WRITE **Write 50–70 words, using all your notes.**

IMPROVE **In pairs, read each other's paragraphs. Check that you have both included all the information you need and have used capital letters correctly.**

LANGUAGES OF THE WORLD   93

LIFE SKILLS LEARNING TO LEARN

EFFECTIVE LEARNING

What was the **first word you said?** 🔊 122

 LIFE SKILLS

To learn something well, you need to
- use a notebook
- practise
- revise
- try

It's normal to make mistakes when we are doing something new. But we can learn from our mistakes as well.

1 Think about how you learn and answer the questions.

1 How did you learn that 2 x 2 = 4, 2 x 3 = 6, 2 x 4 = 8, etc.?
2 How did you learn to ride a bicycle?
3 How do you learn to remember names and dates in history?

2 Match questions 1–3 in Exercise 1 to answers a–c. Then match them to one of the ideas in the *Life skills* box.

a At first, I couldn't do it, but my brother helped me to go along our street every day until one day I could do it by myself.
b We said it in class and repeated it lots and lots of times.
c I work with a friend and we ask each other questions about the things we learn in class.

3 Did you learn to do these things in the same way? In pairs, discuss how you learn.

4 Read the text. Circle the language skills it mentions.

a reading   **b** listening
c speaking   **d** writing

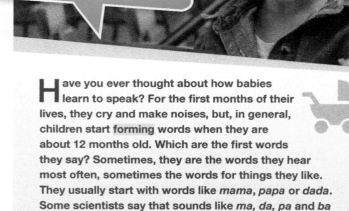

Have you ever thought about how babies learn to speak? For the first months of their lives, they cry and make noises, but, in general, children start forming words when they are about 12 months old. Which are the first words they say? Sometimes, they are the words they hear most often, sometimes the words for things they like. They usually start with words like *mama*, *papa* or *dada*. Some scientists say that sounds like *ma*, *da*, *pa* and *ba* are the easiest sounds to make, so when parents are very happy because their child is saying *mama*, in fact the baby is just experimenting with making noises!

All children begin learning their language first by listening and then speaking. They start with words for objects, like *car* or *dog*, then verbs for actions, like *drink* or *eat*, slowly adding other kinds of words to make sentences. They can understand more difficult words and sentences, but they can't say them. Some children speak more than others (just like adults!) and some children speak earlier than others, but by practising, they all learn in the end.

One mother tells the story of her son who didn't speak until he was four years old. Before then, he pointed when he wanted something or just made strange noises. One day, he came into the kitchen for breakfast and said, 'Can I have some chocolate cereal, please?' And then, he never stopped chatting.

So when you start to learn another language, remember that it took years for you to learn yours! If you keep listening and trying hard to speak, you improve, just like in your own language.

LIFE SKILLS

Learning Objectives

- The students learn how children learn their first language and what makes second language learning effective.
- In the project stage, students make an information page about an English-learning resource and add it to a class file.

Vocabulary

forming experimenting adding practising chatting trying hard

BACKGROUND INFORMATION

Linguists agree that all children are able to learn a first language perfectly but there is disagreement first about how this happens and second about how similar this process is to people, children and adults, learning a second language. One position is that humans, uniquely in the animal world, are genetically wired to learn language and just need input from people speaking around them to construct a language system. So language learning is automatic and unconscious – anyone can and will learn any language. In this way the development of language is similar to general physiological development (all normal children also naturally learn to walk and naturally develop the ability to digest solid food). An alternative explanation is that we learn language through social interaction because we need language to do things. In this approach, language is part of the way that children see the world, build relationships and develop an identity, and its primary purpose is to communicate.

The big difference between learning a first and second language is that most people do not learn a new language perfectly despite putting a lot of time and effort into it. There is a theory that there is a critical age, usually before teenage years, after which it is much more difficult to become a native speaker of a language. Those who believe in a language gene argue that our biological instinct to learn a language switches off at the end of childhood. On the other hand, it is never too late to learn, for example Joseph Conrad, one of the greatest English novelists, was born in Poland and didn't speak English fluently until his 20s. There is also a myth that the earlier you start to learn a second language, the better. This is not true – research shows that teenagers who start learning a language overtake those who started learning it pre-school. The language learning debate continues.

WARMER

Put students into pairs. Tell them they each need to teach their partner something. Give some examples: how to tie a tie, how to count to ten in another language, how to cook or prepare something, some lines of a poem or song, the rules of a game.

Give students time to teach one another. Then put students into small groups to discuss how easy it was to learn and to teach these things.

LIFE SKILLS
EFFECTIVE LEARNING

Tell students to read the information and check vocabulary as necessary. Invite students to say if they agree or disagree with any of the points in the text and to give their reasons. Encourage open-class discussion and help students make connections between their contributions.

1 Ask students if they agree that we never stop learning. Tell students to answer the questions in small groups. Share ideas as a class.

2 Tell students to match the questions to the answers and then to the *Life skills* box. Check as a class.

Answers
1 b – practise   2 a – try   3 c – revise

3 Ask students, 'Which of these is/was the most difficult to learn?'. Have students discuss how they learn(ed) these skills in pairs. Share ideas as a class.

4 Ask students if they can remember what the first word they said in their own language and in English was (if they don't know about the first word in their own language they could ask their parents after class as parents often remember). Give students a time limit to read the text and circle the language skills. Check as a class. Ask students to name languages which have a word similar to *mama* for mother (for example, *English – mum, Greek, Russian and Spanish – mama, Swedish – mamma*).

Answers
The text mentions listening (b) and speaking (c).

FAST FINISHERS

Tell fast finishers to write down an example of an activity using each of the four language skills that they do in English classes. For example, *reading – matching headings and paragraphs.* Some activities could involve more than one skill, for example role-play involves listening and speaking. When the rest of the class have finished, put all the fast finishers' ideas on the board and have the other students add to them so that you have a taxonomy of task types. Put students into small groups to discuss which activities they find most useful, interesting and challenging.

The Reading text is recorded for students to listen, read and check their answers.
122

5 Demonstrate with 'ba is a difficult sound for children to make.' (*Wrong*). Tell students to read the text again, decide if the sentences are right or wrong and correct the wrong ones. Check as a class. Ask students which languages they think are most difficult to learn as second languages.

> **Answers**
>
> 1 ✗ Babies make noises in their first few months.
> 2 ✓
> 3 ✓
> 4 ✗ They start with words for objects.
> 5 ✗ He made strange noises.
> 6 ✗ You need to try hard to speak.

6 Tell students to match the words to the definitions. Check as a class. Ask students why they think the boy suddenly produced a whole sentence after four years of silence. (Tell students that there is a similar story about Albert Einstein and the Einstein syndrome describes children who start talking late.)

> **Answers**
>
> 1 trying hard 2 experimenting 3 practising 4 chatting
> 5 forming 6 adding

🔊 **7** Ask students what would motivate them to learn English
123 better, for example, to pass the Key for Schools test. Play the recording and ask students if Mario mentions any of their reasons.

> **Answers**
>
> Because he met some boys who spoke English and wanted to communicate with them

🔊 **8** See if students can complete the sentences without
123 listening again. Tell students to listen again and check. Ask students, 'How many hours of English did Mario have a week?' (*three hours*). 'How many do you have?'. 'Is this enough?'.

> **Answers**
>
> 1 vocabulary, sounds 2 beach 3 drew pictures 4 an email
> 5 online dictionary 6 stay with

MIXED ABILITY

Go through all the gaps with weaker students before they listen and elicit what could go in each gap, the word class and possible words. For example, in 1 *the two words must be nouns because they come after* the *and they must be connected to the English language.*

🔊 **9** Books closed, ask what words and expressions Mario
123 used to structure his presentation to the class. Books open, have students check if any of their words and expressions are in the exercise. Play the recording and check as a class. Ask students to add any more useful words and expressions for a presentation, for example, *I also want to say …*

> **Answers**
>
> Expressions 1, 2, 5, 6 and 8

» **AUDIOSCRIPT TB PAGE 302**

10 Put students into pairs to discuss their experiences. Share ideas as a class.

PROJECT *Sharing resources*

Tell students that they are going to work in groups and prepare some information pages about resources for learning English. Ask the class for examples of things they have read and watched in English and write them on the board. Ask students to be specific, for example, the website or the name of the cartoon, and give a brief explanation to the rest of the class. Put students into small groups. Each student should choose a resource or think of one that hasn't been mentioned and make an information page about it. Tell students to read the *Funland* example. The page should include full details about what the resource is, how students can access it and why it is effective. Each group takes it in turns to present their information pages to the class. If they have time, they could even demonstrate the resources, for example, show part of a video on a computer. Encourage students to use the expressions in Exercise 9 and answer questions. Each group then puts their pages into a class file – this could be paper or electronic or both. Each week a different group should be responsible for updating the file by adding new resources and comments on existing resources, for example, a link to a similar resource. If you have several English classes, you could put all the files together for a school resource. (Be careful to make sure activities are not repeated.)

PROJECT EXTENSION

Ask students to work in groups and create their own English activity for the class file. Tell them it could be a speaking, listening, reading or writing activity and ask them to look at the class file and their Student's Book for examples. (It could be a variation on an activity rather than something new.) First, students should think of different activities and choose the best one. Then, they should design it. Next, they should ask you to check it. Then they should try out the activity on other groups to see if it works. Finally, they should add it to the class file.

COOLER

Tell students to write down three things that they would like to learn. Give some categories: languages, games, sports, practical skills. Put students into pairs to compare and discuss why and how they want to learn them.

Did you know?

- Babies can learn any language. No language is more difficult than another.

- Most children say their first words between 11 and 14 months old.

- A boy from the USA, Michael Kearney, spoke his first words when he was four months old and finished secondary school when he was six years old.

5 Read the text on page 94 again. Are the sentences right (✓) or wrong (✗)?

1 Babies make their first sounds when they are about a year old.
2 Their first words are often words they have heard a lot.
3 Some scientists think that babies aren't thinking about their mother when they say *mama*.
4 Babies use verbs before nouns when they start speaking.
5 The boy who didn't speak until he was four didn't make any sounds at all.
6 You can learn a new language better if you listen more and talk less.

6 Match the highlighted words in the text to the definitions.

1 making an effort to do something
2 doing new things to find out something
3 repeating something again and again
4 talking
5 making the shape of something
6 increasing the number of something

7 Listen to Mario talking to his class about learning English. Why did he improve?

8 Listen again and complete the sentences.

1 Mario didn't like English at first because he couldn't remember the _____ and _____.
2 He met the brothers at the _____.
3 He wrote the words in a book and _____ to show the meaning.
4 After the holiday, he sent his new friends _____.
5 When he needed a new word, he used an _____.
6 He's going to _____ his friends next summer.

9 Listen again and tick (✓) the expressions Mario uses to make his presentation.

! USEFUL LANGUAGE

1 Hello, my name's Mario.
2 I'm going to talk about …
3 The first thing I want to tell you about is …
4 Next,
5 For example,
6 Finally,
7 To sum up,
8 Does anyone have any questions?

10 Do you know any people who speak English? Do you try to talk to them in English? In pairs, discuss your experiences.

PROJECT
Sharing resources

Funland
Description: This is a vocabulary game. You have to read definitions or words and match them to the pictures.
Opinion: It's a fun game, but you have to be good at fishing!

- Work in small groups.
- Individually, think of something you read in English that was interesting – a web page, a blog, a game, an article, a book, etc. or something you enjoyed watching in English – a video, a film, a series, a cartoon, an activity from your coursebook, etc.
- In your group, prepare a short information page about each idea.
- Include: the title, what it is, where you can find it (the link to a web page or a video etc.), your opinion, photos, screenshots or drawings.
- Present your idea to the class. Try to use some of the expressions from Exercise 9 and be ready to answer any questions about it.
- Create a class file for everyone and add new pages when you find other interesting things to read or watch in English.

EFFECTIVE LEARNING   95

VOCABULARY

1 Complete the sentences with a word from the box.

dollars	grams	litres	metres	pair	pounds	set	slices

1 I've lost my _____ of coloured pens. Can I borrow yours?
2 There are ten of us, so let's cut the melon into ten _____.
3 I think I've lost my new _____ of gloves. My mum won't be pleased!
4 The jacket was on sale for 30 _____ and 99 cents.
5 We need 250 _____ of flour to make the cake.
6 My dad's nearly two _____ tall. That's much taller than me.
7 In our family, we drink two _____ of milk a day. We all have it on our cereal.
8 I haven't got any money for the bus. Can you lend me two _____ 50 pence, please?

2 Match words from A to words in B to make verb phrases about life experiences.

A	B
1 camp	a cave
2 climb	under the stars
3 explore	wild animals
4 kayak	in the snow
5 look for	down a river
6 pick	a tree
7 play	wild fruit
8 track	fossils

Now, write a sentence using each verb phrase.

3 Look at the photos and complete the names of the places.

1 d_____ s_____   2 s_____ s_____

3 m_____

4 c_____ s_____   5 b_____   6 s_____

Overview

VOCABULARY	Outdoor activities; past participles; shops; units of measurement and money; free-time activities; collocations about having fun; words to describe language learning; large numbers
GRAMMAR	Present perfect with *ever* and *never*; present perfect with *just, yet* and *already*; present perfect with *for* and *since*; present perfect and past simple
EXAM TASKS	Listening Part 5; Writing Part 6; Speaking Part 1

Resources

PHOTOCOPIABLE WORKSHEETS: Grammar worksheets Units 13–16; Vocabulary worksheets Units 13–16; Review game Units 13–16; Literature worksheet; Speaking worksheet; Writing worksheet

WARMER

Write VOCABULARY vertically down the middle of the board. Tell students that you will give definitions of words from Units 13–16. All the words will use one letter from *vocabulary* and students should write them down horizontally to include the letter from *vocabulary*.

it has the past participle *had* (ha*V*e)

animals which died a long time ago inside rocks (f*O*ssils)

a shop where you can buy medicine (*C*hemist's)

talking in a friendly way (ch*A*tting)

a thousand million (*B*illion)

what you have when you enjoy yourself (f*U*n)

keeping lots of things of the same type (co*L*lecting)

for example, 2 + 2 = 5 (mist*A*ke)

a shop where you can buy meat (butche*R*'s)

an adverb used in present perfect questions and negative sentences (*yet*)

You could repeat this exercise with the word GRAMMAR, finding words which have one of the letters in *grammar* and making definitions. Students could even work in groups to make the exercise themselves. (Check the words and definitions before they test other groups.)

VOCABULARY

1 Books closed, ask students, 'Which is heavier – 500 grams of gold or 500 grams of sugar?' (*Neither, they weigh the same!*). Go through the meanings of the units of measurement. Ask students, 'Which is worth more, a dollar or a pound?' (*a pound*), 'A pair is how many?' (*two*) 'Do we say a slice or a set of cake?' (*slice*), 'How many metres is a running track?' (*400*), 'Do we measure liquids or solids with litres?' (*liquids*) and 'Is a gram of something heavy?' (*no*). Books open, ask students to complete the

sentences. Check as a class. As an extension activity, have students work in pairs and expand these sentences into short dialogues. Write an example on the board:

Student A: *I've lost my set of coloured pens. Can I borrow yours?*

Student B: *You lost your ruler last week. Why do you lose things so often?*

Student A: *I don't know but I need the pens to draw a map.*

Student B: *No problem but please don't lose mine!*

Ask some pairs to perform their dialogues at the front of the class.

> **Answers**
> 1 set 2 slices 3 pair 4 dollars 5 grams 6 metres 7 litres
> 8 pounds

2 Tell students to cover up column B and try and remember what goes with each verb. Then ask students to look at column B and match the words. Check and then tell students to make a sentence using each verb phrase. Give an example: 'I love camping under the stars in summer.'. Ask some students to read out their sentences. As a variation, ask students to make a story including all the verb phrases (they don't need to be in the same order as in the exercise). Begin a story as an example: 'I was tracking some wild animals and I saw a cave. I decided to explore the cave and …'.

> **Answers**
> 1 camp under the stars
> 2 climb a tree
> 3 explore a cave
> 4 kayak down a river
> 5 look for fossils
> 6 pick wild fruit
> 7 play in the snow
> 8 track wild animals
> Students' own answers

3 Books closed, ask students to tell you which places they have been and bought things in the last week. Write all the places on the board and, books open, tell students to check if they have mentioned every place from Exercise 1 on page 80. Ask students to describe each picture on page 96. Then students name the places. Check as a class. Ask students, 'Why do people go to smaller shops when they can get everything in a supermarket?' and 'What is your favourite smaller shop and why?'.

> **Answers**
> 1 department store 2 sweet shop 3 market 4 clothes shop
> 5 bookshop 6 supermarket

FAST FINISHERS

Tell fast finishers to write down things which you can buy in each place, for example, *furniture, clothes and electrical goods in a department store.*

1   This grammar section covers uses of the present perfect and the difference between the present perfect and the past simple. Before students do the exercises, spend some time revising the form and meaning of the present perfect. For form, elicit that we need *have/has* + past participle to make the present perfect and read out some regular and irregular verbs and have students tell you the past participle, for example, *decide-decided, break-broken*. For meaning, ask these questions and add examples to show each point: 'Do we use the present perfect to talk about past experiences?' (*yes*), 'If we say exactly when something happened, do we use the present perfect or the past simple?' (*past simple*), 'Do we use *already* in present perfect negative sentences?' (*no*), 'Do we use *just* in present perfect positive sentences?' (*yes*) and 'Do we use *since* and the present perfect about points in time like dates?' (*yes*).

Then ask students to complete sentences 1–4 in Exercise 1 and correct sentences 5–8. Check as a class and have students say why sentences 5–8 are wrong.

Answers

1   have never seen   2 has already bought   3 for   4 left
5   I **have** never been to a wedding and I want to come.
6   Tom left his science book at school and he needs it because he **hasn't done** his homework yet.
7   My mum has played the violin **since** she was six.
8   I **have** texted you an hour ago but you didn't answer.

2   Tell students to write a question for each answer. Check, then have students write their own answers. Put students into pairs to ask and answer the questions.

Answers

1   Have you finished your homework (yet)?
2   How long have you lived in this town?
3   Have you ever visited Russia?
4   Have you read any English books this year?
5   Have you ever cooked a pizza?
6   How long have you known your best friend?
Students' own answers

3   Tell students to complete the text. Check as a class.

Answers

1 have loved   2 was   3 spoke   4 began   5 moved   6 went
7 learned   8 haven't started

MIXED ABILITY

Weaker students will have trouble with the difference between the present perfect and the past simple. Give them more practice by writing this text which is similar on the board and having them choose the form:

I was born near Paris but I lived / have lived (*have lived*) *in Barcelona since I was eleven. We* moved / have moved (*moved*) *to Spain in 2016. I am fourteen now so I* was / have been (*have been*) *here for three years. I* travelled / have travelled (*travelled*) *to France last year to see my grandparents but I* didn't stay / haven't stayed (*didn't stay*) *there long.*

A2 KEY FOR SCHOOLS Listening Part 5

 1   Briefly review what students need to do in this part of the exam and if necessary read out the A2 Key for Schools box on TB page 74. Give students time to read the questions and then play the recording twice. Check as a class.

Answers

1 B   2 C   3 A   4 E   5 G

≫ **AUDIOSCRIPT TB PAGE 302**

A2 KEY FOR SCHOOLS Writing Part 6

2   Briefly review what students need to do in this part of the exam and if necessary read out the A2 Key for Schools box on TB page 118. Give students time to write their email and take it in for checking.

Model answer

Hi Sam,
Can you come camping with us next weekend? We're going to camp next to the lake. Please bring some of those great biscuits you make.
Thanks!
Jane

A2 KEY FOR SCHOOLS Speaking Part 1

3   Briefly review what students need to do in this part of the exam and if necessary read out the A2 Key for Schools box on TB page 22. Have students make the questions then check as a class. Put students in pairs to ask and answer the questions. Monitor and collect examples of good language and errors for feedback.

Answers

1   How many languages do you speak?
2   How long have you studied/spoken this/these languages?
3   Do your parents and grandparents speak the same language?
4   What language(s) do they speak?
5   Which languages would you like to learn? Why?
6   Have you ever visited (any) countries that speak a different language?
7   Do you like learning English?
8   What's the most difficult thing about English?
9   What's the best thing about learning English?

COOLER

On one side of the board write about ten regular verbs. On the other side write about ten irregular verbs. Arrange students into pairs and give each pair a dice (or a sugar cube to write a number on each side). One student rolls a dice. If the number is even, they choose a regular verb, if it is odd, they choose an irregular verb. The student has to ask a present perfect question using that verb and their partner has to answer, for example:

Student A: *Have you sent a text today?*

Student B: *Yes, I texted you!*

Tell students to take it in turns rolling the dice, choosing a verb (they must choose a different verb each time) and asking one another present perfect questions.

GRAMMAR

1 Choose the correct options to complete the sentences.

1 They *have never seen / never don't see* a city like it.
2 My dad *has already bought / already buy* the paint.
3 I have had it *since / for* one year.
4 Last night, my sister *left / have left* her bag on the train.

Correct the mistakes in the sentences.

5 I never been to a wedding and I want to come.
6 Tom left his science book at school and he needs it because he doesn't do his homework yet.
7 My mum has played the violin for she was six.
8 I have texted you an hour ago, but you didn't answer.

2 Write questions for the answers. Then, answer the questions about yourself. Use *never, just, yet* or *already* in your answers.

0 *Have you ever done a Saturday job?*
No, I've never done a Saturday job.

1 Yes, I've just finished my homework.
2 I've lived in this town for five years.
3 Yes, I have. I visited Russia in 2018 for the World Cup!
4 Yes, I've already read three English books this year.
5 No, I've never cooked a pizza.
6 I've known my best friend since I was three years old.

3 Complete the text with the correct form of the verbs in brackets. Use the past simple or present perfect.

I **(1)** _____ (love) languages since I **(2)** _____ (be) a little boy. My dad is English and my mum is Spanish, and when I was young, they **(3)** _____ (speak) both languages to me at home. So I **(4)** _____ (begin) learning English and Spanish as a baby. Then we **(5)** _____ (move) to Turkey for my dad's work, and I **(6)** _____ (go) to primary school there. I **(7)** _____ (learn) Turkish quite quickly in school. Now, we live in Japan. I **(8)** _____ (not start) learning Japanese yet. But I'm going to learn it soon.

PREPARE FOR THE EXAM

Listening Part 5

1 For each question, choose the correct answer.

You will hear Ella and Tom talking about people's hobbies. What is each person's hobby?

PEOPLE		HOBBIES
0 Suzy	*F*	**A** collecting things
1 Jason		**B** cooking
2 Laura		**C** doing sport
3 Tom		**D** horse riding
4 Ella		**E** listening to music
5 Maria		**F** photography
		G playing an instrument
		H shopping

Writing Part 6

2 You would like to go camping next weekend.

Write an email to your English friend, Sam.

- Ask Sam to come with you.
- Say where you want to go camping.
- Tell Sam what to bring.

Write **25 words** or more.

Speaking Part 1

3 Make questions. Then, in pairs, ask and answer the questions.

1 How many languages / you speak?
2 How long have you studied / spoken this / these languages?
3 your parents / grandparents / speak / same language?
4 What language(s) / they speak?
5 Which languages / would / like / learn? Why?
6 ever visit countries that speak / different language?
7 like / learn / English?
8 What / most difficult thing / about English?
9 What / best thing / about learning English?

17 STAYING HEALTHY

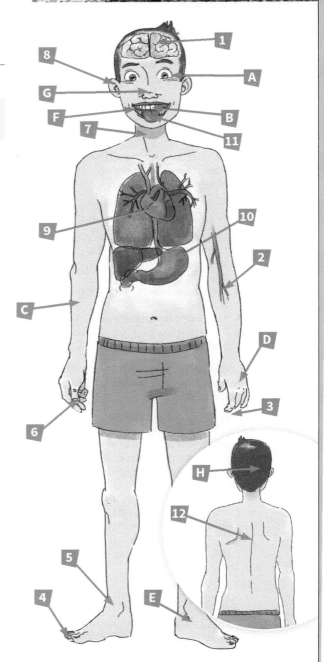

? ABOUT YOU

▶ 13 **Watch the video and discuss the questions.**
Have you ever hurt yourself? What happened?
Have you ever had an accident?
Have you ever broken a bone?

VOCABULARY AND READING

Body parts

1 Match the words in the box to the body parts 1–12.

(EP)

ankle	back	blood	brain	ear	finger
heart	neck	stomach	thumb	toe	tongue

🔊 125 **Listen and check. Then repeat.**

🔊 126 **2** Name the body parts A–H. Listen and check.

3 Work in pairs. One of you says a letter or a number, the other says the body part.

4 Match the definitions with the words from Exercise 1. You may need to make some of the words plural.

1 You've got ten of these on your feet. _____
2 Your food goes into here when you eat. _____
3 You think with this. _____
4 This joins your leg to your foot. _____
5 You've got four of these on each hand. _____
6 This carries things that keep us healthy around our bodies. _____
7 This joins your body to your head. _____
8 You've got one of these on each hand. _____
9 You hear with these. _____
10 This is opposite to the front of your body. _____
11 This sends blood around your body. _____
12 You use this to talk. _____

5 Read Ben's blog on page 99 about what happened to him yesterday. Which parts of his body did he hurt?

6 Are these sentences right (✓) or wrong (✗)?

1 Ben got a bike for his birthday.
2 There were often quite a lot of people on the cycle path.
3 The two cyclists knocked Ben off his bike.
4 The two cyclists came back to help Ben.
5 Ben was able to ride his bike after the accident.
6 Ben had blood on his clothes when he got home.

17 STAYING HEALTHY

Unit Overview

TOPIC	Health
VOCABULARY AND READING	Body parts
	Accident!
GRAMMAR	Reflexive pronouns
READING	Teen health
PRONUNCIATION	/uː/ and /ʊ/
VOCABULARY	Adjectives to express emotion
LISTENING	Five short conversations
SPEAKING	Giving advice
EXAM TASK	Listening Part 1

Resources

GRAMMAR REFERENCE AND PRACTICE: SB page 163; TB page 267

PREPARE FOR THE EXAM: SB pages on TB pages 244–245;
TB page 256

WORKBOOK: pages 68–71

VIDEO AND VIDEO WORKSHEET: Health

PHOTOCOPIABLE WORKSHEETS: Grammar worksheet Unit 17;
Vocabulary worksheet Unit 17

TEST GENERATOR: Unit test 17

WARMER

Dictate these six sentences (or write them on the board for weaker students). Three of them have grammar mistakes with the past simple or present perfect. Students write all of the sentences down and correct the ones which are wrong.

I've always wanted to be a doctor. (*right*)

Have you done your biology homework yesterday? (*Have you done* – *Did you do*)

Tim hasn't taken his medicine yet. (*right*)

She waited for two hours but the doctor is still not here. (*waited* – *has waited*)

Once I went to hospital to visit one of my friends. (*right*)

My sister has worked in a chemist's before she went to university. (*has worked* – *worked*)

⍰ ABOUT YOU

▶ You can begin the class and introduce the topic of the unit
13 by showing the video and asking students to complete the video worksheet. Then, read the questions in the *About you* box and students answer questions in pairs. If their answer to all the questions is 'no', they should think if any of these have happened to friends or anyone in their family. Share ideas as a class. Ask, 'In what situations can accidents happen?'.

VOCABULARY AND READING

Body parts

1 Books closed, point to parts of your body and elicit the words, including the ones in the box. Books open, students match the words in the box to parts of the body.

125

Answers

The answers are recorded for students to check and then repeat.

1 brain 2 blood 3 finger 4 toe 5 ankle 6 thumb 7 neck 8 ear 9 heart 10 stomach 11 tongue 12 back

2 Tell students to name the body parts A–H.

🔊 **Answers**
126

The answers are recorded for students to check and then repeat.

A eye B teeth C arm D hand E foot F mouth G nose H head

3 Put students into pairs to test themselves on the body parts. You could also do this the other way round: students say a body part and then their partner says the letter or number.

MIXED ABILITY

Pair a stronger student with a weaker student for this stage and encourage the stronger student to explain to their partner why they think their answer is correct.

---

4 Have students match the definitions with the words in Exercise 1. Check as a class. Books closed, say one of the words and have students say the definition.

Answers

1 toes 2 stomach 3 brain 4 ankle 5 fingers 6 blood 7 neck 8 thumb 9 ears 10 back 11 heart 12 tongue

5 Tell students to look at the picture of Ben and ask, 'Why do you think he looks so happy?' and 'Where is he cycling?'. Pre-teach **cyclist** (someone who rides a bike) and **brake** (the part of a vehicle or bike that makes it stop or move more slowly). Ask students, 'What could go wrong when you are cycling?' and 'Where are dangerous places to go cycling?'. Give students a time limit to read the blog and find out what happened. Check as a class. Ask students, 'Do you think this was Ben's fault?' and 'Why didn't the cyclists stop and help him?'.

Answer

his ankle and his ear

CONTINUED ON PAGE 194

6 As an example, say 'Nobody knew it was Ben's birthday.' (*Wrong – people sent him texts.*). Tell students to answer the questions. Check as a class and have students correct the wrong sentences. Ask students, 'What do you think Ben did next?', 'Have you ever fallen off a bike?' and 'Is cycling dangerous?'. As an extension activity, put students into pairs and have them role-play a conversation between Ben and one of the cyclists the next day, for example:

Ben: *Why didn't you stop?*

Cyclist: *Sorry but we didn't see you. Are you all right now?*

Ben: *Yes, but …*

Answers

1 ✓ 2 ✗ (The path isn't usually busy.)
3 ✗ (Ben fell off himself.) 4 ✗ (they rode away) 5 ✓ 6 ✓

🔊 The Reading text is recorded for students to listen, read
127 and check their answers.

GRAMMAR Reflexive pronouns

1 Books closed, take a few students to a mirror or the window. Say, 'Look in the mirror/window. Can you see yourselves?'. Write the question on the board and ask: 'What is the subject of this sentence?' (*you*), 'What is the object?' (*yourselves*) and 'Are they the same or different people?' (*the same*). Books open, students read and complete the sentence in the box. Check as a class. Point out that some verbs, like *wash* and *dress*, often take reflexive pronouns in other languages, but not usually in English. We say *get washed/dressed*.

Answer

the same

2 Tell students to complete the table. Check as a class. Drill the reflexive pronouns: you say a subject pronoun, students say the object and reflexive pronoun (e.g. *she – her – herself*).

Answers

a himself b herself c ourselves d yourselves

>> **GRAMMAR REFERENCE AND PRACTICE ANSWER KEY TB PAGE 267**

3 Have students match the sentences to their meanings. Check as a class. Ask students to think of three things that they like to do themselves and three things that they cannot do by themselves, and ask them to explain why. For example, *I like to tidy my room myself. You can't play football by yourself because you need a team.*

Answers

1 a 2 b

4 Demonstrate with an example: *We did it _____ because no one would help us.* (*ourselves*). Have students complete the sentences in the book. Check as a class. Explain that *Help your selves* in question 7 has a special meaning: you invite somebody to take something, especially food or drink, without asking.

Answers

1 himself 2 ourselves 3 myself 4 herself 5 themselves
6 yourself 7 yourselves

5 Write these sentences on the board and ask students to complete them with the right pronoun and explain why.

Dan knows Klara is an actress. He saw _____ in a film. (*her = Klara, subject and object are different*)

Klara is an actress. She saw _____ in a film. (*herself, subject and object are the same*)

Tell students to look at the first sentence and say why it's wrong (*the shirt is for the person who bought it so the subject and object are the same*). Students correct the sentences in the book. Check as a class.

Answers

1 I bought a new shirt for **myself** which was very nice.
2 Our friends had a really good time together and everybody enjoyed **themselves**.
3 You need to bring a photo of **yourself** with your name.
4 She went **by** herself. No one went with her.
5 We were both hungry so we went out and bought **ourselves** some sandwiches.

>> **GRAMMAR WORKSHEET UNIT 17**

6 Tell students to read and answer the questions. Check as a class. Ask students, 'How do you think Sara hurt her big toe?' and 'How can the doctor help her?'. Put students into pairs to read out the conversation.

Answers

1 She's hurt her big toe. 2 She's going to the doctor.
3 Anna's going with her.

7 Ask students to tell you of different (not too serious!) accidents and write them on the board, for example, hitting your head on a low ceiling, slipping on some ice. Tell students to look at the word pool and ask in what situation each phrase could be used, for example: *Help yourselves!* (*a birthday party at home*), *They didn't enjoy themselves that day* (*a school trip*). Put students into pairs to write conversations using phrases from the word pool and looking at Exercise 6 as a model. Give students time to practise their conversations and then ask pairs to perform in front of the whole class. Listen and make a note of any mistakes with reflexive pronouns and write the mistakes on the board for students to correct at the end of the activity.

COOLER

Write these sentences on the board and have students complete them with their own ideas:

This weekend I'm going to _____ by myself.

Most teenagers like to enjoy themselves _____.

Once my best friend hurt her/himself _____.

I've never _____ myself.

ACCIDENT!

Posted by Ben09 on Monday 13th May

This is me with my new bike – before the accident! Have you ever fallen off your bike and hurt yourself? Well, here's my story.

It was my birthday (thanks for all the texts) and this amazing bike was my present. I went for a ride by myself along the bike path. The path isn't usually busy. But that day there were two cyclists coming towards me. I slowed down as quickly as possible but I forgot it was a new bike with good brakes! I stopped really suddenly and fell off. I hit my ankle and it really hurt. The two cyclists rode past and didn't stop. I sat on the ground and watched their backs as they rode away. They were enjoying themselves too much to think about me! I got up by myself and picked up my bike, which luckily was OK. My heart was beating fast as I cycled slowly home and people were looking at me! When I got there I found out why – there was blood all over my T-shirt from a cut on my ear.

GRAMMAR Reflexive pronouns

1 Look at the examples from Ben's blog and complete the Grammar box.

Have you ever fallen off your bike and hurt yourself?
They were enjoying themselves too much.

2 Complete the table with reflexive pronouns: *himself, yourselves, herself, ourselves.*

We use *-self* when the subject and the object of the verb are *the same / a different* person.

I		myself	we	c	
you		yourself	you	d	
he	a		they		themselves
she	b				

≫ GRAMMAR REFERENCE AND PRACTICE PAGE 163

3 Look at two more examples from Ben's blog and match sentences 1 and 2 to meanings a and b.

1 I went for a ride by myself.
2 I got up by myself.

We use the expression *by myself, yourself etc.* to mean **a** *alone* or **b** *without any help.*

4 Complete the sentences with the correct reflexive pronouns.

1 Peter wasn't badly hurt and drove _____ to the hospital.
2 Simon and I really enjoyed _____ at the party.
3 I hurt _____ when I fell off the chair.
4 Zoë told _____ that she wasn't ill.
5 Ben and Sara prepared all the food by _____.
6 Be careful! Don't cut _____ with that knife!
7 'You can help _____ to paper and pens,' the teacher said to the students.

5 Correct the mistakes in the sentences.

1 I bought a new shirt for me which was very nice.
2 Our friends had a really good time together and everybody enjoyed.
3 You need to bring a photo of you with your name.
4 She went herself. No one went with her.
5 We were both hungry, so we went out and bought us some sandwiches.

6 Read the conversation and answer the questions.

1 What's Sara done?
2 Where's she going?
3 Who's going with her?

Anna: Hi, Sara, are you ok?
Sara: Hi, Anna, no, not really. I've hurt my big toe. Look!
Anna: Oh no, that's horrible! Are you going to the doctor?
Sara: Yes.
Anna: Are you going by yourself?
Sara: Yes, but I'll be fine.
Anna: No, you won't. I'll come with you.

7 In pairs, write your own conversations about an accident.

Use the conversation in Exercise 6 to help you. Choose different sentences from the box to include in each conversation.

Practise your conversations. Then role-play a conversation in front of the class.

Help yourselves!
I tried it myself and it was delicious.
They didn't enjoy themselves that day.
He couldn't do it by himself.
We bought ourselves new clothes after that.
Did she cut herself?

STAYING HEALTHY 99

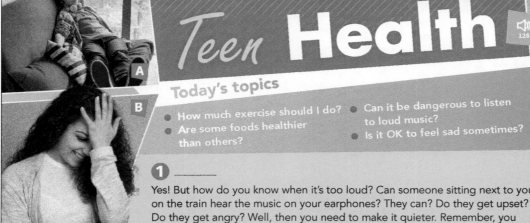

Teen Health

Today's topics

- How much exercise should I do?
- Are some foods healthier than others?
- Can it be dangerous to listen to loud music?
- Is it OK to feel sad sometimes?

1 _____

Yes! But how do you know when it's too loud? Can someone sitting next to you on the train hear the music on your earphones? They can? Do they get upset? Do they get angry? Well, then you need to make it quieter. Remember, you need to look after your ears, so you'll be able to hear well when you're older.

READING

1 Work with a partner. Look at Today's Topics on the *Teen Health* website. What do you think the answers to the questions are?

2 Look at the questions on the *Teen Health* website. Match them to the paragraphs.

3 Work with a partner. Read the texts again. Tell your partner what they say about:

1 earphones	5 feelings
2 hearing well	6 a friend, parent or teacher
3 too much sport	7 a plate of chips
4 playing sport after meals	8 variety

4 In pairs, ask and answer the questions.

1 Do you listen to loud music on your headphones?
2 Do you eat healthily? What do you like to eat?
3 Do you do too little or enough exercise?

PRONUNCIATION | /uː/ and /ʊ/

5 Listen and repeat the sentence. Do both the *oo* words have the same sound?

These types of f<u>oo</u>d are g<u>oo</u>d for you.

What other words sound like:

a *food*?   b *good*?

6 In pairs, discuss whether you agree with the website's answers to the teenagers' questions.

TALKING POINTS

Do you worry about any of these things?
What do people your age usually worry about?
What do you worry about? Why?

VOCABULARY — Adjectives to express emotion

1 Match the words in the box to photos A–J.

angry	confident	embarrassed
friendly	lazy	lonely	surprised
unhappy	upset	worried

2 Complete the sentences with the adjectives in Exercise 1.

1 I feel very _____ today. All I want to do is sit here and read my book. I don't want to do any exercise.
2 I was so _____ when the teacher asked me to read my story. My face went red!
3 It was my first day at the new school today and everyone was really _____. It was great!
4 I read a lot of French magazines, so I'm really _____ about my French exam.
5 My brother doesn't have any friends and he gets very _____ by himself.
6 You look _____. You didn't think you'd get 100% in that test did you?
7 That woman over there is very _____. She's shouting really loudly.
8 I can't find my phone anywhere. I'm really _____ that I've lost it.
9 You look _____ today. Usually, you're smiling and laughing! What's the matter?
10 He was very _____ when he failed the exam. He didn't want to talk to anyone.

3 In pairs, tell each other about different situations when you had some of the feelings in Exercise 1.

READING

WARMER

Tell these jokes:

Patient: *Doctor, Doctor, nobody listens to me!*

Doctor: *Next please!*

Patient: *Doctor, Doctor, I think I need glasses.*

Doctor: *Yes you do, you came in through the window.*

Tell these other 'Doctor, Doctor' jokes for students to guess the last line (i.e. what the doctor replies).

Patient: *Doctor, Doctor, I've broken my arm in two places. (Don't go there again.)*

Patient: *Doctor, Doctor, everyone thinks I lie. (I can't believe that.)*

Patient: *Doctor, Doctor, I feel like a dog. (Sit!)*

1 Scratch your head and look worried. Ask, 'How do I feel?' (*worried*) and 'What do you think my problem is?' (*Your car didn't start today? etc.*). Put students into pairs to describe the photos and say what they think the problems are. Then ask them to read the questions and say what the answers might be. Share ideas as a class.

2 Pre-teach **ache** (a feeling of pain over an area of your body which continues for a long time). Tell students to match the questions to the paragraphs. Check as a class. Ask students to suggest other important topics or questions they would like answered, for example bullying.

Answers

1 Can it be dangerous to listen to loud music?
2 How much exercise should I do?
3 Is it OK to feel sad sometimes?
4 Are some foods healthier than others?

3 Put students into pairs and ask them to tell one another what the text says about each item. Check as a class.

Possible answers

1 Sometimes on a train the person next to you can hear the music on your earphones. / Listening to loud music on earphones can be dangerous.
2 If you play music too loudly now, you won't be able to hear well when you're older.
3 Too much sport can be bad for you – you can hurt something.
4 It's not a good idea to play sport just after you've eaten. You can get a stomach ache.
5 It's normal for feelings to change – everyone feels unhappy sometimes.
6 Talk to a friend, parent or teacher if you feel sad / about your problems.
7 A plate of fruit is healthier than a plate of chips.
8 If you eat a bit of everything, you'll be healthier.

◁)) The Reading text is recorded for students to listen, read
128 and check their answers.

4 Put students into pairs to discuss. Share ideas as a class.

◁ PRONUNCIATION | /uː/ and /ʊ/

◁))
129
5 Play the recording for students to listen and repeat. Elicit that the sounds are different. Explain and demonstrate that the sound in *food* is longer and the lips are usually rounder. Give students a time limit to find other words that include /uː/ and /ʊ/.

Answers

The sounds are different.

Possible answers

a *food*: blue, move, school, room, two, shoe, cool
b *good*: put, could, would, wood, sugar, woman

MIXED ABILITY

Read out the possible answers, mixed up, to weaker students and have them decide whether the words contain /uː/ or /ʊ/.

6 Put students into pairs to discuss. Ask students as a class what they agree with most and least. Have students tell you what information they would change, delete or add to on the website.

💬 TALKING POINTS

Ask students to discuss the questions. Share ideas as a class. Write the things students worry about on the board. Ask students to rank them in order of how serious they are.

VOCABULARY | Adjectives to express emotion

1 Tell students to match the words to the photos. Check as a class. Ask, 'Which three of these adjectives have a positive not negative meaning?' (*confident, friendly, surprised*). Act out some of the emotions and have students say what the adjective is. For example, yawn and prop your head up on the desk (*lazy*), strut down the corridor (*confident*).

Answers

A lazy B embarrassed C upset D lonely E angry F worried
G confident H surprised I friendly J unhappy

2 Read out this example to demonstrate:

I was _____ when I got to the front of the queue in the supermarket and then remembered that I didn't have enough money to pay. (*embarrassed*)

Tell students to complete the sentences. Check as a class.

Answers

1 lazy 2 embarrassed 3 friendly 4 confident 5 lonely
6 surprised 7 angry 8 worried 9 unhappy 10 upset

3 Remind students that many adjectives have *-ed* and *-ing* forms and that *-ed* forms usually describe how you feel. Write these examples on the board:

I was <u>surprised</u> when I came first in the test.

A <u>surprising</u> number of teenagers never watch TV.

Put students into pairs to compare experiences. Share ideas as a class.

≫ **VOCABULARY WORKSHEET UNIT 17**

LISTENING

BACKGROUND INFORMATION

There are health factors which teenagers can't control, for example, the genes they inherit from their parents or the environment they live in, but lifestyle choices have a very big impact not just on teenagers now but on their adult lives. A sensible balanced diet is very important as about 20% of teenagers are obese. The amount of calories teenagers need depends on their age, gender, build and level of activity. Dieting is more effective than physical exercise in reducing weight (you would need to swim fast for an hour to use up the calories in a 100-gram bar of chocolate) but dieting needs to be carefully monitored, especially fasting (not eating any food for an extended period of time) and skipping meals. Most teenagers need more calcium, fibre, protein and iron and less of the added sugar found in soft drinks and sweets. Tips for controlling your diet include eating with your family rather than separately, cutting down on fast food and having fruit and vegetables for snacks.

Teenagers need to be physically active for about 60 minutes a day but this does not have to be done all at once and it can include moderate exercise such as climbing the stairs or walking at a good pace. There are many apps which calculate what you do each day and allow you to set goals and compare with previous days and other people. Some teenagers take sport very seriously, for example professional gymnasts are at their peak in their teens, but doing too much too young can damage the body when it is still developing. Moderate but regular exercise is more effective for general health.

PREPARE FOR THE EXAM

A2 KEY FOR SCHOOLS Listening Part 1

1 Briefly review what students need to do in this part of the exam and if necessary read out the A2 Key for Schools box on TB page 50.

Point out that the questions are often about numbers so they should 'say' the number in each of the three pictures, for example the times in question 1, in their heads to help them know what to listen for.

Put students into pairs to tell one another what is in each picture. Check as a class. Ask students more questions before they listen:

Question 1: 'Who do you think is speaking to who?' (*a trainer and someone in the team or two people in the team*)

Question 2: 'Where do you think the girl is?' (*in a café*)

Question 3: 'How much are the cheapest earphones?' (*£10.20*)

Question 4: 'What season do you think it is?' (*autumn*)

Question 5: 'Will this dialogue be about the future or the past?' (*future*)

Answers

1 three clocks   2 three pictures of food
3 three prices in pounds and pence
4 three pictures of the weather   5 three activities

---

2 Play the recording twice for students to choose the correct pictures. Check as a class. Ask students which of the three activities in question 5 they would rather do that evening.

Answers

1 B   2 A   3 C   4 A   5 A

» AUDIOSCRIPT TB PAGE 303

SPEAKING

1 Ask students to describe each photo. Pre-teach **pick** (to choose something or someone). Tell students to match the sentences to the photos. Check as a class. Ask students, 'Which situation is most serious?'.

Answers

1 C   2 A   3 B   4 D

FAST FINISHERS

Tell fast finishers to think of one more thing the teenagers are worried about to go with each photo. For example: Photo A – *I played badly and my team lost an important match.*

2 Put students into pairs. Tell them to role-play being one of the teenagers in the photos and someone giving them advice. Tell students to use the language in the box and the Teen Health website. Weaker students could write down their dialogues before they say them. As feedback, have some pairs role-play their dialogues at the front of the class.

COOLER

Write these sentences on the board or, for stronger students, read them out. Ask students to make them more natural by using reflexive pronouns.

Thomas looked at his body in the mirror. (*Thomas looked at himself in the mirror.*)

Don't cut your hand with that knife. (*Don't cut yourself with that knife.*)

I did it without the help of other people. (*I did it by myself.*)

Nobody took us to the station but we still got there. (*We got to the station by ourselves.*)

Paula doesn't think about anybody else. (*Paula only thinks about herself.*)

②

Everyone tells you it's not healthy to sit at the computer all day. For one thing, it's very lonely and can make you feel lazy. But doing too much sport can also be bad for you. Your body is still young, so you shouldn't do too much exercise. You can easily hurt something. About an hour of sport a day is right for a teenager. You should also think about when you do sport. For example, you can get a stomach ache if you play tennis just after you've eaten.

③

Everyone feels unhappy from time to time, so you're not alone. Don't be surprised. It's normal for your feelings to change at your age. Is there something you're worried about? Find a friendly person to talk to, like your mum or dad or a teacher. You might get a bit embarrassed, but you'll be glad that you did. If you talk about your problems, they aren't so bad.

④

The answer to this is yes! I'm sure you know that a plate of fruit is better for you than a plate of chips! But what your growing body, your heart and your brain need is variety. If you are careful and eat a bit of everything, then you are healthier. Don't forget fresh fruit, vegetables and eggs! Eating a variety of healthy food gives you energy and can help you feel confident about studying and doing exams.

LISTENING

✓ PREPARE FOR THE EXAM

Listening Part 1

1 Look at the pictures. In pairs, discuss what you can see in each one.

2 For each question, choose the correct picture.

130 **1** What time is basketball practice today?

2 Which food does the girl choose?

3 Which earphones does the boy buy?

4 What's the weather like?

5 What are they going to do?

SPEAKING

1 Look at photos A–D below and match them to the things the teenagers are worried about 1–4.

  1 I failed my exam.
  2 They haven't picked me for the team.
  3 My parents don't understand me.
  4 I think it's broken.

2 Work in pairs. Take turns to be the teenager asking a question about one of the problems in Exercise 1 and the person giving advice. Use the ideas in the *Teen Health* website and the phrases in the box to help you.

> How about …   Why don't you …
> Why not …   You should …

> I failed my exam. What can I do?

> You should ask the teacher what you need to work on. You're always listening to music. Maybe you should spend more time studying.

Exam F **STAYING HEALTHY** 101

18 FROM COVER TO COVER

ABOUT YOU

Write a list of all the things you've read in the last three days.

How many books are included in your list? What kind of books are they?

VOCABULARY AND READING

Books and reading

1 Look at the messages, signs and notices. Where would you see 3, 4, 5 and 6?

1
Kat
I've just finished an amazing book – the kind you pick up and then can't put down again! I'll lend it to you, if you want.
Amber

2
To: All students
From: School secretary
Reply Forward
Everyone – please remember! If you don't return your library books by the end of term, you will have to pay for them.

3
HILLCREST SCHOOL
The writer Jill Hadfield is speaking here next Tuesday! If you buy a book after her talk, she'll write in it for you.

4

Put books back on the right shelves when you've finished with them.
Library receptionist

5
If you buy two books today, we'll give you another from this table
FOR FREE!
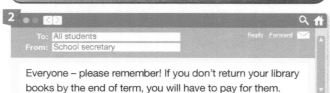

6
Class 9A

Everyone who took a maths textbook home, please bring it back to school tomorrow. If you don't, I won't be able to lend them to 9B.

Miss Taylor

PREPARE FOR THE EXAM

Reading Part 1

2 For each question choose the correct answer.

1 What is Amber doing in this message?
   A telling Kat when she'll finish her book
   B asking Kat for some advice about a book
   C finding out if Kat wants to borrow a book

2 What must students do?
   A take the books they've borrowed back to the library
   B collect the books they've ordered from the library
   C choose which books they want to take out of the library

3 Next Tuesday, students will be able to
   A find out how to write a book.
   B listen to a well-known writer.
   C get some books at a special price.

4 The receptionist wants people to
   A ask if they cannot find the right book.
   B return books to the correct place after using them.
   C give books back to him when they've finished them.

5 A Every customer will get a free book today.
   B There's a discount on all books for today only.
   C You can get three books for the price of two today.

6 A Miss Taylor wants to give the books to another class.
   B Miss Taylor has new maths books to lend to the class.
   C Miss Taylor would like to know who borrowed her books.

3 In pairs, compare your answers. Discuss why you chose each answer and change any you think are wrong.

18 FROM COVER TO COVER

Unit Overview

TOPIC	Literature
VOCABULARY	Books and reading
AND READING	Signs, notices and messages
GRAMMAR	First conditional
PRONUNCIATION	Sentence stress
READING	Books to make you laugh this summer
VOCABULARY	Words about books
LISTENING	A talk about a reading competition
WRITING	A story
EXAM TASKS	Reading Part 1; Reading Part 2; Writing Part 7

Resources

GRAMMAR REFERENCE AND PRACTICE: SB page 164; TB page 267

PREPARE FOR THE EXAM: SB pages on TB pages 236–237, 238 and 243; TB pages 252, 253 and 255

WORKBOOK: pages 72–75

PHOTOCOPIABLE WORKSHEETS: Grammar worksheet Unit 18; Vocabulary worksheet Unit 18

TEST GENERATOR: Unit test 18

WARMER

Read out the titles of these books (you could also include some famous books in your language) and ask students to say the author. You could also do it the other way round by naming authors and having students say what books they have read (if they say the titles of English books in L1, help them to translate them into English.)

Harry Potter and the Goblet of Fire (*J.K. Rowling*)

The Adventures of Huckleberry Finn (*Mark Twain*)

The Hobbit (*J.R. Tolkien*)

Charlie and the Chocolate Factory (*Roald Dahl*)

Frankenstein (*Mary Shelley*)

Animal Farm (*George Orwell*)

Treasure Island (*Robert Louis Stephenson*)

Ask students if they have read any of these books or know anything about them or the authors.

ABOUT YOU

Ask students what kind of things they read at school, at home and outside and write them on the board. Examples: books, websites, emails, signs, leaflets. Elicit different types of books, for example, *adventure, children's, crime, horror, science-fiction, thriller*. Then have students write down a list of what they have read and name the type of books. Put students into pairs to compare. You could also organise this as a whole-class activity (or large groups if you have a big class) by giving students a time limit to collect information from the other students in the class about what they have read and then compare this in small groups. As a class see what books and other things most people have read recently and why they have read them.

VOCABULARY **AND** **READING**

Books and reading

1 Tell students to read the first message and ask, 'Whose book is it?' (*Amber's*) and 'Did Amber like the book?' (*yes*). Have students read the second message and ask, 'Is the secretary giving the students some new information?' (*no*) and 'Do students need to give back the books today?' (*no*). Ask students where they would see texts 3–6.

> **Answers**
> 3 school 4 library 5 bookshop 6 classroom

✓ PREPARE FOR THE EXAM

A2 KEY FOR SCHOOLS Reading Part 1

2 Briefly review what students need to do in this part of the exam and if necessary read out the A2 Key for Schools box on TB page 129.

Tell students to think about the purpose of each text, for example, 4 is giving an instruction and 5 is making an offer.

Make sure that students understand the difference between *lend* and *borrow*. Give a book to a student and say, 'I'm lending Maria the book. Maria is borrowing it.' Tell students to read and choose the answers.

3 Put students into pairs to compare their answers to Exercise 2. Model the discussion:

Student A:	What do you have for 1?
Student B:	I put A because she writes about finishing a book.
Student A:	Yes but she says she has finished the book, not that she will finish it.
Student B:	You're right, so A is wrong. What answer do you have?
Student A:	C because 'if you want?' means 'Do you want to borrow the book?'
Student B:	Yes, you're right!

Check as a class. Ask students to tell you ways that they can improve on this exam task, for example, learning more vocabulary, reading signs and notices on the internet and trying to understand them.

> **Answers**
> 1 C 2 A 3 B 4 B 5 C 6 A

◀)) The Reading text is recorded for students to listen, read
131 and check their answers.

CONTINUED ON PAGE 202

4 Remind students that a phrasal verb is a verb + preposition/adverb and elicit some examples: 'What do you do first in the morning?' (*wake up and get up*) and 'What does a plane do?' (*take off*). Tell students to find the phrasal verbs and match them to the meanings. Check as a class.

> ### Answers
>
> **a** give back **b** pick up **c** bring back **d** find out **e** take back **f** put down **g** put back **h** take out

5 Tell students to complete the sentences. Check as a class.

> ### Answers
>
> **1** find out **2** pick up **3** brought back **4** take out **5** put, down **6** give, back **7** take, back **8** put, back

6 Put students into pairs to choose a situation from page 138 and write a conversation using phrasal verbs. Ask students to perform their conversations in front of the class. The other students should say what phrasal verbs were used.

7 Ask students, 'Do you prefer to buy books or borrow them from a library?' and 'How often do you go to the library?'. Put students into pairs or groups to ask and answer the questions in the book. Share ideas as a class. Ask students, 'Do we still need paper books and libraries now that many books are electronic?'

GRAMMAR | First conditional

1 Tell students to read the examples and find more examples in the texts. Check as a class.

> ### Answers
>
> If you don't return your library books by the end of term, you will have to pay for them.
> If you buy a book after her talk, she'll write in it for you.
> If you don't, I won't be able to lend them to 9b.

2 Tell students to complete the rules. Check as a class.

> ### Answers
>
> **1** No, it doesn't **2** Present simple **3** Very sure

>> **GRAMMAR REFERENCE AND PRACTICE ANSWER KEY TB PAGE 267**

3 Books closed, write the beginning of a conditional sentence on the board and get ideas on how to finish it: *If I feel bored, …* (*I'll call my friend, watch a DVD*, etc.). Books open, students match the sentence halves. Check as a class.

> ### Answers
>
> **1** b **2** a **3** e **4** d **5** c

4 Tell students to complete the sentences. Share ideas as a class.

5 Tell students to correct the sentences. Check as a class.

> ### Answers
>
> 1 If I ~~will~~ go, I will play with my friends.
> 2 I**'ll be** happy if you come to my party.
> 3 If you join this class, you**'ll/will** like it.
> 4 If you like, we**'ll/will** go by car.
> 5 My mum **will be** angry if I don't wear these trousers.

>> **GRAMMAR WORKSHEET UNIT 18**

PRONUNCIATION | Sentence stress

6 Ask students why the words in the example are stressed (*They are important because they show the contrast: I'll/you* and *cake/sandwiches.*). Play the recording for students to listen, mark the stress and repeat.

132

> ### Answers
>
> 1 They'll **come** if you in**vite** them
> 2 If you **pass** the exam, I'll **buy** you a **pre**sent.
> 3 You'll **miss** the bus if you **don't hurry**.
> 4 If **you** help **Tom**, I'll help **Pet**e.

7 Tell students to go to page 138 and write three sentences following the instructions. Then put students into pairs to compare their answers before sharing ideas as a class.

4 Find and underline the phrasal verbs in the texts in Exercises 1 and 2. Then match each one to its meaning a–h.

bring back	find out	give back
pick up	put back	put down
take back	take out	

a return something to a person
b lift something with your hands
c return from somewhere with something
d learn something new
e return something to the place you borrowed or bought it from
f put something you are holding onto the floor or a table, for example
g return something to a place
h remove something from somewhere

5 Complete the sentences with phrasal verbs from Exercise 4 in the correct tense.

1 Did you _____ what we need to do for homework?
2 Can you _____ all the books and clothes from the floor, please?
3 My mum went to China and _____ some great presents for us.
4 How many books are you allowed to _____ of the school library?
5 My book is so exciting. I can't _____ it _____!
6 Thanks for lending me this magazine! I'll _____ it _____ to you tomorrow.
7 My new book had several pages missing, so I'm going to _____ it _____ to the shop.
8 When you've finished with my book, can you _____ it _____ in my room?

6 ≫ In pairs, go to page 138. Choose one of the situations and write a short conversation. Use at least three phrasal verbs in your conversation.

7 In small groups, ask and answer the questions.

1 What's your school library like? What sort of books can you borrow from it?
2 Is there a library in your town? Do you borrow books from it? What else do you do there?
3 How do you feel about lending other people your books or other things?
4 Do you ever borrow books or other things from friends? Do you look after them carefully?

GRAMMAR First conditional

1 Look at the examples of first conditional sentences. Then, find and underline all the examples in Exercise 1 on page 102.

If you buy two books today, we'll give you another from this table for free!
I'll lend it to you, if you want.

2 Read the information and choose the correct answers to the questions.

Sentences in the first conditional have two clauses:
if + verb … , *will* + infinitive
1 Does the *if* clause have to come first?
Yes, it does. / No, it doesn't.
2 What tense do we use after *if*?
Present simple / Future simple

We use first conditional sentences to talk about a possible future.
3 How sure are we about that future?
Very sure / Not very sure

≫ **GRAMMAR REFERENCE AND PRACTICE PAGE 164**

3 Match the two halves of the sentences.

1 We'll miss the film
2 If I find your book,
3 I won't tell anyone
4 If you don't eat fast food,
5 I'll lend you my earphones

a I'll give it to the teacher.
b if you don't hurry.
c if you can't find yours.
d you'll be healthier.
e if you don't want me to.

4 Complete these sentences with your own ideas.

1 You won't get into the football team if …
2 If our team get into the final, …
3 If I have time this weekend, …
4 I'll lend you my jacket if …

5 Correct the mistakes in the sentences.

1 If I will go, I will play with my friends.
2 I'm happy if you come to my party.
3 If you join this class, you like it.
4 If you like, we would go by car.
5 My mum is angry if I don't wear these trousers.

PRONUNCIATION | Sentence stress

6 Listen to the sentences. Mark the stressed words, then practise the sentences.
132

0 I'll bring cake if you bring sandwiches.
1 They'll come if you invite them.
2 If you pass the exam, I'll buy you a present.
3 You'll miss the bus if you don't hurry.
4 If you help Tom, I'll help Pete.

7 ≫ In pairs, go to page 138 and play the *If* game.

READING

1 Look at the pictures of the books and try to guess what they are about. Read the texts quickly to check your ideas.

BOOKS TO MAKE YOU
laugh this summer

We asked three readers to tell us about a funny book they enjoyed – here's what they told us.

A NATALIE

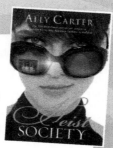

My mum bought this for me for my birthday and I knew from the picture on the front and the title that I was going to love it. I read it in just two days and I was really sad when I got to the end. The story is about a girl who has to help her family by getting back some stolen paintings – I found it really exciting! I'm now a huge fan of the author, Ally Carter – I have all her other books on my shelf ready for the summer.

B HEIDI

In my opinion, this is one of the funniest books ever written for teenagers. It's about a 15-year-old boy who wants to start a rock band, but the adults in his life all try to stop him. Nothing goes right for him until the very end of the story. The writer is also an artist and the clever drawings on each page help the story along. Unfortunately, the cover makes it look like it's for little kids, which is a shame as it might stop some teenagers from picking it up.

C DAVINA

I got this book for a great price in my local store. It's a funny story about a terrible girl who has to learn to be a better person. It's the first time I've tried this kind of book, but I really enjoyed it. Of course, it's not perfect – I wasn't happy with what happens in the last few pages. But it was a lot of fun, and I think I'll probably read more like it in the future.

✓ PREPARE FOR THE EXAM

Reading Part 2

2 For each question, choose the correct answer. Write *A* for Natalie, *B* for Heidi or *C* for Davina.

1 Who didn't like the way the book ended?
2 Who plans to read more books by the same writer?
3 Who explains where she bought the book?
4 Who thought the pictures inside were excellent?
5 Who says the book is different from what she usually reads?
6 Who thinks some people may get the wrong idea about the book?
7 Who says it didn't take her long to read the book?

💬 TALKING POINTS

Do you like reading? If yes, what sort of books? What's the best book you've ever read?

VOCABULARY Words about books

1 Read the texts again and <u>underline</u> the words from the box. Then, match them to the definitions 1–9.

author	chapter	cover	drawings
end	opinion	pages	shelf	title

1 This is the last part of the book.
2 The words and pictures on this help you decide if you want to read it.
3 This is the name the writer gives to the book.
4 These pictures are done with a pen or pencil.
5 You can put your books on this.
6 You turn these as you read.
7 This person writes books.
8 This is what you think or believe about something.
9 This is one of the sections of a book that usually has a number or title.

2 Complete the questions with words from Exercise 1. Then, in pairs, ask and answer the questions.

1 Do you listen to other people's _____ when you choose a book to read?
2 Do you think books with _____ in them are just for little kids?
3 Have you ever chosen a book because you think the _____ or _____ look interesting?
4 Do you like books with hundreds of _____ or do you prefer shorter ones?
5 Have you ever got to the _____ of a book and felt sad that it was finished?

WARMER

Arrange students into small groups. They play the *if* game on SB page 138 again, but this time orally. One student says a conditional sentence, the second student makes a second sentence that continues it, and so on. To demonstrate, students begin by repeating the stories they wrote down, then they can make up new stories.

1 Ask students, 'Do you prefer books about serious topics or books which are funny?'. Ask students to describe the covers and say what each book is about. Give students a time limit to read and check if they were right.

Answers

Students' own answers
A a girl who has to help her family get some paintings back
B a boy who wants to start a rock band
C a terrible girl who has to learn to be a better person

PREPARE FOR THE EXAM

A2 KEY FOR SCHOOLS Reading Part 2

2 Briefly review what students need to do in this part of the exam and if necessary read out the A2 Key for Schools box on TB page 41.

Tell students to read each question in turn and find the information which it matches in one of the texts. The matching information will contain a synonym or paraphrase of the question. Students should not spend too long on a difficult question but move on to the next and go back to it when they have finished the other questions. If necessary, students should guess as they don't lose marks for wrong answers.

Ask some general questions about each text: 'How did Natalie feel when she finished her book?' (*sad*), 'Is Heidi's book for children or teenagers?' (*teenagers*) and 'What does the girl in Davina's book need to do?' (*become a better person*). Give students a time limit to do the exam task. (They should spend about 10 minutes on Part 2.) Put students into pairs to compare answers and explain why they have that answer. Check as a class. Ask students, 'Have you ever read a book in two days like Natalie?', 'What kind of books need good drawings?' and 'Can you think of a book with a really good or a really bad ending?'.

Answers

1 C 2 A 3 C 4 B 5 C 6 B 7 A

 The Reading text is recorded for students to listen, read and check their answers.
133

FAST FINISHERS

Tell fast finishers to write down a chapter heading from each of the three books. For example:

Natalie's: The Escape from the Gallery

Heidi's: The Night of the Concert

Davina's: Problems at School

Fast finishers then read their chapter headings to the rest of the class when they've finished the exam task. The other students say which book the chapter comes from and what happens, for example, in *The Escape from the Gallery* Natalie takes the stolen pictures from an art gallery at night.

TALKING POINTS

Ask students, 'Do you prefer to read print or online books?', 'Many books are also films. Can you think of a film which is better than the book and a book which is better than the film?' and 'Would any of these three books make interesting films?'. Put students into small groups to discuss the questions in the book. Share ideas as a class. Ask students how reading can help them learn English or improve their first language.

VOCABULARY   Words about books

1 Books closed, elicit some of the words: 'Books have hundreds of …' (*pages*), 'Your … is what you think about a book.' (*opinion*) and 'The name of a book is its …' (*title*). Books open, tell students to underline the words and match them. Check as a class.

Answers

1 end 2 cover 3 title 4 drawings 5 shelf 6 pages 7 author
8 opinion 9 chapter

2 Books closed. Demonstrate with examples on the board:

Do you always read books by the same _____? (*author*)

Does anyone know what happens at the _____ of Romeo and Juliet? (*end*)

Put students into pairs to discuss the questions. Books open, tell students to complete the questions. Check as a class. Put students into pairs to ask and answer the questions. Share ideas as a class.

As an extension activity, you could bring some books into class, or take students to the school library, and ask students to choose a book and give details about it using the vocabulary, for example who the author is, what their opinions of the cover and drawings are and (if in the library), which shelf the book is on.

Answers

1 opinion(s) 2 drawings 3 title, cover (in any order) 4 pages
5 end

>> VOCABULARY WORKSHEET UNIT 18

BACKGROUND INFORMATION

In 1950 about 55% of the world's population could read and write but this had increased to 85% in 2015. However, literacy rates are unequal across the world. For example, while almost all adults in North America are literate, the figure is only 60% in sub-Saharan Africa. There are also differences between men and women, particularly in the developing world, where two-thirds of the illiterate are female. For example, in South Asia about 75% of men are literate but only 60% of women are. Unfortunately, this fits into a wider picture of gender inequality in education and opportunities generally. An inability to read and write has major effects on health as well as education: children of literate mothers are 50% more likely to survive childhood because these mothers have access to more information about health matters.

 1 Ask students which of these four topics would be most interesting to hear about in class. Tell students to listen and identify the topic. Check as a class.

> **Answers**
>
> The teacher is talking about a competition and a website.

 2 Demonstrate with an example on the board:

The teacher has organised this competition. (Wrong – it's from a website.)

Play the recording again for students to check the sentences. Check as a class and tell students to correct the wrong answers.

> **Answers**
>
> 1 ✗ (it's open to anyone aged 12–15) 2 ✓
> 3 ✗ (you'll be able to borrow all the books)
> 4 ✗ (the instructions are on the website) 5 ✓ 6 ✓ 7 ✓
> 8 ✗ (it is written by writers and book companies)

MIXED ABILITY

Ask weaker students to rephrase or explain the sentences before they listen. This will show that they understand what it means and what they need to listen for. For example:

1 *Only young children can do the competition.*

2 *The person who reads the most books wins.*

3 *You must buy a lot of books to do the competition.*

This is something you could also do with the whole class as it is a good exam strategy, for both listening and reading.

>> **AUDIOSCRIPT TB PAGE 303**

3 Put students into pairs to ask and answer the questions. Share ideas as a class. Ask students, 'Can you think of other ways to get teenagers to read more books?', 'Would you like to write a book one day?' and 'What would it be about?'.

PREPARE FOR THE EXAM

A2 KEY FOR SCHOOLS Writing Part 7

Briefly review what students need to do in this part of the exam and if necessary read out the A2 Key for Schools box on TB page 46.

Tell students that a good way to organise their story would be to have three sections, one for each picture. Students should check their work carefully when they have finished for mistakes in grammar, vocabulary, spelling and punctuation.

PREPARE TO WRITE
Writing Part 7 A Story

GET READY Tell students to describe each picture in turn. Then have students reorder the sentences to tell the story. Check as a class. Go through the meaning of the words in blue before students complete the sentences: 'Which word gives a reason?' (*because*), 'Which word joins parts of sentences?' (*and*), 'Which word says what happens because of something else?' (*so*), 'Which word shows a contrast?' (*but*) and 'Which word says that something bad happened?' (*unfortunately*). You could ask the questions in L1 if students all speak the same language.

Then tell students to complete the sentences with the linking words. Check as a class. Ask students, 'How often do you get a bus?' and 'Have you ever missed your bus like Tom?'.

> **Answers**
>
> The correct order is c, a, b.
> 1 because 2 so (*and* is also possible) 3 but 4 Unfortunately
> 5 and

PLAN Tell students to look at the pictures on page 139 and ask them some questions to elicit the key vocabulary: 'Where is Ali?' (*in the library*), 'What did she want to do?' (*take out lots of books*), 'What happened to them?' (*They fell on the floor.*) and 'How did Ali's friend help?' (*She picked them up.*). Tell students to make notes including the key vocabulary.

WRITE Tell students to use their notes to write the story.

IMPROVE Put students into pairs to check one another's stories. As feedback, ask some students to read out their stories to the class.

> **Model answer**
>
> Yesterday, Ali went to the library because she wanted to take out some books to read in the holidays. She chose lots of books and unfortunately she couldn't carry them all, so they fell onto the floor. The librarian/receptionist was angry but Ali's friend came to help her pick them all up again.

COOLER

Play Pictionary. You whisper a word to a student, who has to draw it on the board, without writing or speaking, for the other students to guess. Begin with easy concrete words like *shelf* and *weather*, then get students to draw the phrasal verbs on page 103.

LISTENING

1 Listen to the teacher talking to his class. Which of these is he talking about?

a new book   a competition   a website   a writer

2 Read the sentences. Then, listen again. Are the sentences right (✓) or wrong (✗)?

1 If you're under 12, you can enter the competition.
2 To win, you need to read more books than anyone else.
3 If you enter, you'll have to buy lots of books.
4 The teacher will give the students all the instructions they need.
5 One of the prizes is a writing course.
6 You can see people's opinions of books on the competition website.
7 You might save money if you buy a book from the website.
8 The website blog is written by teenagers who like writing stories.

3 In pairs, ask and answer the questions.

1 How many books do you usually read in the long school holiday?
2 Would you like to enter a competition like this?

WRITING

PREPARE TO WRITE

Writing Part 7 A story

GET READY

Look at the pictures and read the sentences. Put the sentences in the correct order to tell the story.

a He started to feel a bit bored, so he took his book out of his bag and started reading it.
b Unfortunately, Tom was enjoying the book so much that he missed his bus, and he had to wait for the next one.
c Tom was waiting for his bus, but it was late. There was lots of traffic because the weather was bad.

Complete each sentence with one of the linking words in blue above.

1 I'm tired this morning _____ I read my book until midnight last night.
2 I lost my library book _____ I had to pay for a new one.
3 I liked the writer's first book _____ I hated her second one.
4 _____ the shop didn't have the book I wanted.
5 I like books that can make me laugh _____ cry.

PLAN You are going to write a story about the pictures on page 139.
• Look at the pictures carefully.
• Make notes about the story. Answer the questions *Who?*, *Where?* and *What is happening?*
• Write down key vocabulary and decide what tense to use.

WRITE Now write the story shown in the pictures on page 139. Remember to write about every picture and use linkers. Write 35 words or more.

IMPROVE In pairs, read each other's stories and check you have both used linking words correctly.

FROM COVER TO COVER 105

CULTURE

ENGLISH LITERATURE

1 In pairs, ask and answer the questions.

 1 What books do you like?
 2 Who wrote them?
 3 Can you name some famous authors from your country?

2 Have you heard of R. J. Palacio? Have you read any of her books or seen films of them? Read the text and complete the fact file.

R.J. Palacio

R. J. PALACIO was born in New York and still lives there with her husband, two sons and two dogs. She studied at the High School of Art and Design and worked for many years as a graphic designer, creating book covers. She wrote her first book, *Wonder*, in 2012. R. J. is also the author of several short stories and has recently published a picture book for younger readers called *We're All Wonders*, combining her writing and artistic talents. She wanted to be a writer for many years but never found the time until one day she decided to write *Wonder*. She says, 'This story was something that I wanted to say and I needed to say.' The book is about a boy who looks very different to other teenagers and his experiences when he first goes to school. The film of the book came out in 2017.

FACT FILE R. J. Palacio

Nationality:	(1) _____
First job:	(2) _____
First book (name and date):	(3) _____
Other books:	(4) _____
Date of film:	(5) _____

THE INTERNATIONAL BESTSELLER

My name is August.
I won't describe what I look like.
Whatever you're thinking,
it's probably worse.

'Has the power to move hearts
and change minds'
Guardian

'Destined to go the way of
*The Curious Incident of the Dog
in the Night-Time*
and then some' *The Times*

'It wreaks emotional havoc' *Independent*

3 Look at the cover of *Wonder* and the words on the back cover. What do they tell you about:

 1 the main character's name?   **2** what he looks like?   **3** how good the book is?

4 Put the sentences about the beginning of the story in the correct order.

 a ☐ He feels lonely sitting on his own, but then he meets a friendly girl called Summer.
 b ☐ Jack is sorry and he and August become friends again.
 c ☐ When he arrives, the principal of the school asks three students to look after him,
 d ☐1 It's August's first day at his first school.
 e ☐ He also meets another boy, Jack,
 f ☐ who is nice to him at first but then is horrible.
 g ☐ but they don't sit with him at lunch.
 h ☐ August is upset because his friend isn't nice to him and runs away from school.

106 CULTURE

CULTURE

Learning Objectives

- The students learn about the author R. J. Palacio, read some of her work and talk about literature in general.
- In the project stage, students write a blurb about their favourite book and a fact file about the author.

Resources

CULTURE VIDEO AND CULTURE VIDEO WORKSHEET: How teens read

BACKGROUND INFORMATION

This is the plot of the novel *Wonder*. August has serious medical problems so he is homeschooled until he is in fifth grade (about ten years old). As soon as he starts school, August is bullied by the other children, especially a boy called Julian, because his face is disfigured. August does make some friends but this causes problems for them too as Julian tries to turn the class against them. August also has problems at home as his sister, Olivia, feels neglected because so much attention is given to August. There is hope for August at the end of the book as Julian leaves the school and August is given a special school prize. Best of all, August's mother says that she is proud of her son and calls him a 'wonder'.

WARMER

Write these (unreal!) books and authors on the board and ask the students to match them.

How to get famous	Mark Ed Low
Danger!	Liza Lott
Funny Stories	A. Lone
10 Years on an Island	Luke Out
The Bad Student	B.A. Star
The Truth?	Jo King

Answers

How to get famous – B. A. Star (be a star)
Danger! – Luke Out (Look out!)
Funny Stories – Jo King (joking)
10 Years on an Island – A. Lone (alone)
The Bad Student – Mark Ed Low (marked low)
The Truth? – Liza Lott (lies a lot)

1 Books closed. Elicit different genres of books, for example, science-fiction, horror, romance, children's literature, fantasy. Ask students to tell you about the last book they read. Books open. Put students into pairs to discuss the questions. Share ideas as a class. Ask students, 'Which authors from your country are most famous in other countries?'

2 It's unlikely that students will have heard of R. J. Palacio so have the students discuss books and films for younger readers.

Pre-teach **combine** (if someone combines two or more qualities, they have both of those qualities) and **wonder** (a feeling of great surprise and admiration caused by seeing or experiencing something that is strange and new). Give students time to read and complete the fact file. Check as a class. Ask students if they think it is difficult for a female writer to write about a boy as the main character.

Answers

Students' own answers
1 American 2 Graphic designer 3 *Wonder*, 2012
4 *We're all Wonders* and short stories 5 2017

🔊 135 The Reading text is recorded for students to listen, read and check their answers.

3 Put students into pairs to discuss what information the cover gives them and whether they would like to read the book. Check ideas as a class.

Answers

1 His name is unusual (August).
2 He looks different to other people.
3 It is a very popular book. / It makes people feel strongly.

4 Books closed. Write the first sentence on the board and ask students to predict what happens next to August. Pre-teach **principal** (the head teacher of a school). Books open. Tell students to put the sentences in order. Check as a class. Ask students, 'Do you think the principal was right to tell the students to look after August?' and 'What do you think happened when he ran away?'.

Answers

The correct order is d, c, g, a, e, f, h, b.

MIXED ABILITY

Help weaker students to recognise the cohesive devices that show the sentences are in the right order. Ask, 'Is d a complete sentence?' (*yes*), 'So the second sentence must be the beginning of a new sentence. Does any sentence talk about August and his first day?' (*yes – c*), 'What are the links?' (*August = he and first day = arrives*), 'Is this sentence finished?' (*no*), 'Do you think the students looked after him?' (*no*), 'So find an end of a sentence that shows something went wrong.' (*g*) and 'Which word shows a contrast?' (*but*). If necessary, continue until students have got the correct order and understood how the text links together in terms of meaning and grammar.

5 Books closed. Write the title of the chapter on the board and ask students for reasons why August didn't go to school. There is vocabulary in the text that students will not know. If many students are weak and you think they will find the reading task difficult without this vocabulary, pre-teach some or all of the difficult words. (You could also do this as a post-reading task.)

petrified extremely frightened

surgery the treatment of injuries or diseases in people or animals by cutting open the body and removing or repairing the damaged part

figure out to understand or solve something

illustrator a person who draws pictures, especially for books

fairy an imaginary creature with magic powers, usually represented as a very small person with wings

mermaid an imaginary creature described in stories, with the upper body of a woman and the tail of a fish

stuff things that someone says or does, when they are referring to them in a general way without saying exactly what they are

hot new and exciting

end up to achieve a situation after other activities

kid a child

hang out to spend a lot of time in a place or with someone

Point out that Via is Olivia, August's sister, and Darth Vader is an evil character in the *Star Wars* series of films. Play the recording for students to read and listen. Tell students to answer the questions. Check as a class.

> **Answers**
> 1 because of the surgeries he had
> 2 at home
> 3 because she's busy looking after the family

🔊 The Reading text is recorded for students to listen, read
136 and check their answers.

6 Ask students if they can remember their first day at school and how they felt. Tell students to read the text again and choose the correct options. Check as a class. Ask students what advice they would give to August on his first day at school. They are sensitive issues but you could start a class discussion about bullying and discrimination of different types at and outside school.

> **Answers**
> 1 worried 2 hospitals 3 ill 4 girls 5 make friends

FAST FINISHERS

Tell fast finishers that *kid* is an informal word for *child*. Write these informal words and phrases on the board and have fast finishers write more formal synonyms (they may need to use mobile devices or dictionaries): *Hi* (hello), *loads of* (lots of), *mate* (friend), *bike* (bicycle), *Cool!* (great!), *a bit* (slightly), *my place* (my flat/house), *See you* (goodbye).

When they finish, have fast finishers think of other informal words and expressions and test the rest of the class with them when they finish.

PROJECT *A book blurb and author fact file*

Show students the back of a book and point out the blurb. Ask students what information goes in a blurb (*a description of the contents and why the book is good*). Tell students to work individually, choose their favourite book and write a blurb, 50 words maximum, for it. Write these useful phrases on the board:

This book is about …

The story begins when …

The main characters are …

At the end …

You must read this book because …

You will enjoy this book if you like …

Students should also find out about the author and write a fact file similar to the one for R. J. Palacio. Weaker students could work in pairs: one writes the blurb, the other the fact file. Then each student presents their blurb and fact file to the rest of the class. (This could be a poster presentation if the class is very large and everyone presenting orally would take too long.)

PROJECT EXTENSION

Ask students to choose a book from one of the blurbs (they can't choose their own!). Tell students to read the book (if it is a famous book, in English as an adapted reader, or in their own language) and write a book review about it. The review should describe the book in their own words, not just copy the blurb, and say what they liked about it. Students who wrote the original blurb should read the reviews and say if they agree with them.

 CULTURE VIDEO: How teens read
14 When students have completed the lesson, they can watch the video and complete the worksheet.

COOLER

Arrange students into groups of five. Give each of them a famous person from the present or the past, for example Lionel Messi, Cleopatra, Alexander the Great, Venus Williams and William Shakespeare. Explain that they are in a boat in a bad storm. The boat is too heavy, so four people must get out of the boat and try to swim. Each person should explain why they should stay in the boat and the others should get out. For example, Venus might say, 'I've got a famous sister and she wants to play tennis with me again. Lionel is very fit so he can swim. Cleopatra …'

5 Read and listen to part of Chapter 2 of *Wonder*. Guess any words you don't know, or ignore them! Answer the questions.

1 Why didn't August go to school before fifth grade?
2 Where did he study before?
3 Why doesn't his mother draw anything now?

Why I didn't go to school

Next week, I start fifth grade. Since I've never been to a real school before, I am pretty much totally and completely petrified. People think I haven't gone to school because of the way I look, but it's not that. It's because of all the surgeries I've had. Twenty-seven since I was born. The bigger ones happened before I was even four years old, so I don't remember those. But I've had two or three surgeries every year since then (some big, some small), and because I'm little for my age, and I have some other medical mysteries that doctors never really figured out, I used to get sick a lot. That's why my parents decided it was better if I didn't go to school. I'm much stronger now, though. The last surgery I had was eight months ago, and I probably won't have to have any more for another couple of years.

Mom homeschools me. She used to be a children's-book illustrator. She draws really great fairies and mermaids. Her boy stuff isn't so hot, though. She once tried to draw me a Darth Vader, but it ended up looking like some weird mushroom-shaped robot. I haven't seen her draw anything in a long time. I think she's too busy taking care of me and Via.

I can't say I always wanted to go to school because that wouldn't be exactly true. What I wanted was to go to school, but only if I could be like every other kid going to school. Have lots of friends and hang out after school and stuff like that.

PROJECT
A book blurb and author fact file

A blurb is a short description about a book on the back of its cover. It should make you want to read the book! Write a blurb of no more than 50 words about your favourite book.

Include:
• an outline of what happens in the book
• why it is a good book

Find out about the book's author and write a fact file to go with your blurb. Tell your class about your favourite author and read your blurb.

6 Read the text again and choose the correct options.

1 August feels *worried* / *confident* about going to school.
2 He has spent a lot of his life in *hotels* / *hospitals*.
3 He didn't go to school because he was often *ill* / *unhappy*.
4 His mother is good at drawing pictures for *girls* / *boys*.
5 August wants to go to school to *make friends* / *learn more*.

 TALKING POINTS
Would you like to read the book? Why / Why not?

19 DIFFERENT INGREDIENTS

Breakfast cereals 🔊 137

Breakfast cereals are popular in many countries. They are made from grains, such as corn, wheat and rice. They are usually eaten with milk, or with yogurt and fruit. In the beginning, cereals were health foods, but these days some children's cereals are 50% sugar, and doctors say we shouldn't eat them too often.

There are lots of kinds of cereal. This is how cereals in different shapes, like stars and balls, are made.

First, the grain is taken to the factory, where it is cleaned and checked.

Then it is prepared for cooking. It is made into flour and mixed with other ingredients. Water is added and the mixture is boiled.

When it is soft, it is put into special machines which make it into shapes like stars, circles, or even letters of the alphabet.

The shapes are baked in an oven to dry them. Then, they are 'puffed' in another machine to make them light and full of air.

After that, they are covered with sugar or honey. Some are filled with chocolate. The cereal pieces are then dried in hot air.

Finally, the cereal is packed into boxes, ready for the shops.

VOCABULARY AND READING

Words to describe cooking

❓ ABOUT YOU
Do you eat breakfast cereals?
How often do you eat them?
What kinds do you like?
Do you think they are healthy?

1 Read the text and put photos A–C in the correct order.

2 Look at the verbs in the text. Match them to the definitions below. Write the verbs in the infinitive.

1 Put one thing with another thing.
2 Make something ready.
3 Take the water out of something.
4 Join two or more things together using a spoon or a machine.
5 Cook something like a cake in an oven.
6 Cook in water.
7 Put something on top of something else.
8 Make an empty space full.

3 In pairs, ask and answer the questions.

1 What other kinds of food do you eat for breakfast?
2 How do you prepare them?
3 Describe the best breakfast you have ever had.

⊝ PRONUNCIATION | Ways to pronounce *ea*

🔊 138 **4** Listen to the different ways to say the letters *ea*.

/ɪə/ ear   /e/ head   /iː/ seat

5 In pairs, put these words into the correct column of the table.

beach	bread	breakfast	
clean	eat	healthy	meal
near	ready	teacher	wheat

/ɪə/ ear	/e/ head	/iː/ seat

🔊 139 Listen and check. Then repeat.

19 DIFFERENT INGREDIENTS

Unit Overview

TOPIC	Food and cooking
VOCABULARY	Words to describe cooking
AND READING	Breakfast cereals
PRONUNCIATION	Ways to pronounce *ea*
GRAMMAR	Present simple passive
READING	The taste test
VOCABULARY	Ingredients; *make* and *do*
LISTENING	A cooking competition
SPEAKING	Talking about a recipe
EXAM TASKS	Reading Part 5; Listening Part 2

Resources

GRAMMAR REFERENCE AND PRACTICE: SB page 165; TB page 267
PREPARE FOR THE EXAM: SB pages on TB pages 241 and 245;
TB pages 254 and 256
WORKBOOK: pages 76–79
VIDEO AND VIDEO WORKSHEET: Favourite foods
PHOTOCOPIABLE WORKSHEETS: Grammar worksheet Unit 19;
Vocabulary worksheet Unit 19
TEST GENERATOR: Unit test 19

WARMER

Oral food and drink anagrams. Say, don't write, or let students write down, some short food and drink words with the letters mixed up. The students must say the word. For example, z i a p z (*pizza*), m e o n l (*lemon*), t r a w e (*water*), f u i t r (*fruit*).

To make it easier, or if you introduce longer words, say the first letter first. Students could then do this in pairs. Give students time to think of food and drink words and write them down as anagrams. They take it in turns to tell one another the anagrams.

ⓘ ABOUT YOU

Books closed, ask students, 'What is your favourite meal of the day?' and 'Which is the most important?'. Write *a box of* _____ on the board and see if students can guess *cereal*. It would be good to bring in a box of cereal to set the context for the discussion. Books open, have students answer the questions in pairs. Share ideas as a class. Ask students, 'Why are cereals so popular?' and 'Are there any healthy cereals?'.

VOCABULARY AND READING

Words to describe cooking

1 Ask students to give you examples of grains (*corn, wheat, rice*). Tell students to look at the pictures, describe them and try to put them in order. Then give students a time limit to read and check the order. Check as a class. Ask students, 'What do you think is the most difficult stage?'

(*Maybe when the grain is cleaned and checked as this could take a long time if humans rather than machines do it.*).

Answers

The correct order is B, C, A.

2 Tell students to match the verbs to the definitions. Check as a class. Ask more comprehension questions about the text: 'How much of some cereals is sugar?' (*50%*), 'Where is the grain checked?' (*in the factory*) and 'What different shapes is cereal made into?' (*many, for example, stars, balls, circles*). As a follow-up question to prompt discussion, ask students, 'Why do you think cereal is made into these different shapes?' (*To make it more interesting for children.*).

Answers

1 add 2 prepare 3 dry 4 mix 5 bake 6 boil 7 cover 8 fill

FAST FINISHERS

Tell fast finishers that *cereal* is a homophone: different words, *cereal* and *serial*, have the same pronunciation /ˈsɪə.ri.əl/. Tell them to think of as many different homophones as they can while the other students are finishing. Examples: *ate/eight, hear/here, our/hour, sea/see, wood/would, write/right*. If students have time, they could try and put pairs of homophones into one sentence, for example, *I ate breakfast at eight o'clock*.

3 Ask, 'Is it important to have a good breakfast?' and 'Should schools serve breakfast?'. Put students into pairs to discuss the questions in the book. Check ideas as a class. As an extension activity, and preparation for Exercise 5 on page 109, in groups, students think of a new cereal. They should say what it is made of, what shape(s) it has, what it is called and why people would buy it. Groups could present their ideas to the class.

🔊 137 The Reading text is recorded for students to listen, read and check their answers.

⊖ PRONUNCIATION | Ways to pronounce *ea*

🔊 138 4 Write on the board *Eat bread for every meal* and ask the students to say it. Ask, 'How many words are there with *ea*?' (*three*) and 'How many different pronunciations are there?' (*three*). Play the recording and have students repeat the words. Tell them that there is no rule for which pronunciation to use, for example, *clean* has /iː/ but *cleanse* has /e/. There are words with other pronunciations of *ea*, for example, *great* /eɪ/ and *heart* /ɑː/.

5 Ask students to put the words into the correct columns in the table. Play the recording for students to listen, check and repeat. Make sure that students distinguish between /iː/ and /ɪ/, as in *seat* vs *sit*. The /iː/ vowel sound is longer and the lips are spread. Next have students make a sentence with an example of each pronunciation of *ea*, for example *Clean your ears before breakfast*, and see who can make the most interesting sentence.

CONTINUED ON PAGE 214

GRAMMAR Present simple passive

1 Books closed, write on the board:

1 People eat cereal everywhere.

2 Cereals are eaten everywhere.

Ask the students, 'What is the subject of sentence 1?' (*people*), 'What is the subject of sentence 2?' (*cereals*) and 'In sentence 2, why don't we say who eats cereals?' (*It's not necessary because it is obvious or because we don't know exactly who eats them.*). Explain that in sentence 1 the verb is 'active' and in sentence 2 it is 'passive'.

Books open, tell students to find examples of the passive in the text and complete the rules. Check as a class. Tell students that only verbs which take an object have a passive form so we can't say *was died, was come,* etc.

As an alternative presentation, or if students need more help with the meaning of the passive, dictate, or write on the board, these amazing facts with the numbers missing for students to guess. (They could look up the answers on their mobile devices or in reference books.)

Every day, people around the world …

make _____ phone calls. (*12 billion*)

eat _____ bananas. (*1.6 billion*)

drink _____ litres of water. (*14 billion*)

buy _____ cars. (*200,000*)

cut down _____ trees. (*40 million*)

kill _____ sharks. (*250,000*)

Ask students, 'What is the subject of all these sentences?' (*people*) and 'Is this clear?' (*yes*). Explain that it would be appropriate to use the passive in this case and write the corresponding passive forms on the board.

Every day around the world …

12 billion phone calls are made.

1.6 billion bananas are eaten.

14 billion litres of water are drunk.

200,000 cars are bought.

40 million trees are cut down.

250,000 sharks are killed.

Then students do the language analysis in Exercise 1. As a follow up, students could find their own amazing facts on their mobile devices or in reference books and write them in the passive to quiz other students.

Answers

1 to be, past participle
2 don't always have to

≫ **GRAMMAR REFERENCE AND PRACTICE ANSWER KEY TB PAGE 267**

2 Books closed, ask students, 'What's your favourite juice?' and 'How many oranges do you think you need to make one litre of orange juice?' (*about 10*). Write these sentences on the board for students to complete with the active or passive form of *need*.

Ten oranges _____ for one litre of juice. (*are needed*)

You _____ ten oranges for one litre of juice. (*need*)

Elicit that the first sentence is passive because the oranges are the subject and the passive verb says what they are used for.

Books open, tell students to complete the text with active or passive forms of the verbs. Check as a class. You could ask students to write a similar description of how another juice, for example apple juice, is made.

Answers

1 are pulled off 2 are put 3 are sent 4 makes
5 is washed and dried 6 are thrown away 7 is cut
8 is removed 9 heat 10 is put 11 take 12 are sold

MIXED ABILITY

Go through the past participles of all the verbs in the text with weaker students before they begin.

3 Demonstrate with an example on the board:

They give you a free drink with it. (*A free drink is given with it.*)

Tell students to rewrite the sentences in the passive. Check as a class.

Answers

1 Loud rock music is played in my favourite café.
2 Bread is often eaten with butter and jam.
3 Lunch is served at 12.30 every day at my school. / At my school lunch is served at 12.30 every day.
4 Our paintings are always put on the classroom wall.
5 A lot of sweets and chocolates are eaten in Britain.

4 Demonstrate with an example on the board:

My mum makes / is made *great pizza.* (*makes*)

Tell students to choose the correct form. Check as a class.

Answers

1 is painted 2 cost 3 is called 4 are called 5 is broken
6 includes 7 is always cooked

≫ **GRAMMAR WORKSHEET UNIT 19**

5 Put students into pairs to invent a snack. They should draw the snack and write a description using the passive and verbs from page 108. Each pair then takes it in turn to tell the class about their snack. The other students can ask questions after each presentation, for example, *How healthy is your snack?* or *How much does it cost?*

6 After each pair has presented their snack, the class can vote on the best snack for the factory.

COOLER

Write /ɪə/, /e/ and /iː/ on the board (or say them) and see if students can remember from page 108 all the words with *ea* which are pronounced in these ways.

1 Look at the sentence from the article. The verbs are in the present simple passive. Find other examples of the present simple passive in the text on page 108 and complete the rules.

The grain is taken to the factory, where it is cleaned and checked.

> **1** To make the passive, we use the verb _____ and the _____ of the main verb.
> **2** When we use the passive, we *always have to / don't always have to* say who does the action.

>> **GRAMMAR REFERENCE AND PRACTICE PAGE 165**

2 Complete the text with the present simple or present simple passive form of the verbs in brackets.

How orange juice is made

The oranges (1) _____ (pull off) the trees and then they (2) _____ (put) into boxes. These (3) _____ (send) to a factory which (4) _____ (make) juice.

At the factory, the fruit (5) _____ (wash and dry) and any bad oranges (6) _____ (throw away). After that, the fruit (7) _____ (cut) in half and the juice (8) _____ (remove) by a machine. Most factories then (9) _____ (heat) the juice to 94 °C. This makes it last a lot longer (6–8 months outside the fridge). The hot juice (10) _____ (put) into cartons or bottles and then left to cool. Finally, lorries (11) _____ (take) the cartons to supermarkets, where they (12) _____ (sell).

3 Rewrite the sentences in the passive. You don't need to say who does the action.

0 People throw away a lot of food these days.
A lot of food is thrown away these days.
1 They play loud rock music in my favourite café.
2 People often eat bread with butter and jam.
3 At my school, they serve lunch at 12.30 every day.
4 Our teacher always puts our paintings on the classroom wall.
5 People in Britain eat a lot of sweets and chocolates.

4 Choose the correct options to complete each sentence.

1 My house *paints / is painted* red and blue.
2 These trousers *are cost / cost* only £15!
3 Do you know that girl? She *calls / is called* Sarah.
4 My sister's children *call / are called* Charlie and Karen.
5 The kitchen drawer *breaks / is broken* and the cooker is not working.
6 The price of the ticket *includes / is included* lunch.
7 Dinner *is always cooked / always cooks* by my dad.

5 Work with a partner. Invent a snack, for example a new kind of ice cream, cake or biscuit. Draw a picture of it and describe what it is like and how it is made. Read your description to the class.

6 While you are listening to the other students' descriptions, imagine you are the manager of a food company. Decide which new snack you are going to make in your factory.

DIFFERENT INGREDIENTS 109

READING

1 Look at the website. Whose blog is this? What is it about? What information can you find on the website?

🔊 140

THE TASTE TEST

About me

Hello everyone!

Thank **(0)** ___you___ for visiting my blog. My name's Caitlin and I'm 14. I've always loved cooking. **(1)** _____ I was nine, I told my parents I wanted to be **(2)** _____ chef and that's still my plan today. I especially love making cakes and baking.

On this blog, I want to show people **(3)** _____ much fun it is to cook. I also want to show them that cooking a meal can **(4)** _____ quick and easy, and that it tastes better **(5)** _____ food that is made in a factory.

And remember, if you do the cooking, you don't have to do the washing-up. That's my rule anyway. So go on – make a mess! I always do.

Don't forget **(6)** _____ leave me a message if you like anything on my website. Happy reading!

The best steak!

YOU NEED:

1 steak per person
some garlic
a little butter
salt and pepper

HOW TO MAKE IT

1 Cover the steak in salt and pepper.
2 Heat the grill. It needs to be hot!
3 Grill the steak for two or three minutes on each side.
4 Fry the garlic in the butter.
5 Serve the steak with garlic butter, fried potatoes and green beans or carrots.

Pancakes

YOU NEED:

2 eggs
300 ml milk
100 g flour

HOW TO MAKE THEM

1 Mix the eggs and milk together.
2 Add the eggs and milk to the flour.
3 Put some oil in a pan.
4 Cook the pancake on both sides.
5 Cover it with lemon and sugar, chocolate sauce or cream, or with pieces of fresh fruit, such as banana and raspberries.

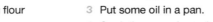

3 Read the two recipes. Match each recipe to one of the photos A–G. Which recipe would you like to make? Do you know any other recipes?

✅ PREPARE FOR THE EXAM

Reading Part 5

2 Complete the *About me* text on the web page. For each question, write the correct answer. Write one word for each gap.

💬 TALKING POINTS

▶ 15 Watch the video, then discuss the questions.

What's your favourite food?
Do you like to cook?
Tell me about your favourite breakfast.

110 **UNIT 19**

WARMER

You say a sentence in the active. Students must say it in the passive (and vice-versa if you wish).

They sell cakes. (*Cakes are sold.*)

We need food. (*Food is needed.*)

I cook them every day. (*They are cooked every day.*)

Do we serve it here? (*Is it served here?*)

People don't want it. (*It isn't wanted.*)

You dry them in an oven. (*They are dried in an oven.*)

Do people sell them online? (*Are they sold online?*)

BACKGROUND INFORMATION

Early humans wouldn't have cooked their food but eaten it raw. The history of cooking probably starts with the controlled use of fire, about a million years ago. Archaeological evidence, for example, basic tools and burned animal bones, shows food was being cooked 300,000 years ago. The advantage of cooking food was that it made it easier to swallow and digest and generally tastier. Cooking allowed a greater variety of food to be eaten because some food, especially meat, is dangerous or inedible when raw. The increase in the range, quantity and quality of food available was probably connected to the increase in the brain size of humans and the development of language.

Cookery evolved from a survival tool to a hobby and art form and the first cookery books, or rather tablets, date back to Mesopotamia around 1700 BC. Apicius, a collection of recipes from ancient Rome, survives and contains sections on sea food and four-legged animals. This book was aimed at the very wealthy as the ingredients are often exotic and expensive and this trend continued until very recently. The first cookery book aimed at ordinary people was probably *Modern Cookery for Private Families,* written in 1845 by the American, Eliza Acton.

1 Ask students, 'Do you have a blog or do you read any?', 'Why do people have blogs?' and 'If you started a blog, what would you write about?'. Give students a time limit to read the blog and answer the questions.

Answers

The blog is written by Caitlin, a teenage chef. It's about cooking. You can find recipes and photos.

 **PREPARE FOR THE EXAM**

A2 KEY FOR SCHOOLS Reading Part 5

2 Briefly review what students need to do in this part of the exam and if necessary read out the A2 Key for Schools box on TB page 153.

Tell students to look at each gap and think about what the whole grammatical construction is and which word is missing from it. For example, for gap 5 students should see that *better* is a comparative and the construction is comparative + *than*.

Tell students to complete the text. Check as a class. Ask students, 'Why did Caitlin start this blog?' (*To show that cooking is fun.*), 'What does she say is the advantage of cooking your own food?' (*it's tastier,*). 'Does she wash up after she cooks?' (*no*) and 'If you like what she writes, what should you do?' (*send her a message*).

Answers

1 When 2 a 3 how 4 be 5 than 6 to

🔊 The Reading text is recorded for students to listen, read
140 and check their answers.

FAST FINISHERS

Tell fast finishers to underline Caitlin's rule *if you do the cooking, you don't have to do the washing-up*. Tell fast finishers to write down three personal rules which they have, using the first conditional. For example:

If I finish all my homework, I can play computer games.

If my sister borrows my scarf, she has to give it me back the next day.

If time, put fast finishers together to compare sentences.

3 Ask students what information you find in a recipe (*a list of food and some instructions*). Ask students to say what the food is in each photo and how it is usually cooked or prepared. Tell students to read the recipes and match them to two of the photos. Check as a class. Put students into pairs to discuss the questions. Share ideas as a class. As an extension activity, students could write out their recipes with the stages in a different order. They then swap recipes with other students and have to put the stages in order.

Answers

The best steak – G, Pancakes – A

💬 **TALKING POINTS**

▶ Show the video and ask students to complete the video
15 worksheet. Then, read the questions in the *Talking points* box and students answer the questions. Share ideas as a class. Ask students, 'How is the food you eat today different from the food your grandparents ate?'. If students don't know, they could ask their grandparents, or older people, and report back in the next lesson.

1 Tell students to match the words to the photos at the bottom of the page. Play the recording for students to listen, check and repeat.

141

Answers

The answers are recorded for the students to listen and repeat.
A salt and pepper **B** carrots **C** potatoes **D** melon **E** steak
F beans **G** pears **H** garlic

2 Ask, 'Which heading would you put apples under?' (*fruit*) 'Cheese?' (*other*) Students write the names of the ingredients under the correct headings. Check and drill the words. Give the students two minutes to add as many words as they can to the table. Share the extra words as a class.

Answers and possible answers

Meat: steak, *fish, chicken, beef, ham*
Fruit: melon, pears, *oranges, bananas*
Vegetables: beans, carrots, garlic, potatoes, *tomatoes*
Other: salt and pepper, *rice, egg, bread, pasta*

3 Tell students to check the meaning of the words. They could use monolingual dictionaries if they are illustrated. Ask students for the translation in your language. They then match the words to the pictures on page 110.

Answers

baked – photo C, boiled – photo D, fried – photos A and F, grilled – photo G, roast – photo E

4 Books closed, ask students to write down as many words as they can for things you use when you are eating and drinking. Books open, they check if their words are included in the exercise. Show students the example and then let them do the rest. Check understanding by saying a food or drink and getting the students to choose what you eat or drink it with, for example ice cream: *spoon* and *bowl*; roast chicken: *knife, fork* and *plate*.

Answers

1 You use a **spoon** to drink soup with, or for dessert, for example ice cream.
2 A **mug** is a kind of cup. It's usually big and heavy. You use a mug for coffee or hot chocolate. You use a **glass** for water or juice. A **cup** is usually for hot drinks like tea.
3 A **bowl** is a round deep dish for eating soup or cereal or for serving vegetables or salad. You usually eat your main course from a **plate**. A **dish** is bigger – it is used for serving food. A dish can also mean a particular food served as a meal.

5 Ask students 'When all the things in Exercise 4 are dirty, what do you do?' (*wash them up*) and 'Do you *do* or *make* the washing-up?' (*do*). Students then categorise the words. Drill all the words with *make* or *do*.

Answers

make: a cup of tea, the bed, a cake, a mess, a mistake
do: the cleaning, the dishes, your homework, the shopping, the washing

6 Arrange students into pairs to discuss. Share ideas as a class.

» **VOCABULARY WORKSHEET UNIT 19**

 **PREPARE FOR THE EXAM**

A2 KEY FOR SCHOOLS Listening Part 2

 1 Briefly review what students need to do in this part of the exam and if necessary read out the A2 Key for Schools box on TB page 86.

Tell students to write numbers as numbers rather than words, so *12* not *twelve*, so that there is no chance of a spelling mistake.

Tell students to listen and complete the text.

142

2 Students check in pairs then listen again to check.
142

Answers

1 2nd/2/second 2 8/eight 3 university 4 Wright (not Right)
5 money

» **AUDIOSCRIPT TB PAGE 304**

SPEAKING

1 Put students into small groups to decide on the recipe. Refer students to the useful language and the recipes on page 110.

2 Groups take it in turns to present their recipes and the class votes for the best dish.

MIXED ABILITY

Help weaker students with the useful language. Tell them that *Why don't we …?* and *Let's …* are followed by the base form of the verb; *What about …?* is followed by the *-ing* form; *I'd prefer …* is followed by the *to-*infinitive.

COOLER

Ask students to tell a story about their day using as many phrases from Vocabulary Exercise 5 as they can. For example, *I woke up and* **made my bed**. *My sister* **made a mess** *so we* **did the cleaning**. *Then …*

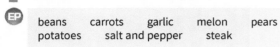
1 Match the words in the box to photos A–H below.

beans	carrots	garlic	melon	pears
potatoes	salt and pepper	steak		

Listen and check. Then repeat.
141

2 Now, write them in the table under the correct headings. Add more words you know to each column.

Meat	Fruit	Vegetables	Other
steak			

3 Check the meaning of these words in a dictionary. Can you find pictures of foods cooked like this on the web page on page 110?

baked	boiled	fried	grilled	roast

4 In pairs, say what you use each thing for.
1 knife / fork / spoon
   You use a knife to cut food. You use a fork to pick food up. You use a spoon to …
2 mug / glass / cup
3 bowl / plate / dish

5 Put the words and phrases with *make* and *do* in the correct column in the table.

the bed	a cake	~~the cleaning~~
~~a cup of tea~~	the dishes	your homework
a mess	a mistake	the shopping
the washing		

make	do
a cup of tea	the cleaning

6 Which of the things in Exercise 5 do you sometimes/often/never do?

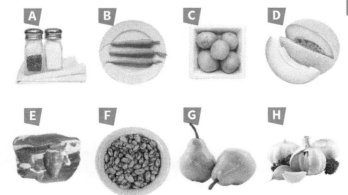

 PREPARE FOR THE EXAM

Listening Part 2

1 For each question, write the correct answer in the gap. Write one word or a number or a date or a time.
142

You will hear a woman giving information about a cooking competition.

SCHOOL CHEF COMPETITION

For students aged:	12–15
Last date to enter:	**(1)** _____ June
Number of teams:	**(2)** _____
Where competition will be:	**(3)** the _____
Name of chef:	**(4)** John _____
Prizes:	**(5)** T-shirts, cookbooks and _____

2 In pairs, compare your answers. Then, listen again and check.
142

SPEAKING

1 You are going to enter the Junior Chef cooking competition. Work in teams of three or four and decide on your recipe.

- What ingredients will you need for your recipe? Make a list together.
- How you will cook it? Write a simple recipe. Look at the ones on page 110 to help you.
- Who will do the different jobs, such as shopping, cutting the vegetables, cooking on the day of the competition, washing up … ?
- Why is it a good meal to serve in a school café? Try to think of three reasons.

USEFUL LANGUAGE

Can you cut the vegetables?	Let's …
	That's a great idea.
I'd prefer not to do the dishes.	That sounds good!
	What about …?
I'll buy the ingredients.	Why don't we …?
I'm not sure about that.	

2 Present your ideas to the class. Choose the best dish for your school café.

20 LIFE CHANGES

LIFE CHANGES 🔊 143

❓ ABOUT YOU
Have you moved house or changed schools recently? Talk to your partner about it.

VOCABULARY AND READING

change as a verb and noun

1 Match sentences 1–4 to the meanings of *change* a–d.

EP
1 I'm sorry, I can't change a ten-pound note.
2 You've really changed your life.
3 Please can I change this jacket? It's too small.
4 We had to change planes in San Francisco.

a take something back to a shop and get something else in its place
b give someone smaller coins when they have paid with a larger coin or note
c move from one kind of transport to another
d do something very different from when you were younger

Now look at sentences with the noun *change* (5–8) and match them to meanings e–h.

5 Remember to bring a change of shoes. It might be wet.
6 I'll email you my change of address.
7 That will make a change.
8 My grandparents hate change.

e new contact details
f something interesting because it's new
g something becoming different
h another item of similar clothing

2 ≫ Go to page 139.

3 Look at pictures A–F in the article. In pairs, discuss the life changes they show.

4 Read the article. Which picture is about Joe's life change?

5 Read the post again and answer the questions.

1 What did Joe remember about his bedtimes as a little boy?
2 Why did they move from London?
3 How did Joe feel about the move?
4 What happened in Dublin that changed their lives?
5 Did people like his mum's first album? How do you know?
6 What was the new apartment like?
7 Which does he prefer, his new life or his old life?

Hi, my name's Joe and I'm 15. I want to tell you about something which changed my life. My mum always sang me songs at bedtime when I was a little boy. The songs weren't written by other people. They were all her own work. Anyway, Mum changed her job and it meant we had to move from London to New York. I was very excited but sad to leave my friends. When we were changing planes in Dublin my mum started talking to a man who worked for a record company. She told him about her songs, and he asked her to send him some of them. When we got to New York, Mum sent him some songs, and he loved them. A year later, her first album was released and it sold a million copies in a week! She recorded another and soon she was rich.

Our old apartment wasn't very comfortable and because mum had lots of money we moved to a really big apartment with a great view of Central Park. Then, our lives really changed. Suddenly, everything was done for us, our food was cooked by someone else, our apartment was cleaned, I was driven to school, Mum and I were flown everywhere in a private plane. I know it sounds amazing and it is, but actually I'd like to go back to my old life in London.

20 LIFE CHANGES

Unit Overview

TOPIC	Changes
VOCABULARY AND READING	change as a verb and noun
	Life changes
GRAMMAR	Past simple passive
PRONUNCIATION	Sounds and spelling
READING	Kevin Pearce
VOCABULARY	Life changes
LISTENING	A conversation about a new school
WRITING	A biography
EXAM TASKS	Listening Part 3

Resources

GRAMMAR REFERENCE AND PRACTICE: SB page 166; TB page 267
PREPARE FOR THE EXAM: SB page on TB page 246; TB page 257
WORKBOOK: pages 80–83
PHOTOCOPIABLE WORKSHEETS: Grammar worksheet Unit 20;
Vocabulary worksheet Unit 20
TEST GENERATOR: Unit test 20; Term test 3; End of Year test

WARMER

Tell students to change these words into new words by adding a letter at the beginning or a letter at the end or both, for example *cat, seat, towns*. (Other answers may be possible for the examples given.)

how (*show*)

ran (*rang*)

pea (*speak*)

ten (*tent*)

anger (*danger*)

one (*money*)

hear (*heart*)

Put students into groups to find more examples and test the other groups on them.

(?) ABOUT YOU

Books closed, ask students to write down any changes in their lives over the last six months, for example, *I have joined a basketball club*. Share ideas as a class. Books open, have students answer the question in groups. If students haven't done either of these things recently, ask them to think what the positive and negative sides of these changes could be. Share ideas as a class.

VOCABULARY AND READING

change as a verb and noun

1 Tell students that *change* is a verb and a noun and have them give you more examples of words which can be both verbs and nouns (*run, sleep, work*). Have students match the sentences to the meanings. Check as a class.

Ask some concept-checking questions: 'Where can you always change money?' (*in a bank*), 'Why might a footballer have a change of shirt?' (*The shirt she is wearing might get wet during the first half of the game.*), 'If something changes your life, is this positive or negative?' (*could be either or both*).

Answers

1b 2d 3a 4c 5h 6e 7f 8g

2 Tell students to turn to page 139 and write a sentence for each of the situations. Then put students into groups to discuss their sentences. Share ideas as a class.

3 Ask students questions about the pictures, for example: 'Where is the plane going to and from?' (*It's going to the USA from Britain.*) and 'What happened when he played football?' (*He broke his leg.*). Then tell students to work in pairs and discuss what changes they show. Share ideas as a class.

4 Pre-teach **release** (if a company releases a film or musical recording, it allows the film to be shown in cinemas, or makes the musical recording available for the public to buy). Give students time to read the article and decide which picture is about Joe's life change. Check as a class.

Answers

c

5 Give students time to re-read the article and answer the questions. Check as a class. Ask students, 'How do you think Joe's life will change in the future?', 'How do you think Joe's mother feels about the changes?' and 'How would your life change if you became very rich?' As an extension activity, you could ask students to work in groups and think about another story showing a change in life. Groups can then take it in turns to tell their story to the rest of the class.

Answers

1 He remembered his mum always sang him songs.
2 They moved because his mum got a job in New York.
3 He was (very) excited but sad to leave his friends.
4 His mum met a man who worked for a record company.
5 Yes, it sold a million copies in a week.
6 It was very big and looked out onto Central Park.
7 His old life.

(♪)) The Reading text is recorded for students to listen, read
143 and check their answers.

FAST FINISHERS

Ask fast finishers to write down questions they would like to ask Joe about his new life, for example,

Do you go to a private school?

What kind of music does your mum write?

When everyone has finished, fast finishers could ask these questions to the class and they should reply as if they were Joe.

GRAMMAR Past simple passive

1 Books closed, write these two sentences on the board.

Mum's records are sold in the USA.

Mum's records were sold in the USA.

Ask students, 'Which sentence is passive?' (*Both of them are.*) and 'What's the difference between them?' (*the first is present simple, the second is past simple*).

Books open, tell students to look at the sentences and complete the rule. Check as a class. You could write some more sentences in the present simple passive on the board and ask students to change them into the past simple passive.

Answers

past simple, past participle

>> **GRAMMAR REFERENCE AND PRACTICE ANSWER KEY TB PAGE 267**

2 Books closed. See if students can remember any other examples from the text. Books open. Tell students to check in the text and then answer the questions. Check as a class.

Answers

1 The songs weren't written by other people.
2 A year later, her first album was released
3 our food was cooked by someone else
4 our apartment was cleaned
5 I was driven to school
Only numbers 1 and 3 mention the agent. It is not always necessary to say who did the action. Sometimes nobody knows who did it. We only say who did it if we think that information is important.

3 Tell students to make the sentences past simple passive. Check as a class. See if students can add more sentences about what happened the day before Joe's birthday, for example, *A birthday card was bought.*

Answers

1 The clothes were made. 2 The music was chosen.
3 The cake was decorated. 4 The food was prepared.
5 The presents were bought.

4 Ask students if they have a favourite park and what they like to do there. Tell them to read the text about a park in Beijing and ask some comprehension questions, for example 'What was its original name?' (*the Garden of Clear Ripples*). Get students to look up the translation of *ripple* in a dictionary. 'What is it now?' (*a park*). Have students rewrite the text using the past simple passive and decide if they need to add *by* …. Check as a class.

Answers

1 The Garden of Clear Ripples *was designed by* the Qing Emperor Quinlong … – needed, new information
2 … and some of the garden *was destroyed.* – not needed because it is not important who/what destroyed the garden
3 So the garden and the buildings *were built* again by the Emperor Guangxu … – needed, new information
4 … and *were given* a new name … – no need for *by him* because Emperor Guangxu has already been mentioned
5 The Summer Palace *was used by* the Empress Dowager Cixi. – needed, new information
6 In 1924 it *was changed* into a public park. – no need for *by someone*, this is obvious
The picture of the Garden of Clear Ripples.

MIXED ABILITY

Weaker students may need extra practice so ask them to rewrite the verbs in the orange juice text on SB page 109 to describe what happened at the factory yesterday: *The oranges <u>were pulled</u> off the trees and then they <u>were put</u> …*

5 Tell students to correct the sentences. Check as a class.

Answers

1 It **was given** to me by my uncle.
2 My bike **was** stolen last year.
3 They ~~were~~ cost £25.
4 All those things **were** sold in yesterday's sale.
5 The school **was opened** five years ago.

>> **GRAMMAR WORKSHEET UNIT 20**

ǝ PRONUNCIATION Sounds and spelling

🔊 6 Demonstrate with an example on the board:
144

wait walk weight

(*walk* because the vowel is pronounced /ɔː/; in *wait* and *weight* there is a diphthong /eɪ/).

Tell students to choose the word which sounds different from the other two in each set. Put students into pairs to listen and check. Play the recording. Check as a class and have students repeat all the words.

Answers

1 boy 2 watch 3 hair 4 word 5 now 6 met 7 own 8 they
9 toe 10 were

7 Have students take it in turns to read the sentences aloud. Monitor and make sure they are pronouncing the sounds correctly.

8 Tell students to turn to page 139, work in pairs and decide which thing is the most important and what they would add to the list. Share ideas as a class.

COOLER

Read out this 'passives' quiz. Students could guess the answers or look them up on mobile devices or in reference books.

The 2018 World Cup was won by …? (*France*)

Which new country was discovered by Captain Cook? (*Australia*)

Don Quixote was written by …? (*Cervantes*)

What language was spoken in ancient Rome? (*Latin*)

Why were cereals first made? (*as a health food*)

The *Mona Lisa* was painted by …? (*Leonardo da Vinci*)

In groups, students could make more questions for other groups to answer.

GRAMMAR — Past simple passive

1 Look at the example sentences from the article. Choose the correct words to complete the rule.

1 Everything was done for us.
2 Mum and I were flown everywhere in a private plane.

The past simple passive is formed with the *present simple / past simple* of the verb 'be' plus the *past simple / past participle* of the main verb.

>> **GRAMMAR REFERENCE AND PRACTICE PAGE 166**

2 Find other examples of the past simple passive in Joe's post. How many examples tell you who did the action? Why isn't it always necessary to say who did the action?

3 Write sentences in the past simple passive about what happened before the day of Joe's 16th birthday.

0 The guests / invite.
   The guests were invited.
1 The clothes / make.
2 The music / chose.
3 The cake / decorate.
4 The food / prepare.
5 The presents / buy.

4 Rewrite the text, changing the verbs in italics into the past simple passive. Decide if you need to say who did the action. Which of the four photos is best for the new text?

5 Correct the mistakes in the sentences.

1 It gave to me by my uncle.
2 My bike is stolen last year.
3 They were cost £25.
4 All those things are sold in yesterday's sale.
5 The school open five years ago.

PRONUNCIATION | Sounds and spelling

6 Choose the word in each group which has a different sound to the other words.

1	buy	boy	by
2	which	witch	watch
3	hear	hair	here
4	would	word	wood
5	know	now	no
6	meat	meet	met
7	own	one	won
8	their	there	they
9	toe	too	to
10	were	wear	where

144 In pairs, compare your answers. Then listen and check.

7 In pairs, take turns to read these sentences aloud.

1 The boys went to buy some food in the shop by the river.
2 Did you see which witch had a watch?
3 Did you hear that? You can get your hair cut here.
4 Would you write a word on the wood, please?
5 I know there are no books there now.
6 You met Sophie at that café, but we can't meet there because I don't eat meat.
7 She won one of her own.
8 They arrived there in their car.
9 My toe hurts too much to put on those shoes.
10 Where were you yesterday? Did you wear that coat?

8 >> Work with a partner. Go to page 139.

A CHANGING GARDEN

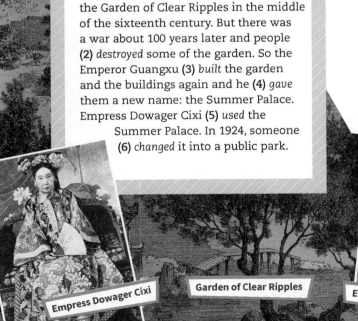

The Qing Emperor Qianlong (1) *designed* the Garden of Clear Ripples in the middle of the sixteenth century. But there was a war about 100 years later and people (2) *destroyed* some of the garden. So the Emperor Guangxu (3) *built* the garden and the buildings again and he (4) *gave* them a new name: the Summer Palace. Empress Dowager Cixi (5) *used* the Summer Palace. In 1924, someone (6) *changed* it into a public park.

Empress Dowager Cixi

Garden of Clear Ripples

Emperor Qianlong

Emperor Guangxu

LIFE CHANGES 113

READING

1 Look at the photos. What do you learn about Kevin Pearce from the fact file?

2 Read the fact file to check your ideas from Exercise 1.

FACT FILE Kevin Pearce

Born: New Hampshire, 1st November 1987
January 1997: entered first snowboarding competition
2002: moved to California with brother Adam
August 2006: won Slopestyle event in New Zealand
January 2008: won open halfpipe in Switzerland.
December 2009: received serious brain injury training in Utah
2010: had to relearn how to walk, talk and swallow
2010: his brother Adam left work to help look after Kevin
2013: the Sundance Film Festival showed documentary film about his life, *The Crash Reel*
2014: Adam and Kevin set up *Love Your Brain Foundation*
2014 – today: giving talks at schools and hospitals
2017: moved back to Vermont

KEVIN PEARCE was born in **(1)** _____ on 1st November 1987. He grew up where there was plenty of snow in the winter and loved snowboarding from when he was young. He entered his first snowboarding competition when he was **(2)** _____ years old. He moved to California with his brother in **(3)** _____ and started training full-time at Mammoth Mountain. Over the next **(4)** _____ years, he travelled a lot and won events in New Zealand and Switzerland. He was a star of the snowboarding world.

In December 2009, when Kevin was training in Utah, he crashed and was very badly **(5)** _____. He spent three months in hospital and it took him a year to learn basic skills like **(6)** _____, talking and swallowing again. His brother Adam left work to help look after Kevin.

Kevin slowly got better, but he was not able to take part in snowboarding competitions any more. In 2013, a documentary film about his life called *The Crash Reel* was **(7)** _____. A year later, a foundation called **(8)** _____ was started by Kevin and his brother Adam. This helps people who have had brain injuries and teaches activities like yoga and meditation.

(9) _____ 2014, Kevin has been busy visiting schools and hospitals. He talks about how important it is for people to look after their brains and to wear helmets. In 2017, he moved to **(10)** _____ in Vermont.

3 Read the fact file again and complete Kevin's biography.

4 Answer the questions about Kevin.

1 What sport did he start doing when he was a small boy?
2 Who did he go to California with?
3 What did he do at Mammoth Mountain?
4 How well known was he in the sport of snowboarding before his accident?
5 Which part of his body did he hurt worst in the crash?
6 How long did it take before he could do basic things again?
7 Was Kevin able to return to competition snowboarding after his accident?
8 What is *The Crash Reel*?
9 What kinds of things does *Love Your Brain* teach?

💬 TALKING POINTS

How has Kevin's life changed from when he was a teenager? In pairs, discuss what you think he learned from the accident.

WARMER

Tell students to leave the room. Make five changes in the room, for example put a chair on a desk and write *Hello!* on the board. Tell students to come back in. Students must describe the five things that were changed, using the past simple passive, for example, *My chair was put on the desk. Something was written on the board.* Repeat by asking one student to make changes while the rest of the class are outside.

BACKGROUND INFORMATION

Brain injuries can be categorised into mild, moderate and severe. People with mild injuries do not suffer long-lasting injury and after about three weeks of treatment are able to return to normal life. Kevin's injuries would be classified as severe as they are long-term and have a serious impact on his quality of life. The most common causes of brain injuries are violence, transport accidents, especially motorbikes, construction and extreme sports. Men are twice as likely as women to have brain injuries.

Prevention is the most effective way of avoiding brain injury and transportation in particular is regulated in most countries so that equipment like seat belts and air bags are standard features of vehicles. Sports authorities also try to protect competitors taking part in high-risk sports, for example, American football players have to wear helmets and clothing designed to reduce the impact of collisions; in football, the referee must tell players who get a head injury to leave the field of play.

For those like Kevin who have to live with serious brain injuries, there is now more psychological and social support to go with the ongoing physical treatment sufferers have. For example, sufferers are given support in finding employment which they can still do and companies are given incentives to employ this category of workers.

1 Have students describe the photos and how they might relate to Kevin Pearce.

Possible answer

He was snowboarding and he had an accident which affected his brain.

2 Tell students that *slopestyle* is an event where snowboarders race downhill around different obstacles; *halfpipe* is an artificial ramp like a raised swimming pool where snowboarders can jump and do tricks at high speed. You could show these events on Youtube to set the scene. Explain that *reel* in the title of the film *The Crash Reel* has two meanings: as a noun it is the round wheel-like object which camera film is wound on and as a verb it means to move from side to side as if you are going to fall. Give students a time limit to read the fact file and check their predictions from Exercise 1. Ask students if they have ever been snowboarding or if they would like to try it.

3 Pre-teach **swallow** (to cause food, drink, pills, etc. to move from your mouth into your stomach by using the muscles of your throat). Tell students to cover up the fact file and see if they can complete the biography from memory or say what kind of words they need, for example, gap 5 comes after *was* and an adverb so they will need an adjective. Then tell students to complete the biography using the fact file. Check as a class.

Answers

1 New Hampshire 2 ten 3 2002 4 seven 5 hurt / injured
6 walking 7 shown 8 Love Your Brain 9 Since 10 live

4 Tell students to answer the questions. Check as a class. As a variation, and practice in making questions, you could give students the answers and ask them to make the questions then check with the actual questions in the book.

Answers

1 snowboarding
2 his brother Adam
3 He started training full-time.
4 He was very well-known: he was a star.
5 his brain
6 a year
7 No, he wasn't.
8 It is a film about Kevin's life.
9 Yoga and meditation and how to look after your brain.

FAST FINISHERS

Tell fast finishers to try and find a word beginning with every letter of the alphabet in the text. For example: *about, basic, competition, documentary, ...*. See which student can get the most letters of the alphabet. Very fast finishers might have time to also find words ending with each letter of the alphabet, for example *yoga*, (no word ending in b), *basic, ...*.

💬 TALKING POINTS

Ask students what other sports are dangerous and how people can reduce the risks. Put students into pairs to discuss the questions in the book. Share ideas as a class. Ask students if they know of any other people, celebrities or people they know personally, who have overcome serious injuries which have changed their lives.

VOCABULARY Life changes

1 Books closed, have students work in pairs and make a list of the major changes in life. Books open, students compare their ideas with those in the book. Students may have other changes, for example, *go to university, have children.* Tell students to put the phrases in order and then compare with their partner.

> ### Possible answer
> be born, learn to walk and talk, start school, change schools, become a teenager, go to high school, find part-time work, take exams, travel, start working or training, get married. *move house* could come at any point, or not at all, as the case may be.

2 Put pairs together to compare lists. Students should make up a life story using the phrases in the past simple and tell another pair. Ask some students to tell their stories to the whole class. As a variation, students could make a text about a real person, using a mobile device or reference book to find out the details. They then tell their story to the rest of the class who try to guess who the person is.

> ### MIXED ABILITY
> Give weaker students extra practice by writing the verbs on one half of the board and nouns on the other half, in a different order, and tell students to match them. Then rub out either the verbs or nouns and have students read out the phrases.

>> **VOCABULARY WORKSHEET UNIT 20**

PREPARE FOR THE EXAM

A2 KEY FOR SCHOOLS Listening Part 3

146

1 Briefly review what students need to do in this part of the exam and if necessary read out the A2 Key for Schools box on TB page 138.

Tell students to listen for specific information, for example dates and prices, as well as feelings and opinions. Ask students to underline the key words and phrases in the question before they listen, for example *time* and *arrive* in question 1, because the listening will probably give several different times, and *at the moment* in question 2, as the correct answer depends on the time they are talking about.

Ask students to read the questions carefully. Ask, 'How do you say the times?' (*for example, eight thirty, half past eight*) and 'Does Jon want to go to a new school too?' (*no*). Play the recording twice for students to answer the questions. Check as a class. Ask students, 'What is the most interesting school trip you have been on?'

> ### Answers
> 1 A 2 C 3 A 4 A 5 B

>> **AUDIOSCRIPT TB PAGE 304**

WRITING

✏️ PREPARE TO WRITE
A biography

GET READY Books closed, write this beginning of a biography on the board and ask students what the problem is.

Kevin Pearce was a great snowboarder. Kevin Pearce won many competitions. People gave him many prizes.

(*There is repetition of Kevin Pearce. The first two sentences could be combined. The third sentence would be better in the passive.*)

Have students rewrite it. (*Kevin Pearce was a great snowboarder who won many competitions. He was given many prizes.*)

Books open. Students re-read the text about Kevin Pearce and answer the questions.

> ### Answers
> 1 There are four paragraphs.
> 2 The topics are: early life, accident, life after the accident, what Kevin does now
> 3 Kevin's name is used in the first sentence of each paragraph.
> 4 His full name is used in the first sentence of the text.
> 5 The pronoun *he* is used in the rest of each paragraph.

PLAN Ask students to read the fact file about Serena Williams. Do they know anything else about her? What do they think about her life?

Students make notes for a biography about Serena Williams using the Kevin Pearce one as a model. They can choose which details to include.

WRITE Students can write individually or in pairs, each being responsible for specific paragraphs. Tell them to divide their work into paragraphs and think carefully about when to use Serena's full name, when to use her first name and when to use a pronoun. Remind them that a paragraph should have a minimum of two sentences.

IMPROVE Students should check their own work and then compare with a partner.

> ### COOLER
> Give a vocabulary quiz on Units 16–20. Read out the questions for students to answer individually or in groups.
> 1 To find a word in a dictionary. (*look up*, Unit 16)
> 2 You do this if you're not sure of the answer. (*guess*, Unit 16)
> 3 The part of the body where your food goes when you eat. (*stomach*, Unit 17)
> 4 You feel this when you've done something silly or bad. (*embarrassed*, Unit 17)
> 5 You … a book from a library. (*take out*, Unit 18)
> 6 The person who writes a book. (*author*, Unit 18)
> 7 We often eat this for breakfast. (*cereal*, Unit 19)
> 8 How you cook meat in an oven. (*roast*, Unit 19)
> 9 Please … here for the train to Oxford. (*change*, Unit 20)
> 10 A job where you work fewer hours than normal. (*part-time*, Unit 20)

VOCABULARY Life changes

1 Look at the phrases about things that happen in people's lives. Can you put them in order? Some might happen more than once. Work with a partner and then compare your list with another pair.

> be born   become a teenager
> change schools   find part-time work
> get married   go to high school
> learn to walk and talk   move house
> take exams   travel   start school
> start working or training

2 In pairs, compare your lists. Now, invent a story of someone's life which uses all these phrases. Use the text about Kevin Pearce to help you. Tell your story to another pair.

LISTENING

PREPARE FOR THE EXAM

Listening Part 3

1 For each question, choose the correct answer. You will hear Tanya talking to her friend Jon about her new school.

1 What time did Tanya arrive for her exam at her new school?
  A 8.30
  B 8.40
  C 9.00

2 How does Tanya get to her new school at the moment?
  A by bike
  B on foot
  C by car

3 What can Tanya take home from school?
  A a musical instrument
  B sports kit
  C a science textbook

4 What has Jon just started doing?
  A playing in a band
  B playing hockey
  C working

5 What reason does Jon give for wanting to stay at his school next year?
  A friends
  B a school trip
  C his mum and dad

WRITING

PREPARE TO WRITE
A biography

GET READY Look at the text about Kevin Pearce again.

1 How many paragraphs are there?
2 What are the topics of each paragraph?
3 When in each paragraph is Kevin's name used?
4 When is his full name used?
5 When is the pronoun *he* used instead of *Kevin*?

FACT FILE Serena Williams

Born: 26th September 1981 in Michigan in the USA

Early 80s: family moved to Los Angeles

1984: began to play tennis

1995: her father became her coach

1999: won her first tournament, the US Open tennis title

2002: won the Wimbledon tennis tournament

2002: became the number one player in the world

2004: started her own designer label, Aneres (Serena spelt backwards)

2005 & 2007: won the Australian Open

2008: opened Serena Williams Secondary School in Kenya

2011: made International Goodwill Ambassador for UNICEF

2012: won the singles gold medal at the Olympic Games

Languages: English, some French, Spanish and Italian

Family: husband – Alexis Ohanian, one daughter, born 1st September 2017

PLAN Read the fact file for Serena Williams. You are going to write a short biography about her. Think about:

- how many paragraphs you will write
- what the topic of each paragraph will be
- when you will use her full name, first name and the pronoun *she*.

WRITE Write your biography. Use the passive as well as the active in your writing.

IMPROVE In pairs, read each other's biography and check for mistakes. Check that you have both included all the necessary information and that you used paragraphs and pronouns correctly.

LIFE SKILLS STUDY SKILLS

TAKING EXAMS

LIFE SKILLS

When you have an exam you should:
- organise your time
- prepare what you need
- keep calm and don't worry!

Taking exams can make you feel nervous or worried. If you prepare well and relax, you will do your best.

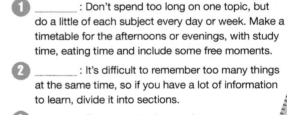

ADVICE – *studying for exams*

1 Look at the statements. Are they true for you?

1 I have a good memory.
2 I find some exams difficult.
3 I don't worry about exams.
4 I can never finish exams in the time.
5 I like doing exams.

In pairs, compare your answers.

2 Do you think these ideas are important when you have to study for exams?

1 how much you sleep
2 what you eat
3 preparing what you need for the exam
4 organising your time
5 talking to your teacher
6 doing physical exercise

Read the text and tick the ideas that are mentioned.

1 .... : Don't spend too long on one topic, but do a little of each subject every day or week. Make a timetable for the afternoons or evenings, with study time, eating time and include some free moments.

2 .... : It's difficult to remember too many things at the same time, so if you have a lot of information to learn, divide it into sections.

3 .... : For example, draw a picture next to a foreign word you want to remember. Or, to remember the formula $E=mc^2$, you could write *The elephant made cakes twice*.

4 .... : We often remember better if we can see a kind of picture of the most important points. This makes it easier to connect the information in our minds.

5 .... : Healthy food gives you energy and helps you to concentrate.

6 .... Stand up every hour and move around. Have a small snack or a short walk to clear your mind.

7 .... : Don't stay up late to send messages on your phone or play video games. It's better to go to bed not too late, get up early the next day and review what you studied the day before.

8 .... : You can test each other on what you need to know. For example, if you are studying history, say the name of an important event and then your friend can say the date, or say the date and he/she can try to say the event.

9 .... : Find time to do some physical activity at the weekend or during the week.

LIFE SKILLS

Learning Objectives

- The students learn strategies for preparing for exams so that they can perform in the exam as well as possible and not get too stressed.
- In the project stage, students prepare a video presentation giving advice and suggestions for exams.

BACKGROUND INFORMATION

There are many ways of assessing performance, for example coursework, but an examination usually means a standardised test. 'Standardised' means that the test conditions, for example the length of the test, the number of questions and what materials, if any, students are allowed to refer to, are the same for all students and the exam is marked in the same way by trained examiners or computers so that the scoring is objective. Some examinations are easier to standardise than others, for example a maths test where the answers are either right or wrong can be marked more objectively than a test of second-language speaking. However, rightly or wrongly, most educational systems in the world rely on examinations to show that students have reached a certain level and to give, or deny, qualifications which they can use for further education or employment. A large part of any school programme consists of preparing students for examinations and in some countries, especially in Asia, children often take private lessons outside school for extra examination practice.

The first country in the world to have a national standardised test was China. This was the Imperial examination and its purpose was to select people for senior positions in the civil service. The exam was introduced in 605 AD, replacing more informal tests such as competitions and interviews, and lasted in various different formats until 1905. The exam covered academic knowledge, like music and law, and military skills, such as archery and horsemanship, and could last up to 72 hours. Because the exam was so long and challenging, mentally and physically, students were allowed to bring their own bed as well as food and water. The examiners had complex procedures to stop cheating and corruption, for example candidates were identified by number not name and their work was rewritten by a scribe so that the handwriting could not be recognised. However, the difficulty of the exam and its importance, meant that some students tried to cheat: long rolls of text exist which dishonest students tried to smuggle into the exam room. The Imperial examination had a major influence on Chinese culture because it set standards in literary style, knowledge of the classics and technical skills. As a standardised test, it influenced other countries in Asia and the European colonial powers in the region.

WARMER

Write this logic problem on the board and ask students to solve it.

Diego said, 'I don't have any brothers or sisters, but this man's father is my father's son'. Who is the man? (*Diego's son*)

Ask students if 20 questions like this would be a fair test of someone's intelligence and in what situations this test could be used.

LIFE SKILLS
TAKING EXAMS

Tell students to read the information and check vocabulary as necessary. Invite students to say if they agree or disagree with any of the points in the text and to give their reasons. Encourage open-class discussion and help students make connections between their contributions.

1   Ask students what the purposes of exams are (for example, *to compare the knowledge and abilities of students by putting them under the same conditions to do the same tasks*).

    Tell students to tick the statements which are true for them. Put students into pairs to compare and discuss. Share ideas as a class. Test how good students' memories are by asking them some questions: 'What was I wearing in the last lesson?', 'What was the first word you learned in English?' and 'What were you doing this time exactly one year ago?'.

2   Tell students to mark each idea from 0 to 5: 0 = not important at all, 5 = very important. Put students into pairs to compare and discuss. Pre-teach **formula** by giving an example: draw a right-angled triangle on the board with $a^2 + b^2 = c^2$ underneath. Then give students time to read the text and check which ideas are included. Check as a class. Ask students how talking to your teacher could be useful, for example, your teacher could explain things that you don't understand.

    Answers
    All of them except 5.

FAST FINISHERS

Tell fast finishers to write down three pieces of strange or funny advice for students preparing for exams. For example: *Don't study in the shower as this will make your books wet and it could damage your mobile device.*

When everyone has finished, ask students to share their advice and the class can decide which is the strangest or funniest.

3 Give students time to complete the texts with the sentences. Check as a class. Ask students which ideas are included in the pictures (*a, c, d, i*).

Answers

1 c 2 g 3 h 4 a 5 e 6 f 7 b 8 i 9 d

 The Reading text is recorded for students to listen, read and check their answers.
147

4 Tell students to answer the questions based on the text. Check as a class.

Answers

1 study time, eating time, free moments
2 draw a picture
3 have a good breakfast / review what you have studied the day before
4 move around, have a snack or a short walk
5 send messages or play video games
6 they can test each other

5 Books closed, ask students to imagine that the next day there will be a vocabulary test of all the new vocabulary in Units 1–20. Give students three options how to prepare for this test and ask them to vote which one they would choose:

A Stay up late revising the vocabulary.

B Do some revision but not too much.

C Do nothing so you will feel fresh for the test.

Have students say the advantages and disadvantages of each option.

Books open, put students in pairs to discuss exam preparation. Share ideas as a class.

 6 Tell students to predict the answers to the open
148 questions (1, 2, 4, 5), for example in 1 Peter and Matty may need a dictionary or a calculator. Have students listen and answer the questions. Check as a class.

Answers

1 Peter: a pen, Matty: a ruler
2 she looked in her book for the answer
3 no
4 check his work / answer question six
5 to organise her time

 7 Tell students to listen again and complete the
148 expressions. Check as a class.

Answers

1 should always 2 Shall 3 could 4 must 5 were you

MIXED ABILITY

Remind weaker students of the meaning of the modal verbs *should, shall, could* and *must* when giving advice: *must* is the strongest, then *should,* then *could; shall* is used in questions to make offers. Tell students that expression 5 is a second conditional and *If I were you,* rather than *If I was you,* is a special form to give advice.

>> **AUDIOSCRIPT TB PAGE 304**

PROJECT *A video presentation*

Tell students that they are going to make a video presentation on exam preparation. If students don't have access to technology, they could make a poster of their ideas and make an oral presentation based on this. Put students into small groups and tell them to use the ideas in the text on page 116 to think of advice for before, during or at the end of an exam. Students should decide who will say what and practise their presentations before they record them. Encourage students to use the expressions for giving advice in Exercise 7. You could check the recordings and give feedback before students present to the whole class. Each group presents and answers questions. As a class, discuss the most useful advice.

PROJECT EXTENSION

Tell students to make a list of the best advice in three categories: before an exam, during an exam, at the end of an exam. Students should keep this and when they have their next exam (any subject, it doesn't need to be English) they should tick what advice they followed and whether it worked. Then put students in small groups to compare and see if there is a connection between following the advice and getting a good result in the exam.

COOLER

Put students into groups to make an exam for parents. The idea is that parents have to take this exam regularly to show that they are good parents. If they fail, they need to go on a special course 'How to be a good parent' and pay a fine. Students need to discuss what questions will be in the exam. Give some examples:

What is your child's favourite music group?

What mark did your child get in their last English test?

What would you say if your child asked you for a new mobile phone?

Give groups time to make the questions and an answer key. Then each group could present their exams to the rest of the class. The class can vote on the ten best questions, put them into one exam then go home and test their parents!

3 Complete the texts 1–9 with the sentences a-i.

a Make mind maps with important information
b Get plenty of sleep
c Organise your study time
d Exercise regularly to help your brain
e Have a good breakfast before you go to school
f Make sure you have breaks
g Try and learn information in small blocks
h Draw pictures or create sentences about information you have to learn
i Revise with a friend

4 Answer the questions. Use ideas from the text on page 116.

1 What information should you put in a study timetable?
2 What can you do to remember foreign words?
3 What can you do in the morning when you have an exam?
4 What should you do when you take a break from studying?
5 What shouldn't you do at night instead of sleeping?
6 How can friends help each other to study?

5 What do you do when you have to prepare for exams? Talk to your partner.

6 Listen to the conversations and answer the questions.

148

Conversation 1: What things did Peter and Matty need for the exam?
Conversation 2: Why did Meg fail her exam?
Conversation 3: Did Sam answer all the questions in the exam?
Conversation 4: What did Tim forget to do in the exam?
Conversation 5: What advice does the teacher give Sophie?

7 Listen again. Complete the expressions for giving advice.

148

(!) USEFUL LANGUAGE

1 You _____ remember to bring an extra pen.
2 _____ I help you study for the next test?
3 You know that you _____ guess?
4 You _____ make sure you've done everything.
5 If I _____ you, I'd look at the clock.

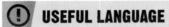

PROJECT
A video presentation

Make a video presentation, giving advice and suggestions for exams.

• Work in small groups.
• Think about what you need to do before an exam, during an exam or at the end of an exam.
• In your group, prepare a short video presentation with the best advice for your class. You can record this on your phones, and you can have a conversation or explain the ideas individually.
• Show your video to the class and be ready to answer any questions about it.
• After you see the video, tell the other groups the ideas you liked.

TAKING EXAMS 117

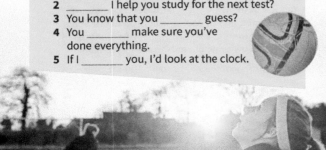

VOCABULARY

1 Put the letters in order to make words for parts of the body.

1 outhm _____
2 mtuhb _____
3 grinfse _____
4 cekn _____
5 esto _____
6 are _____
7 eadh _____
8 ranib _____
9 thare _____
10 dolob _____
11 cakb _____
12 nekal _____

2 Look at the words. Which words are used to talk about books (B) and which words are used to talk about preparing food (F)?

bowl	chapter	cover	knife
plate	shelf	spoon	title

Now, match the words to the definitions.

1 This is a section of a book that has a number or title. _____
2 We put soup in this. _____
3 We use this to cut our food. _____
4 We put books on this. _____
5 We eat our food off this. _____
6 This is the name of a book. _____
7 This is the front and back of a book. _____

8 We use this to eat soup and ice cream. _____

3 Complete the sentences with the correct form of the words in the box.

be born	change schools	find out
find part-time work		give back
take back	take exams	take out

1 He only _____ the name of the book yesterday. He didn't know it before.
2 Please can I borrow your maths book? I _____ it _____ to you tomorrow.
3 We _____ our English _____ last week. I hope everyone passed.
4 I (not) _____ last year. We moved house, but I stayed at the same school.
5 Please can you _____ the forks from the drawer and put them on the table?
6 My grandmother _____ on 15th June 1962.
7 Some teenagers like to _____ in the holidays so they have money to buy things.
8 (you) _____ your library book yesterday?

GRAMMAR

1 Choose the correct options to complete the sentences.

👁 1 You must bring your pyjamas and clean clothes for *you / yourself*.
2 If it *will be / is* all right, I'll meet you in the restaurant.
3 The batteries *include / are included* in the price.
4 This present *gave / was given* to me by my father.

👁 Correct the mistakes in the sentences.

5 I bought a blue shirt for me, which is very nice.
6 If you like, we go by car.
7 You like the class if you come.
8 You need to bring a photo of you with your name on the back.

2 Complete the sentences with the verbs in the box. Use the past passive.

bake	find	make	open	sell	write

1 That book _____ by my mother. She's an author.
2 Her bike _____ in the park after she lost it.
3 The cakes _____ for too long!
4 The new school _____ last week.
5 My phone _____ (not) in this country. It's from South Korea.
6 The paintings _____ for a lot of money.

3 Complete the text with the correct form of the verbs in brackets. Use the present simple active or present simple passive.

WHAT HAPPENS IN AN ICE CREAM FACTORY?

First, the cream, eggs and sugar **(1)** _____ (mix) together in a big machine. Then, the mixture **(2)** _____ (cook) to kill any bacteria and make it safe to eat. After this, the flavourings **(3)** _____ (add). These **(4)** _____ (include) chocolate, vanilla, coffee, mint and of course fruit of all kinds. Some ice cream makers also **(5)** _____ (put) pieces of marshmallow or whole nuts in their ice cream.

The next step is very important. The ice cream **(6)** _____ (freeze) and mixed at the same time in a special machine. After it **(7)** _____ (come) out of the machine, it **(8)** _____ (put) into boxes and then into a big freezer. When it is very cold and hard, it **(9)** _____ (send) to the shops for us to buy. Around 13 billion litres of ice cream **(10)** _____ (sell) every year around the world.

Overview

VOCABULARY	Body parts; adjectives to express emotion; books and reading; words about books; ingredients; *change* as a verb and noun; life changes
GRAMMAR	Reflexive pronouns; first conditional; present simple passive; past simple passive
EXAM TASKS	Reading Part 5; Speaking Part 1; Listening Part 2

Resources

PHOTOCOPIABLE WORKSHEETS: Grammar worksheets Units 17–20; Vocabulary worksheets Units 17–20; Review game Units 17–20; Literature worksheet; Speaking worksheet; Writing worksheet

WARMER

Have a grammar and vocabulary auction. Tell students that they each have €1,000 and they have to decide whether the sentences which you read out are right or wrong. If students are right, they double their money. If they are wrong, they lose it. Students can put as much money as they like on a sentence, if they have it (so they need to keep a note of how much money they have as the activity goes on). The student with the most money at the end is the winner.

1 You have one thumb on each hand. (*Right*)

2 You have one toe on each foot. (*Wrong* ~~one toe~~ – five toes)

3 We looked at us in the mirror. (*Wrong* ~~us~~ – ourselves)

4 I felt really embarrassed when I dropped the ice cream on myself. (*Right*)

5 You can take it out from the library. (*Right*)

6 If I will pass, I will be lucky. (*Wrong* I ~~will~~ pass)

7 The first chapter has 26 pages. (*Right*)

8 The soup was baked for 20 minutes. (*Wrong* ~~baked~~ – cooked)

9 They are sending them to a factory by lorry. (*Wrong* ~~sending~~ – sent)

10 A melon is a kind of fruit. (*Right*)

11 Were the boys found? (*Right*)

12 I want to find half-time work. (*Wrong* ~~half~~ – part)

VOCABULARY

1 Books closed, point to parts of your body and ask students to name them. Books open, tell students to reorder the letters to make parts of the body. Check as a class.

> **Answers**
> 1 mouth 2 thumb 3 fingers 4 neck 5 toes 6 ear 7 head
> 8 brain 9 heart 10 blood 11 back 12 ankle

2 Tell students to put the words in the two categories, books and food. Check then have students match the words to the definitions. Check as a class.

> **Answers**
> Books: chapter, cover, shelf, title
> Food: bowl, knife, plate, spoon
> 1 chapter 2 bowl 3 knife 4 shelf 5 plate 6 title 7 cover
> 8 spoon

3 Tell students to complete the sentences. Check as a class.

> **Answers**
> 1 found out 2 'll give, back 3 took, exams
> 4 didn't change schools 5 take out 6 was born
> 7 find part-time work 8 Did you take back

GRAMMAR

1 Ask students to choose the correct words. Check as a class.

> **Answers**
> 1 yourself 2 is 3 are included 4 was given

Have students correct the mistakes. Check as a class.

> **Answers**
> 5 I bought a blue shirt for **myself** which is very nice.
> 6 If you like, we'll go by car.
> 7 You'll like the class if you come.
> 8 You need to bring a photo of **yourself** with your name on the back.

2 Before Exercises 2 and 3, briefly review the form and meaning of the present simple passive and past simple passive. Ask students to write the passive equivalent of these sentences and explain why they are more natural.

People call him Jim. (*He is called Jim. It doesn't matter who calls him Jim.*)

Somebody found the key. (*The key was found. We don't know or care who found it.*)

Tell students to complete the sentences using the past simple passive form of the verbs in the box. Check as a class.

> **Answers**
> 1 was written 2 was found 3 were baked 4 was opened
> 5 wasn't made 6 were sold

FAST FINISHERS

Tell fast finishers to write another past passive sentence for each of the verbs in the box. You could ask students to make two of the sentences positive, two negative and two questions.

CONTINUED ON PAGE 234

3 Ask students, 'What is your favourite kind of ice cream?' and 'How do you think it is made?' Pre-teach **bacteria** (very small organisms that are found everywhere and are the cause of many diseases), **flavouring** (something that is added to food or drink to give it a particular taste), and **marshmallow** (a soft, sweet, pink or white food). Ask students to complete the text. Check as a class.

> **Answers**
>
> **1** are mixed **2** is cooked **3** are added **4** include **5** put
> **6** is frozen **7** comes **8** is put **9** is sent **10** are sold

A2 KEY FOR SCHOOLS Reading Part 5

1 Briefly review what students need to do in this part of the exam and if necessary read out the A2 Key for Schools box on TB page 153. Tell students to read the text quickly and ask, 'Who are Sally and Dave?' (*friends / students*), 'Where is Sally going?' (*London*) and 'Has she been there before?' (*no*). Ask students to complete the text. Put them into pairs to check their answers then check as a class. Ask students, 'What famous places do you know in London?' and 'Which would you like to visit?'

> **Answers**
>
> **1** with **2** 'll / will **3** to **4** but **5** be **6** you

---

MIXED ABILITY

Go through each question with weaker students and ask questions to guide them towards the answer.

Question 1: 'Read the whole sentence. What preposition could connect *holiday* and *family*?'

Question 2: '*Be* is the main verb. What other verbs can there be before a main verb?' (*modal verbs*), 'Is Sally talking about now or the future?' (*future*) and 'What modal verb is often about the future?'

Question 3: 'What do you need after the verb *want*?' (*an infinitive or a noun*) and 'Is *see* a noun?' (*no*)

Question 4: 'What punctuation is there before this gap?' (*a comma*), 'Does this mean there is a new clause?' (*yes*), 'So what kind of word could it be?' (*a linking word*), 'Is the idea in this clause agreeing with or contrasting with the idea in the first clause?' (*contrasting*) and 'What linking word shows a contrast?'

Question 5: 'What kind of word is before the gap?' (*a modal verb*) 'What do we need after a modal verb?' (*a main verb*) 'What form will this verb be?' (*the base form*)

Question 6: 'What kind of word do you often have after a verb?' (*an object*) and 'Sally is writing to Dave so what could the object be?'

A2 KEY FOR SCHOOLS Speaking Part 1

2 Briefly review what students need to do in this part of the exam and if necessary read out the A2 Key for Schools box on TB page 22.

Books closed, write the three topics on the board: *health and fitness, books, food*. Put students in groups to write down four questions for each topic.

Books open, students compare their questions to the actual questions. Put students into pairs to take turns asking and answering the questions. Encourage students to give full answers and use a range of grammar and

---

vocabulary. Put students into different pairs to repeat the activity. Monitor and note down good language use and mistakes for feedback. Then ask some of the questions to the whole class.

A2 KEY FOR SCHOOLS Listening Part 2

3 🔊 **149** Briefly review what students need to do in this part of the exam and if necessary read out the A2 Key for Schools box on TB page 86.

Books closed, put students into groups to say what they know about the history of their town: when it was founded, if it had a different name, important people who lived there, historical events, etc. Share and compare information as a class.

Books open, give students time to read the questions. Make sure students understand that the answer can only be one word or a number or a date or a time: ask, 'Why would "two pounds" be wrong in question 5?' (*It is two words and the pound sign is already there.*) Play the recording twice. Put students in pairs to check, then check answers as a class. Ask students what their grandparents would probably say about how their town has changed in their lifetimes, for example the shops, prices and transport.

> **Answers**
>
> **1** 850 **2** 54,000 **3** Thursday(s) **4** Regent **5** 1.75

» AUDIOSCRIPT TB PAGE 305

COOLER

Write this quiz on the Student's Book on the board (or dictate the questions). Put students into small groups to look back through the book and find the answers. The group which completes the quiz first with all the correct answers is the winner.

1 How many parts of the Duke of Edinburgh's Award are there? (*four*, page 10)

2 Do most pandas live in zoos or in the wild? (*in the wild*, page 16)

3 What unusual house do Paula and Gary have? (*a lorry*, page 24)

4 What exams do sixteen-year-olds in England do? (*GCSEs*, page 40)

5 Which football team does eSport star Koen Weijland play for? (*Ajax*, page 56)

6 How old was Catherine Cook when she started myYearbook.com? (*15*, page 61)

7 What is pocket money in the US called? (*an allowance*, page 82)

8 What language group is English in? (*Germanic*, page 92)

9 Who is the main character in the book *Wonder*? (*August*, page 106)

10 What sport did Kevin Pearce do before his accident? (*snowboarding*, page 114)

PREPARE FOR THE EXAM

Reading Part 5

1 For each question, write the correct answer.

Write one word for each gap.

Example: **0** *of*

To: Dave
From: Sally
Subject:

Reply Forward

I'm sorry I didn't see you on the last day **(0)** _____ term to say goodbye. I hope you have a really lovely summer holiday in the mountains **(1)** _____ your family. I'm sure it **(2)** _____ be sunny and warm. We're going to London for a week. I'm very excited because it's my first visit there. I want **(3)** _____ see all the famous places. We went to Madrid last year, and that was really interesting, **(4)** _____ it was too hot for me. I hope London won't **(5)** _____ so warm.

See **(6)** _____ next term!

Sally

Speaking Part 1

2 **Work with a partner. Take turns to ask and answer the questions.**

Tell your partner about health and fitness.
What exercise do you do to stay healthy?
Which foods keep you healthy?
Have you ever hurt any part of your body?
How do you get to school every day?

Tell your partner about books.
What kind of books or comics do you like reading?
Where is your favourite place to read?
Do you prefer reading on a screen to reading real books? Why?
What is the best book you have read?

Tell your partner about food.
Describe your favourite meal.
What food can you cook?
Who's the best cook in your family?
Which country's food do you like best?

Listening Part 2

3 For each question, write the correct answer in the gap. Write one word or a number or a date or a time.

149

You will hear a woman talking to a class of students about the history of her town.

Mrs Smith's town

Years Mrs Smith has lived in the town:
(0) _60_ years

Age of town: **(1)** _____ years

Town in 1980

Number of people: **(2)** _____

Day shops closed: **(3)** _____

Name of old cinema: **(4)** the _____

Cost of cinema seat: £ **(5)** _____

PREPARE FOR THE EXAM
A2 KEY FOR SCHOOLS

READING AND WRITING

Reading Part 1   Multiple-choice signs, notices and messages
(Unit 11, Unit 18, Review 3)

 EXAM INFORMATION

What is Part 1?
There are six short texts to read.
They may be emails, text messages,
signs, notices, postcards, etc.

What do I have to do?
Each text has a multiple-choice question
for you to answer.

 EXAM TIPS

- Look at each text and think about where you would see it.
- Decide what the main message of the text is.
- Read all the options carefully. Think about the meaning of each one. Don't just choose an option because it has words or ideas from the text.

1 Look at the exam task and read question 1. What kind of message is it?
Which option is the correct answer? Why are the other two wrong?

1

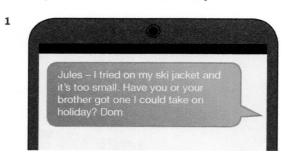

Jules – I tried on my ski jacket and it's too small. Have you or your brother got one I could take on holiday? Dom

Dom would like Jules to

A find a jacket that Dom can borrow.

B tell Dom what size jacket is best.

C ask his brother to return Dom's jacket.

2 Now you try. Complete the Reading Part 1 task. Use the *Exam tips* to help you.

For each question, choose the correct answer.

2

SCHOOL CAFÉ

What do you think of
our new menu?

Leave a note in the box!

A Students can get information about the new menu here.

B The café is asking for ideas for new dishes to add to the menu.

C This is how students can give their opinion of the menu.

3

To Mia
From Abby
Fantastic news! Mr Wilson has agreed to start a climbing club on Friday evenings if enough students are interested. Email him immediately!

A Abby is excited about how good the climbing club was.

B Abby wants Mia to contact Mr Wilson as soon as possible.

C Abby and Mia are the only students who like climbing.

4

Year 9 art exhibition

15th–25th July

Anyone who wants their painting included in this must give it to Miss Evans by Friday, 12th.

What do students find out from this message?

A what kind of painting can go into the exhibition

B how long they've got to finish their paintings

C why the art exhibition is taking place in July

5

BRIDGETOWN SHOPPING CENTRE

Restaurants, shops and cinema open until 10 pm!

Tuesdays and Thursdays only

A The shopping centre closes later than usual two days a week.

B You can see films here from Tuesday to Thursday.

C Some places in the centre close earlier than others.

6

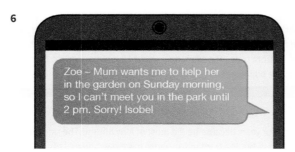

Zoe ~ Mum wants me to help her in the garden on Sunday morning, so I can't meet you in the park until 2 pm. Sorry! Isobel

A Isobel will ask her mum if she can go to the park.

B Isobel won't be able to meet Zoe this weekend.

C Isobel will see Zoe later than they planned.

PREPARE FOR THE EXAM
A2 KEY FOR SCHOOLS

Reading Part 2 Multiple-choice three short texts
(Unit 3, Unit 12, Unit 18)

 EXAM INFORMATION

What is Part 2?
There are three short texts to read.
They might be about people, places,
books, films, etc.

What do I have to do?
There are seven questions to answer.
You match each question to one of the texts.

EXAM TIPS
- <u>Underline</u> the important words in the questions.
- Read the texts and find the information which matches the question exactly. The meaning will be the same, but the words will be different.
- Don't worry if you don't understand every word in the text.

1 Look at the title of the article and read the questions. Then, read the article and find the answer to question 1. <u>Underline</u> the part of the text that gives you the answer.

2 Now you try. Complete the Reading Part 2 task. Use the *Exam tips* to help you.

For each question, choose the correct answer.

		Sarah	Andrea	Trudi
1	Who knows other people who live in homes like hers?	A	B	C
2	Who says that she feels safe in her home?	A	B	C
3	Who is happy with the size of her home?	A	B	C
4	Who says that her house is bright?	A	B	C
5	Who says that guests enjoy spending the night in her home?	A	B	C
6	Who needs a lift when she wants to visit friends?	A	B	C
7	Who feels less comfortable when she is in other people's homes?	A	B	C

 THREE *UNUSUAL* HOMES

SARAH

My home is a houseboat on a river. My parents and I have lived here since I was four, and I can't remember living anywhere else. Lots of my friends live on houseboats too, so it feels normal to me. We haven't got much space, but we don't mind — it's enough for us. Visitors love staying here and are surprised by how comfortable it is. They always sleep really well and love being on the water.

ANDREA

My friends at school think my lighthouse home is very cool. I like it, but it's not easy living here. The rooms are round, so it's hard to fit furniture in, and they're not very big. Also, my parents have to drive me everywhere as we are so far from town. The sea is only about 10 metres away, so it gets very exciting when there is a storm. But the building is very strong, and I never feel afraid.

TRUDI

My dad built our house. It took him four years because he did most of it by himself. The sides and the top are covered with earth and grass, but the front of the house has big windows. Lots of light comes in and it's lovely and quiet. There's always lots of fresh air, too. When I am at my friends' houses, I often get too hot and want to open a window.

122 PREPARE FOR THE EXAM

Reading Part 3   Multiple-choice one long text
(Unit 5, Unit 9, Unit 15)

 EXAM INFORMATION

What is Part 3?
There is a newspaper, magazine or website article to read.
What do I have to do?
You have five multiple-choice questions to answer.

 EXAM TIPS

- One or two questions will test your understanding of the text as a whole.
- The other questions will test details, opinions or feelings in the text.
- The detail questions will follow the order of information in the text.
- Don't just match words in the options with words in the text. Think carefully about the meaning.

1 Read the text and the questions, but don't answer the questions yet. One question tests your understanding of the whole text. Which question is it?

2 For each question, choose the correct answer. Use the *Exam tips* to help you.

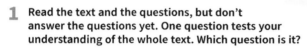 *Luke Thill*

When he was 12, Luke Thill was at home during the school holidays. He was bored and looking for a fun activity, but he didn't want to play computer games or ride his bike. Then, he heard about people who build, and live in, very small wooden houses. 'I decided that I wanted to build one in my garden,' he said. 'I thought if I made enough money doing jobs for my neighbours, it might be possible.'

Luke's dad agreed to help, but he had a few rules. Luke had to pay for everything himself and had to do most of the work. Luke describes his dad as his 'coach' and says that working as a team brought them closer together. It took them a year and a half to finish the house and it cost $1,500.

The house is three metres long and two metres wide. Downstairs, it has a kitchen and sitting area with a TV, and upstairs there's a little bedroom. When he began, Luke was already quite good at repairing things, but there was a lot he didn't know. 'It all seems very simple to me now,' he said. 'But at the time, I had no idea what to do.'

Luke sleeps in his house about twice a week, does homework there after school and invites friends round. He enjoyed building his little house so much that he plans to build a second, bigger one soon, and in a few years' time he'd like to live in it full time.

1 What is the writer doing in this text?
  A giving advice to teenage builders
  B describing an interesting project
  C saying why small houses are popular

2 Why did Luke decide to build a little house?
  A He needed something to do.
  B He liked the one his neighbour had.
  C It was a way to meet new people.

3 Luke's dad was happy to
  A do most of the building work.
  B lend Luke money for the house.
  C show Luke how to do things.

4 What does Luke say about building the house?
  A He was surprised it was so easy.
  B He learned a lot while he was doing it.
  C He broke some things at the beginning.

5 What would Luke like to do next?
  A make another little house
  B build houses for his friends
  C move out of the family home

PREPARE FOR THE EXAM
A2 KEY FOR SCHOOLS

Reading Part 4   Multiple-choice cloze factual text
(Unit 8, Unit 10, Review 2)

 EXAM INFORMATION

What is Part 4?
There is a short newspaper, magazine, website or encyclopaedia article to read.

What do I have to do?
Complete the text by choosing the correct word for each gap.
There are six multiple-choice questions.

 EXAM TIPS

- Before choosing an answer, read the whole sentence so you understand what it is about.
- Look at the words around the space carefully before choosing the one you think is best.
- With some questions, you need to think about grammar as well.

1 Read the article and try question 1. What is the answer? Why?

2 Now you try. Complete the Reading Part 4 task. Use the *Exam tips* to help you.

For each question, choose the correct answer.

THE CITY WHERE PEOPLE CAN SEND EMAILS TO TREES

A few years ago, workers in Melbourne, Australia, gave each of the city's 70,000 trees ID numbers and email addresses. They did this so that people had a way of **(1)** _____ workers know when there was a **(2)** _____ with a tree or if it was dangerous. They could then send someone to work on it and make it **(3)** _____.

The emails soon started arriving. However, workers got a big **(4)** _____ when they read them because many people were using the email addresses to send love letters to the trees. They **(5)** _____ the trees stories, asked them questions and said how beautiful they were. The workers joined in by sending replies from the trees. The email conversations are **(6)** _____ to read and show how important trees are to the people of Melbourne.

1 **A** making   **B** letting   **C** getting
2 **A** mistake   **B** trouble   **C** problem
3 **A** safe   **B** correct   **C** well
4 **A** adventure   **B** surprise   **C** experience
5 **A** spoke   **B** told   **C** explained
6 **A** popular   **B** glad   **C** wonderful

Reading Part 5   Open cloze email
(Unit 13, Unit 19, Review 5)

 EXAM INFORMATION

What is Part 5?
There is a short text, such as an
email, postcard or internet post.
Sometimes, there may be two emails.
What do I have to do?
You have to complete the text by
writing one word in each space.

EXAM TIPS

Read the text once without thinking about the gaps, so you
know what it is about.
- Think about what kind of word is needed for the gap,
  e.g. preposition, pronoun, article.
- Read the whole sentence carefully.
- Only write one word in each space or you will not get
  the mark.
- Spell each word perfectly or you will not get the mark.

1 Read the texts once. What kind of words are missing, grammar or vocabulary?

2 Now you try. Complete the Reading Part 5 task. Use the *Exam tips* to help you.

For each question, write the correct answer.
Write **one** word for each gap.

Example: 0   *my*

| To: | Bart |
| From: | Shammi |

Guess what? Mum says I can paint the walls in **(0)** _____ bedroom. I'm really happy

(1) _____ I hate the colour it is now! **(2)** _____ you want to come and help me? I'm free on
Saturday afternoon and **(3)** _____ day on Sunday.

| To: | Shammi |
| From: | Bart |

Of course! I know **(4)** _____ much you hate your pink walls! Is it OK **(5)** _____ I come at
ten on Sunday morning? By the way, **(6)** _____ colour are we going to use? I painted my
room black a few weeks ago, and it looks fantastic!

Writing Part 6   Guided writing email or note
(Unit 10, Unit 14, Review 4)

 EXAM INFORMATION

What is Part 6?

There is a short writing task.

What do I have to do?

You have to write a short email or note to a friend. You may get some instructions to follow, or you may have part of a message with some questions to reply to.

 EXAM TIPS

- <u>Underline</u> the important words in the email so you understand the topic and the three questions.
- When you have finished, check for spelling and grammar mistakes and that your email or note clearly includes answers to all three questions.
- Check you have written at least 25 words.

1   Read the exam task question and the four example answers. Which one is perfect? What is wrong with the other three?

Read the email from your English friend, Danny.

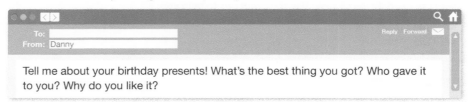

To:

From: Danny

Tell me about your birthday presents! What's the best thing you got? Who gave it to you? Why do you like it?

Write an email to Danny and answer the questions.
Write **25 words** or more.

A

> I got lots of fantastic presents for my birthday. The best thing was my bike, which my parents gave me. I love it because it's fast and a really cool colour. Lets go for a ride together soon!

B

> My birthday was great. All my friends came to my party and we had a great time. We all missed you a lot! When can we see you?

C

> I got lots of presents including a new mobile phone it's the best one I've ever had

D

> My best present is earring from my frend. is bautiful I loving it and waring always

2   Now you try. Write your own answer to the Writing Part 6 task. Use the *Exam tips* to help you.

Writing Part 7 Picture story
(Unit 4, Unit 18, Review 1)

 EXAM INFORMATION

What is Part 7?
There is a story writing task.
What do I have to do?
You have to write a story based on three pictures.

 EXAM TIPS

- Look at all three pictures and get an idea of the whole story before you begin.
- Include something about every picture in your story.
- Use the past tense for the events of the story.
- Try to use linking words such as *so, and, but, because,* etc. in your story.

1 Read the exam task and the sample answer. Is there something about every picture? What tense is the story in? Why?

Look at the three pictures.
Write the story shown in the pictures.
Write **35 words** or more.

Last week, Jim saw a poster at school about a cooking competition. He loves baking, so he decided to enter it. He went home and baked an amazing chocolate cake. Jim took his cake to the competition and was very happy and surprised when he got first prize for it.

2 Now you try. Do the Writing Part 7 task below. Use the *Exam tips* to help you.

Look at the three pictures.
Write the story shown in the pictures.
Write **35 words** or more.

LISTENING

Listening Part 1   3-option multiple choice five short dialogues
(Unit 4, Unit 17, Review 1)

 EXAM INFORMATION

What is Part 1?
There are five short conversations.
What do I have to do?
Each conversation has a multiple-choice question for you to answer. The options are pictures.

 EXAM TIPS
- You will hear something about each picture, but only one picture answers the question, so only give one answer.
- You hear the conversation twice, so don't worry if you miss the answer the first time.

1 Look at the pictures for question 1. Write down some words you think you are going to hear in the conversation.

2 Read the question carefully. Is it asking about what Ted has got or what he wants?
Now, listen and answer the question.

1 What would Ted like to get for his room?

A

B

C

Listen again to check your answer.

3 Now you try. Complete the Listening Part 1 task. Use the *Exam tips* to help you.

For each question, choose the correct picture.

2 What is still in the car?

A

B

C

3 How much is the bag?

A

B

C

4 Where did they go camping last year?

A

B

C

5 What are the boys going to do now?

A

B

C

Listening Part 2   Gap fill notes
(Unit 7, Unit 19, Review 5)

ⓘ EXAM INFORMATION

What is Part 2?
There is a person giving some information on a subject.

What do I have to do?
You need to listen and complete some notes. There are five pieces of information you need to write down. These will be words, numbers or spellings.

✅ EXAM TIPS

- Before you listen, think about the kind of information you need for the gap.
- Sometimes, you will hear two possible answers. Listen carefully to understand which one is correct.
- It's best to write numbers as numbers and not as words, so you don't make a mistake with spelling.
- You hear the recording twice, so don't worry if you miss the answer the first time.

🔊 152 **1** Read the exam task. Then, listen to the first part and look at the example. You hear two days – Saturday and Friday. Why is Saturday correct and Friday wrong?

🔊 153 **2** Now you try. Complete the Listening Part 2 task. Use the *Exam tips* to help you.

For each question, write the correct answer in each gap. You will hear someone talking about a gym. Write one **word**, or a **number** or a **date** or a **time**.

Bodyfit Gym
Club for teenagers

Day:	*Saturday*	Teacher's name:	**(3)** _____
Price:	**(1)** £ _____ per month	What **not** to wear:	**(4)** _____
Start time:	**(2)** _____ am	What to bring:	**(5)** _____

PREPARE FOR THE EXAM
A2 KEY FOR SCHOOLS

Listening Part 3   3-option multiple choice dialogue
(Unit 12, Unit 20, Review 3)

 EXAM INFORMATION

What is Part 3?
There is a conversation between two people.
What do I have to do?
Listen and answer five multiple-choice questions.

 EXAM TIPS

- Read the questions before you listen so you know what information to listen for.
- You will hear something about all three options, so listen carefully to catch the meaning of what the people are saying.
- The answer can come from either speaker.
- At least one question will ask about the opinion or feelings of one of the speakers.
- You hear the conversation twice, so don't worry if you miss the answer the first time.

🔊 154 **1** Read the questions and the instructions so you know what the conversation will be about. Then, look at question 1. Listen to the first part of the recording and answer the question below.

Why is C the answer? Why are A and B wrong?

🔊 155 **2** Now you try. Complete the Listening Part 3 task. Use the Exam Tips to help you.

For each question, choose the correct answer.
You will hear Callum talking to his friend Stella about going to a skatepark.

1 Callum says the new skatepark is close to
   A the cinema.
   B Callum's house.
   C the swimming pool.

2 Stella does not like skateparks that are
   A old.
   B small.
   C dirty.

3 What will the skatepark have in the future?
   A a shop
   B a roof
   C a café

4 How much does it cost to use the skatepark at the moment?
   A £7
   B £5
   C £3

5 The friends will see each other at the skatepark at
   A 10 o'clock.
   B 12 o'clock.
   C 1 o'clock.

130   PREPARE FOR THE EXAM

Listening Part 4 3-option multiple choice main idea, message, gist or topic
(Unit 8, Unit 16, Review 2)

ⓘ EXAM INFORMATION

What is Part 4?
There are five short conversations or monologues.

What do I have to do?
Listen and answer five multiple-choice questions.

☑ EXAM TIPS

- Read the focus question carefully as this will tell you what to listen for.
- The kind of things you'll be listening for include the topic, an opinion, someone's reasons for doing something, someone's likes and dislikes, activities, events, etc.
- Don't worry if you don't understand every word.
- Listen for the meaning, don't just match words in the question and answer.
- You hear the recordings twice, so don't worry if you miss the answer the first time.

🔊 **156** **1** Look at question 1. Then listen and choose the correct answer. Compare with a partner and say why you chose the answer you did.

🔊 **157** **2** Now you try. Complete the Listening Part 4 task. Use the *Exam tips* to help you.

For each question, choose the correct answer.

1 You will hear a girl talking to her mother. What does she want to eat?
  A a sandwich
  B some biscuits
  C a large meal

2 You will hear a girl talking to a friend about a TV programme. What does she say about it?
  A It was funny.
  B It was long.
  C It was exciting.

3 You will hear two friends talking about a walk they did together. What happened on the walk?
  A They got wet.
  B They got lost.
  C They hurt themselves.

4 You will hear a boy leaving a message for a friend. Where would he like to meet his friend?
  A at the bus stop
  B at the ticket office
  C at the big stage

5 You will hear a teacher talking to her class. What is she talking about?
  A a story they'll write
  B a book they'll read
  C a film they'll watch

Listening Part 5   Matching
(Unit 2, Unit 6, Review 4)

 EXAM INFORMATION

What is Part 5?
There is a longer dialogue.
What do I have to do?
You need to listen and match five people / days / times, etc. to eight possible answers.

EXAM TIPS

- Before you listen, read the list A–H carefully and think about the kinds of words you may hear.
- Often the words in A–H will be different in the listening, e.g. *get ready for the concert = music practice*.
- You will hear the conversation twice, so don't worry if you cannot answer all the questions the first time.
- The information in the recording will be in the same order as the questions.

 1 Read the exam task instructions and the example. Then, listen to the first part of the dialogue while you read the recording. <u>Underline</u> the part of the text that gives you the answer to the example.

Grandma:	How was your half-term holiday, Jasmin? What did you and your friends do?
Jasmin:	Well, Grandma, I played the guitar a lot. I'm in the school concert next week and I need to get ready for it.

 2 Now you try. Complete the Listening Part 5 task. Use the *Exam tips* to help you.

For each question, choose the correct answer.

You will hear Jasmin telling her grandmother about her half-term holiday. What activity did each person do?

Example: **0**   Jasmin   `C`

People		**Activities**
1 Sophie	☐	**A** cooking
2 Sam	☐	**B** going online
3 Joe	☐	**C** music practice
4 Emily	☐	**D** photography
5 Gemma	☐	**E** shopping
		F studying
		G sport
		H travelling

SPEAKING

Speaking Part 1 Examiner led questions
(Unit 1, Unit 16, Review 1, Review 4, Review 5)

 EXAM INFORMATION

What is Part 1?
There are questions about you.
What do I have to do?
You need to talk to the examiner and answer the questions you are asked.

 EXAM TIPS

- Listen carefully to the examiner's questions. You and your partner will get questions on different topics.
- You can ask the examiner to say the question again if you don't understand.
- When the examiner says *Tell me about ...* try to answer in two or three sentences.
- This part will take three to four minutes.

1 The examiner will ask you questions like these. Which need short answers and which need longer answers?

1 What's your name?

2 Where do you come from?

3 What's your best subject at school?

4 Do you like studying science?

5 What do you wear to school?

6 How much homework do you get?

7 Tell me something about your favourite teacher.

8 How much free time do you have?

9 Who do you spend your free time with?

10 Do you play computer games?

11 Do you like reading?

12 Tell me something about a hobby you enjoy.

2 Match the answers a–e to the questions in Exercise 1. Which are good answers and which are not so good? Why?

a No, I don't.

b No, not really. I find it quite difficult.

c Just my normal clothes. I don't have to wear a uniform.

d She's nice. I like her.

e I haven't got any hobbies.

3 Listen to some more answers and match them to the questions in Exercise 1.

4 Now you try. Take turns to ask and answer the Speaking Part 1 questions. Use the *Exam tips* to help you.

Speaking Part 2   Discussion with visual stimulus
(Unit 3, Unit 7, Review 2)

 EXAM INFORMATION

What is Part 2?
There is a conversation with your partner and the examiner about some pictures.

What do I have to do?
You need to answer the examiner's questions and talk to your partner as well.

 EXAM TIPS

- Don't forget to say what you can see in the pictures. Let the examiner see how much vocabulary you know. Don't just say *yes* or *no*. Use some adjectives.
- Try to make correct sentences and questions if you can. Don't worry about making small mistakes.
- Let your partner speak too and ask him/her questions. You will get marks for that, too.
- Try to relax and enjoy yourself!

1 **Look at the pictures. They are all places you can visit.
   Work with a partner and say what each one is.**

2 **Listen to two students doing this exam task. Number the pictures in the order the students speak about them.**
161

3 **Write the places in the table in the correct order. Then listen again and complete the table with
   (✓) for 'likes it' and (✗) for 'doesn't like it'. The first one has been done for you as an example.**
161

Place	Girl	Boy
Shopping centre	✓	✗

4 **What adjectives did you hear the speakers use about each place?**

5 **Now you try. Take turns to ask and answer the Speaking Part 2 questions.
   Look at the pictures on the opposite page. Use the *Exam tips* to help you.**

   Here are some pictures that show different places to visit. Do you like these different places to visit? Say why or why not.

6 **Now ask and answer these questions together.**

   Do you think:
   going to a museum is boring?
   visiting a castle is interesting?
   going to the cinema is expensive?
   shopping is fun?
   going to a park is pleasant?

   Which of these places do you like visiting best? Say why.

7 **Listen to the last part of the test. Number the questions below in the order you hear them.**
162

   ☐ Do you prefer visiting places that are inside or outside? Why?

   ☐ Do you like places that teach you about history? Why?

   ☐ Do you prefer visiting places on your own or with other people? Why?

8 **Listen again. What happens if the candidate gives a very short answer to a question?**
162

9 **Ask and answer the questions in Exercise 6 with your partner. Ask Why? / Why not?
   if your partner gives a short answer.**

Do you like these different places to visit?

READING AND WRITING

Reading Part 1 Multiple-choice signs, notices and messages (Unit 11, Unit 18, Review 3)

Remind students of the format of Reading Part 1 and refer them to the exam information and tips boxes. This part is also practised in the Student's Book on pages 66, 75 and 102 and in the Workbook on pages 46 and 73.

1 Tell students to read the text in question 1. Ask students what is in the picture (*a phone screen*) and who is writing to whom (*Dom is writing to Jules*). Ask students what kind of message it is. Then tell students to look at the answers and decide which is right and why the others are wrong.

Check as a class. Ask students what the key word is in A that gives them the answer (*borrow*) and tell them that it is a good idea to underline key words as they go through the options.

Answers

It's a text message between two friends.
The answer is A. Dom needs to borrow a ski jacket – his is too small for him.
B is wrong because he's telling Jules about the size of his own jacket – it's too small.
C is wrong because he is asking if Jules or his brother has a jacket he can borrow – he hasn't lent one to Jules' brother.

2 Give students time to do questions 2–6 by themselves. Put students into pairs to check and say why they have chosen their answers. Then check as a class. Give detailed feedback so that students understand why the correct answers are correct and what exam strategies were useful.

Question 2: Ask, 'What is this box for?' (*To get notes from students.*) 'What should the notes be about?' (*What students think about the new menu.*) 'Which answer is closest in meaning to this?' (*C*) 'Why?' (*It says 'opinion of the menu.'*) 'Why is A wrong?' (*The box does not give any information.*) 'Why is B wrong?' (*There is nothing on the box about adding new dishes to the menu.*)

Question 3: Ask, 'Why is Abby writing to Mia?' (*She wants Mia to email Mr Wilson.*) Which word in the correct answer B means the same as *email*? (*contact*) Point out to students the importance of looking for synonyms and words or phrases which have similar meanings in the answers and texts. Ask, 'Why is A wrong?' (*The climbing club hasn't started yet.*) 'Why is C wrong?' (*Abby thinks there are several people interested, enough to start a club.*)

Question 4: Ask, 'What kind of message is this?' (*a notice for students*) 'What do students have to do?' (*Give in their painting by July 12th.*) 'Why is B correct then?' (*It shows there is a deadline.*) 'Why are A and C wrong?' (*This information is not in the notice.*) Tell students not to consider answers which contain information that is not included in the text, or contradicted by it.

Question 5: Ask, 'What is the purpose of this notice?' (*To give information about opening times.*) 'Which two answers are about opening hours?' (*A and C*) 'Why did you choose A not C?' (*The two days in A are the Tuesdays and Thursdays in the text. C is wrong because days are compared, not places.*) Point out to students that they need to read each part of the text carefully – here the *Tuesdays and Thursdays only* was key to getting the correct answer.

Question 6: Ask, 'What does Isobel need to do on Sunday morning?' (*Help her mum.*) 'Can Isobel still meet Zoe in the park?' (*Yes*) 'Which answer says this?' (*C*)

Ask students to tell you ways that they can improve on this part of the exam, for example by trying to find a synonym for each word or phrase they learn (tell students that this works with grammar too, for example, *must = have to*).

Answers

1 A   2 C   3 B   4 B   5 A   6 C

Reading Part 2   Multiple-choice three short texts
(Unit 3, Unit 12, Unit 18)

Remind students of the format of Reading Part 2 and refer them to the exam information and tips boxes. This part is also practised in the Student's Book on pages 22, 70 and 104 and in the Workbook on pages 14, 50 and 74.

1 Tell students to read the title and ask, 'What information do you think will be in each text?'. (*For example, why these homes are unusual, who lives there and why, the advantages and disadvantages of living there.*) Ask students to say what kind of homes are in the photos (teach *lighthouse*) and have them predict what the people will say about what it is like to live in each place.

Give students time to read the questions. Ask students to think of synonyms or words and phrases close in meaning to the words and phrases in the questions.

1 other people (*friends*)
2 safe (*comfortable*)
3 happy with (*satisfied by*)
4 bright (*not dark*)
5 spending the night (*sleeping over*)
6 needs a lift (*has to ask for help getting somewhere*)
7 feels less comfortable (*isn't very happy*)

Give students a time limit to read the article. Ask some general comprehension questions, for example, 'How old was Sarah when she started living on the houseboat?' (*four*) 'What shape are the rooms in the lighthouse?' (*round*) 'What is a lot of the front of Trudi's house made of? (*glass*) Then, tell students to answer question 1 and underline the information that gives the answer. Check as a class and ask why (*friends are other people she knows*).

Answers

Lots of my friends live on houseboats too (in Sarah's text)

2 Give students time to complete the task. Tell students to underline the information that gives them each answer. When you go through the answers, have students read out what they have underlined. Ask students which house they would prefer to visit or live in.

Answers

1 A Lots of my friends live on houseboats too
2 B But the building is very strong, and I never feel afraid.
3 A We haven't got much space, but we don't mind – it's enough for us.
4 C Lots of light comes in
5 A They always sleep really well and love being on the water.
6 B my parents have to drive me everywhere
7 C I often get too hot and want to open a window.

Reading Part 3   Multiple-choice one long text
(Unit 5, Unit 9, Unit 15)

Remind students of the format of Reading Part 3 and refer them to the exam information and tips boxes. This part is also practised in the Student's Book on pages 34, 56 and 88 and in the Workbook on pages 22, 38 and 62.

1 Books closed, ask students if there are any advantages of living in a very small home and any disadvantages of living in a very large home. Which would they prefer? Books open, tell students to look at the photo and ask what rooms and furniture they think are in the house. Give students time to read the text. Ask some general comprehension questions, for example, 'Is this the first small house?' (*no*), 'How much did it cost to build this house?' (*$1,500*) and 'How many rooms does the house have?' (*two – a kitchen and sitting area downstairs and a bedroom upstairs*). Tell students to read the questions. Ask students, 'How many questions are there?' (*five*) and 'How many paragraphs are there?' (*four*). Tell students that there is one question for each paragraph and a general question. Ask, 'Which is the general question?' (*the first question*) and 'How do you know?' (*It asks about the purpose of the text, not a specific detail.*).

Answer

Question 1

2 Give students time to answer the questions. When you go through the answers, ask students to refer to the text to show how they got the correct answer and why the other answers are wrong. Then ask students, 'What kind of house would you like to design or build?'.

Answers

1 B The text is a description of his personal project. A is wrong because the focus is not on how teenagers can build small houses. C is wrong because the text doesn't say what other people think about small houses.
2 A *He was bored and looking for a fun activity* during the school holidays. B is wrong because there is no information about his neighbours. C is wrong because the text doesn't say he met anybody.
3 C Luke's dad was his *coach*. A is wrong because the text says that Luke did most of the work. B is wrong because Luke had to pay for the house himself.
4 B *there was a lot he didn't know*. A is wrong because he *had no idea what to do* when he started building it. C is wrong because the text doesn't say he broke anything.
5 C *he'd like to live in it full time*. A is wrong because his next house will be bigger. B is wrong because there is no information about this.

Reading Part 4 Multiple-choice cloze factual text
Unit 8, Unit 10, Review 2

Remind students of the format of Reading Part 4 and refer them to the exam information and tips boxes. This part is also practised in the Student's Book on pages 48, 53 and 61 and in the Workbook on pages 34 and 42.

1 Books closed, put students into pairs to say who they wrote their last email to and why. Check ideas as a class. Write the title of the article on the board and ask students, 'Why would people want to send emails to trees?', 'What would they write in their emails?' and 'What would the trees answer?'. Tell students to read the article. Ask some general comprehension questions, for example, 'Why did the trees have email addresses?' (*So people could tell workers if something was wrong with the tree.*), 'But what kind of emails did people send?' (*Messages to the trees saying how great they were.*) and 'Did the trees reply?' (*Yes, through the workers.*). Tell students to do question 1 and explain their answer. Ask, 'Are there any other ways people could let workers know about problems?' (*There could be a special telephone line.*)

> **Answer**
>
> B The expression is *let someone know*. Other similar expressions are *make someone aware* and *get to know* but they don't fit.

2 Pre-teach **join in** (to become involved in an activity with other people). Give students time to complete the rest of the questions. Then have students check with one another. Then go through the answers as a class and ask students to explain why each answer is correct. Ask students if trees are important in their town and if people would do the same thing if your trees had email addresses. As an extension activity, you could ask students to take a photo of a tree near their home and write an email to it.

> **Answers**
>
> 2 C *problem* means something wrong (*trouble* is either uncountable or used in the plural).
> 3 A The expression is *make something safe*.
> 4 B The emails were unexpected.
> 5 B You *tell somebody/something* but *explain something to somebody* and *speak to somebody about something*.
> 6 C This means very nice. *Glad* also goes with an infinitive but this means very pleased, for example *I'm glad to meet you*.

Reading Part 5 Open cloze email
(Unit 13, Unit 19, Review 5)

Remind students of the format of Reading Part 5 and refer them to the exam information and tips boxes. This part is also practised in the Student's Book on pages 78, 110 and 119 and in the Workbook on pages 54 and 78.

1 Books closed, put students into pairs and ask them to describe their bedrooms to one another. Tell them to say what they like most, what they dislike and how they would like to change their bedrooms. Share ideas as a class.

Books open, tell students to read the texts. Ask some basic comprehension questions, for example, 'Why is Shammi happy?' (*He's going to change the colour of his bedroom walls.*), 'What colour are the walls now?' (*pink*) and 'Do we know what colour he is going to paint the walls?' (*no*). Ask students to look at the gaps and say what kind of words are missing. Elicit from students some kinds of grammar words (for example, *determiners, prepositions, pronouns*).

> **Answer**
>
> grammar words

2 Do the example together to demonstrate. Ask, 'What kind of word often goes before a noun?' (*a determiner or preposition*) 'Do we already have a preposition here?' (*yes, in*), 'So if it's a determiner, what word would show it's Shammi's bedroom?'. Give students time to complete the rest of the questions. Then have students check with one another. Then go through the answers as a class and tell students to explain why each answer is correct. Ask students if they think the colour of a room can affect how you feel. Ask them, 'What colour walls would be good for someone to study hard in?' and 'What colour walls would make people feel relaxed?'.

> **Answers**
>
> 1 because/as/since – The second clause is giving an explanation for the first clause so we need a conjunction.
> 2 Do – This is a question so we need an auxiliary.
> 3 all – This means *the whole* (day).
> 4 how – This is part of the phrase *how much*.
> 5 if – This is a request.
> 6 what/which – These are determiners before *colour*.

Writing Part 6 Guided writing email or note
(Unit 10, Unit 14, Review 4)

Remind students of the format of Writing Part 6 and refer them to the exam information and tips boxes. This part is also practised in the Student's Book on pages 61, 83 and 97 and in the Workbook on pages 43 and 59.

1 Books closed, put students into small groups to talk about their last birthday. Did they have a party? If so, where? What presents did they get? Which was the most interesting? How else did they celebrate? Share ideas as a class. Tell students to read the exam task and underline the three questions. Ask, 'What verb tenses should you use?' (*past simple for the first two questions and present simple for the third.*), 'What is the minimum length for an answer? (*25 words*) and 'If you write more than 25 words, will you get a better score? (*no*).

Tell students to read the example answers and say which one is the best and what the problems with the other three are. You could ask students to correct the mistakes in D (My best present **was an** earring from my **friend**. **It is** beautiful. I **love** it and always **wear it.**)

> **Answers**
>
> A is perfect.
> B does not answer any of the questions in the email.
> C has bad punctuation, only answers one of the questions and it doesn't have enough words.
> D has spelling mistakes, grammar and tense mistakes and not enough words.

2 Give students time to write their own answer using A as a model. When students finish tell them to check that they have answered all three questions clearly as this is the most important requirement of this part of the exam, in at least 25 words. Students should also make sure they have as few mistakes as possible in grammar, vocabulary, spelling and punctuation.

Students can read one another's emails and also check. Take in the emails, mark them and give feedback. When you return the emails, students could write a second draft using your feedback to make a better version.

> **Model answer**
>
> Hi Danny
> I had a great birthday. My favourite present was a new winter coat, which my uncle bought for me. I like it because it's my favourite colour and it's really warm.
> Sam

Writing Part 7 Picture story
(Unit 4, Unit 18, Review 1)

Remind students of the format of Writing Part 7 and refer them to the exam information and tips boxes. This part is also practised in the Student's Book on pages 25, 31 and 105 and in the Workbook on pages 19 and 75.

1 Ask students if they or anyone in their family is good at cooking and what they can cook. Elicit *bake* by asking, 'You roast potatoes; you … a cake'. Tell students to look at the three pictures and ask questions about them in the past tense. 'What did Jim see?' (*a poster*), 'What did the poster say?' (*There was a baking competition.*), 'What did he make?' (*a cake*) and 'Why was Jim so happy?' (*He won the competition.*).

Tell students to read the sample answer, check that every picture is included, say what tense is used and why. Ask, 'Why is the boy given a name?' (*It makes the story read more naturally and it means that there can be sentence variation between his name and pronouns.*). Ask, 'Is the story longer than 35 words?' (*yes*) and 'Which linking words are used?' (*so, and x2, when*). Ask students what *it* refers to at the end of the second sentence and why it is used (*it = the competition; this avoids repetition*).

> **Answers**
>
> Yes – every picture is mentioned. Events in the story are told in the past tense. The past tense is the best tense for telling a story.

2 Ask students past simple questions about the story: 'What kind of competition was this one?' (*a music competition*), 'What was the girl doing in the second picture?' (*She was practising the guitar.*), 'How did the other people feel?' (*Annoyed because the music was too loud.*) and 'Did the competition go well?' (*Yes, everyone was enjoying themselves.*).

Tell students to write their story. Remind students to use the past simple tense and to include linking words. Take students' answers in to check and write the sample answer on the board for students to compare with their answers. 'What adjectives in the sample answer make it more effective?' (*terrible, amazing, great*). Ask students if they have ever entered a competition and how well they did.

> **Model answer**
>
> Last month Charlie saw a poster at school about a music competition. She loves playing the guitar, so she decided to enter it. She went home and practised a lot. Her family put their hands over their ears because they thought she sounded terrible. However, when she played on stage in the competition, everyone thought she was amazing. Charlie had a great night.

LISTENING

Listening Part 1   3-option multiple-choice five short dialogues (Unit 4, Unit 17, Review 1)

Remind students of the format of Listening Part 1 and refer them to the exam information and tips boxes. This part is also practised in the Student's Book on pages 27, 31 and 101 and in the Workbook on pages 19 and 71.

1   Tell students to look at the pictures for question 1 and write down words that could be included in the conversation. Get students' suggestions then ask how all the pictures are connected (*They are all objects that could be in a room.*).

> **Possible answers**
>
> *desk, sofa, posters*

🔊 150   2   Tell students to read the question carefully and say if they need to choose what Ted has now or what he plans to get. Play the recording for students to choose the answer. Check around the class to see what answers students have and what they base this on. Play the recording again to check as a class. If necessary, read out the section of the audioscript which gives the answer: *The only thing I need now is a sofa.* Ask students what they need for their room.

> **Answers**
>
> The question asks about what he wants.
> The answer is B.

>> **AUDIOSCRIPT TB PAGE 305**

🔊 151   3   Give students time to look at the pictures and read the questions. Ask some questions to check that students know what to listen for.

Question 2: 'Where are all these things in the car?' (*on the back seat*), 'Is the question about what to take in the car?' (*No, it is about what has been left in it.*)

Question 3: 'What information does each picture give?' (*the price of the bag*)

Question 4: 'What do pictures A and C have in common?' (*They both show water.*)

Question 5: 'Is the question about what the boys plan to do?' (*yes*)

Play the recording twice. Check answers as a class and ask students to say how they know. (Use the audioscript if necessary to show the answers.)

> **Answers**
>
> 2   C   The other one [bag of shopping]'s on the back seat I think.
> 3   A   from today that one is £15
> 4   A   It was lovely by that lake, wasn't it?
> 5   B   Let's go to that new café in town.

>> **AUDIOSCRIPT TB PAGE 305**

Listening Part 2   Gap fill notes (Unit 7, Unit 19, Review 5)

Remind students of the format of Listening Part 2 and refer them to the exam information and tips boxes. This part is also practised in the Student's Book on pages 45, 111 and 119 and in the Workbook on pages 31 and 79.

🔊 152   1   Books closed, ask students, 'How do you keep fit?' and 'Do you go to a gym?' If any students use a gym, ask them for information such as how much membership costs, what equipment the gym has and how they use it. Books open, tell students to read the instructions and notes. Play the recording with the example and ask students why the answer is Saturday not Friday.

> **Answers**
>
> Saturday is the day of the club and Friday is the last day you can book.

>> **AUDIOSCRIPT TB PAGE 305**

🔊 153   2   Ask students what information they expect to hear for the other answers. (1 *a price*, 2 *a morning time*, 3 *a first name or surname* (not both as there can only be a one word answer), 4 *an article of clothing*, 5 *something connected to sport*) Tell students that 3 will probably be spelled out and that there is a negative in 4, so they need to listen for something that is not necessary.

Play the recording twice. Have students check in pairs, then check answers as a class. Use the audioscript if students are unsure about what they heard. Ask some more questions about the recording. (You may want to play the recording again.) For example, 'How much are other clubs?' (*£15 or £20*), 'Why should people arrive by 10 o'clock?' (*So they can meet the teacher.*), 'What should people wear?' (*shorts*) and 'Why don't they need to bring water?' (*The gym has it.*).

Put students into small groups to think of ways that gyms could attract more teenagers, for example *they could offer a discount if friends go together; trainers from local gyms could go to PE classes in schools and tell the students about their gyms.* Share ideas as a class.

> **Answers**
>
> 1 12.50   2 10.20   3 Hughie   4 trousers   5 towel

>> **AUDIOSCRIPT TB PAGE 306**

Listening Part 3   3-option multiple-choice dialogue
(Unit 12, Unit 20, Review 3)

Remind students of the format of Listening Part 3 and refer them to the exam information and tips boxes. This part is also practised in the Student's Book on pages 71, 75 and 115 and in the Workbook on pages 50 and 83.

🔊 154 **1** Books closed, elicit from students some ideas for spending an afternoon, for example, going to the zoo, watching a film, playing table tennis. Have students work in groups to rank the activities according to how much fun they would be.

Books open, tell students that Callum and Stella are going to a skatepark. Ask students if there is a good skatepark near them and if they go there. Tell students to read the instructions and questions. Ask some questions to see that students understand what they are going to listen to: 'Who knows about the skatepark – Callum or Stella?' (*Callum*), 'Are there going to be any changes to the skatepark?' (*yes*) and 'Do they decide to go to the skatepark?' (*yes*). Tell students to re-read question 1. Play the recording for students to say the answer. Ask students why the answer is C not A or B.

Answers

C
A is wrong because he doesn't say how close it is to the cinema.
B is wrong because it's on the other side of town, so it's not close.
C is correct – it's opposite it so it must be close.

» AUDIOSCRIPT TB PAGE 306

🔊 155 **2** Tell students they are going to do the rest of the task and give them time to re-read the questions. Play the recording twice. Have students check in pairs then check answers as a class. Use the audioscript if students are unsure about what they heard. Ask some more questions about the recording (you may want to play the recording again): 'Is there another skatepark in town?' (*yes*). 'Why is the weather not a problem?' (*The skatepark has a roof.*) and 'Where does Stella need to be in the afternoon?' (*her auntie's house*). Ask students if their town has enough places for teenagers to spend time and what extra things the town could have, for example a zoo.

Answers

2 B it has to have enough space
3 A they're going to put a shop there too
4 C when it's finished, it'll be £5, but it's only £3 until then
5 A 'We could meet there at ten…' 'Yes, sure'

» AUDIOSCRIPT TB PAGE 306

Listening Part 4   3-option multiple-choice main idea, message, gist or topic (Unit 8, Unit 16, Review 2)

Remind students of the format of Listening Part 4 and refer them to the exam information and tips boxes. This part is also practised in the Student's Book on pages 49, 53 and 90 and in the Workbook on pages 35 and 67.

🔊 156 **1** Ask students to read the first question and answers. Ask students, 'If the girl just wanted a snack, what answer could it be?' (*A or B*). Play the recording for students to choose the answer. Put students in pairs to compare. Ask students why they chose this answer and not the others. Ask students, 'Which word in the conversation is the same as very hungry?' (*starving*).

Answers

The answer is C. She is hungry but doesn't want the other things her mother offers her. She wants something big.

» AUDIOSCRIPT TB PAGE 306

🔊 157 **2** Ask students to read the questions and answers. Then play the recording twice. Have students check in pairs, then check answers as a class. Use the audioscript if students are unsure about what they heard. Ask some more questions about each conversation. (You may want to play the recording again and pause after each conversation to ask the question.)

Question 1: 'What is mum cooking?' (*roast chicken*)

Question 2: 'How long was the show?' (*two hours long*)

Question 3: 'What happened to the boy's boots?' (*They got very wet.*)

Question 4: 'What are the friends going to?' (*a music festival*)

Question 5: 'Is the writer famous?' (*no*)

Answers

2 C There was so much action – I wasn't bored for a minute.
3 A Just because of a tiny bit of rain?
4 B I need to go to the ticket office first so why don't you wait for me there?
5 B The writer's not very well known but the story …

» AUDIOSCRIPT TB PAGE 307

PREPARE FOR THE EXAM
A2 KEY FOR SCHOOLS

Listening Part 5   Matching
(Unit 2, Unit 6, Review 4)

Remind students of the format of Listening Part 5 and refer them to the exam information and tips boxes. This part is also practised in the Student's Book on pages 17, 39 and 97 and in the Workbook on pages 10 and 26.

158 1 Books closed, put students into pairs to compare how they spent their half-term holidays. See which student had the most interesting time. Books open, ask students to read the instructions then the example. Ask students, 'What kind of music practice do you think Jasmin did?' Play the recording and then have students underline the part of the audioscript which gives the answer.

> **Answers**
>
> Grandma: How was your half-term holiday, Jasmin? What did you and your friends do?
> Jasmin: Well, Grandma, I <u>played the guitar a lot. I'm in the school concert next week and I need to get ready for it.</u>

159 2 Ask students to give you an example of each activity, for example cooking (*making a cake*), going online (*checking emails*). Play the recording twice for students to answer the questions. Have students check in pairs then check answers as a class. You could then ask students to underline their answers in the audioscript as they did in the example. Ask some more questions about each person (you may want to play the recording again).

Question 1: 'Why did Jasmin do a lot of music practice?' (*She has a concert next week.*)

Question 2: 'What sport did Sophie do?' (*hockey*)

Question 3: 'Who did Sam travel with?' (*his parents*)

Question 4: 'What is Joe going to do with his best photos?' (*enter a competition*)

Question 5: 'Why didn't Emily go shopping?' (*She didn't have enough money.*)

Question 6: 'What did Gemma plan to do?' (*study*)

Ask students, 'Who had the most interesting half-term?' and 'What advice would you give to someone like Emily who doesn't have much money but still wants to have an interesting time?'.

> **Answers**
>
> 1 G She played hockey
> 2 H He went away with his parents.
> 3 D He spent a lot of time taking pictures.
> 4 B She went on the internet a lot
> 5 A she spent the whole week baking

» **AUDIOSCRIPT TB PAGE 307**

SPEAKING

Speaking Part 1   Examiner-led questions
(Unit 1, Unit 16, Review 1, Review 4, Review 5)

Remind students of the format of Speaking Part 1 and refer them to the exam information and tips boxes. This part is also practised in the Student's Book on pages 13, 31, 93, 97 and 119.

1 Books closed, write these two questions on the board:
How old will you be on your next birthday?
What do you usually do at the weekends?

Ask students, 'Which question needs a short answer and which needs a longer answer?' (*The first needs a short answer; the second needs a longer answer.*). Books open, tell students to do the same for the list of questions. Check as a class.

> **Answers**
>
> Questions 7 and 12, the 'Tell me about' questions, need longer answers – try for three sentences.

2 Ask students, 'What makes a good answer to a question?' (*not too short, plenty of detail, correct grammar, interesting vocabulary*). Ask students to think of good answers for the second question on the board and tell one another. Then tell students to match the answers to the questions in Exercise 1 and decide how good they are. Check as a class.

> **Answers**
>
> a An answer to 'do you' questions like questions 4, 10 and 11. It is not so good because it is too short. You need to say why. See answer b for a better way to answer.
> b This is a better way to answer 'do you' questions like questions 4, 10 and 11.
> c Question 5. This is a good answer because it gives plenty of detail.
> d Question 7. It is not so good because it is too short. You need to say why.
> e Question 12. It is not so good because it is too short. It doesn't let the examiner hear any of the English you know. Even if you just go online, talk about that. Or make something up!

160 3 Tell students to listen and match the answers to the questions. Check as a class. You could also ask questions about details in the answers. For example, (Speaker 1) 'What does he do with his friends?' (*play sport or go to the park*)

> **Answers**
>
> Speaker 1 – question 9
> Speaker 2 – question 3
> Speaker 3 – question 8
> Speaker 4 – question 7
> Speaker 5 – question 6

» **AUDIOSCRIPT TB PAGE 307**

4 Put students into pairs. Tell them to take turns asking and answering the questions. Then ask some students to answer the questions in front of the whole class.

Speaking Part 2   Discussion with visual stimulus
(Unit 3, Unit 7, Review 2)

Remind students of the format of Speaking Part 2 and refer them to the exam information and tips boxes. This part is also practised in the Student's Book on pages 21, 42 and 53.

1 Books closed, ask students what kind of places they usually visit when they have free time. Books open, put students into pairs to see if any of the places they mentioned are in the pictures on page 135 and to name them. Check as a class. Ask questions about the pictures to encourage students to give details when it is their turn to do the task.

Question 1: 'What are they looking at in the museum?' (*maybe Greek vases*)

Question 2: 'What are they doing in the park?' (*chatting and reading*)

Question 3: 'What are the people looking at?' (*a castle*)

Question 4: 'Why are they wearing glasses in the cinema?' (*it is a 3D film.*)

Question 5: 'Which shop has special low prices?' (*Bags and Accessories*)

> **Answers**
> a museum, a park, a castle, a cinema, a shopping centre

🔊 **161** 2 Tell students to listen and put the pictures in order. Check as a class. Tell students that it is not necessary to talk about the pictures in the same order they are in on the page. A good strategy is to begin with the most interesting picture, the one which they can say the most about, so that they start the task well and feel confident.

> **Answer**
> They speak about the shopping centre, the museum, the park, the castle and the cinema in this order.

🔊 **161** 3 Tell students to write the places in order in the table. Then play the recording again for students to mark who likes and doesn't like each place. Check as a class.

> **Answers**
> Girl: likes shopping centres, museums, parks and cinemas
> Boy: likes parks, castles and cinemas; doesn't like shopping centres and museums

>> **AUDIOSCRIPT TB PAGE 308**

4 Ask students what adjectives were used about each place. If necessary, play the recording again for students to check. You could also ask students to write down the phrases which were used to get their partner's opinion and include them in the conversation. (*What about you? And you? How about you? Do you agree?*)

> **Answers**
> shopping centre – boring
> museum – interesting
> park – fun
> cinema – expensive

5 Put students into pairs and give them two minutes to say whether they like visiting the places in the pictures and giving their reasons. To make the activity similar to the test, you could repeat the examiner's instructions (note that the examiner who speaks to the students is called the interlocutor): 'Now, in this part of the test you are going to talk together. Here are some pictures that show different places to visit. Do you like these different places to visit? Say why or why not. I'll say that again. Do you like these different places to visit? Say why or why not.' Repeat the task with students in different pairs. Monitor and give feedback on examples of ambitious language and mistakes.

6 Books closed, ask students to write down three follow-up questions which an examiner could ask about the same topic. Give an example: 'Which places can you visit for free?'. Books open, tell students to answer the questions in pairs. Check as a class.

🔊 **162** 7 Have students read the questions then listen and put them in order. Check as a class.

> **Answers**
> The order in which the questions are asked is:
> Do you like places that teach you about history? Why?
> Do you prefer visiting places that are inside or outside? Why?
> Do you prefer visiting places on your own or with other people? Why?

🔊 **162** 8 Play the recording again and ask students to say how the examiner deals with short answers. Check as a class. Ask students for good ways to reply to *Why?* or *Why not?* and write them on the board, for example: *Because ... , I'm not sure but ... , I think ... , It seems to me that ... .*

> **Answers**
> The examiner will ask 'Why?' or 'Why not?' and you should expand your answer.

>> **AUDIOSCRIPT TB PAGE 308**

9 Put students into pairs and tell them to ask and answer the questions in Exercise 7. Then ask some students to answer the questions in front of the whole class.

EXTRA ACTIVITIES

PAGE 17, EXERCISE 3

Student A
Ask your partner for information about the sand cat to write a fact file. Make a note of the answers. Then, answer your partner's questions about the kakapo. Use the information on the right:

FACT FILE Kakapo

What is it: A kind of parrot

From: New Zealand

Lives: only on two small islands

Eats: plants, fruit and nuts

Adult weight: 2–4 kg

Numbers: about 127 kakapos left in the wild, none in zoos

Kakapo babies are called chicks. Females have 2–3 chicks every two years. The chicks stay with their mother for 10 weeks.

UNIT 5 **PAGE 33, EXERCISE 6**

Work with a partner. Take turns to make sentences.

Use one of the verbs in box A and the correct form of a comparative or superlative adverb made from the adjectives in box B.

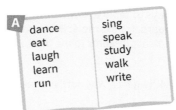

A
dance · sing
eat · speak
laugh · study
learn · walk
run · write

B
bad · loud
careful · noisy
dangerous · quick
fast · quiet
good · slow

UNIT 8 **PAGE 49, EXERCISE 3**

Complete the sentences with the words in the box. Use each word twice.

book   kind   picture   ring   watch

1 Sorry, I'm busy now. I'll _____ you later.
2 You can draw a _____ of your time capsule, if you like.
3 She's really _____. She lent me her favourite jacket for the party.
4 I don't want to _____ TV. I'd prefer to listen to some music.
5 When you phone the cinema, can you _____ a ticket for me, too, please?
6 What _____ of soup would you like? Vegetable or chicken?
7 That's a beautiful _____ you've got on your finger.
8 Can I borrow your maths _____? I left mine at home.
9 I'll take a _____ of it with my phone.
10 I'm sorry, I don't know what the time is. My _____ is broken.

136 EXTRA ACTIVITIES

UNIT 9 — PAGE 55, EXERCISE 10

In pairs, imagine you are setting up a sport or activity club at your school. Choose the sport or activity, then think of a name for your club. Write some rules for your club. Tell another pair about your club. Whose club sounds most fun?

UNIT 11 — PAGE 67, EXERCISE 3

Play this game. Work in pairs. Student A chooses an uncountable noun from Exercise 1. Student B must ask a question beginning *How many …?* using a related countable noun. Student A answers the question.

A: *homework*
B: *How many maths exercises did you do last night?*
A: *Eight!*

UNIT 12 — PAGE 69, EXERCISE 7

In small groups, design your own cinema. Think about:

- where your cinema will be
- the kind of films you'd like to show
- extra activities you might offer
- what you could sell
- the kind of seats you'll have.

Choose one person from your group to present your ideas to the class.

We'll have shops that sell …
We'll show films that …
People who come to our cinema will …
Our cinema will be in a place which …

UNIT 16 — PAGE 90, EXERCISE 2

Scores:

Add up your scores

A 4

B 3

C 2

D 1

12–16 You are a very serious language learner. You will do very well in your studies, but remember you can have fun when you are learning English! It's not all about getting the best mark in the class.

8–11 You enjoy learning English. You are happy to try new ways of learning and you are not afraid to make mistakes. You like using the language in real situations.

4–7 English probably isn't your favourite subject, but if you work hard, you can be good at it. Study a little but often, and you'll soon see the difference!

>> EXTRA ACTIVITIES

UNIT 2 | PAGE 17, EXERCISE 3

Student B
Answer your partner's questions about the sand cat. Use the information on the right. Then ask your partner for information about the kakapo to write a fact file. Make a note of the answers.

FACT FILE **Sand cat**

What is it: a kind of cat

From: Africa, Asia

Lives: in deserts

Eats: insects, birds and other small animals

Adult weight: 1–3 kg

Numbers: No one knows how many there are in the wild; 200 in zoos.

Sand cat babies are called kittens.

Females have 18 kittens every year. The kittens stay with their mother for about six months.

UNIT 18 | PAGE 103, EXERCISE 6

1 **Student A**   Student B has got one of your books and you want it back by tomorrow at the latest.

   Student B   You don't know where the book is! Don't tell Student A the truth! Try to get more time to return the book.

2 **Student A**   You want a book that Student B has borrowed from the library. You think Student B has had it for a very long time and want him/her to return it to the library so you can borrow it.

   Student B   You borrowed a book from the school library and Student A wants it. You haven't finished with it yet and want to keep it for as long as possible.

UNIT 18 | PAGE 103, EXERCISE 7

The *If* game. Choose a sentence from 1–3 below and complete it.
Then start a new sentence with the second part of your first sentence. Then write two more sentences.

If I have a party on my birthday, I'll ...
If I have a party on my birthday, I'll ask all my friends.
If I ask all my friends, we'll make a lot of noise.

1 If I have enough money, I'll buy ...
2 If I pass all my exams, I'll ...
3 If I move to a new class next year, I'll ...

In pairs, compare your answers.

138 EXTRA ACTIVITIES

UNIT 18 PAGE 105, WRITING

UNIT 20 PAGE 112, EXERCISE 2

Write a sentence for each of these situations.

A time when you:
- changed something in a shop.
- changed from one kind of transport to another of the same type.
- made a big or small change in your life, either because you wanted to or because someone else made it happen. For example, had a hair cut, moved things around in your bedroom.
- had to take a change of clothes somewhere.
- had to give someone a change of email address or change of phone number.
- enjoyed something because it was new or different.
- talked to someone who liked things in the past and didn't like life changing today, e.g computers, smartphones.
  Last year, my parents bought me a jacket for my birthday, but I didn't like it. So, I changed it for a different jacket that I really liked.

In groups, discuss your sentences for Exercise 2. Are any of them the same?

UNIT 20 PAGE 113, EXERCISE 8

All these things have changed people's lives. In pairs, discuss each one and decide how important it is for our lives today. Decide which is the most important. What other things would you add to the list?

DNA was discovered.
The internet was created.
Electricity was discovered.
The steam engine was developed.
Air conditioning was invented.

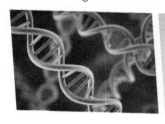   

GRAMMAR REFERENCE AND PRACTICE ANSWER KEY

UNIT 1 — PRESENT SIMPLE AND PRESENT CONTINUOUS

1
1 'm (am) painting
2 don't (do not) like
3 are playing
4 hate
5 do (you) enjoy
6 go
7 plays
8 prefer
9 'm (am) not doing

2
1 My dad usually goes to work by car.
2 We're (are) learning how to play the guitar today.
3 I always watch TV after dinner.
4 My friends aren't (are not) swimming in the sea now.
5 My cousin doesn't (does not) have breakfast every day.

UNIT 2 — VERBS WE DON'T USUALLY USE IN THE CONTINUOUS

1

Verbs we can use in the continuous	Verbs we don't normally use in the continuous
buy, climb, make, sing, work	believe, feel, hate, like, mean, own, understand, want

2
1 know
2 's learning
3 need
4 are you thinking
5 aren't playing
6 don't understand
7 Can you hear

3
1 I don't (do not) understand this exercise.
2 My friends think football is boring.
3 What are you doing right now?
4 We don't (do not) want to watch the film.
5 That dog belongs to my cousin.
6 Penguins don't (do not) feel the cold weather.
7 I don't (do not) like this book very much.

UNIT 3 — PAST SIMPLE

1
1 flew
2 went
3 asked
4 wanted
5 didn't want
6 went
7 walked
8 saw
9 didn't go
10 was
11 had

2
1 did the boy see
2 happened
3 ate
4 did you go
5 did

UNIT 4 — PAST CONTINUOUS AND PAST SIMPLE

1
1 It was raining.
2 Dad was cooking dinner.
3 My brother and I were watching TV in the living room.
4 My sister was reading.
5 My grandparents were leaving their apartment.

2
1 started
2 were playing
3 had
4 was doing
5 were packing

3
1 got up
2 was shining
3 decided
4 were sitting
5 saw
6 wasn't

UNIT 5 COMPARATIVE AND SUPERLATIVE ADVERBS

1
  1 more cheaply, the most cheaply
  2 heavily, more heavily, the most heavily
  3 fast, faster, the fastest
  4 badly, worse, the worst
  5 seriously, more seriously, the most seriously
  6 wonderfully, more wonderfully, the most wonderfully

2
  1 the most beautifully
  2 more often
  3 better
  4 more easily
  5 the most quickly

3
  1 as late as
  2 as quietly as
  3 as slowly as
  4 as often as
  5 as well as

UNIT 6 POSSESSION

1
  1 Terry's gold coins are on the table.
  2 The children's shoes are near the door.
  3 Both boys' lunches are in the kitchen.
  4 I can't find my sister's necklace. She'll be angry.
  5 My cousins' names are Ana and Eva.

2
  1 hers
  2 Our
  3 Their
  4 yours
  5 mine

3
  1 hers
  2 ours
  3 mine
  4 theirs
  5 yours

UNIT 7 PRESENT CONTINUOUS FOR FUTURE

1
  1 're going paddle boarding (F)
  2 Are (you) listening (N)
  3 isn't (is not) coming (F)
  4 'm (am) doing (N)
  5 are (you and your friends) getting (F)

2
  1 I'm going to the dentist
  2 're (are) having pizza at Paolo's Pizzas
  3 I'm (am) playing basketball
  4 I'm (am) studying

3 **Possible answers**
  1 I'm going to school tomorrow morning.
  2 I'm meeting my friends on Friday afternoon.
  3 I'm playing football on Saturday morning.
  4 We're having lunch at my grandparents' house on Sunday.
  5 I'm going to school next week.

UNIT 8 FUTURE WITH WILL

1
  1 I'll (will) have a big house and a fast car.
  2 My friends will move away.
  3 My cousin will become a famous film star.
  4 There'll (will) be cities on other planets.
  5 We won't (will not) buy things in shops.

2
  1 Will students go to school in the future? (*Possible answer*) I'm sure they won't go to school.
  2 Where will we buy clothes and shoes in the future? (*Possible answer*) I think we'll buy clothes and shoes online.
  3 How will people travel from one place to another? (*Possible answer*) I'm certain people will travel in rockets.
  4 Will there be more wars? (*Possible answer*) I hope there won't be more wars.
  5 Will scientists discover new things? (*Possible answer*) I'm sure scientists will discover new things.

FUTURE WITH MAY / MIGHT

1
  1 I'm sure I'll go swimming.
  2 We may have pizza or we may have a hamburger.
  3 My mum might be able to drive us to the concert, but she isn't sure.
  4 I'm certain they won't be late.
  5 Where will you go on holiday?

2
  1 I may / might not go to the beach.
  2 I may / might turn off the air conditioning.
  3 It may / might not rain later.
  4 Her parents may/ might buy her a new smart phone.
  5 You may / might not understand this teacher because she talks very fast.

UNIT 9 MUST, MUSTN'T, HAVE TO, DON'T HAVE TO

1
  1 They must fill in the form.
  2 We mustn't forget Mum's birthday.
  3 My cousin mustn't wear large earrings to school.
  4 You must practise for an hour every day.
  5 You must be careful.

2
  1 don't (do not) have to go
  2 has to work
  3 does (your sister) have to come
  4 has to go
  5 don't (do not) have to watch

3
  1 had to
  2 mustn't
  3 Do you have to
  4 don't have to
  5 mustn't

UNIT 10   VERB PATTERNS – GERUNDS AND INFINITIVES

1   **1** seeing   **2** to study   **3** getting up   **4** Making   **5** writing
  6 downloading

2   **1** making   **2** playing   **3** failing   **4** uploading   **5** joining

3   **Possible answers**
1. When I leave school, I hope to go to university.
2. I don't mind doing homework, but I don't like writing stories.
3. I started playing the piano when I was younger.
4. I prefer watching TV to reading books.
5. I'm thinking of going to the cinema next weekend.

UNIT 11   DETERMINERS

1   **1** a   **2** the   **3** the   **4** a   **5** the   **6** a   **7** the   **8** the

2   **1** another   **2** Both   **3** another   **4** the other   **5** all   **6** both

3   **1** other   **2** an   **3** All   **4** another   **5** the   **6** both

UNIT 12   RELATIVE PRONOUNS *WHO, WHICH, THAT*

1   **1** which   **2** who   **3** who   **4** which   **5** which   **6** who

2   **1** The festival which is here in the summer is good fun.
  2 The friend who went to a musical had a good time.
  3 There's a shop near my house which sells jazz CDs.
  4 We went to a cinema which had 12 screens.
  5 The neighbour who likes watching drama films acts as a hobby.

3   **1** c, who   **2** e, which   **3** b, which   **4** a, who   **5** d, which

UNIT 13   PRESENT PERFECT WITH *EVER* AND *NEVER*

1   **1** arrived   **2** enjoyed   **3** repaired   **4** stopped   **5** travelled
  6 walked   **7** broken   **8** bought   **9** fallen   **10** grown
  11 lent   **12** worn

2   **1** 've (have) never kayaked
  2 've (have) never grown
  3 have never met
  4 's (has) never learned
  5 've (have) never explored

3   **1** Has your brother ever written a blog? No, he hasn't.
  2 Have your friends ever ridden a horse? Yes, they have.
  3 Has your teacher ever forgotten your name? Yes, she/he has.
  4 Have you ever sold things you don't want? No, I haven't.
  5 Have you and your friends ever won a competition? No, we haven't.

UNIT 14   PRESENT PERFECT WITH *JUST, YET* AND *ALREADY*

1   **1** I've just seen my best friend outside the library.
  2 Let's see a different film. I've already seen that one.
  3 I'm hungry. I haven't eaten yet.
  4 Rob can't play football. He's just broken his foot.
  5 Have your friends arrived yet?

2   **1** just   **2** already   **3** yet   **4** yet   **5** just   **6** already

3   **1** I haven't seen the Statue of Liberty yet.
  2 Have you had lunch yet?
  3 I've already read that book.
  4 I've already bought the bread.
  5 Have you chosen a film yet? / Have you chosen a film already?

UNIT 15   PRESENT PERFECT WITH *SINCE* AND *FOR*

1

since	for
13th April 2011, breakfast, I was young, May, my birthday, Tuesday	ages, ever, five days, four months, three minutes, two hours, two weeks, a year, years

2   **1** 's (has) had, since
  2 hasn't (has not) eaten, for
  3 've (have) liked, since
  4 haven't (have not) seen, for
  5 have been, since

3   **Possible answers**
1. We haven't (have not) had maths since 10 o'clock.
2. My best friend has lived in his/her house for a long time.
3. My mum hasn't cooked a meal since last Sunday.
4. My friends have known each other since they were young.
5. I haven't eaten anything for four hours.

4   **Possible answers**
1. How long have your parents lived here? They've (have) lived here for 20 years.
2. How long has your best friend had his/her school bag? He/She's (has) had it for six months.
3. How long have you studied in this school? I've (have) studied in this school since I was 12.
4. How long has your favourite shop been open? It's (has) been open since last year.
5. How long has your English teacher worked in your school? He/She's (has) worked in my school since September.

UNIT 16   PRESENT PERFECT AND PAST SIMPLE

1

Present perfect	Past simple
already, ever, for 18 weeks, never, recently, since 5th May, yet	in 2008, last week, three days ago, when I was younger

2 **1** bought
  2 haven't (have not) been
  3 missed
  4 sent, hasn't (has not) answered
  5 have known, went
  6 've (have) made

3 **Possible answers**
  1 How long have you known your English teacher? I've known him/her for six months.
  2 How long have you liked your favourite band? I've liked them since I was 12.

4 **Possible answers**
  1 When did you learn to swim? I learned to swim when I was six.
  2 When did you use a computer for the first time? I used a computer for the first time in 2004.

UNIT 17   REFLEXIVE PRONOUNS

1 **1** himself **2** myself **3** themselves **4** yourselves
  5 yourself / yourselves **6** ourselves

2 **1** by
  2 -
  3 by
  4 by
  5 -
  6 -

3 **1** by itself **2** by myself **3** ourselves **4** themselves
  5 by themselves **6** yourself

UNIT 18   FIRST CONDITIONAL

1 **1** 'll **2** don't **3** won't **4** don't **5** doesn't

2 **1** 'll (will) go, snows
  2 aren't (are not), 'll (will) fall
  3 'll (will) get, doesn't (does not) stop
  4 don't (do not) leave, won't (will not) catch
  5 won't (will not) stay, 's (is)
  6 doesn't (does not) come, 'll (will) miss

3 **Possible answers**
  1 If I'm late home, my parents will be angry.
  2 If it's cold tomorrow, I'll wear a coat.
  3 If I pass all my exams, I'll be happy.
  4 If I go shopping on Saturday, I'll buy a new T-shirt.
  5 No, I won't cook dinner if I get home before my parents tonight.
  6 Yes, I'll watch TV if I finish all my homework.

UNIT 19   PRESENT SIMPLE PASSIVE

1 **1** is sold
  2 are given
  3 isn't made
  4 is watched
  5 'm not paid
  6 aren't invited

2 **1** is called
  2 are downloaded
  3 aren't (are not) needed
  4 'm (am) given
  5 aren't (are not) worn
  6 are baked

3 **1** is spoken
  2 aren't (are not) used
  3 isn't (is not) cooked
  4 are sent to me by
  5 aren't (are not) grown
  6 is made into different shapes by

UNIT 20   PAST SIMPLE PASSIVE

1 **1** This photo was taken by my sister.
  2 The cakes were eaten by my friends.
  3 The Summer Palace was made into a public park in 1924.
  4 We weren't invited to Megan's party last week.
  5 We were shown around the library by the tour guide.
  6 You weren't given a present by your brother.

2 **1** was built
  2 am driven
  3 was stolen
  4 is visited
  5 were made
  6 was written

3 **Possible answers**
  1 I was born in 2001.
  2 I was given some new clothes.
  3 Many different types of fruit are grown in my country.
  4 My house was built in 1972.
  5 We're given a lot of homework.
  6 I was 5 when I was taught how to read.

WORKBOOK ANSWER KEY AND AUDIOSCRIPTS

UNIT 1 It's a challenge!

VOCABULARY

1 **1** polite **2** helpful **3** friendly **4** popular **5** active **6** kind
   7 lazy **8** quiet **9** creative

2 **1** lazy **2** friendly **3** polite **4** helpful **5** popular **6** active
   7 creative **8** kind **9** quiet

GRAMMAR

1 **Present simple:** every Monday, often, twice a week

   Present continuous: at the moment, now, this week, today

2 **1** plays; 's playing

   2 listens; 's listening

   3 does; 's doing

   4 has; 's having

3 **1** do you usually do

   2 is teaching

   3 don't go

   4 Are you having

   5 don't play

4 **1** They're playing football in the park now.

   2 My brother goes to the cinema on Friday evenings.

   3 He visits his cousin on Sunday afternoons.

   4 My parents are shopping in the supermarket at the moment.

   5 We meet in the café every Saturday.

   6 She usually sees her friends at the weekend.

5 **1** Every day in the morning we **eat** soup.

   2 She **studies** medicine at Odessa University.

   3 Anna goes to college every day. She **is** / She**'s** learning English this term.

   4 I **am** / I**'m** writing this email because I want to tell you about my last trip.

   5 My brother **is** / **'s playing** a board game at the moment because he's bored of computers.

VOCABULARY

1 **1** Adam

   2 Price

   3 15

   4 English

   5 – (none / doesn't have one)

   6 07662012976

   7 adampr45@kmail.com

2 **1** What's your surname / family name

   2 what's your first name

   3 What's your address

   4 What's your phone number

   5 What's your email address

READING

1 **1** B **2** A **3** B **4** B

2 **1** Sofia

   2 Marcos

   3 21 / twenty-one

   4 28 Spring Street

   5 Spanish

   6 history

   7 swimming

   8 the violin

LISTENING

1 B, D

2 **1** 4B **2** France **3** five **4** 180 **5** 52 **6** badminton
   7 awards **8** Monday

 Teacher: Good morning, Class 4B. Can you listen carefully, please, because I've got some information about this year's camping trip for you and for Class 4A?

First, where are we going? Well, I know some of you wanted to go to Spain, but as you are learning French this year, we're going to France. We'll be away on the trip for five nights, but only three of the nights will be at the campsite. We'll travel on the first and last nights.

Now the cost. This year each person will need to pay £180 for the whole trip. We know it's a lot of money, but you don't have to pay it all at one time. You can pay £60 a month in March, April and June.

As you know, two classes from our school are going together this year. 27 students from this class can go, and 25 students from the other class. So that's 52 of you. There will be three teachers, too.

The campsite's great. There's lots to do there: you can play volleyball and tennis outside, and badminton inside. There's a great sports hall for that. You can also learn new skills at the campsite. Students will get awards for cooking and art on the last night. There will also be sports competitions.

If you want to come on the trip, please take a form from my desk today. Take it home, ask your parents about it and fill it in. Then, bring your form back next Monday. I will put up a list of everyone that is coming on the trip in the classroom next Friday.

WRITING

1 **1** e **2** f **3** d **4** h **5** b **6** i **7** a **8** g

2 Students' own answers

UNIT 2 Our changing planet

VOCABULARY

1 forest: ×, hill: A and B, sea: B, mountain: A and B, volcano: B, valley A, lake: A, river: ×

2 **1** river **2** volcano **3** hills; valley **4** sea **5** desert **6** forest

GRAMMAR

1

Verbs that we use in the present continuous	Verbs that we don't usually use in the present continuous
happen read walk watch write	belong to hate have hope know like love mean need own think understand want

2 **1** 'm doing
2 belong
3 like
4 's working
5 understands
6 Do you know
7 'm looking for
8 don't own

3 **1** There is a concert on Saturday. I **want** to go.
2 correct
3 I think you **like** reading.
4 correct
5 We **want** to tell you what we think of Rio de Janeiro.

VOCABULARY

1

	1 d		2 e									
	o		l			3 w						
	l		e			h			4 p			
	p		5 p	o	l	a	r	b	e	a	r	
	h		h			l			n			6 m
7 g	i	r	a	f	f	e			g			o
	n		n						u			n
			8 t	i	g	e	r		i			k
								9 s	n	a	k	e
												y

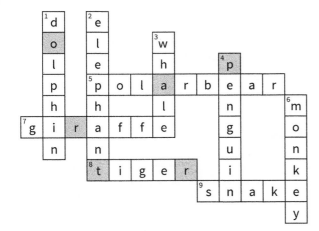

2 parrot

READING

1 **1** younger **2** animals **3** the book **4** some things

2 **1** B **2** C **3** E **4** A; Not needed: D

LISTENING

1 **1** F **2** D **3** B **4** A **5** H

02 You will hear Martha talking to a friend about a trip to the zoo. Which animal was each person most interested in?

Boy: Did you have a good time at the zoo, Martha?

Martha: Yes, we really enjoyed it. My brother loved the monkeys.

Boy: They're very funny to watch. What about your sister?

Martha: Well, she hated the snakes! We only watched them for about one minute! But we spent a long time watching the penguins, because they were her favourite thing at the zoo.

Boy: And did your dad have a good day?

Martha: Yes. He enjoyed looking at the giraffes the most. He didn't like the elephants very much – I don't know why.

Boy: That's interesting. What about you and your mum?

Martha: Oh, I liked the dolphins best. Mum did too, so we went to look at them again after the penguins.

Boy: Did your grandad have a favourite animal?

Martha: He liked the giraffes a lot, but he preferred the bears. He liked them most because they're so strong and clever.

Boy: Really? And what about your grandma?

Martha: She quite liked the snakes, but for her, the wild dogs were the most interesting. She even bought a book about them in the shop!

Boy: Great – you all had a great day, then.

Martha: Yes, we loved it.

WRITING

1 **1** grass and insects
2 between 90 kg and 270 kg
3 two or three
4 cubs
5 about two years
6 around 600,000

2 **Paragraph 1: where they live / food**
leaves, grass, fruit
Paragraph 2: size / what they weigh / age they live until
adults very big – 2,268 kg – 6,350 kg / live in wild until around 70
Paragraph 3: babies / how many wild African elephants today
females have one baby ('calf') every two–four years, heavy – about 91 kg when they're born / now 470,000–690,000 wild elephants

3 Students' own answers

UNIT 3 On holiday

VOCABULARY

1 **1** plane **2** bike **3** boat **4** coach **5** helicopter **6** on foot **7** motorbike **8** scooter **9** ship **10** tram **11** underground

2 **on the sea:** boat, ship
on a road or path: bike, coach, on foot, motorbike, scooter
on a railway line or track: tram, underground
through the sky: helicopter

3 **1** d **2** c **3** e **4** a **5** b

GRAMMAR

1 **1** was **2** went **3** knew **4** did; get **5** Was **6** didn't have **7** weren't

2 **1** were **2** did **3** travelled **4** spent **5** started **6** waited **7** didn't stop **8** arrived

3 **1** I went to Mar del Plata. I **had** a lovely day.

   2 Last night I **left** my history book in your house.

   3 I went shopping yesterday. I **bought** a very nice skirt and a sweater.

   4 I liked the weather last week because it **was** hot.

4 **1** did **2** did **3** – **4** did **5** – **6** –

VOCABULARY

1 **1** map **2** guest **3** visitor **4** suitcase **5** luggage **6** receptionist **7** tourist **8** guidebook

2 **1** guest **2** luggage **3** visitor **4** map **5** guidebook **6** receptionist

READING

1 **Possible answer**

The sea enters the bookshop in the winter. The books are in boats and baths and some books are furniture and art. Not all the books are for sale. It's not very tidy, but it's full of wonderful things.

2 **1** C **2** R **3** E **4** C **5** R **6** E **7** E

LISTENING

1 **1** d **2** a **3** b **4** c

2 **1** short **2** 10.00 **3** famous **4** modern art **5** theatres

🔊 03

Assistant: Hello, there. Can I help you?

Ross: Hi. I'm here in Liverpool with my parents and my sister for three days. I'd like to get some information about things to do for all of us.

Assistant: OK. Let's see … do any of you like looking at old buildings?

Ross: Hmm, Dad doesn't enjoy doing that, but Mum loves it.

Assistant: She'll be happy then. There are two amazing cathedrals to visit.

Ross: Oh, great.

Assistant: Just a minute, I'll give you a map so you can find them. Here you are. And what about going on the river on a boat? That's fun. You can go on a short trip around Liverpool for 50 minutes or on a long one to Manchester. But that takes six hours.

Ross: A short boat trip's a really good idea.

Assistant: And what about football? Liverpool's football club is very famous, of course.

Ross: Oh yes. My sister Jessica's a big fan.

Assistant: Great. You can go and have a tour between 10 and 3, every day of the week.

Ross: She'll like that.

Assistant: Oh, good! And do you like music?

Ross: I love it!

Assistant: Do you know The Beatles? They were a very famous group from Liverpool from the 1960s. You can find out all about them at a special place called The Beatles Story.

Ross: Sounds great! Are there any places to look at art in Liverpool? My dad loves looking at paintings.

Assistant: Yes, there certainly are. For modern art, there's Tate Liverpool, and for art from every century, there's the Walker Gallery. But I can give you a list of the others, too. Here you are.

Ross: Thanks! Dad'll love this. Thanks very much for your help.

Assistant: That's all right. Oh, and by the way, there are some great shows on at the theatres tonight. Here's some information about them, too.

Ross: Thanks!

WRITING

1 **1** C **2** E **3** A **4** D **5** B

2 Students' own answers

UNIT 4 My place

VOCABULARY

1 **1** ✗ **2** ✗ **3** ✓ **4** ✓ **5** ✗ **6** ✗ **7** ✓ **8** ✗ **9** ✓

1 **1** sink **2** garage **3** gate **4** balcony **5** ceiling **6** ground floor **7** cupboard

GRAMMAR

1 **1** c **2** a **3** d **4** e **5** b

2 **1** was swimming; started

   2 phoned; were playing

   3 was walking; saw

   4 bought; was playing

   5 was watching; took

   6 were flying; began

   7 was making; was talking; was cleaning; were playing

   8 was doing; arrived

3 **1** I watched it with my family.

   2 We danced, ate and drank.

   3 We lay on the beach every day.

VOCABULARY

1

p	u	n	u	s	u	a	l	q	t	c
r	d	l	q	e	p	c	o	l	d	o
t	o	l	u	j	n	n	d	g	a	o
i	e	i	b	r	i	g	h	t	r	l
n	d	g	w	e	z	c	s	j	k	c
y	f	h	a	t	t	e	t	e	n	o
a	t	t	r	a	c	t	i	v	e	s
l	a	d	m	o	v	b	o	k	m	y
p	e	a	c	e	f	u	l	i	x	t

2 comfortable

3 **1** cool **2** peaceful **3** unusual **4** light **5** attractive **6** comfortable **7** bright

4 Students' own answers

READING

1 **1** B **2** A **3** C

2 **1** 1 **2** 3 **3** 2,3 **4** 2,3 **5** 1,2 **6** 1,3 **7** 3 **8** 2

LISTENING

1 **1** B **2** C **3** B **4** C **5** C

🔊 **1**

What was Richard doing when his mum got home?

Richard: My mum was surprised when she came home yesterday.

Girl: Why was that, Richard?

Richard: I was in the kitchen, making some soup. I don't like cooking, but there was no bread for a sandwich and I was hungry.

Girl: Wow! Was it difficult?

Richard: No, not really.

2 What do Charlie and his family use their garage for?

Charlie: Our house has a garage, but we don't keep our car in it.

Sally: What do you use it for, then?

Charlie: Well, I really want a table tennis table in there but it's full of boxes of old things. And my brother wants to practise in there with his band.

Sally: You'll have to take all the boxes away.

3 What did Rosie's dad buy yesterday?

Dad: Rosie – are you at home this afternoon? I bought something yesterday, and the shop is bringing it at two.

Rosie: I'll be here. Have you bought a new sofa?

Dad: We don't need one! It's a sink for the new kitchen. We just have to find the right cooker now, then we'll have everything we need.

4 Who is on the balcony?

Man: Who's that talking outside on the balcony?

Woman: Bethan and her friends. One's Catherine, but I don't know the other girl with them.

Man: I can hear a boy laughing, too.

Woman: That's the TV! Hannah's watching it in the sitting room.

5 What did Emma paint on her ceiling?

Emma: I finished painting my ceiling last night. It looks great.

Boy: Oh yes? What did you decide to paint on it? The sun or the stars?

Emma: Well, you know my ceiling's light grey? So the stars weren't right. I decided to do clouds instead.

Boy: Good idea!

WRITING

1 **Possible answer**

The boy was watching TV when his two friends came to his house with four pizzas. The boys ate all four pizzas, but later they felt sick. The boy's sister thought it was funny and took a photo of them.

UNIT 5 School

VOCABULARY

1 **Possible answers**

1 b + h = biology

2 d + f = maths

3 e + p = geography

4 g + o = drama

5 j + i = physics

6 l + c = science

7 m + k = chemistry

2 **1** B **2** B **3** C **4** C **5** B

3 **1** PE

2 geography

3 history

4 design and technology

5 maths

6 biology

7 physics

8 ICT

9 foreign languages

GRAMMAR

1 **1** ✗ **2** ✓ **3** ✓ **4** ✗ **5** ✓ **6** ✗ **7** ✗ **8** ✓

2 **1** more quietly

2 the best

3 more quickly

4 (the) worst

5 (the) hardest

3 **1** most **2** more **3** more **4** most **5** most

4 **1** Jacob finished the meal more quickly than his friends.

2 Davina wrote her name the most carefully.

3 Louis works harder than the other art students.

4 Marta always sleeps the worst in her family.

5 **1** better

2 easily

3 like the best

4 carefully

5 more clearly

VOCABULARY

1 **1** catch **2** carry **3** use **4** go along **5** make **6** study

2 **1** He is taking an umbrella

2 She is taking (some) medicine.

3 She is taking an exam.

4 He is taking the/a bus.

READING

1 Students' own answers

2 **1** B **2** B **3** C **4** A **5** A

LISTENING

1 **1** Ben **2** Lorna **3** Mrs Black

2 **1** chemistry **2** physics **3** farm **4** sister **5** drama
6 market **7** 500 **8** jeans **9** month

🔊 **A** Mrs Black
05

Mrs Black: Quiet please. Thank you. I'm Mrs Black, your new teacher. Good morning Class 8A. I'm going to teach you chemistry this year. I also teach biology, but to the younger students. Your biology teacher won't change this year. But you will have one other new teacher this year. He's called Mr Hill. The only science subject I don't teach is physics. So he'll teach you that.

B Lorna

Lorna: Hi, I'm Lorna. I'm homeschooled because we live on a farm, a long way from the nearest school. But it's not just me – I have a brother and a sister, and my sister is homeschooled with me. My brother's too young for school. My mum teaches us. She's really good at maths, and teaches it well. But she teaches us drama better than any other subject – when she was younger, she wanted to be an actor.

C Ben

Ben: My name's Ben Rogers. My son's 11 and he's leaving his school at the end of this year. I'm looking at schools for him. We're lucky – there are three good ones near our home in King Street. I think the best school's the one in Market Street. It's quite small – only 500 students go to it. And the teachers are great. Students don't have to wear a uniform but they can't wear jeans. Students there have to work hard. They have tests every month and homework every night of the week, too.

WRITING

1 **1** G **2** D **3** C **4** A **5** F **6** B

2 Students' own answers

UNIT 6 Favourite things

VOCABULARY

1 **1** ✗ **2** ✗ **3** ✓ **4** ✗ **5** ✓

2 **1** wool; leather
2 wood
3 gold; silver
4 glass
5 plastic
6 wood; cotton

3 **1** The box isn't made of wool. It's a wooden box.
2 The bottles aren't made of silver. They're glass bottles.
3 The bag isn't made of leather. It's a cotton bag.
4 The table isn't made of wood. It's a glass table.

GRAMMAR

1 **1** a **2** b **3** b

2 **1** mine **2** their **3** your **4** mine **5** yours **6** ours **7** hers

3 **1** 's **2** s' **3** s **4** 's **5** s; 's

4 **1** I watched a **volleyball** game last Friday.
2 The colour of **my** bedroom is blue.
3 I bought a smartphone. You can take great photos with **its** camera.
4 I went to the football match with my father and two friends of **ours**.
5 I bought a pair of jeans because **mine** are small.

VOCABULARY

1 **1** c **2** e **3** b **4** f **5** a **6** d

2 **1** b **2** c **3** a **4** e **5** d

3 **1** heavy **2** colourful **3** round **4** smooth **5** hard **6** soft

READING

1 B

2 **1** scooter **2** wood **3** leather **4** brother's (jacket)
5 evening **6** dad **7** 6 / six

LISTENING

1 **1** H **2** E **3** D **4** B **5** C

🔊 You will hear Alicia talking to her Aunt Jane about packing
06 things in boxes to take to a new house. Who does each thing belong to?

Alicia: Thanks for helping me put everything in boxes for our new house, Aunt Jane.

Aunt Jane: That's all right, Alicia. Hmm, is this old tennis racket your dad's?

Alicia: Of course! He wants to keep it – don't ask me why!

Aunt Jane: And this phone? I think that's yours, Alicia?

Alicia: Er, that one's my brother Daniel's. Can you put it in his box?

Aunt Jane: OK. Now I know this book about motorbikes is George's. It's got his name in it.

Alicia: Actually, he gave it to Ryan. Ryan's more interested in motorbikes. So can you put it in his box?

Aunt Jane: Wow! Look at all these DVDs. And these video games!

Alicia: Ben loves them. They're his. He plays them with Daniel all the time.

Aunt Jane: I love this photo of you and your mum, Alicia.

Alicia: It's great. Dad took it, but he gave it to me.

Aunt Jane: I'll put it in your box, then.

Alicia: Oh, but who do these keys belong to? They're not mine. Perhaps they're Mum's. She's got lots of keys.

Aunt Jane: Oh, they're mine, Alicia. Don't put them in any of the boxes!

WRITING

1

Opinion	Size	Physical quality	Shape	Age	Colour	Material
lovely	large	hard	round	new	black	glass
pretty	little	heavy		old		metal
	small	smooth				silver
						wooden

2 Possible answers
  1 lovely, big, soft
  2 pretty, new, silver
  3 ugly, heavy, metal
  4 large, new, glass

3 1 It's an old wooden bowl.
  2 It is from Germany.
  3 beautiful, old, wooden, strong, smooth
  4 Because it belonged to his / her grandmother's mother.
  5 He / She likes it because it is strong and smooth and feels like part of the family.

4 Students' own answers

UNIT 7 Adventure holidays

VOCABULARY

1 1 f **2** c **3** b **4** e **5** d **6** a
  Waterskiing is not a two-word phrase.

2 1 sailing **2** diving **3** camping **4** hiking

3 1 e **2** d **3** b **4** c **5** a

4 1 to **2** up **3** on **4** lost **5** back

GRAMMAR

1 1 's / is meeting
  2 are playing
  3 'm / am studying
  4 're / are taking
  5 's / is having
  6 's / is visiting

2 A 3 **B** 6 **C** 5 **D** 1 **E** 2 **F** 4

3 1 I'm going to the airport. My mum**'s / is arriving** at 3.30 pm.
  2 My father**'s / is taking** us to the sports centre at six o'clock. Don't forget to bring your racket!
  3 Would you like to help me paint my bedroom? We**'re / are starting** on Sunday morning at 10.
  4 My friend Jacek is from Poland. Next week he**'s / is coming** to see us in England.
  5 Don't forget we**'re / are meeting** at 3 pm at my house.

4 Students' own answers

VOCABULARY

1

Crossword answers:
- 1 across: towel
- 5 across: sleeping bag
- 6 across: backpack
- 8 across: tent
- 9 across: map
- 11 across: sun
- 13 across: first aid kit
- 1 down: torch
- 2 down: washbag
- 3 down: trainers
- 4 down: snacks
- 7 down: cooker
- 10 down: waterproof
- 12 down: jacket

2 1 backpack
  2 sleeping bag
  3 walking boots
  4 waterproof jacket
  5 towel
  6 wash bag
  7 snacks
  8 map

READING

1 A, C, D, E

2 1 ✓ **2** ✓ **3** ✓ **4** ✗ **5** ✗ **6** ✓ **7** ✗ **8** ✗

LISTENING

1 1 11.30 **2** beach **3** 900 **4** kayaking **5** Murphy

🔊 07 You will hear a teacher telling students about a trip.

Teacher: Good morning everyone! Before we get on the bus, I need to tell you some things about today. As you know, we're going to Dolphin Island. It's called that because you can often see these beautiful animals swimming there. The bus is leaving soon to take us to the boat, and that goes at eleven thirty. We'll get to the island at about twelve o'clock.

We're having a picnic lunch. We'll eat on the beach, and then walk through the forest to Woodside Castle. A rich family built the castle 900 years ago, and it was the only building on the island for 200 years. Now, there are holiday homes and hotels, as well as the activity centre. We're going there for our activity: kayaking. While we're there, look out for the zip wire – it's fantastic! Maybe we'll do that next time. After that, we're coming home.

If you have any problems today, you need to phone Mrs Murphy – that's M-U-R-P-H-Y. She and Mr Brown are coming with us. I'll text you all her number in a minute, so you've got it on your phones. Any questions?

WRITING

1 **A** 4 **B** 2; 3 **C** 1

2 Students' own answers

UNIT 8 Life in the future

VOCABULARY

1 **1** ✗ **2** ✗ **3** ✗ **4** B **5** B **6** ✗ **7** ✗ **8** A **9** A and B
10 A and B **11** B

2 **1** washing machine
  2 heating
  3 air conditioning
  4 stairs
  5 lights
  6 fridge
  7 bookcase
  8 roof

GRAMMAR

1 **1** I don't think I'll go to the cinema.
  2 Will Chelsea win the Champions League?
  3 I think the weather will get better.
  4 Do you think Chris will pass his history exam?
  5 Our team won't win the Championship.
  6 Will life in the future be very different? / Will life be very different in the future?

2 **1** 'll / will; be
  2 won't / will not live
  3 won't / will not have
  4 'll / will turn
  5 'll / will use

3 **1** will
  2 won't
  3 might/may
  4 will
  5 might / may
  6 won't

4 **Possible answers**
  1 Gerry might watch *Cloud Thirteen* at the cinema.
  2 Gerry may walk to the cinema.

5 **1** Just come to my house and we**'ll** / we **will** have a great time together.
  2 Wear old clothes because we**'ll** / we **will** probably get paint on them.
  3 What time **will** you come?
  4 I**'ll** / I **will** arrive at eleven o'clock.
  5 I think that you**'ll** / you **will** only need £5 for the skatepark.

VOCABULARY

1

Verbs	Nouns	Adjectives
book	book	kind
picture	kind	
ring	letter	
watch	picture	
	ring	
	watch	

2 **1** kind; kind
  2 letters; letters
  3 book; booked / 'll book / 'm going to book
  4 watching; watch
  5 ring; ring
  6 picture; picture

READING

1 B

2 **1** B **2** B **3** C **4** A **5** C **6** B

3 **1** B, D
  2 B, D, G

LISTENING

1 **1** B **2** C **3** C **4** A **5** B

🔊 **1** You will hear two friends talking on the way to school. What did the girl forget to do before she left home?
08

Girl: Oh no! I forgot to do something before I came out.

Boy: What? You've got all your school things – I saw you get them.

Girl: I know but the air conditioning's still on. I needed it while I washed the plates and cups from breakfast.

Boy: Oh dear!

2 You will hear a girl talking about some train tickets. What is she explaining?

Girl: When Mum and I were at Grandma's, we needed train tickets to come home. Mum usually gets them online, but Grandma hasn't got access to the internet at her cottage and I couldn't use my phone there. Mum tried to use Grandma's phone, but the train company number was always busy. So she went to the station and got them there.

3 You will hear a boy and his mother talking about tomorrow evening. Who does the boy need to talk to?

Mum: Michael don't forget it's your brother Sam's birthday tomorrow, so you can't go to basketball practice in the evening.

Michael: Oh. The other players think I'm playing. Are we going to Sam's house?

Mum: I told you yesterday - we're going to the Castle Restaurant. We booked it weeks ago!

Michael:	All right, Mum, I'm still coming. I just need to phone one of my teammates this evening and make other arrangements.
4	You will hear a boy telling his friend about breaking something. What is he worried about?
Boy:	I broke my grandmother's old wooden box yesterday, I'm really annoyed. I stood on it to get a book from a high shelf.
Girl:	Oh no. What did your mum say?
Boy:	She doesn't know yet! She won't be angry, but Grandma will be really sad about it. I don't know how I'm going to tell her!
Girl:	Perhaps you can repair it.
Boy:	I don't think so.
5	You will hear a woman talking about the weather. How will it change next week?
Woman:	The weather will change a lot next week. The good news is that there'll be some rain for the first time in three weeks! And the wind we're having this week will stop late this evening or early in the morning – I know a lot of you will be delighted about that. Temperatures will stay the same.

WRITING

1 **1** D **2** A **3** B **4** C

2 Students' own answers

UNIT 9 Sports, games and activities

VOCABULARY

1 **1** A **2** B **3** B **4** B **5** B **6** A **7** A

2 **1** g **2** h **3** c **4** f **5** d **6** a **7** e **8** b

GRAMMAR

1 **1** b **2** c **3** a

2 **1** don't have to

  2 mustn't

  3 must

  4 must

  5 mustn't

  6 don't have to

3 **1** You **don't have** to bring anything because the teacher will give you what you need.

  2 correct

  3 correct

  4 Tomorrow night you must come to my house. To get to my house you **have** to take the number 15 bus.

  5 You don't **have to** bring anything because I've got everything.

4 **James**

  1 He didn't have to eat everything on his plate at meal times.

  2 He had to go to bed at 7.30.

  3 He didn't have to wear his brother's old clothes.

  4 He had to walk to school with one of his parents.

  You

  Students' own answers

VOCABULARY

1 **1** fans **2** champions **3** tournaments **4** take part **5** prize **6** professional

2 **1** swimmer **2** singer **3** skier **4** runner **5** photographer **6** golfer

READING

1 a professional gamer

2 **1** B **2** B **3** B **4** A **5** A

LISTENING

1 **1** ✗ **2** ✗ **3** ✓ **4** ✓

2 **1** Wednesday(s)

  2 five / 5

  3 first

  4 (professional) golfer

  5 walk

  6 glove

  7 email

🔊 09 Matt:	Emma, you can come to my golf class now. It's on a different day.
Emma:	So it's not on Tuesdays now?
Matt:	That's right, it's on Wednesdays at seven o'clock every week. I know you're busy on Tuesdays.
Emma:	Oh great. I'd like to try a class.
Matt:	Ah, but you can't book just one class. You have to book five of them.
Emma:	That's OK. How much is it?
Matt:	We pay £40 for five lessons, but you'll get your first class free. So you'll pay £32 if you come.
Emma:	Right. So who's the teacher?
Matt:	She's called Tanya Maple. She was a professional golfer when she was younger, and she's a great teacher.
Emma:	And she teaches at the sports centre?
Matt:	She does. We practise at a special area at the back of the sports centre.
Emma:	So I can walk there really easily from home.
Matt:	Yes, I know, it's perfect for you. I usually go on my bike.
Emma:	What do I have to wear for the classes?
Matt:	No special clothes really – I play in shorts and a T-shirt. The only thing I bought for the class is a special glove for playing golf. It really helps.
Emma:	And what about the clubs and the balls?
Matt:	We use kit from the sports centre.
Emma:	OK. How do I join the class? Do I have to fill in a form online before I go to it?
Matt:	I think you can, but I just emailed the teacher, and she said 'Come to a class'.
Emma:	OK, I'll do the same. Have you got her address?
Matt:	It's on my phone. I'll send it to you.
Emma:	Great. Thanks, Matt.

WRITING

1 **1** no **2** *I don't agree

2 Students' own answers

UNIT 10 Useful websites

VOCABULARY

1 **1** neighbours **2** member **3** guests **4** contacts
 5 relatives **6** classmate

2 **1** B **2** B **3** A **4** A **5** B **6** B **7** B **8** B **9** A

GRAMMAR

1 **1** doing **2** playing **3** to learn **4** to buy **5** studying
 6 Sleeping

2 **1** c **2** d **3** e **4** b **5** a

3 **1** to live
 2 seeing
 3 to study
 4 losing
 5 to go
 6 Listening

4 **1** a **2** a **3** b **4** b **5** a

VOCABULARY

1 **1** link
 2 web
 3 site
 4 blog
 5 menu
 6 message boards

2

x	s	u	p	l	o	a	d	r
p	a	z	n	t	g	k	q	e
o	v	q	i	w	v	m	p	c
s	e	s	e	a	r	c	h	o
t	r	a	n	w	v	m	d	r
r	d	o	w	n	l	o	a	d

3 **1** save
 2 uploaded
 3 to post / posting
 4 downloaded
 5 recorded
 6 search

READING

1 Music videos and funny videos of children and pets.

2 **1** C **2** A **3** B **4** C **5** A **6** B

3 **1** Music **2** December **3** Harry **4** grandfather **5** 2017

LISTENING

1 **1** S **2** C **3** C **4** C **5** S

2 **1** ✗ **2** ✓ **3** ✗ **4** ✓ **5** ✓ **6** ✗

🔊 10

Cathy: What are you listening to, Stuart?

Stuart: It's a band I didn't know. I'm listening to them for the first time now. They're good.

Cathy: Oh, is it music from the website you told me about the other day?

Stuart: No, it's a different one. I'll show you the site on my phone. Look, it only has very modern music. There's no music on the site from before 2015.

Cathy: Oh, yes. Looks interesting. Is it an American website?

Stuart: Actually it's Australian but it has music on it from all over the world. I like it – it's really fun.

Cathy: So can you download songs from it for free?

Stuart: At the moment I can, but only for the first 30 days I use the site. After that, I have to pay £18 a month.

Cathy: Oh dear, that's not cheap. So do you like a lot of the music on there?

Stuart: Quite a lot of it, yes. Some of it's a bit crazy.

Cathy: Do you know how many songs there are on there?

Stuart: It's got about ten thousand – sorry, a hundred thousand – songs to choose from. Some are videos and some of them you can only listen to.

Cathy: Wow! That's a lot. Can you upload songs as well?

Stuart: That's the best thing. All the songs on the site are by normal people, not pop stars or big bands.

Cathy: Really? Well what about our band, then? We could record one of our songs and put it up there.

Stuart: We could. But we need to practise a lot first.

WRITING

1 **1** watch videos on video-sharing websites
 2 search for information
 3 upload videos / photos, etc.

2 Students' own answers

3 Students' own answers

UNIT 11 City living

VOCABULARY

1 **1** yes **2** yes **3** yes **4** no **5** no **6** yes **7** no

2 **1** f **2** d **3** e **4** a **5** b **6** c **7** g

GRAMMAR

1 **1** the; the; a
 2 the; the; both
 3 all; Another
 4 a; other

2 **1** Amsterdam **2** New York **3** London **4** Moscow

3 **1** I live on ~~the~~ Black Street at Number 10.
 2 correct
 3 correct
 4 We had **a** sports competition today.
 5 I want a penfriend in **another** country.

4 **1** the **2** a **3** the **4** a **5** both **6** All **7** Both **8** the

VOCABULARY

1 **1** luggage **2** wildlife **3** information **4** money **5** staff
6 jewellery **7** furniture

2 **1** projects; homework

2 meal; food

3 electricity; batteries

4 car; traffic

5 news; articles

READING

1 stadium, palace, café, art gallery, skyscraper, museum

2 **1** B **2** C **3** A **4** B **5** A **6** B

LISTENING

1 **1** ✓ **2** ✗ **3** ✗ **4** ✓

2 **1** meal **2** *Honey* **3** 45 **4** five **5** restaurant **6** under
7 young adults

Man: There's more than just sporting events happening at the Harlake Stadium this January. It's going to be a really exciting month. We start with our New Year's family party on the 5th of January in the stadium's events venue. The cost of the party is just £50 for a family of four, and there will be a fantastic lunch for every member of your family, as well as live bands, dancing and games. It's the city's biggest party – don't miss it!

On the evening of the 11th of January, we've got the top band Money Talks, playing songs from their number one album, *Honey.* Tickets are £45 when you buy them online, or only £43 when you buy them at the stadium ticket office at least a week before the concert.

In the afternoon of the 14th of January, Professor Clinton Richards will be here to talk about his wonderful new book, *Know Everything.* Tickets for this are £35. And the first five people to buy one will be able to meet Professor Richards after the talk, in the stadium's new restaurant – above the cinema.

From the 18th until the 21st of January, there's an amazing tennis tournament. This will be for players aged under 16 on the 18th and 19th, and then for young adults – including some professional players – on the 20th and 21st – the tennis stars of the future! Tickets sell quickly for this as they are only £10 every day of the tournament, so book your tickets soon.

We really hope to see you at the Harlake Stadium this January!

WRITING

1 **1** the one to Mr Greg

2 Dear; surname; could you; I'm afraid; did not (also use of email rather than message)

3 Hi; can; didn't; thanks

UNIT 12 Films

VOCABULARY

1 **1** action

2 animated

3 adventure

4 musical

5 science-fiction

2 **1** musical

2 animated film

3 science-fiction

4 thriller

5 drama

3 **1** A, C **2** C **3** A, C **4** C **5** B **6** C **7** C

GRAMMAR

1 **1** which **2** who **3** who **4** who **5** which **6** which

2 **1** The Arts Centre cinema has large seats which are really comfortable.

2 I don't like films that are longer than three hours.

3 The stars of action films are usually actors who are very fit.

4 Scarlett Johansson is the actor that plays Black Widow in the Avengers films.

5 My oldest brother is the only person in our family who likes horror films.

Sentence 3 matches the photo.

3 **1** b **2** b **3** a **4** b **5** a

VOCABULARY

1 **1** when **2** where **3** so **4** while **5** If **6** that **7** or

2 **1** that; if

2 when; while

3 when; where

4 that; when

5 if; when

6 so; or

READING

1 two

2 **1** F **2** W **3** F **4** F **5** M **6** W **7** M

LISTENING

1 **1** C **2** B **3** A **4** B **5** C

You will hear Marina telling her friend Lucas about a film she is going to make.

Lucas: Marina – are you coming with me and Sarah to the cinema on Friday evening?

Marina: I'm busy I'm afraid, Lucas.

Lucas: Oh – are you going out with friends from school?

Marina: That's right, from my film class at school. We're planning a film for a competition. It's about a large family.

Lucas: OK. So is it a film competition just for school students?

Marina: That's right. Schools from around the country are entering, so it's really important. If we win this one, our school club can enter an international competition.

Lucas:	So what kind of film is it? Another comedy, like your last one?
Marina:	Actually, it's going to be a thriller. This week, we're planning the music, and deciding how it might end.
Lucas:	So when's the competition?
Marina:	We have to send our film to the competition office before the 12th of June, and they'll post the winner on their website on the 19th of June. Then, they'll show the winning film at a film festival on the 30th of June.
Lucas:	Right. So where is the film festival? Is it at the cinema in town?
Marina:	Not this year. It's at the new film school. It's not far from the Arts Centre.
Lucas:	Great! I can't wait!

WRITING

1 **1** the town library
  2 4 pm
  3 *Leave before midnight*
  4 the first Monday of every month / Monday(s)
  5 thriller
  6 5.30 pm
  7 exciting

2 **1** in Art Room 3
  2 at 2.30 pm
  3 *Spirited Away*
  4 on the first Friday of every month
  5 an animated film
  6 at 4 pm

3 Students' own answers

UNIT 13 Life experiences

VOCABULARY

1 **1** B and C **2** B and C **3** C **4** C **5** A **6** B and C **7** A and C
8 B **9** A and B

2 Students' own answers

GRAMMAR

1 **1** listened **2** watched **3** visited **4** camped **5** played
6 explored

2 **1** Have you ever kayaked down a river?
  2 Have you ever picked an orange from a tree?
  3 Have you ever played the drums?
  4 Have you ever watched a really scary film?
  5 Have you ever climbed a mountain?
  6 Have you ever camped next to a river or lake?
  7 Have you ever tried horse riding?

3 Students' own answers

4 **1** correct
  2 I have to tell you that this **has** never happened before.
  3 correct
  4 Ayrton Senna was the best Formula 1 driver that **has** ever lived.
  5 I really like *Call of Juarez*. It's the best video game that I have **ever** played.

VOCABULARY

1

s	e	d	g	r	o	w	n	d
t	a	o	l	h	a	d	b	i
e	a	t	e	n	b	s	e	g
p	g	r	s	t	r	w	e	r
m	i	n	t	k	o	s	n	i
e	d	x	v	m	k	e	s	d
t	m	a	d	e	e	n	l	d
b	w	c	m	u	n	t	e	e
l	s	w	u	m	n	c	p	n
f	l	o	w	n	p	f	t	t

2 **1** D **2** B **3** E **4** A **5** C

3 **1** Have you ever flown ...? (Students' own answers)
  2 Have you ever eaten ...? (Students' own answers)
  3 Have you ever swum ...? (Students' own answers)
  4 Have you ever ridden ...? (Students' own answers)
  5 Have you ever broken ...? (Students' own answers)

READING

1 Students' own answers

2 **1** am / 'm **2** Have **3** be **4** was **5** and **6** never / not

3 **1** B **2** A **3** A **4** A and B **5** B **6** A **7** A and B

LISTENING

1 B, C, E

2 **1** ✗ **2** ✗ **3** ✓ **4** ✓ **5** ✗ **6** ✓ **7** ✓

🔊 13

Rick:	I'm Rick Thomas and with me on *Active World* today is the amazing climber, Agnes Jay. Welcome, Agnes.
Agnes:	Hi. Thanks, Rick.
Rick:	Now Agnes, this is the first time you've ever been on a TV show. Is that right?
Agnes:	That's right, Rick. I've never been on TV before. It's a bit scary for me!
Rick:	Scary? But you're a climber, Agnes – you're not scared of anything, are you? But actually, have you ever been scared when climbing?
Agnes:	I always get excited, but not scared. You can't let yourself feel like that, because you always need to think really clearly when you're climbing.
Rick:	Yes, I see. Now, you usually climb with your husband, George, who's also a great climber. And you have a son who's six years old. Does he climb?
Agnes:	Yes. His name's Billy. He loves climbing smaller rocks and the wall at our local sports centre.
Rick:	You and your husband often climb in other countries. Has Billy ever been on a climbing trip with you?
Agnes:	No, he stays with my mum, his grandma. He might come with us when he's a bit older.
Rick:	Right. So, Agnes. What's the highest rock you've ever climbed?
Agnes:	Er, well, I've climbed 300 metres in a day. That's the most, I think.
Rick:	Wow! That's amazing.

Agnes: Yes, I was really tired after that!

Rick: Have you ever had a more 'normal' job?

Agnes: Well yes, I worked in a museum once, and I've also worked in a sports centre. But I much prefer being a climber.

Rick: Well thanks, Agnes. Let's look at some videos of you climbing …

WRITING

1 **1** *YOLO!*

  2 last month

  3 on the magazine's website

  4 6,126

  5 Students' own answers

2 **1** 6,126

  2 flown somewhere for a school trip

  3 eaten something in a classroom

  4 grown plants at school

  5 ridden a bike to school

UNIT 14 Spending money

VOCABULARY

1 **1** department store

  2 a shoe shop

  3 a clothes shop

  4 a market

  5 a supermarket

  6 a bookshop

  7 a café

  8 a chemist

  9 a sweet shop

2 **1** a video game

  2 a map

  3 cameras

  4 trousers

  5 a piano

  6 tomatoes

  7 jewellery

  8 grapes

GRAMMAR

1 **1** yet **2** just **3** already **4** just **5** yet **6** already

2 **1** yet **2** yet **3** already **4** yet **5** yet **6** already

3 **1** She's just played a tennis match.

  2 He's just got home.

  3 We've just seen a concert.

  4 They've just left a shoe shop.

4 **1** correct

  2 Yesterday, I left a book at your house and I need it because I **haven't done** my homework yet.

  3 I**'ve** just watched the football game with my family. It was really fun.

  4 correct

  5 I'm in England. I haven't seen much **yet** because it's rained every day.

VOCABULARY

1 **1** h **2** i **3** d **4** a **5** f **6** l **7** k **8** c **9** b **10** e **11** g **12** j

2 **1** ml / millilitres

  2 £

  3 euros

  4 km / kilometre

  5 c / cents

3 **1** pair **2** variety **3** set **4** slices

READING

1 B

2 **1** C **2** G **3** B **4** A **5** D **6** E **7** F

LISTENING

1 A, C, D, E

2 **1** trainers

  2 department store

  3 25 / twenty-five

  4 grandad

  5 month

  6 brother

  7 never / not

🔊 **14**

Marie: Hey, Harry. So how was your shopping trip last weekend?

Harry: It was great thanks, Marie. It's a shame you couldn't come.

Marie: Yes, I know. Did you get the jeans that you wanted?

Harry: Well, I looked in hundreds of shops but I couldn't find any nice ones, so I bought some trainers instead.

Marie: Right. Did you get them at that sports shop you always go to?

Harry: They didn't have my size, so I got them at that department store.

Marie: What, that one by the river?

Harry: Yes, Marley's. The trainers I got were quite cheap there, too. Only 25 euros. Most of the other trainers in the shop were 50 euros or more.

Marie: That's good. Did you buy them with your pocket money from your parents?

Harry: Actually, it was money that my grandad gave me – I've cleaned his car three times this month and he paid me for doing it.

Marie: Well done, Harry! I wanted to go shopping today, but I haven't got any money – I've spent it all.

Harry: Oh? What have you bought?

Marie: A ticket for the football match on Saturday.

Harry: Oh great. Have you been to a match before?

Marie: Of course! I go about once a month with my brother.

Harry: OK! I didn't know you liked football. We've never talked about it before.

Marie: I like it. Have you ever been, Harry?

Harry: Never. And I've got no money now, so I can't go this week.

Marie: Perhaps you can do some more jobs for your grandad and then come with us next time?

Harry: Yeah, I'd like to.

WRITING

1   1 What time shall we meet?
    2 Let's go home.
    3 I need to buy something from the market.
    4 I saw **M**r Smith yesterday.

2   1 **D**ear **V**ictor,
    I can't wait to see *Quiet Lake*. **I**t sounds really good. **S**hall we meet at the cinema at six**?**
    See you soon**,**
    Ivan

    2 **H**i **P**aloma,
    On Friday**,** my train will arrive in the town centre at ten o'clock. **I**'d like to meet you at the café in **M**arket **S**treet. **I** need to go to the chemist first to get a new hairbrush.
    Love**,**
    Stella

3   1 ten o'clock
    2 the café in Market Street
    3 buy a hairbrush from the chemist

UNIT 15 Free time

VOCABULARY

1   1 c 2 d 3 a 4 b 5 i 6 e 7 h 8 g 9 f

2   1 spending 2 chatting 3 listening 4 making
    5 photography 6 Cooking 7 going 8 playing
    9 watching 10 reading 11 playing 12 collecting
    13 acting 14 singing 15 going

GRAMMAR

1   1 for 2 since 3 since 4 for 5 for 6 since

2   1 b 2 b 3 a 4 a 5 b

3   1 I've had a headache since 4 pm.
    2 Josh has had that camera for four months.
    3 Aysha and Faruk have been out with their friends for five hours.
    4 Davina's only played the violin since July.
    5 You haven't phoned me for a week.
    6 The rain hasn't stopped since last night / since 7 pm last night / yesterday.

4   1 for 2 for 3 has 4 since 5 have 6 since 7 has 8 since

VOCABULARY

1   1 B 2 C 3 C 4 A 5 C

2   Students' own answers

READING

1   making shoes

2   1 C 2 B 3 C 4 A 5 B

LISTENING

1   C

2   1 ✗ 2 ✗ 3 ✓ 4 ✗ 5 ✗ 6 ✗ 7 ✓ 8 ✓ 9 ✓ 10 ✗

🔊 **Dilek:**   Hi, I'm Dilek and I come from Edirne in Turkey. I've been a dancer for about six years – I started when I was ten. I do other free-time activities, but I like this one best. I dance in a group which usually meets once a week, but sometimes we meet twice or more in a week if we need to practise for a competition. We haven't won any competitions yet, but that doesn't matter. As well as dancing in competitions all around Turkey, our group dances at weddings and birthday parties. We dance to Turkish folk music, which I love. When we practise, we wear normal jeans and T-shirts, but at parties and competitions we wear special dresses and shoes.

Burak: Hi, I'm Burak and I'm from Konya, in Turkey. The free-time activity I enjoy most is playing a wooden Turkish musical instrument called an oud – that's spelt O-U-D. It's very difficult to play, but it makes a beautiful sound. It's really good to play for sad songs! I've played it since I was six. My dad plays it too, and he taught me. I enjoyed learning because Dad likes the instrument so much and plays so well. He plays in concerts and in a restaurant in my town, and sometimes I play with him. I learned to play the guitar as well, but I prefer playing the oud. I play it every night and I'd like to be a professional oud player when I'm older.

WRITING

1   1 D 2 B 3 E 4 A 5 C

2   Students' own answers

UNIT 16 Languages of the world

VOCABULARY

1   1 c 2 f 3 d 4 g 5 a 6 h 7 b 8 e

2   1 articles 2 topics 3 mistakes 4 exercises 5 spell 6 list
    7 guess 8 look it up 9 translate

GRAMMAR

1   1 Have 2 Did 3 Has 4 did 5 have

2   Students' own answers

3   1 I've / I have never met anyone from the USA.
    2 We went to Cyprus last year.
    3 He studied Chinese and Arabic two years ago.
    4 She watched a great cricket match on Saturday.
    5 He hasn't / has not won any chess competitions since 2009.
    6 We didn't see my grandparents last month.
    7 I've / I have never eaten Mexican food.

4   Hi David,
    It's been ages since I (1) <u>haven't</u> heard from you! I'm in London now. I'm studying at the Camden School of English! I (2) <u>met</u> lots of people from all over the world here. The teacher is good and the textbook she gave us at the beginning of the course is very interesting. I (3) <u>learn</u> a lot of things from it since then.
    Every day, after class, we go into the centre of London. I've already done lots of things! I (4) <u>'ve</u> the British Museum. It was great! I (5) <u>'ve went</u> shopping in a market yesterday and bought some clothes. I (6) <u>'ve bought</u> three T-shirts in the market because they were very cheap and they look really nice. They (7) <u>have only cost</u> me £20.
    Right, I must go now. I've got to study for an English test tomorrow – it's on the present perfect.
    Love,
    Danuta

5 **1** 've / have

  2 've met / have met

  3 've learned / have learned

  4 've been to / have been to / 've visited / have visited

  5 went

  6 bought

  7 ~~have~~ only cost

VOCABULARY

1 **1** c **2** d **3** a **4** b

2 **1** 7,100 **2** 4,000,000,000 **3** 50,000,000

3 Students' own answers

READING

1 **1** 3 **2** 1 and 2 **3** 1 and 2 **4** 1

2 **1** g **2** c **3** a **4** f **5** e **6** d **7** b

LISTENING

1 **1** A **2** B **3** C **4** C **5** B

🔊 16 **1** You will hear a girl called Lucy talking to her mum. What are they discussing?

Mum: I'm working a bit later than usual today, Lucy.

Lucy: OK, Mum. But can we have dinner before five thirty? I've got basketball practice.

Mum: But I won't finish work until five thirty.

Lucy: Never mind, I'll just have a snack before I go out, then.

Mum: OK. You can have a proper meal when you get back.

2 You will hear a girl called Sam talking to her friend about playing musical instruments. Why does she prefer the piano to the guitar?

Boy: You play the piano well, Sam.

Sam: Thanks, I like it much more than the guitar. I don't play that now. All my friends play guitar so it seems really boring. And it's possible to play lots of different types of music on the piano. I can't yet, though, I'm still learning. But hopefully I will in the future.

3 You will hear a girl talking about her Chinese homework. What is she explaining?

Girl: We've got three exercises for our Chinese homework: one's a listening exercise, one's writing and one's reading. I only had an hour for homework this evening and I did the easiest one first – that, for me, is reading. I love writing Chinese but it takes a lot of time and effort. I'll have to do that tomorrow, and I'll do the listening exercise then as well.

4 You will hear a boy talking about his English lesson today. What does he say about it?

Boy: I had to read a long text in my English lesson today and there were lots of words in it that I didn't understand, so I couldn't answer any of the questions about it. I had to ask my teacher the meanings of the words because I didn't have my dictionary with me. We're not allowed to use the internet in class so I couldn't look them up online.

5 You will hear a girl called Sophie talking to a friend about an article she read. What was the topic of the article?

Boy: Did you go to the gym at lunchtime?

Sophie: No, I read an interesting article in a magazine. It was about learning languages.

Boy: Oh yes?

Sophie: Yes, a man who knows 52 languages wrote it. He was saying he thinks children should learn more languages at school because it really helps you – it makes you more intelligent!

Boy: Really?

WRITING

1 My name is **C**arys and I am from **W**ales, which is a country in the **UK** (the **U**nited **K**ingdom of **G**reat **B**ritain and **N**orthern **I**reland). The **UK** is in **E**urope. **W**ales has two languages: **W**elsh and **E**nglish. **M**ost people in **W**ales speak **E**nglish, but many also speak **W**elsh. At home I speak **E**nglish because my parents are from **S**cotland. I learn **W**elsh at school. I also learn **S**panish and **F**rench at school.

2 Students' own answers

3 Students' own answers

UNIT 17 Staying healthy

VOCABULARY

1 **1** blood **2** back **3** brain **4** heart **5** tongue **6** thumb **7** finger **8** ankle **9** neck **10** stomach

2 **1** ear **2** brain **3** stomach **4** heart **5** brain **6** back

3 **1** ears **2** fingers **3** Blood **4** stomach **5** brains **6** neck **7** back **8** toes **9** heart **10** ankle

GRAMMAR

1 **1** d **2** g **3** b **4** f **5** h **6** c **7** e **8** a

2 **1** himself **2** yourself **3** ourselves **4** themselves **5** herself **6** myself

3 **1** herself **2** yourself **3** yourselves **4** himself **5** ourselves **6** myself **7** themselves **8** itself

4 **1** correct

  2 Yesterday I went to buy **myself** some clothes.

  3 I'm so happy that I'm coming to your house tomorrow. We'll enjoy **ourselves**.

  4 You take care of **yourself**.

  5 correct

VOCABULARY

1 **Across**

  2 worried **5** unhappy **6** surprised **8** lonely **10** friendly

  Down

  1 confident **3** embarrassed **4** upset **7** angry **9** lazy

READING

1 **1** school work

  2 staying healthy

  3 friends

  4 sport

  5 family

2 **1** ✓ **2** ✗ **3** ✗ **4** ✓ **5** ✓

LISTENING

1 **1** B **2** A **3** B **4** C **5** A

1   How much did Monica pay for her keyboard?

Boy: You play your keyboard well, Monica. Do keyboards cost a lot of money?

Monica: My friend William bought this one for £450 a few years ago. He sold it to me for £120 last month.

Boy: That's still a lot of money.

Monica: Yes. I had £90 from my job in my uncle's café and Mum gave me some pocket money.

2   What time will the football match finish?

Mum: I'll be at the sports field at five o'clock to pick you up after the match, Mark.

Mark: That's too late, Mum. It ends at quarter past four today.

Mum: What about quarter to five, then?

Mark: Yes, that's better. Thirty minutes is enough time to have a shower and get changed. Thanks.

3   When is the history test?

Girl: I need to study for next week – the history test's on Wednesday, isn't it?

Boy: We've got a geography test on Wednesday, but not a history test.

Girl: Oh, really? When is it then? On Tuesday?

Boy: That's right. And it's maths next Monday morning, OK?

4   Where is the girl's purse?

Girl: Have you seen my purse, Mum? I need to take it to school.

Mum: Is it on the sofa? You often leave it there.

Girl: I've looked there. Oh, here it is: under the chair!

Mum: Really? Why don't you keep it in your bag?

5   What is the girl's father doing now?

Girl: Where's Dad, Tom? Has he already gone to the office?

Tom: Not yet. He's in the garden cutting the grass. Why?

Girl: I'd like him to fix my computer. It's stopped working again.

Tom: Well, he won't have time to do that now.

WRITING

1 **1** ✗ **2** ✗ **3** ✓ **4** ✗ **5** ✓

2 **Possible answers**

A good advice – your brain works better after a rest

B bad advice – in this situation, studying even more could make him more stressed

C good advice – exercise helps you feel better and sleep better; working with other people can help you study more effectively

3 Students' own answers

UNIT 18 From cover to cover

VOCABULARY

1 **1** pick it up
   2 find out
   3 take it back
   4 bring back
   5 put the food down

2 **1** take out
   2 pick; up, put; back
   3 bring; back
   4 take; back
   5 give / bring; back
   6 find out

GRAMMAR

1 **1** rains
   2 don't / do not like
   3 get
   4 works
   5 'll be / will be
   6 won't see
   7 will feel / 'll feel
   8 will go / 'll go
   9 eat

2 **1** If I don't finish my project, I won't come to the cinema with you.
   2 We'll get fitter if we do more exercise each week.
   3 She'll learn Portuguese if she moves to Brazil.
   4 They'll be late for the dentist if they don't leave now.
   5 If we don't win the match on Saturday, we'll be very upset.
   6 If he works hard, he'll pass his Russian exam.

3 **1** If you come too, you'**ll** love it.
   2 I think it **will** be OK if we meet at the park at ten o'clock in the morning.
   3 I will bring some banana pancake for you if my mum **makes** it for me.
   4 If you don't have any, I'**ll** give you some.
   5 If you can visit Vietnam, I'll **take** you to Vũng Tàu and lots of beautiful places.

VOCABULARY

1 **1** c **2** h **3** a **4** g **5** e **6** i **7** d **8** b **9** f

2 pick up, take back, take out, put down

3 **1** B **2** B **3** A **4** C **5** B **6** C

READING

1 Uri: mountain climbing books and magazines
   Ned: He doesn't read books.
   Mike: comics, science magazines, funny ebooks

2 **1** M **2** N **3** U **4** M **5** N **6** M **7** U

LISTENING

1 **1** B **2** A

2 **1** family **2** window **3** two/2 **4** title **5** first **6** Market

🔊 18

Man: Hello, can I help you?

Girl: Oh yes, please. I'm looking for a book about South Africa. Can you tell me where I can find one?

Man: Er, do you mean a guidebook about places to see when you're visiting South Africa?

Girl: That's right. Me and my family are going there next month.

Man: Lucky you! You'll find the books you want in the travel section.

Girl: Where's that, please?

Man: On those shelves over there, by the window. Do you see where I mean?

Girl: Yes, I can see. Thank you.

Man: You're welcome. And don't forget: if you buy two books today, you'll get one half price.

Girl: Oh yes. There *is* another book I might get, actually, for my sister. I'm not sure of the title, but it's by Jan Blair. Do you know what her newest book's called? It's about photography.

Man: No, but I can find out. Come over to the computer and I'll search for it.

Girl: OK, thanks.

Man: OK … Ah, Jan Blair's new book is called *Pictures for Life*.

Girl: Great, thanks for that. And where will I find it?

Man: Her books are up on the first floor, right next to the stairs up to the second floor.

Girl: OK. But if my sister's already bought the book herself, can I bring it back?

Man: Yes, you can bring it back here to Queen Street, or take it back to our larger shop on Market Street. You can do that any time in the next six weeks.

Girl: Great. Thanks for all your help.

Man: You're welcome.

WRITING

1 **1** 2 **2** 1 **3** 2 **4** 1 **5** 3 **6** 2 **7** 1

2 **Possible answer**

A boy was sitting on the sofa, trying to read a book. Unfortunately, his younger brother was hitting a drum and the noise the drum made was very loud. Then his little brother started playing a keyboard and the music was terrible! The boy stopped reading and put his book down on the sofa. The boy read a book to his little brother and the little brother was quiet so both boys were happy.

3 Students' own answers

UNIT 19 Different ingredients

VOCABULARY

1

p	r	e	p	a	r	e
h	t	s	f	d	q	c
a	l	n	k	d	u	o
d	b	o	i	l	p	v
r	g	e	d	z	m	e
y	b	a	k	e	i	r
f	i	l	l	m	x	b

2 **1** dry **2** boil **3** Cover **4** baked **5** mix **6** added
7 prepared **8** fill

GRAMMAR

1 **1** c **2** d **3** e **4** a **5** b

2 **1** Tomatoes are often grown inside.

2 Jam is made from fruit.

3 My favourite biscuits are covered with chocolate.

4 The cakes are put into a very hot oven.

5 The pasta is filled with cheese and mushrooms.

3 **1** Tea is drunk by people in most parts of the world.

2 Too much sugar is eaten by many children.

3 Pineapples are grown by farmers in warm countries.

4 Bread is made in different ways by people in different countries.

5 Coffee is drunk with ice by some people.

4 **1** The art lesson **starts** at ten o'clock.

2 You start off from your house, turn left, go straight on, take the second right, and you **arrive** there.

3 correct

4 You can get the number 12 bus. It **stops** near my house.

5 The class lasts two hours and we **spend/spent** the time painting.

VOCABULARY

1 **1** vegetable **2** round **3** meat **4** white **5** meat **6** orange
7 chips **8** soup

2

	Cooked in water	Cooked inside the cooker	Cooked on top of the cooker	Cooked in some oil or butter
a fried fish			✓	✓
a baked potato		✓		
a roast chicken		✓		✓
a grilled burger		✓		
a boiled egg	✓		✓	

3 **1** make **2** do **3** make **4** do **5** do **6** make **7** make **8** do
9 do **10** make

4 **1** doing **2** make **3** makes **4** do **5** made **6** made
7 doing **8** do **9** done **10** make

5 Students' own answers

READING

1 family life

2 1 am / 'm 2 the 3 with 4 of 5 and 6 There

3 1 E 2 B 3 D 4 C

Not needed: A

LISTENING

1 1 Thursday 2 6.45 3 20 4 Yardley 5 museum

🔊 **Narrator:** You will hear a boy telling his friend about
19 another friend's birthday meal.

Richard: Hi, Nina, it's Richard here. I'm phoning to let you
know the details about Jason's birthday meal.
Mum's booked us a table at Roberto's restaurant
– we all like eating there. As you know, Jason's
birthday is on Friday, but he's going away for
the weekend, so the meal will be on Thursday.
It will be dinner, so in the evening, of course.
We wanted to book for seven thirty, but we
could only get a table for earlier, at six forty-
five. I hope that's all right for you. Mum says it's
£20 each – that's for a starter, main course and
dessert. It's a special price for our group – three
courses usually cost £25. The address of the
restaurant is 74 Yardley Street. That's Y–A–R–D–
L–E–Y. It's the restaurant across the road from
the museum, and next to the theatre. Let me
know if you have any questions about any of
this. Bye.

WRITING

1 1 how about

   2 Why don't you

   3 could one of you

   4 I'm not sure about

   5 It's a good idea

2 Students' own answers

UNIT 20 Life changes

VOCABULARY

1 1 g 2 h 3 c 4 a 5 e 6 b 7 d 8 f

2 1 to change

   2 a change

   3 to change

   4 a change

   5 to change

   6 a change

   7 to change

   8 a change

3 1 N 2 V 3 V 4 N

GRAMMAR

1 1 a 2 a 3 b 4 a 5 b

2 1 was given

   2 was made

   3 were visited

   4 was completed

   5 was decorated

   6 were taken

   7 was built

3 1 The LoveYourBrain foundation was set up in 2014
by Adam and Kevin Pearce. / The LoveYourBrain
foundation was set up by Adam and Kevin Pearce in
2014.

   2 The new museum was opened last summer by the
president. / The new museum was opened by the
president last summer.

   3 The royal gardens were opened to the public in 2002.

   4 I was given this leather bag by my parents when I went
to high school. / I was given this leather bag when I
went to high school by my parents.

   5 These expensive paintings were given to our local
museum.

   6 Last year, the Empire State Building was visited by
over three million people.

4 1 My old shorts **were** eaten by my dog.

   2 I am selling my little home in the centre of town. It was
built 25 years ago.

   3 My birthday party was very enjoyable. All the people
danced / **were dancing**.

   4 My mobile is fantastic. It **was** made in Mexico.

   5 Do you know about my new flat? I **moved** there two
weeks ago.

VOCABULARY

1 1 You learn to talk.

   2 You go to high school.

   3 You start school.

   4 You learn to walk.

   5 You are born.

2 1 born 2 moved 3 change 4 became 5 take 6 work
7 travel 8 found 9 training

READING

1 1 c 2 a 3 d 4 b

2 1 e 2 h 3 c 4 f 5 a 6 d 7 g 8 b

LISTENING

1 1 C 2 C 3 A 4 B 5 C

🔊 **Narrator:** You will hear Robert talking to his friend Penny
20 about moving house.

Robert: I've got something to tell you, Penny. We're
moving house.

Penny: What, Robert? When?

Robert: In about three months, at the beginning of July.
I've got my exams in May so we can't go then,
and in June my sister has exams.

Penny: I can't believe it! Are you staying here in
Liverpool?

Robert: No, but the new house is in York – that's not too
far. You can come and visit me when you go to
see your grandma in Leeds.

Penny: Yes, I'd like that. I can't drive yet and it's a bit far
to get a lift. So it'll have to be the train. The bus
would probably take too long.

Robert: Yes, I suppose so.

Penny: Yes. So why are you moving? Is your dad
changing jobs again?

Robert: It's my mum this time. She's going to work at the
university. Dad will travel to his old job.

Penny: Oh, really? And how do you feel about moving, Robert?

Robert: Well, I'll miss my friends, but I'm not unhappy about it. Starting a new life is exciting. Meeting new people and things like that don't worry me.

Penny: You'll have to take lots of photos and send them to me.

Robert: I will!

WRITING

1 **1** d **2** a **3** b **4** c

2 Students' own answers

STUDENT'S BOOK AUDIOSCRIPTS

Unit 1, Student's Book page 13
07

Daniel: So, Grace. What activities are you going to choose for your Duke of Edinburgh?

Grace: I'm going to do art for my skill, of course! I love it and I really want to improve. And for my fitness, I'd like to do modern dance. I'm not sure about the volunteering yet. What about you, Daniel?

Daniel: For my fitness I'm going to do hockey. There's a club near my house, so I'm going to join that. And for my skill I'm going to learn the drums.

Grace: But Daniel, you're already learning the guitar and the keyboard. You can't learn three instruments, can you?

Daniel: Why not?

Finn: Excuse me! I'm Finn. I heard you talking about the DofE. I'm a new student at this school, and I'm going to do the award too.

Daniel: Oh, hi Finn. I'm Daniel and this is Grace.

Grace: Hi Finn. So, do you know what activities you're going to do?

Finn: No, not yet!

Grace: Well, what do you like doing in your free time?

Finn: I like computer games. And I'm quite good at chess.

Daniel: So, you could do chess for your skill. Look, it's here on the website.

Finn: Oh, brilliant!

Grace: And what about your fitness? What sports do you like?

Finn: That's the problem. I don't really like sports – well, I don't like team sports anyway.

Grace: You don't have to do a team sport. You can do something like dance. Or swimming? Or running?

Finn: Running sounds good! Oh, thanks guys – you're so helpful!

Daniel: No problem. But the volunteering's more difficult.

Finn: Well, why don't you both come round to my house at the weekend and we can talk about it then?

Daniel: OK! Where do you live?

Finn: Just around the corner from school. My address is 33 Alloway Road. That's A-DOUBLE L-O-W-A-Y.

Grace: Great. Got that. I need to ask my mum first and then I can let you know. Can I text or call you tonight? What's your number?

Finn: It's oh seven three four, double six seven, three seven eight.

Daniel: Thanks. And what's your email address? I can let you know if I find any good websites about volunteering.

Finn: Yes, f dot townsend 56 at facemail dot com.

Daniel: f dot ... How do you spell Townsend?

Finn: T-O-W-N-S-E-N-D

Daniel: OK ... f dot townsend fifty-six at facemail dot com. Thanks!

Unit 2, Student's Book page 17
15

You will hear Gina talking to her uncle about some photos of animals. Where did he take each photo?

Gina: You're really good at photography, Uncle Liam!

Liam: Thanks, Gina.

Gina: Did you take this picture of a lion when you were in Kenya last year?

Liam: That's right.

Gina: You're so lucky – I never go to exciting places like that! Did you take that picture of a monkey there too?

Liam: I took that in India. We were at a market and they were eating all the fruit.

Gina: I can't believe you took this picture of a snake! Weren't you afraid?

Liam: No, I was excited! Anyway, it's not dangerous, like the ones you see in Africa or India. I took that picture in England, when I was hiking.

Gina: Really?! Oh, and this is such a great picture of a penguin! Did you take it in New Zealand?

Liam: That was in South Africa. It's funny, isn't it?

Gina: Yes! This dolphin picture's good too.

Liam: Oh, yes. I saw dolphins in Mexico and Argentina, but I took that photo in Scotland.

Gina: Ah, and finally eh this amazing elephant. You took that in a forest in India, I suppose?

Liam: Er ... I took that in Mexico.

Gina: What??

Liam: In a zoo, Gina!

Gina: Oh, right!

Man: Today there are two walks you can join.

The first one takes you up to Mount Washburn.

The group leaves at 10 am from the hotel entrance, and we take you to the start of the walk by bus.

It's a two-hour walk to the top where we have lunch. We take sandwiches, fruit and cold drinks for you. It can be windy so take a light jacket. Oh, and don't forget your camera – there are amazing views of the Grand Canyon of Yellowstone and the Teton mountains in the distance. You can also see wild sheep and maybe foxes on the hills.

We should be back in the hotel at four o'clock when you can have a rest before joining everyone in the meeting room at five to watch a film about the geography of the area. This describes the volcanic rock formations and geysers.

Our second option is to visit the Mystic Falls area. The bus leaves at 9 am and takes about an hour to the start of the walk at 10. The first part of the route goes through forest to the camping area where we cook lunch. The hotel kitchen provides hamburgers and chicken for this.

We will then go through more open fields where there are many fine examples of wild flowers. Take a notebook so the guide can help you draw some of the beautiful plants in this area.

Then we visit Biscuit Basin, which is full of geysers and hot water pools. And finally, we go on to the Mystic Falls where you can see the 25-metre waterfall. There are also lots of animals to observe, especially the bison that are typical in Yellowstone Park.

You get back to the hotel about 6 pm and there is a meeting at 6.30 for everyone to share their pictures.

So, please let me know which trip you would like to do.

John: Hello. We arrived this morning. I'm a guest here with my mum and dad, and my sister.

Receptionist: Oh yes, I remember. John, isn't it? How can I help you?

John: It's our first time here in Moscow and we want to do some sightseeing this afternoon. Can you give me some information about things to see, please?

Receptionist: Yes, certainly. I can give you a small street map Em, here it is. We're here … and the tourist information centre is … here. It's not very far. You can easily get there on foot.

John: That's perfect. Thank you. Do you have a guidebook? My mum and dad like having a guidebook. My sister and I think guidebooks are boring – we think it's much more fun to use the internet to read about things to do in a city.

Receptionist: Yes, we have some guidebooks here. You have to pay for them, though.

John: OK, I'll tell Mum and Dad. Oh, and do you have a metro map?

Receptionist: Yes, look. It's on the other side of the street map. The best way to get around Moscow is by metro or by bus. You can get day tickets for both.

John: What about taxis? Aren't they quicker?

Receptionist: Taxis are OK, but they can be expensive and quite slow. There's always a lot of traffic, so they often take a long time!

John: Thank you. That's really useful information for mum and dad. Bye.

Receptionist: Goodbye … Oh, excuse me. You left your suitcase.

John: Pardon?

Receptionist: Isn't that your suitcase there on the floor?

John: No, that isn't mine. Mine's in our room. I saw a man here at the desk before me. He had lots of luggage. Perhaps it belongs to him. He went up in the lift.

Receptionist: Ah yes. I remember. I'll call his room. Thank you.

1   What is the number of Maria's house?

Boy: Excuse me, do you live on this street?

Maria: Yes, I do. It's the fifth house on the right. The white one.

Boy: Oh yes, I can see. It's really pretty. It's opposite ours. Is yours 15 then?

Maria: Yes, that's right, it is. And yours is 25?

2   Which is Jason's house?

Jason: When you come to my party on Saturday, Sally, you can see our new house.

Sally: Great. Is it much bigger than your old one?

Jason: Yes, it is. The living room's on the first floor and the bedrooms are on the ground floor.

Sally: Wow. I'd like to live on two floors. Our house has just one floor.

3   What time is Jenny going to leave school today?

Dad: Hi Jenny. You don't usually call me at ten past three. Is everything OK?

Jenny: Yes dad. I'm calling because I finish school at a different time today.

Dad: It's usually ten past four on Friday isn't it?

Jenny: No, dad, it's ten past four on *Thursday*! Please come at ten to four today, that's 20 minutes earlier than usual.

4   What colour does Ben want to paint his bedroom?

Girl: Hello, Ben. Are you going to help your dad paint your bedroom?

Ben: Yes. He prefers red, but I don't like that colour very much. I like blue.

Girl: Oh, I don't like blue. How about green? It's nice and bright.

Ben: I'm sorry. I don't agree! I don't like green bedrooms.

5   What is Sarah going to do this afternoon?

Tom: Hi Sarah, can we finish our homework project together this afternoon?

Sarah: Oh, sorry Tom, I can't. I'm going to make my mum's birthday cake after lunch.

Tom: Well, what about tomorrow then? I'm going to play football in the morning but I can come round after that.

Sarah: Great! See you then.

David: So, Jenny, what are we going to do for Martha's birthday this Saturday?

Jenny: We can have a surprise party. We did it last year and it was fun.

David: Maybe, but why not do something different? It's boring to do the same thing every year.

Jenny: I know! Martha likes films. We could go to the cinema.

David: Yes, but the cinema is expensive.

Jenny: You're right. Mmm. Do you like the idea of a picnic in a park?

David: Yes, I do. That's a great idea. I think it's going to be sunny on Saturday and I know Martha loves being outside. Do you think she wants to go to the park in the centre for her birthday?

Jenny: I'm sure that's the best place. So, we could buy some food and drink in the supermarket in the morning.

David: OK. And we can ask everyone to give us some money.

Jenny: But not Martha because it's *her* birthday. We can get bread, cheese and crisps.

David: We need to buy drinks as well. Do you think Martha likes orange or lemon?

Jenny: I'm not sure. What do you think is best?

David: Mmm, we can get lemon and orange, then everyone is happy.

Jenny: Excellent idea! So, who shall we invite?

David: I'll ask Martha. She can make a list, then I can send a text to her friends to invite them.

Jenny: Of course. Now we have to think of a present.

David: That's more difficult. What ideas have you got?

Jenny: I saw a fantastic T-shirt in the sports shop. Maybe she'll like that!

David: Great. We can go to the shop now.

1 What day does Antonio play football?

Anna: Hi Antonio. Do you want to come to the cinema this week? The new film *Tuesday's Child* is on.

Antonio: Hi Anna. Yes I'd love to see it. I'm not busy except for football practice.

Anna: That's Thursday, right? So, let's see the film on Friday.

Antonio: Great. Text me the time and we can meet there.

2 How much is a family ticket to the zoo today?

Man: Hello, we'd like to come to the zoo today.

Woman: Well, you're very lucky! Our family tickets are usually £28, but this week we have a special offer of £25.

Man: But we only paid £22 last year.

Woman: Yes, that's right. It's a bit more this year, but we have more animals.

3 What time does the girl's coach arrive?

Girl: Dad, can you pick me up from the coach station later?

Dad: Yes, sure. But I can't leave work until a quarter past three.

Girl: That's fine. I get in at five past three, but I've got some shopping to do, so let's meet at the coach station at half past three.

Dad: Perfect, see you later.

4 What is the number of Rosa's house?

Rosa: Hi Phil. Do you want to come to my house this evening to finish the geography project?

Phil: That's a good idea. Are you number 16 or 18 Green Street?

Rosa: We're on the other side of the road at 17. My friend lives at 16, and I don't know the people at 18.

Phil: Well it's a good thing I asked! See you later.

5 What did Marco buy for his bedroom?

Marco: I went shopping today. I wanted to get something for my bedroom.

Girl: Did you get some new posters?

Marco: The posters weren't very interesting, but I saw some great desk lamps. I got a white one.

Girl: Now all you need is a bookshelf for all your books!

Ava: And now it's time for 'What's new?' This week we have Ethan Grant, who's 13, joining us from Bali in Indonesia. Hi Ethan.

Ethan: Hi Ava.

Ava: So, Ethan, I read your blog. Could you tell us about it?

Ethan: Yes, it's called World Schooling.

Ava: Is that like homeschooling?

Ethan: OK, well, em basically, yes it is, but school isn't at home – it's … the world.

Ava: Right!! Tell us from the beginning.

Ethan: OK. That was two years ago. My sister, Ruth, and I were doing OK at school. Mum lost her job and Dad loved travelling, so one day our parents said to us, 'We're taking you out of school for a year and we're going to see the world'. Ruth and I thought it was a great idea.

Ava: A big change for your parents! What did your family and your neighbours think?

Ethan: They all thought mum and dad were mad!

Ava: So what happened next?

Ethan: Mum and dad planned things carefully. They sold the house and lots of their things. Then they bought a camper van and … we left.

Ava: So what about your schooling?

Ethan: Mum and dad taught us things each week – they got material off the internet – but the big thing about world schooling is that travelling is an education in itself. So many subjects connect when you are in a new place. You learn about the history of a place, its geography, its language or languages and you need maths when you are using the money. Ruth and I have been to lots of countries, met so many amazing people and learned so much about the world.

Ava: How long have you been in Bali?

Ethan: Actually, we've been here nearly a year. I wanted to go to school, so I asked if we could stay – I need exams to go to university. Mum and dad like it here in Bali, they've got a little hotel and I go to an international school. Perfect!

Ava: So do you like being at school again?

Ethan: Yes, I do, I've made lots of new friends. School work is fine – in fact, I worked much harder when I was travelling. Ruth's homeschooled but she's going to come to my school next year.

Ava: Thanks, Ethan. Good luck. Bye.

Ethan: Bye.

1

Cam: Hello. My name's Cam. Can I ask you a few questions about your favourite thing, a very special object?

Speaker 1: OK.

Cam: Right. Do you have a favourite thing?

Speaker 1: Yes, I do and I'm wearing them right now!

Cam: Oh, OK – your earrings?

Speaker 1: Yes, that's right!

Cam: Oh yes, I think they're great. They're made of silver right?

Speaker 1: Yes. Actually, they're not really mine. They belong to my mum, but she doesn't wear them.

Cam: Ah, so they were hers and now they're yours.

Speaker 1: You've got it!

2

Cam: Hello, my name's Cam. Can I ask you a few questions please?

Speaker 2: Yes sure. But, be quick. I'm in a hurry.

Cam: OK. I'm asking about people's favourite things. Can you tell me about yours?

Speaker 2: Mmm, I don't really have any. But my parents do. They've got lots.

Cam: OK! So what are theirs?

Speaker 2: Well, my dad's favourite thing's a little wooden elephant.

Cam: Wow. OK. Has it always been his?

Speaker 2: He bought it when he was a student, years ago. I don't know why he likes it so much.

Cam: OK, thank you.

3

Cam: Hello. My name's Cam. Can I ask you a few questions about your favourite thing?

Speaker 3: Yeah, sure.

Cam: OK, so, do you have a favourite thing?

Speaker 3: Yes. I can give you a list. There's my bike, my skateboard, my football kit, my new trainers …

Cam: OK, thanks. I meant one very special thing. What about your parents? Is there something of theirs that's very special to them?

Speaker 3: The birds!

Cam: What do you mean?

Speaker 3: When they got married, their friends made them lots of origami birds to bring them luck. They're made of coloured paper and they're everywhere in the house. I guess they're ours now.

Cam: Wow, that's unusual. Thanks.

You will hear Carmen talking to Murat about some things she has found in her grandparents' house. Who does each thing belong to?

Carmen: I'm looking for a small wooden clock. It belongs to my granddad, and he says I can paint it. I think it's in this box.

Murat: Let's have a look. Oh, here's a heavy old computer. Is that your grandma's?

Carmen: Actually, it's my aunt's. She doesn't use it any more, though.

Murat: And this old hat's cool! Ah, is it your mother's?

Carmen: That was a present from my mum to my uncle. He never liked it!

Murat: Ah, … look, a toy bear! It's really soft! Is this your baby cousin's?

Carmen: That's my brother's. My dad gave it to him when he was little.

Murat: Oh, and look at this painting!

Carmen: Ah, I painted that and I gave it to my dad when I was about eight. I don't know why it's here.

Murat: It's lovely! … And what's this? Oh, it's a colourful, cotton jacket! Is it yours?

Carmen: That thing? That's not mine! My aunt gave it to my grandma.

Murat: Well, the box is empty now. The clock isn't here.

Carmen: Oh no!

Murat: Eh, Carmen?

Carmen: Yes?

Murat: What's that on the wall?

Carmen: Huh? It's the clock! Thanks, Murat!

Aleesha: My school, Woodedge, is a comprehensive with 1,200 pupils. It's a multi-cultural, multi-ethnic school in London. That means we have people from lots of different backgrounds in our school. For example, I'm Asian, but in my class, there are people who are Afro-Caribbean, East European, African, and lots more. It's great because we learn about each other's cultures, festivals and languages – it's really interesting.

My school day begins at 8.35 and ends at 3 o'clock. We have six lessons a day. We also have PDT every day – that's personal development time. We often talk about what's in the news. We sometimes also talk about money – how to open a bank account and that sort of thing.

We have a break in the morning and a break at lunchtime. I eat in the school café every day. The food's quite nice. There's always a hot meal, like beef curry or roast chicken, or you can buy sandwiches. Our parents put money into a school account online for us and then we pay for our lunch with a card.

After school, we have lots of different clubs to choose from. This term I'm doing singing and badminton. Last term I did table tennis and drama club. They're good fun and we don't have to pay for them.

We've got Charity Day next Friday. It's always really good fun. We're all making things to bring to school and sell. I'm making cakes and my friend's making biscuits. I hope we sell a lot and make lots of money for Save the Children!

Tara: Hello?

Dan: Hi. Is that Tara?

Tara: Oh hi, Dan. How's it going? Guess what! I'm going on an adventure holiday next week.

Dan: Me too!

Tara: Oh! Mine's called International Adventure Week and it's in the Pyrenees, but not far from the sea. It's from 31st March to 7th April.

Dan: I'm going on the same one! Cool! How are you getting to the airport?

Tara: My parents are taking me there by car. Can you remember all the things we're doing next week?

Dan: No, but I've got some information here from the website. Um … Hang on … Here it is.

Tara: Great. So when are we going mountain biking and paddle boarding? They're my favourite!

Dan: That's on the 3rd April, … so that's Thursday. It says we're following bike paths through the mountains and then we're going paddle boarding.

Tara: Excellent! What about the other days?

Dan: Let me see. We're going hiking on Monday. We have to get up really early because we're getting on a bus at five o'clock in the morning! It's taking us to somewhere in the mountains and then we have to get back to the activity centre alone. I hope I can find my way back and I don't get lost.

Tara: Me too! And when are we going zip wiring? Is it Tuesday?

Dan: No, it's Wednesday. That looks amazing! It's so high!

Tara: And fast! When are we going sailing?

Dan: That's on Tuesday. But we aren't going sailing on the sea. We're going on a lake near the centre. After that we're going horse riding at the centre. It's a shame we aren't going camping.

Tara: I don't mind. I don't like camping.

Dan: And then there's kite surfing on Friday morning and a barbecue and a party in the evening. Everyone's doing something from their country – cooking food, playing music, things like that.

Tara: I'm taking my guitar, so I can play and sing.

Dan: Good idea! I'm not taking my keyboard with me next week – it's too big!

Tara: OK, I guess I'll see you at the airport next week!

Dan: OK, Tara. Bye.

You will hear a teacher telling students about an adventure holiday.

Teacher: Hello, everyone. I want to tell you about a new adventure holiday for this summer. It's called Across the Water and it's going to be really great! The holiday is from 28th July for a week. Yes, most holidays are in August, but ours is in July *and* August.

I think you're really going to like it because the group isn't too big. We have four rooms, so there is space for 16 students.

Last year's adventure holiday was beside the sea and everyone liked it. This year it's near a river. We're kayaking, zip wiring and even spending a few nights camping.

This holiday is £345 for the week and that includes everything. It's even cheaper than last year, when the price was £375!

Are you interested? Then tell your parents about the holiday and get them to call me on oh-five-three-seven-one two double five nine-four-six. See you there!

Jason: Hello, and welcome to 'Dream Home'. Today we're talking to Professor Suzie Franks about homes of the future. Welcome to the programme, Professor Franks.

Suzie: Thank you, Jason. I'm very pleased to be here. Please call me Suzie.

Jason: OK, Suzie. So, what do you think our homes will be like in the future?

Suzie: First of all, I think they'll be very different from today's homes. We already use technology a lot in our houses and we'll use it more and more in the future.

Jason: Can you give me an example?

Suzie: Sure. Well, today in the house of Microsoft boss Bill Gates, the temperature, music and lights change when different visitors go into a room.

Jason: That's amazing. Will we all be able to do this in our homes soon?

Suzie: Why not? We can already use our smartphones to turn washing machines on or off, but we'll also be able to change channels on TV or control tablets without touching anything. You won't have to use your hands to do it. And you'll even know when your bins are full without looking!

Jason: Will it work for the heating and the lights too?

Suzie: Yes, it will. For example, lights will come on when you step on the stairs.

Jason: Mmm, will furniture change very much, do you think?

Suzie: No, I don't think so. Seats, bookcases and things like that might not look very different. And you can't use a smartphone to talk to a table! But you may have a table or chest of drawers with a computer inside it, so you can look at your photos or play games.

Jason: So will our homes look more like ones we see in movies about the future?

Suzie: Yes, some of them definitely will.

Jason: And, finally, might our homes look different on the outside, too?

Suzie: Oh yes. Perhaps that'll be the biggest change. Some will be underwater, and some might even have grass on the roof. I'll put some pictures of the houses I'm talking about on the programme website. One of them has got an amazing barbecue in the garden.

Jason: Yes, sure. Er … excuse me, Suzie, but you can't use a phone in the studio.

Suzie: Oh sorry. I'm just looking in my fridge to see if I need to buy some food on the way home.

Jason: By smartphone?

Suzie: Yes. Of course.

1   You will hear two friends talking about technology. What do they think they will use in the future?

Boy: I've got a new smartwatch – look how cool it is!

Girl: Yes, but the screen is really small. What about smart glasses, have you heard of those?

Boy: Yes, but I don't think people use those very much.

Girl: You're right. I still like my smartphone best. I think that's what people will use most in the future.

Boy: Yes, I agree!

2   You will hear a teacher talking about an activity students are doing in class. What does she say?

Teacher: Listen please. You're still working on your projects and I know you would like to finish them for homework, but that isn't always the best thing. I'd prefer you do it in class together with your friends. We have some time tomorrow to finish it. We won't have the laptops, so you'll have to write by hand.

3   You will hear a boy talking about his shopping trip. What did he buy?

Boy: I tried on several pairs of trainers. I really liked the blue ones, but they didn't have my size. On the way to a café I stopped at the supermarket and got myself a computer magazine and sat in the park. After that, it started to rain, so I went home to eat.

4   You will hear a daughter talking to her father about a new computer he is buying for her. What does she like best about the computer?

Dad: What do you think about this laptop? It's nice and small.

Girl: That's good – my old one was quite heavy to carry around. But it looks like an old model.

Dad: It's not – it's the latest one, and it comes with all the software you need. But maybe you'd prefer one in a bright colour?

Girl: Yes, I'm not keen on black.

5   You will hear a boy talking to his mother about the weather for his holiday. What will the weather be like tomorrow?

Boy: Can you look up the weather on your phone for me? Will I need to pack sun cream?

Mum: No, you won't need that. But take some jumpers and a raincoat. It might rain a bit over the next few days.

Boy: What about tomorrow?

Mum: Let me see. It'll be cloudy, but it'll stay dry. No rain until the next day.

1

Jack: So, how are we going to get to Ben's house this afternoon?

Ollie: Well, I don't think we should walk. It's very far. What do you think, Mara?

Mara: There's a bus at three o'clock. And you, Jack? Do you agree?

Jack: Yes, the bus sounds good. OK Ollie?

Ollie: That's great. We'll get the bus.

2

Lenny: We have to think of a project for science. I think we should make a poster.

Karl: Well, I think we should do a presentation; we can use pictures from the internet.

Lenny: Maybe, or we could do both.

Poppy: Excuse me, can I say something? We can make a model to show the class.

Karl: Oh sorry, Poppy. We didn't ask you. That's a good idea, too!

3

Grandmother: Hello Archie, how are you? How's school? Are you getting good marks?

Archie: Weeell …

Grandmother: You must study hard. What do you want to study at university?

Archie: Hmm, I'm not sure … er. How are you, Granny?

Grandmother: Oh. Thank you for asking. I'm having problems with …

Teacher:	OK everyone, quiet please. Today we need to choose a country and an object for that country to put in a time capsule. I'd like you to get into groups and decide on one country and one object. Then we can compare ideas.
Josie:	Right. Mr Thompson wants us to choose a country. Let's choose Brazil. It's a very big country and I like their football team!
Sam:	Yes, we could put a football in the time capsule.
Dan:	Maybe, but a football is an object that's important in lots of different countries. It's not really special for only one country. Mmm. What about Russia? It's a big country too.
Josie:	That's a good idea. We studied some Russian history last term and it's an important country.
Sam/Dan:	Yeah/OK.
Laura:	Excuse me! Can I say something? I think Italy is best.
Dan:	Why?
Laura:	It's a beautiful country and it has delicious food.
Sam:	Oh, sorry Laura, we didn't ask you. I like your idea. It's good!
Laura:	Thanks Sam. What about you, Josie?
Josie:	Maybe. But what object can we choose from Italy? Dan, what's your opinion?
Dan:	Italy is famous for pizza. We can put a pizza in the time capsule.
Josie/Laura:	Oh no!
Josie:	Imagine the pizza in two years' time!
Sam/Laura:	Urgh/Yuk!
Dan:	OK, OK. So we need a country with a good object.
Sam:	Well, I like Dan's idea about Russia. You know they have those dolls. You can open them and there is another one inside. That's a good object.
Laura:	Yes, a Russian doll. I've got one in my bedroom we can use. It opens and there are five more dolls inside.
Dan:	That's fantastic! So, do we all agree?
Sam/Laura:	OK/I do.
Laura:	And you, Josie?
Josie:	Yes, OK. Mr Thompson, we're ready!

1	You will hear a teacher talking to students about a school trip. What do they need to bring?
Teacher:	OK class, it's the school trip to Bowland Forest tomorrow. We'll bring food and drink for lunch, but you may want to pack chocolate or crisps for the journey.
Girl:	What about torches, sir?
Teacher:	Don't bother. We won't be out in the dark. Wear comfortable trainers, and don't forget that you'll be carrying your backpacks. Please don't put too much in them!
2	You will hear a girl talking about her history homework. What does she say about it?
Girl:	Well, history's my favourite subject, as you know, Mum. It doesn't usually take me long to do the homework, but I left my history textbook at school, so I had to look up all the information online. It took hours! But you'll be pleased to hear that I did it all. I won't make that mistake again!
3	You will hear a woman talking to her son. What is she most unhappy about?
Mum:	Paul, you really need to have more than fruit before school. Also, I know it's good exercise to run for the bus, but one day you might not catch it! So from tomorrow you need to be out of bed earlier in the morning and then you'll have enough time.
4	You will hear two friends talking about a visit to the sports centre. What did they do there?
Boy:	What a shame we couldn't swim today. The pool at the sports centre is so nice.
Girl:	Yes, it's a pity it was closed today. And then I didn't have my tennis shoes!
Boy:	But you borrowed some and we had a good game!
Girl:	True! And it made me very hungry. Let's go and have something to eat at my house.
5	You will hear a man talking to his daughter. What's the weather like at the moment?
Dad:	Are you going hiking this afternoon?
Girl:	Yes, I hope the weather gets better by then. It'll be awful if it carries on raining.
Dad:	Yes, but at least it's not windy! It's more fun when the sun is shining.
Girl:	True.

1 Players must leave the field now.
2 What must we bring tomorrow?
3 You mustn't wear black shoes.
4 Students must wear school uniform.
5 You mustn't worry about the maths test.
6 You must stop writing now.
7 We mustn't spend too much money.

Dad: How was school today, Lily?

Lily: It was really interesting, Dad! We talked about the Olympics. Did you know that some people want to add eSports and Mind sports to the Summer games?

Dad: Eh? I know what the Olympics are. But eSports? Mind sports? What are they?

Lily: Don't worry, Dad! I didn't know what they were until today. eSports are video games, and mind sports are things like chess and some other board games and card games. Ones that make you think hard.

Dad: I see! Well, I'm not sure, Lily. The Olympic Games are for sport, and surely video games and chess aren't sport! You sit down to play both of those, and you don't use your body at all.

Lily: But sport isn't just about being fit and strong, Dad. You have to use your brain as well if you want to win.

Dad: I suppose so. I play football and it's really important to think about what you're doing when you play. But it's also about running and kicking, and how well you move the ball.

Lily: Well, lots of chess champions and video game stars work hard to stay fit you know. They know it's good for their brains to be fit.

Dad: Well, maybe. But there are lots of important chess competitions already. It doesn't need to be in the Olympics.

Lily: But the other competitions aren't as famous as the Olympics, are they? An Olympic medal is very special.

Dad: That's true, I suppose.

Lily: eSports and mind sports are already in the Asian games you know. I'm sure they'll be in the Olympics in ten years' time.

Dad: Mmm, I don't agree. I don't think they'll ever be in the Olympics.

1

Dr Mandy: I'm very sorry to hear about your problem. Studying alone isn't easy. But it doesn't mean you can't have friends. There are lots of ways to meet people. What activities do you enjoy doing? Maybe you should think about joining some clubs, for example drama or dance. Make sure you have lots of contacts in your phone or online, and remember to call people. Waiting for them to contact you first isn't always a good idea.

2

Dr Mandy: Thank you for writing to the website. I can understand why you aren't happy about what your friend is doing. But don't be too angry. After all, it means she thinks you look great! I think you should try to talk to her about how you feel and explain why you don't want her to do it. Also, why not offer to go shopping with her? If you decide to do this, you can give her advice and help her to find her own way of dressing. Good luck!

3

Dr Mandy: I know that leaving your friends behind is difficult, but if you want to improve, you should be in the higher class. You'll get better at dancing and you'll probably make new friends, too. And here's another idea – why don't you tell your friends to practise a bit more? Offer to help them in your free time. Then maybe the teacher will ask them to move up too.

Speaker 1: I'm 14 now and I wrote my first app when I was 11. It's a physics puzzle called *Catch the Ball*. There are 56 levels and you get different things to help you complete each level, like nets and wheels, and pieces of wood. It costs 99p and it's still quite popular. About 100 people a week download it. I've got lots of ideas for new games, too.

Speaker 2: I'm 16 and I wrote my first app with a friend last year, when I was 15. I got the idea when I was studying for a test and I needed to organise my work. You write a list of all the jobs you have to do into the app, and then it helps you remember to do them, and not be late with everything. It costs £1.50 to download. Some people say it's too expensive, but I don't agree. 30 people a week download it. I'm still working on it – there's always something to improve!

Speaker 3: I'm 15 and the apps I write are all educational, and they are all free. The first one I made was when I was 12. It's all about geography and teaches young children about the countries of the world. Around 70 people a week download it. It has information and quizzes so you can test yourself. At the moment I have 18 apps that people can download, and lots of ideas for more.

Teacher: So, each group is going to tell us about a type of football. Jack, let's start with your group.

Jack: OK. Well, we found out about table football, which probably started in about 1920. You usually have two or four players. It's very popular in youth clubs and some people play it at home. Both men and women play, but the 11 wooden or plastic players in each team are nearly always men! There are international competitions in Europe and the United States and in the future more countries will take part.

Teacher: Thank you. Now Lily, what about your group?

Lily: We want to talk about futsal. This is a sport that people play at a sports centre, usually inside. It began in Uruguay when a teacher organised the game on basketball courts in 1930. At first, it was just for men but now there are a lot of women's futsal teams. There are five players in each team. The best teams are from South America and Spain because lots of people play futsal in these countries.

Teacher: Ah, that's interesting. How about you, Oliver?

Oliver: Well, we think that video game football is a great game. The first FIFA game appeared in 1993. Each weekend, more than 200 million FIFA matches take place all over the world in people's living rooms, bedrooms, and even kitchens. Girls play as well as boys, and on the screen there are men's and women's teams. There are different options for the number of players, but I think the maximum is eight.

Teacher: So this kind of football is popular everywhere! Now, finally Jessie, what kind of football did you choose?

Jessie: Did you know that football for blind people is a Paralympic sport? The ball makes a sound so that they can play by using their ears and feet! It started in Spain in the 1920s and the first World Championship was in 1998. It's a Paralympic sport but there are only men's teams at the moment. There are five players in each team, but only two players can see – the goalkeepers. Nowadays, people play in many countries, but especially Brazil.

Presenter: OK, are you all ready? The quiz will begin in a few moments. All the questions are about cities of the world. Listen carefully to each question and then write down the name of the city.

Here is *question 1.*

This is the second biggest city in China. It's in the north of the country and has some beautiful parks and temples, including the Summer Palace. It also has a very famous stadium, called the Bird's Nest. What is its name?

Question 2

This city is in Europe. The city has a lot of bridges, museums and art galleries, including the Louvre and the Musée d'Orsay. It has one of the most famous cathedrals in the world – Notre-Dame. The cathedral is on an island in a river. There's another beautiful church in the city, called Sacré-Coeur.

Question 3

This city is in the United States of America. It's probably the most famous city in the US, but it's not the capital. It has a statue called The Statue of Liberty. It's on an island, so you can take a boat trip to see it and also the beautiful Brooklyn Bridge. There are many other great places to visit. Central Park and Times Square are both popular.

Question 4

This Latin American city is next to the Atlantic Ocean. It has one of the biggest football stadiums in the world. It's a modern city with many skyscrapers, but it also has a beautiful and very interesting old town. The other really famous thing here is the statue of Jesus on top of a mountain above the city. Oh, and every year there is a big carnival in the city, at the end of February. The Olympic Games were here in 2016.

Question 5

This is the largest city in the world. It's in Asia. It's very modern and busy, and is famous for its bright lights, skyscrapers, shopping areas and restaurants. The city also has many excellent museums, temples and gardens, and, of course, over 150 foreign embassies. There's a beautiful mountain called Mount Fuji, not far away.

Question 6

This is the largest city in India, but it's not the capital. It's in the west of the country by the sea. It has a very large film industry. It's a great place for tourists because it has both beaches and wonderful museums. There's a beautiful fountain called the Flora Fountain in the south part of the city.

You will hear Finley inviting a friend to the cinema.

Finley: Hi Ana … I'm going to Star Cinema with a few friends for my birthday this weekend. Can you come?

Ana: Sure! Which day?

Finley: Well, it'll have to be Saturday because I've got a family dinner on Friday night and a football match on Sunday.

Ana: No problem! What are we going to see?

Finley: *Body Swap*. I hope that's OK?

Ana: Yes, of course! All my friends say it's excellent – good acting, really funny, and nice and short. Most films are so long these days! So, what time does it start?

Finley: We're going to the show at six forty-five. If you like, we can pick you up on our way, at ten past six? We should get there by 6.30.

Ana: Oh, yes please. How much are the tickets?

Finley: We're all 13 now, so it's a bit more expensive – instead of £7.50 it's £10.00. Bring an extra £5.00 if you can, for a drink or some popcorn.

Ana: OK. And how are we getting home? I can get the 263 bus from the cinema I think.

Finley: You don't have to. Mum will come and get us in the car. I wanted to walk, but she says it's too far.

Ana: OK, thanks, Finley.

Sam: Right everyone. Let's start planning our suggestions, for the school party.

Anna: We need to do something really different if we want the class to choose our ideas.

Henry: You're right. So, shall we all write down a list of suggestions first?

Nicky: I think we should draw a line for each topic, you know, like what food we'll have, what the theme of the party will be …

Sam: Good idea!

Anna: Why don't we make a mind map, then we can see the ideas more clearly.

Henry: Yes, I'll get some paper. Mmm. Is this one big enough?

Nicky: That looks fine. So, we can write school party here in the middle. Then, what about the other circles? How many do we need?

Anna: Well, the topics are food, drink, theme and date.

Nicky: OK, that's four for the moment. I'm sure we'll think of some more. So, let's start with the theme. What ideas have you got?

Henry: How about *Under the sea*? Or *Pirates*?

Sam: Maybe *Cinema*, so people dress up like their favourite character.

Anna: Oh, or *Roman times* because we studied that this year.

Nicky: Mmm, what about different nationalities? Like Japanese, French or Spanish, for example.

Sam: Those are some good ideas. Next, we'll have to choose decorations, so that's another circle we need on the mind map.

Anna: That's right. So, have you got any more ideas for the theme?

Henry: Not really. Shall we move on to the food?

You will hear Serena talking to her friend Ed about the new sports centre.

Ed: Serena, what's the new sports centre like?

Serena: It's amazing, Ed! There's a fantastic climbing wall, a hall for fitness classes, and you can do sports like badminton and tennis there. That's the best thing about it, for me.

Ed: Do you know what the opening hours are?

Serena: At the moment, it's open from 7.30 in the morning to 10 o'clock at night, Mondays to Fridays. At weekends and school holidays, it's 8 till 10.

Ed: OK. I might go and try something.

Serena: Try the climbing wall. It's great for people like you, who don't like team sports. I know the teacher and she's great. It might be hard at the beginning because you're not very strong, but it will be fun!

Ed: OK!

Serena: There's also a board games club at the sports centre.

Ed: That's interesting! Board games might not help you get fit, but they are good exercise for your brain. People forget how important that is! In fact, we should play them at school!

Serena: I saw a notice about it with some contact details. I didn't see a phone number but there was an email address.

Ed: Thanks Serena

Juan: Hey Susanna, I've found a great website. It's got lots of ideas of things to do before you're 16. I like the outdoors section. Do you want to hear some of them?

Susanna: OK, but I do lots of things outside, so I've probably done them.

Juan: Let's see about that! OK first one, have you ever camped under the stars – you know, without a tent?

Susanna: Yes, I have camped under the stars. I did that last summer with my mum in Scotland.

Juan: OK another one … Mmm. Have you ever kayaked down a river?

Susanna: Yes, I have. I did that with my dad last year in Spain. It was amazing.

Juan: Mmm. I'd love to do that too. Here's another one. Have you ever explored a cave?

Susanna: Actually, no I haven't. I don't like going underground very much.

Juan: Right … Have you ever recorded birdsong?

Susanna: Yes, I have. I used my phone to record birdsong at school last week for our project.

Juan: So. Let me find another one. Have you ever looked for fossils?

Susanna: No, I've never looked for fossils. I'd like to though.

Juan: Me too. OK, what about this one. Have you ever tracked wild animals?

Susanna: By following their foot prints you mean? No, I haven't but that would be cool!

Juan: Ah yes this is a good one … Have you ever picked wild fruit?

Susanna: Yes, actually, I have. I picked some wild strawberries yesterday in my grandma's garden.

Juan: OK, let me find one more … Mmm. Ah yes. Have you ever tried rock climbing?

Susanna: I've climbed the climbing wall at school. Is that the same thing? I did it a few weeks ago.

Juan: Yeah, it is. OK, I think I'll send you the website link. There are definitely still some things you can do before you're 16!

Jim:	Hi you're listening to *Jim's World* and today's guest is Christina Wells, the explorer. Welcome to the show, Christina.
Christina:	Thank you, Jim.
Jim:	So Christina. You've been to so many amazing places.
Christina:	Yes, I have. And, of course, there are always more to explore.
Jim:	So tell us, have you ever got lost on any of your travels?
Christina:	Well, yes. I have, Jim. It wasn't a pleasant experience. I was in the Brazilian rainforest looking for insects. I had a compass, but somehow I got lost and was walking for two days before I found a village. I didn't want to tell anyone that I, Christina the well-known explorer, was lost in the rainforest for two days.
Jim:	But you're happy to share that with us now.
Christina:	Yes. Because the important thing about that experience was that I found my way through the forest and got to the village.
Jim:	True. Have you ever wanted to come home early from a trip?
Christina:	No, I haven't. But my trip to the North Pole alone was very difficult. I was skiing, pulling all my equipment, and I often had to stop and think about why I was doing it. I kept a diary on that trip. There was no-one to talk to, so I wrote in my diary. That helped me think more clearly.
Jim:	So Christina, what's your next trip?
Christina:	Well, next month I'm taking part in the Tour d'Afrique. It's a cycling trip through Africa from Cairo to Cape Town. I haven't done a trip with other people before.
Jim:	Wow, that's a long way to cycle! How far is it?
Christina:	About 12,000 kilometres, and it'll take us four months. It'll be a fantastic experience. Anyone can come along. Jim, why don't you join us?
Jim:	Me? No, I don't think so. I don't even cycle to work!
Christina:	Well, you should start!
Jim:	Thanks for coming on the show, Christina.
Christina:	Thanks for inviting me, Jim. Bye!
Jim:	Goodbye Christina. Good luck with the ride.

Lana:	Hi, David.
David:	Hi, Lana.
Lana:	Are we ready for Pia's picnic tomorrow?
David:	I think so. I've already got four big bags of crisps and some apples.
Lana:	How many apples did you get?
David:	About a kilo and a half.
Lana:	Perfect. Have you bought the pizzas yet?
David:	Yes, I've got three pizzas, that's twenty-four slices. Have you already done everything on your list?
Lana:	Almost. I haven't got the drink yet.
David:	Maybe my dad can take us to the supermarket this morning to get some. I'll ask him. How much are we going to get?
Lana:	Well, we need a variety of drinks, don't we? How about two litres of lemonade and the same of fruit juice?
David:	Perhaps we need a bit more lemonade.
Lana:	OK, let's get three litres of that. And we need some water too. I'll get a litre.
David:	Fine. What are we going to sit on? Have you got a blanket?
Lana:	Good point! My dad's got an old blanket. It's about one metre by two metres. I'm sure I can use it.
David:	Perfect!
Lana:	I can text everyone who's coming, if you like, and ask them to bring blankets, too. Right. Is that all?
David:	Except for the cake! I'll get a €5 one tomorrow.
Lana:	OK. What present have you bought for Pia?
David:	I've got her a necklace from the market.
Lana:	Great idea! I'm going to get her a pair of sunglasses.
David:	Cool! Let me know about the supermarket.
Lana:	Hey, just a minute, we forgot about …

Dan: Hi Alice. How was your trip to London?

Alice: Hi Dan. We had a great time. We saw Buckingham Palace and went to the Science Museum on Saturday, but the best part was when we went to Camden Lock Market on Sunday.

Dan: Oh yeah, that's famous, isn't it?

Alice: Yes, there were hundreds of stalls and shops. In fact, I think there are more than 1,000 because there's a big market building and then other places in the streets around it.

Dan: Wow, that's enormous! What do they sell there?

Alice: Well, it isn't like a typical fruit and vegetable market, you know. There aren't stalls selling food to take home to cook, just food stalls selling dishes to eat there, like hot dogs, hamburgers or pizzas. We had Mexican food for lunch. It was delicious! There are some shops that famous people, like rock stars, have opened, which are really cool. There's music everywhere.

Dan: So what did you like best in the market?

Alice: The clothes stalls! You know I love shopping for clothes, so that was great. I found really cheap T-shirts, and I bought three. I've got one for you! And I found a really cool green handbag. I'll show it to you. There were antique stalls as well, selling jewellery. I got a ring for my sister's birthday present and a lovely necklace for me.

Dan: So you spent a lot of money!

Alice: Well, I only had five pounds left at the end of that day and I bought a poster with that. I went into a music shop where there was fantastic music and they had posters of bands and singers. I bought one of Justin Bieber. I'm going to give it to my friend Lisa because he's her favourite singer.

Dan: I think Justin Bieber is amazing, too!

Alice: Anyway, why don't you come to my house after school and I can give you your T-shirt?

Dan: Great!

Owen: Some people like dancing or doing sport, but I like using the computer. There are lots of great websites to visit. You can find information, share videos and photographs, keep a blog, download music – and lots more. I've had my own computer for three years. It's in my room on my desk, and I use it after school. Some people say you shouldn't spend a lot of time on the computer, but I don't agree – you learn a lot and it's certainly not bad for you!

Kyle: I like to be busy. I don't like spending time on the computer or watching TV. My sister watches TV for hours – cartoons, films … anything! I have quite a few hobbies – I especially like collecting things. These days, it's badges – I've got 90 of them now and I'm always looking for more. When I was younger, I collected football cards too, but I haven't bought any of those for a long time. I've played football since I was very little, and I started hockey a few months ago.

Erin: I've got lots of hobbies. My favourite is playing the guitar. I've played it for two years now, and I'm improving fast. I've got two guitars – I've had one of them since I was ten. The other one is new – I've had that since January. I also love reading. I've got at least 50 books in my room! I also like taking photos. I use my dad's camera. He's had it since he was a teenager, but it's a really good one. I've taken some great pictures with it.

Mrs Jones: OK everyone, quiet please. As you know, every week a different student is going to tell us all about their hobby. Today, we are hearing from Libby, who keeps bees. Libby, you can start.

Libby: Thanks, Mrs Jones. Yes, my hobby is beekeeping! I started after someone gave my mum some bees as a present. She didn't have time to look after them, so I decided to do it instead. I had to go on a course first to learn all about it. I'm so glad I did that! I was the only teenager on the course, but I had a great time. I knew immediately that beekeeping was the perfect hobby for me.

The bees stay inside the hive for the winter, so I don't have to do much with them. Then in spring, when it's warm enough, they come out and start looking for food. Through the summer I am quite busy looking after them. I love spending time with them. I've heard that they can recognise faces, and I believe that. When I look into the hive, I have the feeling they know who I am and they're happy to see me.

I have to be careful not to let the hive get too crowded. That's because when the number of bees in a hive gets too large, they all fly away. I also have to collect the honey. I do this three times during the summer and get about 50 kilos of honey from my hive. I don't really enjoy taking the honey – it makes me feel bad! The bees work so hard to make it. And did you know that each bee makes less than a gram of honey in its lifetime? So think about how many bees you need to make just one jar of honey!

Anyway, I've been a beekeeper for two years, now and I think it's a brilliant hobby. If you want to know more, just ask!

Mrs Jones: Thanks, Libby – that certainly was an interesting talk. OK – does anyone have any questions?

1 You will hear a boy called Danny talking to his friend. How did Danny improve his Spanish?

Girl: Your Spanish has improved a lot Danny! Did you go to Spain in the holidays?

Danny: Yes, but I didn't speak much Spanish while I was there. It's that website the teacher told us about. I've learned loads from it.

Girl: Oh right.

Danny: It's great. The exercises are really fun, and I think you can even find Spanish penfriends on there.

2 You will hear a teacher talking to her class. What does she want them to work harder on?

Teacher: OK everyone. You're all doing really well in English at the moment. You don't seem to make many mistakes with the grammar, and I've noticed that you're all using a good level of vocabulary these days. However, I would like you to think about how you sound when you speak the language. It's just as important as grammar, you know.

3 You will hear two friends talking about some homework. Why hasn't the boy done his?

Girl: Have you done the German homework yet? I've finished mine already. It wasn't too difficult.

Boy: No! I didn't know we had any German homework. There's nothing in my homework diary.

Girl: The teacher gave it to us three days ago. Did you miss the lesson?

Boy: I haven't missed any lessons this term. Oh dear! I must remember to write it in my diary next time.

4 You will hear a girl telling her mother about her new friend, Yumi. What languages does Yumi speak well?

Mum: How was your first day at school, Nicola? Did you meet anyone interesting?

Nicola: Yes, I met a girl called Yumi who speaks three languages really well! She's spoken Japanese since she was a baby, and she learned Russian last year, when she was in Moscow. She's lived all over the world!

Mum: Wow. So I guess the third language is English?

Nicola: It's Swedish. She lived in Sweden three years ago. She hasn't learned much English yet.

5 You will hear a boy giving a classmate some important news. How did he find out about the news?

Boy: I've just heard some amazing news! Our French teacher has won first prize in a competition!

Girl: That's fantastic. How do you know?

Boy: My brother saw an article in the local paper. He said she's going to be on the radio tomorrow.

Girl: Wow – I'm surprised she didn't tell us herself. We had a lesson with her this morning.

Man: Hello, everyone, and welcome to 'Our Amazing World'. Today I'm going to tell you some things about languages that you probably didn't know. For example, not all languages have the same number of basic colour words. In English there are 11, but in Russian and Greek there are 12. Those languages have two words for blue. Other languages have just one word for green and blue, or one word for green and yellow.

Numbers are also very different in some languages. For example, the Pirahã language of Brazil only has words for 'one', 'two' and 'many'. They just don't need more numbers than that in their daily lives! Several other languages have very few words for numbers.

There are some very interesting languages in Australia and Africa that have two sets of vocabulary – so two words for 'chair', or two words for 'parent'. You use one set when you're talking in the home, with close family, and the other set when you need to be more polite. The grammar is the same, but the vocabulary is different. So people who speak it have to learn two whole sets of vocabulary!

Another amazing group of languages has no words for 'left', 'right', 'in front of', 'behind' and so on. Instead, speakers use north, south, east, west to say where things are. So they say things like 'There's an insect north of your foot.' or 'The book is on the east side of the table.' It's hard to believe, but they know all the time where north, south, east and west are!

Unfortunately, some of these languages only have a few speakers left. It's important not to lose them, because they have a lot of information in them – about nature, and about the culture of the speakers. Luckily, modern technology is helping to keep these languages alive. These days, there are talking dictionaries and smartphone apps to teach pronunciation to younger speakers. People are working hard to keep at least some of these languages alive.

Mario: Hello. My name's Mario and I'm from Italy. Today, I'm going to talk about my experience learning English. When I was small I didn't like learning English. There was too much vocabulary and too many sounds. I couldn't remember them all. I only had classes three hours a week, so we didn't practise much. Really, I didn't understand why I had to say things in a different way when I only needed my own language to have fun with my friends and family.

Everything changed one summer when I was on holiday at the beach. I met two boys about my age who were brothers. We played football on the sand and swam in the sea. But they didn't speak Italian, they only spoke English. I listened carefully when they were talking and slowly I began to understand some words. I really wanted to talk to them, so I pointed at things I wanted to know the vocabulary for. They told me the words and I wrote them in a little book I had and drew pictures to show the meaning. For example, I drew a boat, an ice cream, a fish and a crab.

At the end of the holiday they gave me their email address and we all went home. I started to write to them, but I needed more words. I found lots of useful things in an online dictionary. I also started watching English films and series. It was hard at first, but I learned more and more. Finally, when my friends write to me now, I hardly ever need a dictionary. Next summer I am going to stay with them for a week, and then, they are coming to stay here. I can't wait!

Does anyone have any questions?

You will hear Ella and Tom talking about people's hobbies. What is each person's hobby?

Ella: What did you find out about people's hobbies for the school project, Tom?

Tom: Well, Ella. I asked Suzy first. She was in a hurry because she had a guitar lesson, but she told me that her hobby's taking pictures. She's really good.

Ella: So, I spoke to Jason. He had a bag of things to make a cake with from the supermarket. He makes all the food in their house now. That's his hobby.

Tom: I asked Laura. She's in the football team and was in a tennis match last weekend!

Ella: Yes, she's always doing some kind of exercise. … Tom, is that a new cap?

Tom: Yes, it is. I've got 15 of them now. I bought four when we went to visit the US last year. I'm trying to get as many as I can. So what about you, Ella?

Ella: Yes, I'm interested in hearing songs from all over the world. … Oh, and we mustn't forget Maria!

Tom: Of course! What did she tell you?

Ella: She's started learning the drums. She loves it!

1	What time is basketball practice today?
Boy 1:	Are you going to basketball practice this afternoon?
Boy 2:	Yes, I'll go if it doesn't rain. I'm not sure of the time. Is it at three or three thirty?
Boy 1:	It's at a quarter past three. It was at three thirty last week!
Boy 2:	Thanks. See you there, if it isn't raining!
2	Which food does the girl choose?
Girl:	Hello. What kind of pizzas do you do?
Waiter:	Sorry, we aren't doing pizza today. The oven is broken. But our burgers are very popular. We do lots of different kinds of sandwiches, too.
Girl:	I'll try the burger, thanks. I had a sandwich for lunch. And can I have a lemonade with that?
Waiter:	Certainly. I'll bring your drink now.
3	Which earphones does the boy buy?
Boy:	Hello. I'd like to buy some earphones, please. What have you got?
Assistant:	Well, we've got these for ten pounds twenty, these for fifteen pounds fifty and these for eighteen pounds.
Boy:	The eighteen-pound ones are a little expensive. I'll have the fifteen fifty ones, please.
Assistant:	Certainly. I'll put them in a bag for you.
4	What's the weather like?
Girl:	Hi, Sandy. Do you want to come for a walk in the park with me?
Sandy:	I'm not sure. Isn't it very windy?
Girl:	It was windy earlier, but now it's just a bit cloudy. It's going to rain later.
Sandy:	OK, let's go before it rains.
5	What are they going to do?
Girl:	I'm bored. What shall we do? Let's play tennis.
Boy:	I'm tired, and we have to get the bus there. I've got a new computer game. Let's play that.
Girl:	Oh, I played computer games all morning. I want to do something outside. Oh, how about a bike ride?
Boy:	I can't. My bike's broken. OK, let's do what you want – I'll go and get my racket.

Teacher:	Listen carefully everyone! I want to tell you about a fantastic competition you can enter over the summer. It's called the Reading Challenge and it's open to anyone aged 12 to 15. All you have to do is read as many books as you can over the summer – the winner is the person who reads the most! It doesn't cost anything to enter, and you'll be able to borrow all the books from school or your local library.
	To enter the competition you need to go to the Reading Challenge website and enter your details. After you join, you'll get all the instructions you need to get started. There are some great prizes – books, of course – but also a writing course, where you can learn how to turn your idea into an exciting story that other people will want to read!
	Even if you don't want to do the competition, the website is really useful. It has information about hundreds of books, and tells you what other readers thought of them, so it makes choosing a book really easy. There are lots of special offers and discounts on books too.
	Another part of the website has games and quizzes on it, which are very popular. And there's also a blog. This has really interesting articles about books and reading and is good, if you're interested in writing your own stories. There's lots of fantastic advice there from writers and book companies about what works and what doesn't.
	I hope lots of you will join. Jacob, what about you?
Jacob:	Yes, sounds good!
Emma:	Me too!
Teacher:	Fantastic – I hope the rest of you feel the same. Let me know!

You will hear a woman giving information about a cooking competition.

Woman: The School Chef Competition happens every year, and it's a great way for school students to show what they can do in the kitchen! It's for everyone aged 12 to 15, and you enter the competition in a team. The idea is to think of a dish to serve in a school café.

The competition is in two parts. First you must email us a recipe idea. We need those by 2nd June. We'll look at them all by 4th June. We think about 50 teams will enter, but only eight can go through to the cooking competition. If your idea is chosen, we'll let you know by email.

We will have the cooking part of the competition at the university. They have plenty of space for us there. Oh – and one piece of exciting news – the person who is going to choose the winners this year is top chef John Wright. That's W-R-I-G-H-T. Find out about him on the internet today!

There are great prizes for all the teams that cook. These will include cookbooks, money and T-shirts. Good luck, everyone – fill in the form on our website today!

You will hear Tanya talking to her friend Jon about her new school.

Jon: Hi Tanya, what's your new school like? Did you have to pass an exam to get a place there?

Tanya: Hi Jon. Yes, but I nearly didn't get there in time. The exam was at nine o'clock and we had to be there by half past eight.

Jon: Oh no! Do you get the bus to school?

Tanya: Well, there is a bus, but it leaves quite early, so Mum gives me a lift. I'll cycle when it's warmer

Jon: Mmm, how is it different from your old school?

Tanya: Well, it's got a much bigger science building. And the music lessons are great. They even have instruments we can borrow. Oh, and we play cricket, not hockey. Are you still in the school hockey team?

Jon: No. No time! I've joined a band called The River Boys and I'm starting a part-time job next week.

Tanya: So, do you think you'll change schools and come to mine?

Jon: My parents want me to. I like my classmates, but I can see them at weekends. No, the thing is I'm going to China with the school next year. I definitely don't want to miss that!

Tanya: OK. See you later.

Jon: Bye.

1 What things did Peter and Matty need for the exam?

Teacher: All right, please put your hand up if you have any questions. Yes, Peter?

Peter: My pen is broken.

Teacher: OK. Here's another one. You should always remember to bring an extra pen with you to the exam. Anything else? Yes, Matty, what do you need?

Matty: I forgot my ruler to draw the triangle shapes.

Teacher: I'll give you a ruler, but next time you mustn't forget it.

2 Why did Meg fail her exam?

Emily: Meg, you look worried. What's the matter?

Meg: I've just done my final history exam, but I did something really stupid.

Emily: Oh, what happened? Did you forget an answer?

Meg: No, it was much worse. I thought the teacher wasn't watching and I looked in my book for the answer.

Emily: And she saw you do it!

Meg: Yes, so now I've failed history!

Emily: Oh dear! Shall I help you study for the next test?

3 Did Sam answer all the questions in the exam?

Sam: Well, my French exam went really badly!

James: Why, what did you do?

Sam: Well, I had to choose a, b or c, but I didn't know some of the answers so I didn't write anything.

James: You know that you could guess? You should choose an option for every question. It doesn't matter if you get it wrong but if you write nothing you get no marks.

Sam: Oh no!

4 What did Tim forget to do in the exam?

Tim: Miss, Miss, I've finished now! Can I leave?

Teacher: Have you checked your work? You must make sure you've done everything.

Tim: Yes, it was easy!

Teacher: Mmm. Let me see. And what about question 6? You haven't written anything.

Tim: Oh. I didn't see it. Maybe I won't go yet.

5 What advice does the teacher give Sophie?

Sophie: I hate exams! I never have time to finish all the questions. I'm so slow.

Teacher: Have you tried organising your time better? I mean, if the exam is 60 minutes and you have six questions, then you should spend 10 minutes on each question.

Sophie: You're right. I always try to do the first question perfectly and it takes me a long time.

Teacher: Well, if I were you, I'd look at the clock and move to the next question after ten minutes. Then you'll have time to try and answer all the questions.

Sophie: OK. I'll try that next time.

You will hear a woman talking to a class of students about the history of her town.

Mrs Smith: Hello everyone. My name's Mrs Smith and I'm here to tell you about this town, where I've lived for 60 years. First, let's think about the town's history. Does anyone know how old it is? 400 years? 700 years? Almost! It's 850 years old.

Next, I want to talk about what the town was like in 1980. There are 66,000 people living here now but then there were only 54,000. But, surprisingly, there were more shops in the town centre in 1980 than there are now and oh, a fantastic market. Another thing, today the shops are open every day, including Sundays, but in 1980 all the shops were closed on Thursdays. Strange, isn't it? And, you know, the cinema in the High Street. Well, it wasn't called the Royal then. Its name was the Regent. Ah, sorry, that's R-E-G-E-N-T. I went to the cinema last week and paid £12 for a seat. I couldn't believe it! In 1980 it only cost £1.75.

So, any questions?

1 What would Ted like to get for his room?

Aunt: Wow, your room looks great Ted! I really like your posters.

Ted: Thanks! They were a present from my brother.

Aunt: And this desk looks really useful.

Ted: Yes, it's great for doing my homework. The only thing I need now is a sofa. I want a big comfortable one to go under the window.

2 What is still in the car?

Dad: Did you bring everything in from the car?

Girl: I think so. My tennis kit … your jumper … and you brought in the shopping didn't you?

Dad: One bag, but we had two. The other one's on the back seat I think.

Girl: You're right. OK. I'll get it.

3 How much is the bag?

Girl: I'm looking for a school bag, but I've only got £20 to spend. How much is this one?

Assistant: Mmm … from today that one is £15.

Girl: Oh, great!

Assistant: You're lucky. It *was* £17.75, but it's in the sale now.

4 Where did they go camping last year?

Boy: Mum, can we go camping again this summer? It was great fun last year.

Mum: It was lovely by that lake, wasn't it? Maybe we can find somewhere in the mountains next time.

Boy: I suppose so – or near a beach.

Mum: A beach sounds good! Let's see what Dad thinks.

5 What are the boys going to do now?

Boy 1: Shall we do something else now? I'm bored of playing computer games.

Boy 2: Me too. What about playing football in the park?

Boy 1: I haven't got my trainers with me. Let's go to that new café in town. They do great milkshakes!

Boy 2: Good idea. We can play football another time.

You will hear someone talking about a gym.

Man: Thanks for visiting Bodyfit Gym today. Now I think you're all here because you're interested in our new club for teenagers. Well, it starts next week, and takes place every Saturday, but please book your place by this Friday.

You will hear someone talking about a gym.

Man: Thanks for visiting Bodyfit Gym today. Now I think you're all here because you're interested in our new club for teenagers. Well, it starts next week, and takes place every Saturday, but please book your place by this Friday. Speak to your parents about it as soon as you get home! The cost is £12.50 a month, which is a fantastic price. Other clubs are £15 or even £20 a month.

About the time – the club begins at 10.20, but it's a good idea to arrive by 10 o'clock, so you'll have time to get changed and meet the teacher. His name's Hughie, that's H-U-G-H-I-E. You can find out more about him on our website.

People always ask what they should wear. Most kinds of comfortable sports clothes are fine, but trousers are a bad idea. The gym gets very hot, so shorts are better. Oh, and you don't need water as we have that here, but a towel is a good idea, so you can dry yourself while you're exercising.

OK, now any questions?

You will hear Callum talking to his friend Stella about going to a skatepark.

Callum: Shall we go to the new skatepark tomorrow, Stella?

Stella: OK Callum – but I didn't know there was a new one! Is it near your house?

Callum: It's on the other side of town actually – just opposite the swimming pool. It's much better than the one near the cinema.

You will hear Callum talking to his friend Stella about going to a skatepark.

Callum: Shall we go to the new skatepark tomorrow, Stella?

Stella: OK Callum – but I didn't know there was a new one! Is it near your house?

Callum: It's on the other side of town actually – just opposite the swimming pool. It's much better than the one near the cinema.

Stella: I hope it's bigger too. I don't mind if a skatepark is old or dirty – but it has to have enough space.

Callum: Oh, yes, don't worry about that. And the weather's never going to be a problem either – this skatepark's got a roof! It's also got toilets and a café, and they're going to put a shop there too.

Stella: Wow, fantastic! But how much do we have to pay to get in? I've only got £7 to spend.

Callum: From next month, when it's finished, it'll be £5, but it's only £3 until then.

Stella: Great! Do you mind if we go early? I've got to go to my auntie's for lunch at 1. We could meet there at ten and stay until 12 if that's OK for you?

Callum: Yes, sure. See you then.

1 You will hear a girl talking to her mother. What does she want to eat?

Girl: Mum I'm starving!

Mum: Sorry, dinner's not ready yet. I can make you a sandwich if you like? Or you could have a couple of biscuits?

Girl: Mmm – I don't feel like a snack. I need something big! What are you cooking?

Mum: It's roast chicken.

Girl: OK, I'll wait. That sounds really good.

1   You will hear a girl talking to her mother. What does she want to eat?

Girl: Mum I'm starving!

Mum: Sorry, dinner's not ready yet. I can make you a sandwich if you like? Or you could have a couple of biscuits?

Girl: Mmm – I don't feel like a snack. I need something big! What are you cooking?

Mum: It's roast chicken.

Girl: OK, I'll wait. That sounds really good.

2   You will hear a girl taking to a friend about a TV programme. What does she say about it?

Boy: Did you watch that show I told you about last night?

Girl: Yes! I usually only enjoy things that make me laugh, but this was brilliant. There was so much action – I wasn't bored for a minute.

Boy: You didn't think it was too long?

Girl: You know, there was so much happening I didn't even notice it was two hours long!

3   You will hear two friends talking about a walk they did together. What happened on the walk?

Boy: Oh dear! I'm not sure I want to do a walk like that again! That was awful!

Girl: What?? Just because of a tiny bit of rain? I thought we did really well. No accidents or broken bones, and we had no problems following the map.

Boy: That's true – but I don't think my boots will ever get dry.

Girl: They will!

4   You will hear a boy leaving a message for a friend. Where would he like to meet his friend?

Jackson: Freddie – it's Jackson – just getting in touch about the festival in the park tomorrow. I'm going to get the bus from my house as far as the High Street and then walk from there. I need to go to the ticket office first, so why don't you wait for me there? Then we can go to see the first band at the big stage. I'm really looking forward to it!

5   You will hear a teacher talking to her class. What is she talking about?

Teacher: I'm pretty sure you're all going to love this one! The writer's not very well known but the story has been made into a film, so you've probably all heard of it. Oh and it's not too long – I know how important that is to some of you!

You will hear Jasmin telling her grandmother about her half-term holiday. What activity did each person do?

Grandma: How was your half-term holiday, Jasmin? What did you and your friends do?

Jasmin: Well Grandma, I played the guitar a lot. I'm in the school concert next week, and I need to get ready for it.

You will hear Jasmin telling her grandmother about her half-term holiday. What activity did each person do?

Grandma: How was your half-term holiday, Jasmin? What did you and your friends do?

Jasmin: Well Grandma, I played the guitar a lot. I'm in the school concert next week, and I need to get ready for it.

Grandma: Did Sophie practise with you?

Jasmin: She played hockey all week with her team. She was lucky. No studying!

Grandma: Sounds great! And what about Sam?

Jasmin: He went away with his parents. They drove around the country, staying in different places.

Grandma: Did he take his friend Joe with him?

Jasmin: Joe stayed at home. He spent a lot of time taking pictures. He's going to enter an online competition with his best ones.

Grandma: Oh. And what about Emily?

Jasmin: She went on the internet a lot to play games and listen to music. She didn't have enough money to go shopping or anything. She was a bit bored!

Grandma: Oh dear! And what about Gemma?

Jasmin: Gemma planned to study, but in the end she spent the whole week baking. It's her favourite hobby.

Grandma: Well, it sounds more fun than studying!

Boy: Well, during the week, it's with my family. But at weekends I see my friends. We play sport together or go to the park.

Girl: Maths! Some of my friends don't like it, and they say it's difficult. But I think it's fun. If I have maths homework I always do that first.

Boy: I have a few hours after school, when I can watch TV or go online. And I have quite a lot of free time at weekends. Sometimes I have to go shopping with my parents or do some jobs for them, but not always.

Girl: His name's Mr Wheelan, and he's my history teacher. He knows a lot about his subject and he makes it very interesting. Also he's very friendly and kind.

Boy: I spend about an hour a day doing homework. I usually have three or four things to do, for different subjects.

Interlocutor:	Now, in this part of the test, you are going to talk together. Here are some pictures that show different places to visit. Do you like these different places to visit? Say why or why not. I'll say that again. Do you like these different places to visit? Say why or why not. All right? Now, talk together.
Girl:	Do you like going to shopping centres?
Boy:	Not really. I think it's quite boring and it makes me feel tired. What about you?
Girl:	I like it. I go about once a month with my friends.
Boy:	And what about museums? Do you like museums?
Girl:	Yes, I think they're interesting. And you?
Boy:	Not really. I prefer going to the park. How about you?
Girl:	Yes, parks are fun. I love going in summer. I go to do sports with my friends or just lie on the grass. Do you like castles?
Boy:	Yes, I really like castles. There's one near my home and I often go there with my family.
Girl:	And the cinema? Do you like going to the cinema?
Boy:	Well, yes but I think it's expensive. Do you agree?
Girl:	Yes. I don't go very often. We usually watch films at home, on TV.
Interlocutor:	Thank you.

Interlocutor:	Now, do you like places that teach you about history?
Girl:	Yes, I do. I think it's very interesting.
Interlocutor:	And what about you?
Boy:	No.
Interlocutor:	OK, why not?
Boy:	I think it's boring and I prefer going to other places.
Interlocutor:	Do you prefer visiting places that are inside or outside?
Boy:	I prefer to be outside. My favourite thing is sport, so I don't like looking at old things.
Interlocutor:	And what about you?
Girl:	I also like sport and I like being outside, but I enjoy museums as well. I don't mind spending time indoors.
Interlocutor:	Do you prefer visiting places on your own or with other people?
Girl:	Mmm, with other people.
Interlocutor:	OK, why?
Girl:	It's more fun. You can feel lonely if you are by yourself.
Interlocutor:	And what about you?
Boy:	I agree. Sometimes if my friends are busy, I go to the park by myself to ride my bike. But I prefer to go with other people.
Interlocutor:	Thank you. That is the end of the test.

Acknowledgements

The authors and publishers acknowledge the following sources of copyright material and are grateful for the permissions granted. While every effort has been made, it has not always been possible to identify the sources of all the material used, or to trace all copyright holders. If any omissions are brought to our notice, we will be happy to include the appropriate acknowledgements on reprinting & in the next update to the digital edition, as applicable.

Teacher's Book

All the texts, photographs and illustrations are used from the Student's Book.

Front cover photography by Kevin Dodge/Getty Images.

Videos

Key: C = Culture

Photography

The following photographs are sourced from Getty Images:

C5: M_a_y_a/E+; William Voon/EyeEm; MundusImages/E+.

Video Clips

The following video clips are sourced from Getty Images:

C1: piola666/Vetta; thisnight/Creatas Video; SimonSkafar/Creatas Video; simonkr/Vetta; Onyx Media, Llc - Footage/Archive Films: Editorial; Academic Media Network/Verve+; simonkr/Creatas Video; Gregory B Balvin/DigitalVision; Academic Media Network/Verve+; PeakMystique/Creatas Video; Guillaume749/Creatas Video; Revelation/DigitalVision; milehightraveler/Creatas Video; prasit chansarekorn/Creatas Video; milehightraveler/Creatas Video; Gallo Images/Delimont, Herbig and Associates/DigitalVision; Counter Production/Image Bank Film; Revelation/DigitalVision; Discovery FootageSource; milehightraveler/Creatas Video; WLV Stock/DigitalVision; Gregory B Balvin/DigitalVision; BBC Natural History/BBC Creative; Gregory B Balvin/DigitalVision; Garden Photo World/Verve+; Simonkr/Verve; **C2:** SolStock/Creatas Video; SolStock/Creatas Video; Klaus Vedfelt/one80: Signature; FatCamera/Vetta; Steve Debenport/Vetta; FilmColoratStudio/Creatas Video; selected-takes/Creatas Video; kali9/Creatas Video; JK1991/Creatas Video; Caiafilm/Vetta; CaiaFilmJV/Creatas Video; SolStock/Creatas Video; Constantinis/Vetta; CLIPPN The Professional Clip Network/Verve+; kali9/Creatas Video; CaiaFilmJV/Creatas Video; Caiafilm; Caiafilm/Vetta; Mark Andersen/DigitalVision; Grooters Productions/Photodisc; FatCamera/Creatas Video; Marc Romanelli/Image Bank Film: Signature; FatCamera/Vetta; Yellow Dog Productions Inc/Image Bank Film: Signature; saskam/Creatas Video; jblpictures/Creatas Video; Caiafilm; leventince/Creatas Video; **C3:** LeoPatrizi/Creatas Video; Pressmaster/DigitalVision; kali9/Creatas Video; Purplevideos/Creatas Video; FatCamera/Creatas Video; Aksonov/Vetta; freemixer/Creatas Video; Mageed/Creatas Video; Jin Li/Moment Video RR; Hin255/Creatas Video; The Time Lapse Company/Image Bank Film; Gsmotion/Photolibrary Video; Paul J Lilley/Image Bank Film; Alistair Berg/DigitalVision; Robert Harding Video/Verve+; komisar/Creatas Video; Warner Bros. Studios/Warner Bros. Entertainment; Fluorescent Films Ltd/Photodisc; Vasyl Shulga/Vetta; fatihkeles/Creatas Video; Mageed/Creatas Video; Easy_Company/Creatas Video; hoozone/Vetta; FatCamera/Creatas Video; **C4:** Pigeon Productions Inc./Image Bank Film: Signature; tawattiw/Creatas Video; Laurence Dutton/Creatas Video; Easy_Company/Creatas Video; Fraser Hall/Photodisc; Holly Hildreth/Moment Video RF; giddyuptimelapse/Creatas Video; Yuji Kotani/Photodisc; SimonSkafar/Creatas Video; Gary Conner/DigitalVision; Rudy Maxa's World/Verve; Christian Ender/Photodisc; Rudy Maxa's World/Image Bank Film; Rudy Maxa's World/Image Bank Film; DCR Imagenes S.L.U./Image Bank Film; minemero/Creatas Video; visualspace/Creatas Vide; BBC Universal/BBC Creative; Nikada/Creatas Video; Yamato1987/Creatas Video; Gavin Hellier/Corbis Video; Gavin Hellier/Corbis Video; AK Dobos/Moment Video RR; Robert Harding Video/Photolibrary Video; FatCamera; **C5:** ridvan_celik/Creatas Video; HeroImagesFootage/Creatas Video; gawrav/Vetta; kali9/Creatas Video; ozgurdonmaz/Creatas Video; Bplanet/Creatas Video; JK1991/Creatas Video; Pekic/Creatas Video; saskami/Creatas Video; FilmColoratStudio/Creatas Video; TODCHAMP/Creatas Video; gawrav/Creatas Video; AzmanJaka/Vetta; basketman23/Creatas Video; Frank Rothe/DigitalVision; martin-dm/Creatas Video; Juanmrgt/Vetta; creativeballs/Vetta; jal/wlp/Image Bank Film; Robin Beckham/Creatas Video; Andersen Ross/Verve+.

Audio

The following music clips are sourced from Getty Images:

Intro: LP_MUSIC/SoundExpress; **C1:** juqboxmusic/SoundExpress; **C2:** Skip Peck/SoundExpress; **C3:** juqboxmusic/SoundExpress; **C4:** Anton Evdokimov/SoundExpress; **C5:** run.fire.stop/SoundExpress.

The publishers are grateful to the following contributors: cover design and design concept: restless; typesetting: Mouse Life, S.L.; Videos in units 4, 5, 7, 8, 9, 11, 13, 16, 17 and 19 produced by Purple Door Media Ltd.